MARTYRS AND MURDERERS

MARTYRS AND MURDERERS

THE GUISE FAMILY AND
THE MAKING OF EUROPE

STUART CARROLL

OXFORD

UNIVERSITY PRESS

OXFORD

UNIVERSITY PRESS

Great Clarendon Street, Oxford OX2 6DP

Oxford University Press is a department of the University of Oxford.
It furthers the University's objective of excellence in research, scholarship,
and education by publishing worldwide in

Oxford New York

Auckland Cape Town Dar es Salaam Hong Kong Karachi
Kuala Lumpur Madrid Melbourne Mexico City Nairobi
New Delhi Shanghai Taipei Toronto

With offices in

Argentina Austria Brazil Chile Czech Republic France Greece
Guatemala Hungary Italy Japan Poland Portugal Singapore
South Korea Switzerland Thailand Turkey Ukraine Vietnam

Oxford is a registered trade mark of Oxford University Press
in the UK and in certain other countries

Published in the United States
by Oxford University Press Inc., New York

British Library Cataloguing in Publication Data

Data available

Library of Congress Control Number: 2009924595

Typeset by SPI Publisher Services, Pondicherry, India
Printed in Great Britain
on acid-free paper by

Clays Ltd., St. Ives plc

ISBN 978-0-19-922907-9

1 3 5 7 9 10 8 6 4 2

PREFACE

To understand the Guise is to understand the profound transformations that shook sixteenth-century Europe. So it is mystifying that outside France they are all but forgotten. For in their day the Guise were held in awe throughout Europe. Admiring or appalled, none could ignore them. Enemies at one time or another of the great dynasties of Tudor, Habsburg, Valois, and Bourbon, the Guise were one of the most powerful princely houses of sixteenth-century Europe. With dreams of empire and aspirations to rule several kingdoms, they were the greatest non-royal house of their age. There may have been richer German princes and more cultured Italian dukes, but none had the astonishing range of dynastic interests which they possessed, ranging from Scotland to Sicily and from Ireland to Jerusalem. Their story requires retelling and it is fitting that the first comprehensive biography of the family for a century and half should fall to an Englishman, and not just because Elizabeth I considered for most of her reign that it was the Guise, and not Philip II, who was her foremost enemy.

Today, the main family members are largely remembered outside France as bit players in the drama of one of their brood, Mary Stuart, Queen of Scots. But Mary's story cannot be told fully without reference to her kith and kin. Mary's star certainly burned brightly for a brief while: she was Queen of France for eighteen months, and claimed the thrones of England and Ireland before setting sail for Scotland in 1561. Yet once there, events were soon out of her control and she spent the last nineteen years of her life in prison, a pawn in dynastic politics. She was not the sun around which her kinsfolk orbited. Mary's importance to history lies less in the consequences of her deeds, but more in what she represented at the time and continues to represent, whether as woman, lover, or martyr. Her life has been romanticized and her historical significance overstated. Put simply, in the annals of the Guise family her existence values a few brief pages. There is no need for hyperbole when it comes to retelling the deeds of her uncles and cousins. They shaped the course of European history: rising to prominence around mid-century as the greatest enemies of the House of Habsburg before plunging France into bloody chaos, they refashioned the Catholic Church at the Council of Trent; plotted to invade England and remove Elizabeth I; and made and unmade the kings of France before ending the century as martyrs for the Catholic cause.

All this is true and makes for drama. The story is a good one, but it is also an important one. Their mark on history was not confined to military campaigns, artistic patronage, and diplomatic and court intrigue. The Reformation was not just a religious event; it led to a profound reordering of political thought and practice. The Guise embody the changes wrought by the sixteenth century. As popular movements were mobilized for and against the Reformation, the traditional dynastic politics of the middle ages were utterly transformed. Power was no longer the preserve of a tiny aristocratic elite. What shocked contemporaries about the Guise was that they represented something novel and pernicious. They incited and manipulated popular Catholic feeling and used the new medium of print to create a religious party with mass support. More than fifty years before the English Republic, the Guise led a religious and political revolution in France that overthrew the Valois monarchy.

The Guise story urgently needs retelling for another reason. In an age of religious fundamentalism, it is time to revisit the roots of Europe's own religious violence. The word 'massacre' was first used in its modern context in sixteenth-century France. The French Wars of Religion are of wider significance not simply because France was the most populous state in Europe and because its Calvinist Church was for a decade Europe's largest, or because the conflict sucked in all of Europe's major powers. They were significant because ordinary Catholics and Protestants throughout Europe conceived events in France as part of a wider confessional struggle. France's tribulations were a constant backdrop to domestic affairs and a terrible object lesson in what might happen at home if one's guard was momentarily dropped. The image and actions of the Guise family were on public trial. At home, their appeal to Catholic populism was to make them more powerful than the King of France. In the eyes of the Catholic masses they were charismatic heroes, worshipped in song and woodcut, lauded in a new form of cheap political broadsheet. Protestants replied with their own scurrilous songs and satires. The Black Legend of the Guise was born.

The legend was most ubiquitous in England. Here, fascination with the Guise was intensified by Mary Queen of Scots' execution. And it is no coincidence that the Guise were among the first contemporary figures to be portrayed on the English stage. Christopher Marlowe's

Massacre at Paris set a dark tone, dramatizing the family's 'treacherous violence' (Act I, Scene IV), a Machiavellian pursuit of self-interest in the name of religion. First performed in 1593, barely a decade after the Guise had attempted to invade England and overthrow Elizabeth I, Marlowe gave voice to their vast ambition in the character of Henri, Duke of Guise. It is surely one of the most memorable soliloquies he ever wrote:

> What glory is there in a common good
> That hangs for every peasant to achieve?
> That like I best that flies beyond my reach.
> Set me to scale the high Pyramides,
> And thereon set the diadem of France,
> I'll either rend it with my nails to naught
> Or mount the top with my aspiring wings,
> Although my downfall be the deepest hell.

More whimsically, in *Doctor Faustus* (first performed in 1588/9 or 1592/3), the duke's uncle, the Cardinal of Lorraine, makes a brief appearance with the Pope, both entering the banquet hall only to have an invisible Faustus snatch away their dinners and, in a spectacular exit, scatter the banquet hall with fireworks. The stage popularity of the duke continued in the seventeenth century, making appearances in several plays and culminating in Dryden's *The Duke of Guise* of 1682, which was so controversial that its first performance was delayed by several months and the playwright forced to defend it in a separate *Vindication*.

This interest would be a mere footnote to English history if it were not for another important, hitherto neglected, facet of the Guise. Historians of England are interested in French events in so far as they relate to English foreign policy; dynastic matters, such as the Anjou match; or the development of a distinctly English Protestant national identity. Popular understandings of French affairs rely on the endless production of works on Mary Stuart, or the extraordinary (in all senses of the word) performance of Fanny Ardant as Marie de Guise, regent of Scotland, in Shekhar Kapur's film *Elizabeth* (1998). This is, however, preferable to the position in France, where the importance of British affairs to the development of a distinctive French Catholic identity in contradistinction to the heretical and perfidious English is all but ignored. Part of the *raison d'être* of this book therefore is to bring to a general readership some unjustly neglected aspects of Anglo-French relations during a crucial period—the projected Guise invasions of England, the major role played by the English Catholic refugees in Parisian politics, and the consequences for France of the Jesuit mission to England and Mary's captivity and execution.

The Guise story is a remarkable one, but it has yet to be told fully in any language, principally because it has been distorted by historians, who have cast the Guise as heroes or villains, martyrs or murderers, according to sectarian prejudice. From Marlowe's *Massacre* onwards they have made for stock historical villains; portrayed by their enemies as power-hungry Machiavellian conspirators, history has judged them harshly, accusing them of selling out France to foreigners, of pursuing their own interest to the detriment of the *patrie*, of being slavishly devoted to the cause of religious reaction. It is time to put the record straight.

ACKNOWLEDGEMENTS

Just when I thought I had finally rid myself of the Guise, Luciana O'Flaherty at OUP persuaded me to write this book—I'm glad she did. The finished product owes much to her editorial nouse. I would like to thank Adam Morton, Susan Doran, Jean Braybook, Malcolm Walsby, Simon Ditchfield, and Justine Taylor for their help with enquiries. Bill Sheils listened politely to daily progress reports over coffee and read Chapter 6. Taneth Russell helped to rewrite the preface. John Bossy and Mark Greengrass have inspired many of the ideas that follow. They kindly agreed to read the finished manuscript in its entirety. They not only corrected numerous errors factual and stylistic, but their wisdom and expertise prompted re-thinks and fresh leads. Finally, a huge thanks to the students of my French Wars of Religion special-subject group at York who, over the last decade, have stimulated and challenged me and contributed more than most to the contents of this book. It is dedicated to their enthusiasm.

CONTENTS

CONTENTS

LIST OF MAPS, PLATES, AND
GENEALOGICAL TABLES

Maps

Plates

1. Portrait ou Plan de la Ville de Vassy
2. Massacre at Wassy (March 1562)
3. Portrait of Claude de Lorraine, 1st Duke of Guise
   (Jean Clouet (or Cloet), Galleria Palatina,
   Palazzo Pitti, Florence)
4. Antoinette de Bourbon, Duchess of Guise
5. Mary of Guise and King James V
6. Joinville
7. The Italian garden and new palace at Joinville
8. Anne, Duke of Montmorency
9. Cardinal Charles of Lorraine (El Greco)
10. The Cardinal of Lorraine's device
11. François de Lorraine, Duke of Guise
12. Catherine de Medici
13. Arms of Mary Stuart, Queen of France, England,
    Scotland, and Ireland
14. The executions at Amboise, 15 March 1560
15. View of the grotto of Meudon
16. The Colloquy of Poissy
17. Triumph of the Eucharist, c.1562 (Leonard Limousin)
18. The Duke of Guise is mortally wounded
19. The three Coligny brothers
20. Henri de Lorraine, Duke of Guise, aged 16
21. Henri III (Francois Quesnel the elder)
22. The Massacre of Saint Bartholomew's Day
    (Francois Dubois)

Genealogical Tables

A NOTE ON COINAGE

Two types of money existed side by side in sixteenth-century France: money of account and actual coin. Accounts were kept in the former; actual transactions carried out in the latter. The principal money of account was the livre, the term that readers will encounter most often in this book. The French livre was the equivalent of the English system of pounds, shillings and pence. One livre was worth twenty sous; one sou worth twelve deniers. Readers will also come across the écu or crown, an actual coin, whose value fluctuated. In 1575 it was worth three livres. In the sixteenth century one English pound was worth approximately ten French livres.

I

INVITATION TO A MASSACRE

Early spring is a busy season in the vineyards of France. But on the morning of Saturday 28 February 1562, those toiling on the east-facing hills overlooking the château of Joinville who momentarily stopped pruning their vines and looked below were treated to an impressive sight. Two hundred heavily armed men were mounting up; their lord and master, François de Lorraine, Duke of Guise, ten days after celebrating his forty-third birthday had been summoned to court by the regent of France, Catherine de Medici, on an important matter of state. While at court a superficial state of peace prevailed, the provinces of France were descending into civil war as Protestants fought to defend their right to worship and Catholics to deny them. As head of one of the greatest princely houses of Europe, he was a rare visitor to Joinville these days, but he was immediately recognizable among the throng: 'no more and no less than the tallest, thickest and most honorable oak among all the trees in the forest', as one contemporary put it.[1] And this was no exaggeration: the Guise were uniformly tall in an age when men were on average much shorter than they are today, and when much greater store was placed on physical prowess. Mary Stuart, the duke's niece, was 5 feet 11 inches tall and she shared with her uncle the distinctive blond hair, which made the Guise look so un-French like, and which added fuel to the court gossips, who whispered that the Guise were not true-born French-men, but 'foreigners' from the 'Germanic' lands of Lorraine. The peasants were privileged to catch a glimpse of one of the most famous men alive. As the Venetian ambassador put it, 'he surpasses by his courage, not only all the most celebrated generals of his age, but also any that have come before'.[2]

To the peasants working among the vines, the sights and sounds of a princely retinue on the move was as amazing as it was unusual. An aristocratic retinue was a naked expression of power and, in dangerous times such as these, it had to be seen to bristle with menace. The most impressive men came from the squadron of the ducal gendarmerie company, which at full strength comprised 250 heavy cavalry. This was the elite of the French royal army, on campaign the men-at-arms being required to arm themselves with closed helm; a good cuirass; upper arm and forearm armour; thigh, haunch and knee pieces; and a fully armoured saddle in addition to a pistol and a good, strong lance. Their horses were required to be barded—that is to have head and chest armour as well as flank protection. Each man had to maintain two great warhorses and one nag for his baggage.

Also catching the eyes of those accustomed only to everyday hues was the dazzling clash of colours. Red and yellow were the colours of the House of Lorraine. It was used for the duke's livery, on which was stitched the distinctive ducal badge ‡, today known as the cross of Lorraine, but in those days more properly called the cross of Anjou— a reminder that the Guise claimed descent from one of the greatest of medieval princely houses. Yellow was also the colour of the House of Bourbon, from whom the duke was descended through his mother. But he was most likely dressed in his favourite colour, red, which was traditionally associated with martial prowess, and wearing a hat topped with red plumes, 'for he loved plumes'.[3] The ears of those listening from the vineyards would also have been assailed by the strange and unfamiliar. Foreign sounds mingled with more familiar cadences among the shouts and commands of the officers, as the men prepared to move off. Most of the men-at-arms were local, from the Barrois, Chaumont, Eastern Champagne and the other borderlands where the kingdom of France met the duchy of Lorraine, then part of the Holy Roman Empire. But the following of a great prince was a polyglot entity that reflected his dynastic interests and that made flesh an identity that was not restricted by national boundaries. Along with his soldiers travelled the men who counselled him, dressed him, served at his table, cared for his horses, and checked his accounts. Here were heard accents from Normandy and Picardy, where the duke was a significant landowner, but also from Italy, where all educated Frenchmen believed the centre of the world to be and where the duke had once campaigned; from Germany, whose people were prized for their warlike disposition and whose specialist 'muscle' was called upon for particularly dirty and dangerous work; and from

Scotland, to where Mary Stuart had six months previously been unhappily dispatched. Lackeys provided 'protection' for their lord; they were often employed solely for their ability to intimidate and to project an image of invulnerability. Their swaggering braggadocio was announced by the outlandishness of their appearance: earrings, ruffs, codpieces, trend-setting haircuts, and artfully curled mustaches. At their sides dangled the newly-fashionable long sword, which the English called the rapier but which they knew as a 'verdun', whose elaborate hand guards marked out their owners as men of fashion and distinction. But the rapier was not just for show: it announced that one was a man of honour and prepared to die fighting if necessary to uphold it.

The onlookers' gaze could not have missed the ducal coat of arms, which was everywhere to be seen: on the surcoats of his men, on the carriage which carried his pregnant wife, Anne d'Este, and, not least, on his battle standard, unfurled by the standard bearer of the gendarmes, which depicted three silver eaglets on a red band set on a yellow background. The eaglets were a reminder of his House's imperial heritage—that they were vicars of the Holy Roman Empire in the territories that lay between the Rhine and the Moselle. Coats of arms symbolized the identity of the family and, with the badges, banners, and livery, they were totems representing the bonds of fellowship and mutual obligation which bound the princely host together. The quarters of the duke's coat of arms represented the seven other sovereign houses from which he claimed descent: Hungary, Naples, Jerusalem, Aragon, Guelders, Jülich, and Bar. This was no idle symbolism but a statement of his claim for precedence among his fellow men and of his rights, which he was honour-bound to defend.

As prince of Joinville, François was aware that his ancestors occupied an especially privileged place in the annals of chivalry and, as a Christian knight, a history that he aspired to emulate. Originally built in the eleventh century on a wooded spur of a hill overlooking a bend on the left bank of the river Marne, it had seen the famous Jean de Joinville, companion in arms and chronicler of Saint Louis, ride forth to the crusades; it housed the relics brought back from Palestine and the shield of Geoffroy V de Joinville given to him by Richard the Lionheart; it had sheltered Jeanne d'Arc at the beginning of her mission; during the Hundred Years War it had been a French frontier outpost and partially burnt by the Burgundians. Despite its growth into a bustling market town of 3,000 people and the building of its

Renaissance château surrounded by one of the most magnificent gardens in France, Joinville was still a frontier outpost; as recently as 1544 it had been burned and pillaged by the invading forces of Charles V, Holy Roman Emperor and king of Spain. Guise's loathing for the House of Habsburg was based on personal experience. It was hostility to the Habsburg which had brought the Guise and their neighbours, the Houses of Clèves and la Marck, to the French court. These princely houses occupied a privileged position at the very apex of French society, although it was only in the seventeenth century that they were commonly referred to as *princes étrangers*, which distinguished them juridically from indigenous French princes.

* * * *

Joinville faced east across the Marne. The countryside round about was hilly and wooded with vines on the lower slopes; but higher up the slopes, some of which rose to over 1,000 feet, the gradients were so steep that only grass clung to them. From here, as far as the eye could see, the land belonged to the duke. A land of water, woods and hills, it was neither well populated nor particularly productive, but it made for magnificent hunting, the duke's favourite pastime. Nine miles to the south-east of Joinville, at the limits of his lands, lay one of his many hunting lodges, hidden amidst the forests in the village of Doulaincourt. Just beyond, in the same direction, the onlooker could admire Reynel, the château of the duke's neighbour, Antoine de Clermont-Amboise, who at one time had been a frequent guest at Joinville. The duke found little to admire now that Antoine was a Protestant, a pestilence that everywhere crept closer and closer to his own lands. Turning to the north-east, seven miles from Joinville, was the duke's smaller château at Montiers-sur-Saulx, which lay within the Barrois, not part of the kingdom of France but belonging to the Duke of Lorraine. But the duke was not heading in this direction; he turned west towards Paris, where he had been summoned because of the crisis caused by the Edict of Toleration, which had been promulgated only six weeks before by Catherine de Medici. Although the Edict had only conceded the Protestants limited and temporary rights of public worship, its implications were revolutionary in a monarchy founded on the precepts of 'one king, one faith, one law'. Not since the fall of the Roman Empire had a European state officially permitted the exercise of more than one Christian creed among its subjects; nowhere in sixteenth-century Europe, not even in heterogeneous

Poland, did there exist similar legal protection for religious dissidents. For people in the sixteenth century, toleration lacked the positive connotations that it does today; they prized above all the unity of the body social. To 'tolerate' meant putting up with something that one did not care for. Heresy was another word for sedition. For most Catholics not only was the Crown 'tolerating' something it should be rooting out; it was setting a dangerous precedent in giving in to rebels, who had renounced the true faith into which they had been baptized.

But these abstract principles were less on the duke's mind as he headed to his first stop, his manor at Dommartin-le-Franc, situated in the next major valley, where flowed the river Blaise. No—the man who claimed to be one of the greatest princes of Christendom, who dominated this region of Eastern Champagne known as 'the vallage', was having his authority undermined and his pride injured in his own backyard. The complaints of his mother, Antoinette de Bourbon, about the spread of heretics hereabouts were still ringing in his ears. She was a woman who demanded respect and attention, for it was she, like most aristocratic women who shunned the frivolities of the royal court, who looked after the family finances. While he had little time for local affairs and was often away at court or on campaign, she resided permanently at Joinville and took care of the mundane matters of estate administration both locally and in the extensive Guise domains in the rest of France, busying herself with land deals, overseeing agents and estate managers, making peace between squabbling peasants, dealing with the many requests from clients for preferment and favour, and above all doling out alms to the sick and poor to whom she has devoted herself since the death of her husband in 1550.[4] Now aged 68, Antoinette, who had given birth to the last of her twelve children in 1539, was also responsible for the upbringing of the duke's own children and his nieces and nephews. She presided over a sort of blue-bloodied crèche at Joinville with her daughters-in-law, where her young grandchildren were raised alongside other aristocratic children who had been placed there by parents eager to hitch their fortunes to the Guise star.

Antoinette inspired respect not only because this was a society that viewed disregard of parental authority as a sin, but also because even by the standards of her time she was austerely pious. In the early seventeenth century it was recalled that she was a 'mirror of perfection, a princess of rare virtue, in such a way that the common opinion that she was a saint has lasted until this day'.[5] Her piety was as famous in her own day as it was conventional: King Henry II

5

had charged her with the reorganization of the royal relic collection in the Sainte-Chapelle in Paris, a task which she performed with such care that 'a little part of each [relic] was given to her and encased in a silver reliquary', with typical modesty it was 'a gift which she passed to the parish church of Saint-Laurent, Joinville'.[6] The regime she maintained at Joinville, in which her sons and grandsons were brought up, was far from the festivals of excess usually associated with the Renaissance aristocracy. She went to Mass every day and, in the gallery that connected her apartments to the chapel, placed her own coffin 'in order that the spectacle would serve as a perpetual reminder of the day of her death'.[7] Since the death of her husband she had never worn anything else than mourning clothes and she herself stitched the garments that the poor would wear at her funeral. Hers was a medieval piety, at odds with the new currents of contemplative belief associated with Erasmus and his fellow humanists; she had inherited her father's great psalter and his book of hours, but also his flagellant's hair shirt and scourge. Her confessor, the Dominican Pierre Doré, who had captivated her with his zeal and preaching eloquence when he had come to Champagne to reform a Carthusian monastery, was a prolific writer of works refuting heresy and defender of Catholic orthodoxy, but his brand of Catholicism seemed so naïve to the humanists that he became the butt of clever jokes: Rabelais alludes to his preposterous sermons as Master 'Dungpowder' in *Pantagruel*. Twice, in 1533 and 1557, heretics had burned beneath her eyes in Joinville town square. No wonder that Protestants referred to her as their 'capital enemy'.[8]

For an eldest son charged with the responsibility of family head, the righteous anger of one's mother can be the most chastening of experiences. On François's arrival at Joinville a few days before, Antoinette 'had ceaselessly complained to her son, and begged him continually to sort out such an unpleasant neighbourhood, and she often reproached him for his patience which she saw as excessive, [and] which would, in her words, offend God and do harm to his reputation'.[9] During his absence Protestant worship had spread to the very borders of his domain, and particularly to the royal town of Wassy on the Blaise, seven miles away. Wassy was a moderately prosperous walled market town of 3,000 souls, where the surrounding countryside was more suitable for farming than the higher ground to the east. People from the surrounding area came to do business; there was a market, a notary, and a royal law court. There was also industry: there were many forges in the area, mines, and no less than 120 mills were turned by the Blaise when it was high enough. Above all, like in other parts of urban Champagne, there was weaving and cloth production that linked the town to the major city of Troyes, the regional capital and a cloth manufacturing centre of international importance, employing nearly a quarter of its 30,000 inhabitants.[10] Wassy was not full of rich people, but there were significant numbers who were not completely dependent on agriculture and its traditional rhythms and for whom the economic and cultural Renaissance of France in the first half of the sixteenth century had promoted literacy and provided the where-withal to buy the occasional luxury, such as the new Geneva bible. Its Protestant community had a long gestation: the man burnt at Joinville in 1533 had been caught preaching there, and twelve years later they were confident enough to evangelize in local villages.[11] On 12 October 1561, in the house of a wholesale draper, Wassy held its first properly officiated Protestant service for 120 people. The confident church of Troyes, whose congregation worshipped openly at a number of sites in the town and whose numbers exceeded 2,000, sent representatives to Wassy to advise and help their friends establish a church. The spread of Protestantism was abetted by commercial and kinship networks—the Protestant cells of Troyes had themselves been galvanized to establish a church in 1551 by Michel de Poncelet, a wool-carder and cloth weaver from nearby Meaux. The richer Troyen merchants evangelized and sent books to their kinsmen and business partners in the smaller towns. The local nobility also did much to ensure Protestantism's expansion outwards from its urban base. Most of Champagne's ministers came not from Geneva, but Neuchâtel, a principality beyond the kingdom of France in the Jura Mountains. It was administered in the name of her young son, the Duke of Long-ueville, by Jacqueline de Rohan, a confidante of Calvin who lived at Blandy on the western fringes of Champagne.

Wassy may have been a day's ride away, across the marshes and through the woods of what is called humid Champagne, but for the missionaries from Troyes the route was not a hostile one: the road passed through friendly estates and there were several gentlemen's residences where a friendly welcome was guaranteed, such as the castles of the 24-year-old Jean de Luxembourg at Piney and Brienne. Jean was a great magnate with links to the Troyen Protestant elite, and he attended services in the city.[12] Evidence of his godliness survives in the château of Ligny in the Barrois, where he commissioned a huge iron plaque; at over one square metre in size and weighing 200 kilograms it was positioned in the fireplace in the great hall and depicted his arms and his badge, a mermaid. More unusual were the passages from psalm 72 and two passages from the gospels crucial to Reformation theology. The first reads 'Jesus our Lord...was put to death for our sins and raised for our justification' (Rom. 4, v. 25), referring to the Protestant belief that man is saved by faith in Jesus Christ alone. The second was from Saint Paul's third letter to the Ephesians, 'the Gentiles...are partakers of eternal life through the gospel', which declares the exclusive authority of the word of God against the errors and incertitude of human tradition. Had the Duke of Guise visited his neighbour at Ligny, as his mother did, he would have been as aware as any guest that the errors and traditions referred to belonged to his Catholic faith.

It seems likely that the Protestant cell in Wassy had initially attended services at Brienne, Trémilly and on other noble estates in the vicinity, but this still meant a long journey for a cloth worker on foot, and their growing number and confidence in the autumn of 1561 persuaded them to consider setting up their own church. The advice of Troyes was that such an undertaking was likely to antagonize the Guise, for not only was Wassy too close to their lands but the usufruct of the royal demesne at Wassy had recently been signed over to Mary Stuart as a part of her jointure as dowager queen of France. Her uncle had been charged with its administration. It was considered safer to maintain a secret conventicle serviced by Pastor Jean Gravelle from Troyes. However, numbers grew so rapidly that secrecy became a problem. Perhaps as many as 500 to 600 people, many of them curious Catholics, came to hear Gravelle's sermons, and he was forced to move to the courtyard of the hospital, which lay just beyond the town walls, in order to accommodate them.

Wassy would not at first seem to have been a welcoming place for the Reformation. Indeed, the Duke of Guise had got wind of the public preaching and in early November sent some of his gendarmes to 'snuff out this small church in its infancy'.[13] But reformed ideas incubated well in small towns which prided themselves on their civic independence, where everyone knew each other, where everyone had a relative or neighbour who was a member of the new church, where even those who remained attached to the old faith shared the general antipathy to the overfed monks of Montier-en-Der, who controlled Wassy's parish church and its revenues and exercised jurisdiction over twenty-one parishes in the vicinity. The abbot of Montier was none other than the duke's brother, Charles, Cardinal of Lorraine, head of the Catholic Church in France and the richest man in the kingdom.

Wassy was a microcosm of the complacency that beset the Catholic clergy everywhere: families among the local elite saw benefices principally as a cash cow and a means to social advancement and were only tangentially concerned with the welfare of the laity. Clerical pluralism was an issue at Wassy; the son of the provost, Claude le Sain, was not only curé of the town, a task made much more onerous in recent years by population growth, but also had control of the house of Augustinian hermits, situated among the forests outside the town. Provost le Sain played an important role in the events to come. He was initially a supporter of aspects of the reform movement. Protestants later accused him of 'having revolted against the knowledge he had of the truth of the Gospels'.[14] Like many educated Catholics he desired a more scripturally based religion. But as a royal official he had no desire to challenge the status quo. This explains the particular hostility the Protestants reserved for him, and those they considered to be 'Apostates' or 'Nicodemites', that is those who hid their truth faith. Le Sain's concerns were first expressed to Antoinette de Bourbon when the Protestants began to worship publicly. She urged him to do something, but he would do nothing without the authority of the provincial governor and expected the Guise to help him out of his predicament.

Guise's threats were unsuccessful for another reason. The psychology of Protestantism thrived on adversity; a sense of persecution may even have been essential to its spread, since the righteous expect their faith to be tested by God. Protestants referred to themselves and interpreted events in biblical terms; they were the Israelites, threatened on all sides by the heathen, but sure in the knowledge that if they kept faith they would be saved, while the rest were surely damned. In the land of the king of Babylon, God's chosen people would not be stopped from raising their temple in his honour: on 13 December, in defiance of the duke, Jean Gravelle travelled from Troyes to perform the first Protestant baptisms in the town.

On the advice of the Cardinal of Lorraine, the duke decided to adopt a more conciliatory approach and bring back his subjects and neighbours by force of argument. Four days after the baptismal rites, a delegation arrived headed by the Bishop of Châlons—Guise's creature—Jérôme Bourgeois. He summoned the leading Protestants, each of whom was well known locally, and announced that the following day a monk would preach to them and return them to the fold. The meeting was tense, since the Protestants did not wish to listen to 'false prophets' and the bishop was perturbed by their insolence and suggestion that he should come and hear their pastor, but after two hours of negotiation they agreed to his demand. They saw it as an opportunity to vindicate themselves and spread the Word; that evening they met with pastor Gravelle to plan the bishop's downfall.

When, the following morning, Bishop Jérôme entered the large barn that served as the Protestant meeting house, it was as far removed from the experience of entering his cathedral in Châlons as he could possibly have imagined. In the cathedral, the brightly painted and decorated walls, and the glorious clutter of reliquaries, stained glass, votive candles, tombs of local worthies, pictures of Saint Etienne, the cathedral's patron, and images of the virgin assailed the eye of the beholder. Pews, rails, and screens carefully demarcated sacred space. In contrast, the barn contained only a makeshift pulpit and the gaping holes in the roof, though they would one day prove an unintentional godsend, left the congregation exposed to the elements. With no pews to segregate the social classes, or men from women, the congregation mixed freely, giving credence to Catholic preachers' claims that these meetings were akin to the witches' coven, a breeding ground for social disorder and sexual licentiousness. And it was noisy. When the bishop arrived with his train, consisting of a fifteen-man retinue, the preacher, Provost le Sain, the royal procurator, and the prior of Wassy, it was already crammed full of expectant townsfolk. As they entered, the Protestants opened their psalm books and began singing the hymn to the Commandments:

> Thus spoke the Lord: I am your God,
> who brought you out of Egypt's land.
> One God alone shall you revere
> and so fulfil my command (Kyrie eleison!).[15]

Catholics were unaccustomed to such sounds. The laity did not normally sing during the liturgy and the strangeness of the psalms offended many Catholics: in Troyes in April 1559 a goldsmith had been murdered for having the temerity to sing them in the streets.[16] The congregation followed their hymn with a prayer, which was cut short by the bishop, who wished to have his arrival formally announced. But Pastor Gravelle had no regard for the usual niceties and showed no respect for the bishop's dignity, cutting him short: 'Monsieur, since I am in the chair first, I shall be the first to speak.' Behind this veneer of politesse lurked an insult, it being more correct for a man of his low station to address a bishop with the dignified Monseigneur. Gravelle had seized the initiative and went on to state that they were permitted by law to practise their beliefs and none should prevent them from doing so. In fact, this was untrue: the royal council was at that moment debating the matter, but at this stage such assemblies were still forbidden in law. His argument, however, rested not on the letter of the law but on its interpretation: the provincial governor, who had the power to 'interpret' royal edicts as he saw fit, had recently permitted Protestant worship in Troyes. What he failed to mention was that the governor, the Duke of Nevers, was himself a Protestant.

Gravelle offered the bishop the right to reply, but again in such a manner as to cut the man down to size: 'Speak not in your capacity as a bishop, but as a private individual, for we only recognize you as such.' The event was already slipping from the bishop's control and he was on the defensive. He found himself asking why they would not accept him as a bishop, which simply allowed the pastor to expound on the failings of the Catholic clergy. The pastor mocked him for failing to administer the sacraments and being unable to preach; and when the bishop said he did not need to preach and employed vicars to do so, he trumped his adversary with the precise passages of scripture in which bishops were conjoined to preach in person. Bishop Jérôme was then required to defend Episcopal authority and the concept of apostolic succession—things he had not dreamt of having to do and for which he was unprepared. He was, however, no fool and he tried a couple of jokes to mock and deflate his earnest opponent, a move which contrived only to make the pastor more serious: 'saying that on several occasions he had exposed his life to danger in the name of Jesus Christ, and that... he was ready to seal with his own blood the doctrine that he preached to the poor people'. And he went on to denounce the riches of the Church and the poverty of the people: 'You have taken trouble only to nourish your insatiable greed, and not those souls which were bought so dearly by the blood of the Eternal son of God.' The pastor was now playing to the crowd, asking rhetorically which of the debaters was better suited to care for them. The bishop could not compete with this sort of populism so he now asked the minister to leave; the minister refused, saying that he would now preach the Gospel and that if the bishop wished to he could listen in peace, otherwise he should depart henceforth. Even Protestant sources describe the meeting as angry: the bishop could only conclude that 'fury' reigned among them; the provost had already left in fright. They were pursued on leaving the barn by cries of 'Wolf! Fox! Ass! Get back to school!' The monk bravely went to preach in Wassy church, but, startled by the noise of the Protestants leaving their meeting, soon thought better of it, quitting the pulpit in such haste that he left one of his shoes behind.

Even if the Protestants exaggerated the extent of their victory there is no denying the impact that this drama had on the town. Many new converts were won over that day with the simple message that they should stay and listen to the sermon and afterwards ask any question they wished. This was a young movement responding to a laity hungry for news of the path to true salvation. The congregation grew rapidly. It was claimed that 900 people took communion at Christmas. Although some of them came from the surrounding region—Guise tenants among them (one of the deacons was a Joinville man)—there is no doubt that, as a proportion of the town's population, Wassy compared well with other Protestant strongholds. In percentage terms the congregation was now stronger than the host church at Troyes. It was time to appoint a permanent minister: Jean Gravelle returned to Troyes and on 27 January Léonard Morel arrived from Geneva.

Bishop Jérôme hurried back to Joinville to lick his wounds. Antoinette de Bourbon ordered a report to be drawn up and sent to the king and, in the absence of her eldest son, she set to work to bring this insolent riff-raff to heel. She summoned Provost le Sain and the prior and ordered them to ensure that none of her 'subjects' took part in Protestant services, said anything derogatory about the Holy Roman Church, or failed to attend Mass. She wrote strongly worded letters to the principal townsfolk expressing her (and Mary Stuart's) displeasure. In the meantime, a Lenten preacher, otherwise referred to as the 'cockroach' by Protestants, was dispatched to shore up the Catholic faithful.

* * * *

On 1 March 1562, fifty Protestants were massacred in Wassy. Thus began a conflict that shook Europe for thirty-six years. Historians once disdained the study of events as being the mere flotsam of history that floated on deeper, more impersonal seas. More recently, the ways in which an event can utterly transform and reshape history has been brought into sharp focus by 9/11. Wassy was one of the great transformative events of European history, ushering in the age of the Wars of Religion, which over the next century would engulf the whole of Europe, the legacy of which, until recently, we congratulated ourselves on having been confined to a corner of Ireland.

The Protestant accounts stress premeditation. But the evidence is flimsy. When the Duke of Guise left Joinville he did not make straight for the town; he was accompanied by his pregnant wife in a carriage, suggesting that this was not a whirlwind strike, and we know that his initial plan was to stop the night at Dommartin before heading north-east to another of his residences at Eclaron, stopping briefly at Wassy only to pick up a squadron of gendarmes who were accustomed to lodge in the town. Pro-Guise accounts, on the other hand, overplay the accidental and unplanned nature of events on 1 March. In order to interpret accounts which were written for propaganda purposes, I want to do something that historians largely try to avoid: speculate about the duke's state of mind on that previous evening.

This was the season of Lent, a time of fasting and prayer, and in recent years a season in which a new breed of fiery preacher was gaining celebrity for their vitriolic denunciation of heresy, reminding their audience that God's wrath would inevitably be brought down on Catholics unless they excised this pollution from the community. There was one very important man who sat down with the duke to share his frugal meal that night who was open to such a message: the duke's 77-year-old chief advisor, Jacques de la Brosse. Jacques had a particularly strong devotion to the Eucharist and an intense veneration of the Host and its sacred properties, the product of a Catholic revivalism in reaction to Protestant denials that the consecrated bread turned into the body of Christ. Jacques's Eucharistic piety was unusual even among his fellow revivalists, for he called his daughter by a highly unusual name: Euchariste. No wonder he was chosen as the man to combat Protestantism in Scotland, spending three years there in total and finally returning to France in the summer of 1560. But the Guise were not motivated by blind religious zeal or easily seduced by the counsel of fanatics. The duke was not a man given to excessive devotion; indeed he displayed an aristocratic *hauteur* for any passion that smacked of a loss of control. His brother Louis, Cardinal of Guise, was with him at Dommartin but he was more courtier than priest and more likely than the others to consider breaking the Lenten fast. Known as 'the cardinal of the bottles' in reference to his penchant for booze, he once admitted in a letter to his disapproving mother that a stomach ache had been caused by a surfeit of eating and hunting while at court.[17] The duke's wife, Anne d'Este, was no fanatic either—she had been raised a Protestant and was known for her compassion.

An assault on Wassy is unlikely to have been the dinner-table conversation that night; the duke had other things on his mind. In his governorship of Dauphiné, a province close to Calvin's Geneva and in even greater turmoil than Champagne, he was facing armed insurrection. That evening he dictated a letter to his lieutenant there, la Motte-Gondrin, the tenor of which tells us much about his state of mind: 'I think that if there is large assembly [of Protestants] . . . it would be best to seize the pastor, and to immediately hang him, as the author of the seditions and conspiracies against you, and of the rebellions that they are making now against the edicts and commandments of the King . . . which will curb the madness of the rest.'[18] This letter was intercepted by the Protestants who later published it as evidence of the duke's pre-meditation at Wassy. In fact, it is nothing of the sort. Dauphiné had been experiencing a vicious sectarian civil war for months: there had been attempted coups in several towns. La Motte-Gondrin's opponent there, the Baron des Adrets, was the bloodiest of Protestant captains, whose veins even moderates said coursed with 'black blood'. Des Adrets campaign was fuelled by personal factors: the Duke of Guise had forbidden him to fight a duel, his honour thereby besmirched. His revenge was on a grand scale. The duke's present concern was therefore sedition and revolt; to him Protestants who worshipped openly in large gatherings were rebels and deserved to be treated as such, but he made it clear, in line with royal policy before the Edict of Toleration, that only pastors were to be made examples of. The duke's fears were very real—within two months of writing this letter there was a Protestant coup in Valence; la Motte-Gondrin was killed and his body displayed from a window in the centre of the town.

What gripped the duke as he set off from Dommartin early on Sunday 1 March for Eclaron was not some abstract religious anxiety—the fear of God's wrath lest he act—but the feeling that everywhere his authority was under threat. He was only too aware that the manor in which he had stayed the night was, under France's infinitely complex feudal laws, held in vassalage from his neighbour, the Protestant Count of Brienne. How humiliating it was to do homage to a heretic! He had to cross Wassy, entering through the south and departing through the north gate, in order to reach Eclaron, but there was no need to stop in the town. However, the season demanded that he and his men hear Mass. Eclaron was too far away, so when the troop had done only three miles it stopped at the village of Brousseval, only a mile or so from Wassy, where he could have done his devotions. But he chose not to.

There were certainly those who counselled that the Protestants should be dealt with, but the duke was not initially among them: 'I would not suffer my breakfast to be prepared at Wassy, so I ordered that it should be waiting for me at [Brousseval], expressly to prevent what would come to pass at Wassy... wishing to prevent one of my men from irritating or saying words to the townsfolk, and that neither one nor the other entered into religious disputes, which I had expressly forbidden mine to do'.[19] He quickly lost his appetite when, on arriving at Brousseval, he heard the ringing of bells from the direction of Wassy 'at a time when one was not accustomed to hearing them'.[20] He loudly demanded what the ringing was for and a number of his men, as well as people in the street, replied that the Protestants were being summoned to their Sunday service. The bells had clearly upset him. Were the Protestants making use of Wassy's church? While we would hardly consider bell-ringing an antisocial activity, the sound of bells was often a cause of friction in pre-industrial societies. The right to ring bells at particular times and during particular festivals was a right that was highly coveted. Even in the early nineteenth century there continued to be many disputes over 'the power to decide when the bells were to be rung and when they were to remain silent during the rites of passage'.[21] Bell ringing was an especially contentious issue in the sixteenth century—both Protestants and Catholics rang them to drown out the services of the other. Nuisance noise is still the greatest cause of neighbourly disputes today. For the duke, it was also a direct challenge to his rights of lordship, as protector of the patrimony of Mary Stuart. He decided to summon a council. When an important decision was to be taken, noblemen did nothing in haste. Guise's men were expected to lay down their lives in his service and they expected to be consulted on matters of policy: a noble following had a collective identity and sense of responsibility and the man who acted alone could find himself isolated. Some counsellors did not share the duke's caution. Two men in particular played a key role at this juncture. The master of his household, Jacques de la Montaigne, originally from distant Saintonge, had settled in the vicinity of Wassy ten years previously and was 'a great enemy [of the Protestants and]...author and solicitor of the massacre'.[22] The ultra pious Jacques de la Brosse, whose son was to play a big role in the events that were to follow, was also a key man in that fateful decision. A no-nonsense man of action, he had been present with the duke in all his major triumphs of the past fifteen years and had achieved recognition as the most experienced and respected captains of his day and 'the most sweet and gracious man of war that one had ever known'.[23] The rise of these two out-siders was due to talent: the sentiments of kinship and neighbourliness that were providing the Protestants of Wassy a measure of protection from other ducal servants were entirely lacking. There were many others whose goal in entering Wassy had little to do with faith or thoughts of order, especially 'the lackeys who rejoiced at this enter-prise saying that there'd be pillage for them'.[24]

The duke resolved to go and hear Mass at Wassy. It is here that his protestations of innocence ring hollow. He could have stayed at Brousseval but he was not welcome there, as the local lord of the manor was yet another convert to Protestantism, and he had encour-aged many of the inhabitants of the village to go to the Protestant service at Wassy.[25] By opting to go and hear Mass sung at Wassy with his full retinue, the duke was fully aware of the dangers. But the risks were overridden by the knowledge that everywhere in this region his rights were being challenged. He felt betrayed. If he could not hear Mass at Wassy, his niece's property, where else would soon be off limits? The duke was also aware that the Edict of Toleration provided for Protestant worship outside of towns, and the bell-ringing made it clear that Wassy's Protestants were holding their services inside the town. He may have gone with the intention of arresting Minister Morel, a policy he had backed before the Edict of Toleration. When the duke passed through Wassy's south gate he undoubtedly felt that he was doing his duty in upholding the law. Almost certainly lacking was any sense of the spirit in which those laws were enacted.

As the host entered the town at around 8 am, la Montaigne pointed out a Protestant rope-maker in the street who was interrogated before being released. The duke was apparently looking for the Protestant minister.[26] It is from here that Protestant sources become less reliable. The duke is supposed to have launched a surprise attack on the barn where the Protestants were meeting, but if this were so it was not a particularly successful enterprise: out of a congregation of several hun-dred, the duke's heavily armed retinue, most of them veteran soldiers and hired thugs, could only manage to kill a fraction of that number.

The duke did not head towards the barn, but instead made straight for the parish church of Wassy, where he intended to investigate the bell-ringing and do his devotions. A further irritation to the duke's mood came from the location of the barn. More provocative than the ringing of bells to announce a public service within the town walls was the fact the meeting house lay not one hundred yards from the church along a street that ran to the south-eastern quarter of the town. This part of town fell within the jurisdiction of the imposing royal castle. In his attempts to justify the events that were to follow, the duke made no mention of the fact that Protestants were worshipping within the city walls and therefore acting illegally under the terms of the Edict of Toleration.[27] Rather, he made much of the fact that the barn belonged to him and that they were worshipping on his property. In those days the castle quarter was clearly separated from the rest of the town by a ditch. The Protestants claimed that they were in the castle compound, technically outside the town's jurisdiction and therefore acting lawfully. But legal quibbles were not what provoked the duke's anger. The castle and its environs had been entrusted to his protection by his niece and he was furious that one of his subordinates, the captain of the castle, Claude Tondeur, should permit such an outrage to occur. (The presence of one of the captain's relatives among the Protestant congregation is further evidence of his complicity.)[28]

Most of the ducal host did not enter the church, alighting in the covered market opposite the western aisle, while others were posted in the cemetery, located between the church and the Protestant meeting house. The reinforcement gendarme squadron of fifty men, already fully armed, was in the Market Square and ready to move. Groups of soldiers milled about the streets. Barely one hundred yards away they could hear hundreds of psalm-singing voices. Once inside the church the duke convened the town's anti-Protestant faction, headed by the provost, the prior of Wassy, and the priest. To visit the Protestant meeting would not be without precedent: the Edict of Toleration stipulated that, while royal officials could not hinder Protestant worship, they had the right to oversee assemblies. The provost, opposed by powerful interests in the town, had been unable to stop the services and he must have been delighted finally to be able to press his case in person, persuading the duke to delay his departure for Eclaron. The meeting with the provost confirmed what the duke had already seen and heard that morning. At this point he became very agitated—something had to be done.

A later, moderate account probably has it about right when it says that the duke's 'design was not to do ill to any individual, but to dissipate by his presence these kinds of assemblies'.[29] There is no hint of a premeditated assault. He was determined to reprimand these rebels in person and he sent three men to announce his arrival: Gaston de la Brosse, son of Jacques and standard-bearer of the duke's gendarmes, and two German pages. It was now that events got out of hand; the three envoys arrived at the barn door to find the minister inside delivering his sermon to 500 or so men, women, and children.[30] What happened at the door we will never know, but it seems likely that they were not permitted to enter until the minister had finished and, when they raised their voices to object, were told to be quiet. They then tried to force an entry, but were repulsed. The unarmed Protestants at the door reached for anything that would scare them off—a stone or two were thrown. La Brosse had been humiliated by 'mere peasants' in front of his comrades. Noblemen recognized only one way to repair honour wounded in such a public fashion; his upbringing taught him to respond in only one way. He wanted their blood and now had support on all sides, as the duke's men rushed towards the noise of the scuffle. The first Protestants were killed vainly defending the barn door: a poor wine-seller was asked if he was a 'Huguenot' and when he replied that he 'believed in Jesus Christ' was run through with several sword thrusts; two others were cut down as they tried to make a run for it. Confusion quickly spread through the town: muskets were let off; cries of 'Kill! Kill! By God's death kill these Huguenots' were heard; the trumpets of the duke's gendarmerie company summoned them to the attack; the provost ran over to the Swan tavern and told the duke's lackeys to put down their drinks and run to their master's aid. Chaos reigned in the narrow streets as the duke arrived at the scene, and in the press he was unable or unwilling to hold his men back as they forced their way into the barn to exact vengeance. In this enclosed space the slaughter was face-to-face with swords and daggers, such that the 'posts and walls of the barn were splattered with blood'.[31] Amidst panic-stricken screams the congregation fled the slashing steel blades up the stairs and onto the barn roof, whose feeble covering, a curse during the winter months, now permitted them to clamber away and make their escape by jumping onto the town walls. Some were less lucky. Those who tried to make a run for it in the opposite direction were an easy target for the Cardinal of Guise's arquebusiers, who were lined up behind the cemetery wall. Escapees on the roof were also quickly identified and began to be picked off by sharpshooters. Amid the carnage Léonard Morel continued to preach until bullets began to fly around his improvised pulpit. After ducking down and saying a prayer, he removed his cassock and tried to escape, but he was quickly wounded and, on being recognized by one of the duke's gentlemen, taken prisoner.

The massacre lasted about one hour and led to the deaths of some fifty people, in addition to which up to 200 were wounded. But this was no indiscriminate killing that did not spare women or children, as would occur in other copycat massacres in the coming years: at most, five women and one child were killed at Wassy. The identity of the dead, and some of those lucky enough to escape, tells us much about the nature of Protestantism in the town and why it was proving so hard to root out. Among the toll of murdered vignerons, drapers, and weavers we find the rector of the town's schools, the town procurator, and, among those who escaped, two aldermen and a notary. The Duke of Guise's reaction to events also tells us much. In Protestant eyes the 'butcher of Wassy' had revealed his true self and in propaganda they made much of his cruel and vengeful nature after calm had been restored. His actions tell a different story. The duke was an angry man in the aftermath of this bloodletting. He had lost control of his men; the martial discipline on which his reputation rested had broken down. His wife, who had been reduced to tears by the spectacle, in particular needed comforting. The duke vented his frustration on a Catholic: Claude Tondeur, captain of the castle, was 'fiercely reprimanded for having permitted the assembly and preaching there to take place', arrested, and sent—along with the two Protestant aldermen and the minister—to Eclaron, where they were subjected to a severe rebuke before being released. He did not try to use the events of 1 March politically and play to the gallery of Catholic fanatics who saw the massacre as a manifestation of divine vengeance. Social hierarchy was a more important factor for him. During an interview with the English ambassador in the Hôtel de Guise in Paris on 23 March he complained of the 'arrogance' of vassals who dared to challenge his authority.[32] He referred to the event as an 'accident' caused by seditious elements which contrasted with his own aristocratic stoicism—he had displayed the 'moderation and patience' of a Pericles and the 'magnanimity' of a Scipio. Wassy's Protestants begged to differ, but his behaviour after the massacre does not suggest the workings of a cunning mind; he certainly wished to prevent Protestant worship, but as he himself said 'he despised cruelty and [preferred] to leave the sword and arms to the magistrate'.[33]

* * * *

In an age of religious renewal and violence, Europeans need to look back afresh at their own history of sectarian hatred. Wassy was partly a French affair. But for Protestants and Catholics across sixteenth-century Europe the massacre was not an obscure incident in a far-off foreign town; rather it was a profoundly local event, the first salvo in the greater struggle between good and evil, a reminder of what would happen lest one dropped one's guard at home. The printing presses rolled with news of Wassy not only in French, but also in German, Dutch, English, and Latin. Terrifying woodcuts took the message to the illiterate. Wassy became infamous, a byword for religious bigotry or the evils of sedition, depending on one's confessional persuasion. The town's notoriety was such that its description was added to the later editions of Sebastian Münster's *Cosmographie Universelle*, a guide to the great cities and major topographic features of Europe— a sort of cumbersome sixteenth-century forerunner to the Michelin Guide.

News of the massacre spread terror among Protestants. Throughout the kingdom congregations held hastily organized secret musters, drew up rolls of those able to bear arms, and hatched plots to seize control of towns. The opening chapter in a terrible story and the beginning of a civil war that would last thirty-six years, Wassy continues to reverberate across the centuries. A new word 'massacre' was added to the political lexicon, a sound to which, in recent years, we have become inured. Up until the 1550s, 'massacre' had meant the chopping block used by French butchers, their meat cleaver being termed a 'massacreur'.[34] Within a year the 'butcher of Wassy' was himself dead. Prior to the events of 1 March 1562 there had been at least one attempt to assassinate him but, in the wake of the massacre, the Protestants had even greater cause for revenge. The duke's murder heralded an end to an older form of politics based on knightly chivalric ideals and ushered in a new ideological age in which political assassination was construed as an instrument of divine will. In France, massacres and the assassinations were to become regular occurrences, the Guise fated to be both conspirators and the victims of conspiracy. In the new political age, their image as murderers or martyrs was shaped and manipulated by the opposing religious parties in order to mobilize public opinion across Europe. In order to understand how and why these upheavals occurred we must turn to the origins of the family and chart their rise to power.

2

'ALL FOR ONE: ONE FOR ALL'

The mythic dictum of *The Three Musketeers* is far from original; it was for generations the motto of the House of Lorraine. In 1477, François de Guise's grandfather, René II, Duke of Lorraine, rode into battle against Charles the Bold, Duke of Burgundy, behind the 'banner of his ancestors', which depicted an arm protruding from a cloud and clutching a sword over which was written *Une pour toutes*. François's father, Claude, the second son of René II, who was born at Condé on the Moselle in 1496, changed the emphasis to express solidarity and steadfastness when he took his own motto: *Toutes pour une. Là et non plus* ('All for one. Here and no further').[1] The ideal of family unity is universal, and the reality of family tensions too. Relations between family members in the past were no less passionate than today, the stuff of perennial squabbling and reconciliation. In the past the stakes were even higher because power and wealth was predicated on the possession of land, which was acquired principally by inheritance and marriage. Today's complex families, with their high proportion of step-parents, half-sisters and brothers and multiple sets of in-laws, was much the same as the distant past, where it was high rates of mortality and re-marriage, not family breakdown, that complicated kin relations. Property sharpened the emotional bonds between family members, establishing a sense of dependence or independence, embittering the excluded, and shaping the ambitions of the clever and the cunning. Among the aristocracy the stakes were higher and sibling and generational rivalry had serious political implications: a contested inheritance could result in blood-letting. The genius of *King Lear* is timeless. But for contemporaries, its dissection of the rivalry, treachery, and murder that consumes a family made it no fable.

The Guise rise to power was initially predicated on royal service and the favour of the King of France. But their ability to profit from it in the long term, and to hold on to power once favour was withdrawn, was due to an extraordinary level of family solidarity. The Guise did not suffer from the rivalries and jealousies that tore other families apart—the road to political impotence. Individuals acted in the interests of the group; sons invariably deferred to their father, younger brothers to the eldest male. It was recognized that an individual's status was furthered by working for the collective, meaning that women too had an important role to play in the formulation and implementation of policy. Cooperation was not achieved by the enforcement of patriarchal discipline alone, since this could never by itself ensure harmonious affective relationships. Rather, wealth and power was distributed in such a way as to ensure equilibrium between family members, so good provision was made for younger sons and daughters, who were expected to show deference and loyalty in return. Ecclesiastical property and patronage were crucial to the maintenance of this strategy. The Guise aspired and lived up to their motto, engendering a clan mentality, the nature of which was reinforced by their distinctive origins and status among the princely houses of France.

The Guise descended from the most ancient surviving House of the Franco-Imperial borderlands. During the sixteenth century, genealogists would fancifully trace that descent as far back as the Carolingians and the creation of the kingdom of Lotharingia, the territory that lay between the Meuse and the Rhine, in 855—the implication being that the pedigree of the House of Lorraine was greater than that of the ruling House of Valois, who had replaced the ruling Capetian dynasty as recently as 1328, when the innovation of the Salic law had conveniently prevented succession in the female line. However, in the struggle with the House of Lancaster over this legal technicality, which came to be known as the Hundred Years' War, the dukes of Lorraine were faithful allies of the Valois. An early example was Raoul, Duke of Lorraine, who acquired in 1334, among other French possessions, the seigneury of Guise when he married the niece of King Philip IV; he was killed by the English at Crécy in 1346.

The true origins of the Guise were more recent. The lineage was the product of the dynastic convolutions of the Houses of Lorraine and Anjou in the fifteenth century. The extinction of the elder ducal line of Lorraine in 1428 triggered a conflict into which the great powers of Valois, Lancaster, and Burgundy were drawn: the duchy was recurrently the focus of Franco-Burgundian power politics right down to 1477. The succession war was a classic confrontation between the heir in the female line, Good King René of Anjou, Count of Provence and King of Naples and Sicily; and the heir in the junior male line, Antoine de Lorraine, Count of Vaudémont and sire of Joinville. Despite crushing the Angevins at the battle of Bulgnéville in 1431, Vaudémont could not unseat René. Nonetheless, the very favourable terms which he secured for ending his challenge were the roots of the close association which developed between the two lineages. Particularly important was the marriage of Antoine's eldest son Ferry and René's daughter Yolande d'Anjou: it was through Yolande's right that her son René II claimed the duchy on the death of Nicolas d'Anjou, the last surviving son of Good King René, in 1473.

René II's title was not secure and he now had to confront the greatest power in the region, the Duke of Burgundy. It was only in 1477, after the great triumph of the Lorraine and their Swiss allies at the battle of Nancy, where the body of Charles the Bold, the last Duke of Burgundy, lay humiliatingly unclaimed for two days, that René enjoyed undisturbed possession of Lorraine. René owed much of his success to the support of King Louis XI, and because of this alliance he was unable or unwilling to secure recognition as heir to the duchy of Anjou and county of Provence when Good King René finally died in 1480. Nevertheless, Angevin claims to Provence and the kingdom of Naples and Sicily were never forgotten and were incorporated into his coats of arms. How far his pretensions depended on French support was demonstrated in 1485 when an attempt to remove the Aragonese, who had installed themselves in Naples, ended in dismal failure. In later life he became disillusioned by the unwillingness of Charles VIII and Louis XII to recognize his rights and he did not take part in the French descent into Italy in 1494–5. Nevertheless, the close relationship between the Houses of Valois and Lorraine was destined to continue once the House of Habsburg entered the region between France and the Empire as heirs to the lands of the dukes of Burgundy.

Before he died in 1508, René II drew up his will, dividing his lands among his surviving six sons. The eldest, Antoine, inherited the duchies of Bar and Lorraine. Two sons were sent to be brought up in France and take control of the patrimony held there: the second son, Claude, received the lion's share, the youngest son François being limited to some smaller properties in Provence. Claude's inheritance was a substantial one in its own right, consisting of the seigneuries of Mayenne, la Ferté Bernard, and Sablé in Maine; the counties of

Aumale and Harcourt and the barony of Elbeuf in Normandy; the barony of Boves and the county of Guise in Picardy; and the barony of Joinville and the seigneuries of Ancerville and Montiers-sur-Saulx in Champagne and the Barrois. The use of ecclesiastical benefices to prevent the fragmentation of the patrimony, for which the Guise became renowned, was already a feature of dynastic policy. Although he was also raised at the French court, the third son, Jean, was a key to the consolidation of the duchy of Lorraine. In 1505, at the age of only 7, he was provided with the bishopric of Metz, one of the richest in Europe, to which was added, in 1517, the bishopric of Toul (a benefice initially earmarked for the youngest brother, Louis, before he renounced it in favour of a military career). Jean completed the hat-trick of Lorraine bishoprics when he acquired the see of Verdun in 1523.[2]

Claude was only 9 years old when he left home to fulfil his father's plans. Arriving at the French court in March 1506, he was awarded letters of naturalization. He thus became a Frenchman, took a French title, Count of Guise, and established his residence in France at Joinville in easy reach of both Paris and the capital of Lorraine at Nancy. But in becoming French he did not forget his ancestors. As a boy, his father had recounted tales of their exploits and how God had favoured their House because of its piety, especially the deeds of Godefroy, Duke of Lorraine and Count of Bouillon, on the First Crusade and his election as the first King of Jerusalem in 1099, 'chosen above others...to take in hand the sacred sceptre of Judah'.[3] His father assured him that providence had marked out their house for special consideration. At the battle of Nancy, God had revealed his 'assurance in his well-beloved children' and his scorn for the 'lack of piety' displayed by their enemy, Charles of Burgundy.

A more lasting influence on his life was his mother, Philippa of Guelders, who had been born in Brabant in 1462. Claude was her favourite son, possibly because her eldest, Antoine, had been born before the death of her husband's repudiated and barren first wife. Although rumours that Antoine was a bastard caused some tension between the two eldest brothers, it did not lead to an open rift and in 1530 a transaction was signed, definitively leaving the French possessions to Claude and Lorraine and Bar to Antoine, 'in order to uphold and nourish peace and fraternal love, and to flee and avoid all troubles, questions, debates and quarrels'.[4] For the next eleven years after the death of her husband, Philippa, with the assistance of Nicolas le Clerc, doctor of theology at the Sorbonne, took care of her children and their affairs, and then in 1519 she shocked them by announcing that she was retiring to the convent of Sainte-Claire at Pont-à-Mousson. She became a byword for saintliness. Although, in consideration of her status, the Pope had dispensed her from the novitiate and life of austerity, she insisted on completing her year on probation as the humblest novice, sleeping in the common dormitory, going barefoot, and rigidly observing every fast. Despite her reclusion, she continued to play an important part in Claude's life. Until her death in 1547, she continued to maintain her rights to the Angevin inheritance in Italy and signed herself 'Queen of Sicily'. She received visits by her children and grandchildren, jogging consciences habituated to the frivolities of court. Philippa's renunciation of the world had more immediate consequences for Claude. She renounced her dower and enabled him to take up residence in Joinville and, in an ostentatious show of favouritism, bequeathed all her moveable property to him alone.

Just before his mother entered the cloister, another woman, Antoinette de Bourbon, entered his life. She would play a dominating role in family affairs for the next sixty years, outliving her husband and all her sons. Unusually for an aristocratic match, love seems to have played a part in their union. It was in 1512 that Claude, as part of the suite of the heir to the throne of France, the Count of Angoulême, who was visiting his betrothed, the Duchess of Brittany in the Hôtel des Tournelles, first encountered Antoinette, daughter of Marie de Luxembourg, Countess of Saint-Pol and François, Count of Vendôme, the great-grandfather of King Henry IV. The two were able to talk alone, a rare occurrence for teenagers of the opposite sex in those days; and following this, Claude, aged only 16, asked Angoulême to procure 17-year-old Antoinette's hand in marriage. The dowry was fixed at 40,000 livres and they married in June 1513 in the royal parish church of Saint-Paul in Paris beneath the stained glass which depicted Joan of Arc.

The marriage was a vital step in Claude's political career. He had married into the royal family itself. Members of the House of Bourbon were styled princes of the blood in recognition of their privileged status, as heirs to the throne. Though Antoinette claimed descent from Saint-Louis through eight generations, the counts of Bourbon-Vendôme were in fact cadets of the ducal House of Bourbon, and in many respects her maternal line, the House of Luxembourg, which had provided five Holy Roman Emperors and many queens, was the greater. The Vendôme were very much in the shadow of Charles III, Duke of Bourbon, the king's most powerful vassal who controlled a large swathe of central France. When the Count of Angoulême ascended the throne as Francis I in 1515, Charles was made constable, the highest office in the kingdom, which gave him control of military affairs. The close alliance between the Houses of Lorraine and Bourbon was sealed the same year when Duke Charles's sister, Renée, married Antoine, Duke of Lorraine. Henceforth there was to be a close affinity between the various branches of the Houses of Lorraine and Bourbon, and their fluctuating relationship was a dominating feature of French politics for the rest of the century.

Though he was only two years younger than Francis and had known him from boyhood, Claude did not figure among the young king's confidants. He did however share the king's passion for deeds of chivalry and tales of derring-do. The day after his marriage to Antoinette, Claude fought in a tourney, upending Charles Brandon, Duke of Suffolk, favourite of Henry VIII. Francis too was physically powerful, a man of action who was happiest when riding to hounds, tilting in the joust, or performing in a masque. A young knight like Claude was fortunate to come of age just as the blossom in the Indian summer of French chivalry burst into bloom. Francis was the ideal of the *roi chevalier*: energetic, vigorous, and eager for glory. Since 1494 the Valois had been intervening militarily in Italy in pursuit of their rights to the duchy of Milan and, through the House of Anjou, their claim to the kingdom of Naples—a claim in which the Guise, too, retained an interest. The most recent French intervention in 1513 had ended disastrously; after a crushing defeat at the hands of the Swiss at Novara, Burgundy was invaded and Dijon besieged. By January 1515 France had lost all her possessions in Italy, the House of Sforza had been reinstalled as dukes of Milan, Genoa was an independent republic, and the whole of Naples was under Aragonese control.

French honour and the reputation of the Valois dynasty were at stake. Within a year of his accession, Francis invaded Italy in pursuit of his claim to the duchy of Milan. He faced a formidable league of anti-French forces which included the Duke of Milan, the Pope, the King of Aragon and the Emperor. Recent wars in Italy had shown that campaigns could no longer be won solely with heavy cavalry, the strongest arm of the French army. Until 1510 the King of France had been able to employ Swiss mercenaries, the best infantry in Europe, but they were now in Sforza pay. Instead, Francis raised 23,000 German landsknechts whose tactics were closely modelled on those of the Swiss, but they were notoriously ill-disciplined. The elite of the infantry was the famous 'Black Band' from Guelders, comprising 12,000 pikemen, 2,000 arquebusiers, 2,000 men armed with two-handed swords and

1,000 halberdiers.⁵ Claude de Guise was initially seconded to the unit as an officer under his uncle, the Duke of Guelders. But on the eve of battle, the duke was called home and Guise was elected by the landsknechts, in preference to their current lieutenant, as their new captain. His knowledge of German may have been a reason for choosing him ahead of other, more experienced, French princes. At the age of eighteen and still a minor (he was not released from his mother's charge until October 1518), the count found himself a general on his very first campaign.

At midday on the 13 September 1515 the Swiss swarmed out of Milan and tried to catch the French army whilst it was camped in the vicinity of Marignano, attacking in three compact echelons of pike-men, each containing about 7,000 men. The first square encountered the French at 4 pm and though the German landsknechts were pushed back they did not break. Fighting continued by moonlight until midnight in one of the bloodiest battles of the sixteenth century. Next morning, the battle raged with renewed fury. The decisive factors were the French artillery, whose 74 guns did great damage to the tightly packed ranks of the Swiss, and the timely arrival of Venetian reinforcements. As the Swiss began to retreat, Guise rashly charged forward and was hit on the right arm and on the thigh by arquebus shots, and a third killed his horse. Unhorsed, lying prone and defenceless, the count's armour resounded with dozens of pike and halberd blows; he would have been killed had not one of his German squires, Adam Fouvert from Nuremberg, hurled himself forward and taken the blows, giving his own life to save his master's.

It was only with difficulty that the household officers of the king were able to locate the duke's body among the 16,000 corpses that littered the battlefield, his wounds so severe that his recovery was regarded as a marvel of contemporary medical practice. A month later, his arm in a sling, he was able to accompany Francis into Milan as captain-general of landsknechts. The House of Lorraine had once again provided valiant service to the kings of France: Claude's elder brother, Antoine, was signalled out for his command of a gendarmerie company and his younger brother, Ferry, was killed. Claude's visceral experience and his miraculous recovery confirmed his trust in divine providence. When he regained consciousness after the battle, he made a vow to go on pilgrimage on his return home. In early 1516 he was greeted by Antoinette and their first child, 3-month-old Marie, future queen consort of Scotland. Two days later, dressed in full armour 'as if he were in battle', he walked the twenty-five leagues to the shrine of Saint Nicholas, the patron saint of Lorraine, close to Nancy. Claude's solemn reverence for his ancestors was a feature of traditional Catholic practice; Claude's father had attributed his victory over Charles the Bold to the saint, in recognition of which work had begun in 1481 on a magnificent basilica dedicated to Saint Nicholas, where he housed the relics accumulated over the centuries by the House of Lorraine.

Marignano dramatically revived French fortunes in Italy: returning Milan to French control; forcing the Swiss, in return for an annual subsidy, to agree to serve no other master than France; and encouraging Pope Leo X to consider supporting the French claim to Naples. And yet French hegemony in Italy was a mirage. On 23 January 1516 King Ferdinand of Aragon died, an event which seriously upset the new balance of power in Europe. Ferdinand left his kingdom, comprising Castile, Aragon and Naples, to his grandson the Archduke Charles of Habsburg, who already ruled the Burgundian lands, which included the Netherlands and the Franche-Comté. Initially, Charles's position was weak. In Aragon and Castile there was support for a return to separate rulers, and he had to buy off Francis. On 13 August he signed the Treaty of Noyon, by which he agreed to take Francis's daughter Louise as his future bride with Naples as her dowry, pending completion of which he undertook to pay an annual tribute of 100,000 crowns for Naples—implicitly recognizing the French king's claim to the kingdom. He even agreed to discuss the future of the kingdom of Navarre, the Spanish portion of which had been wrested from its king, Jean d'Albret, by Ferdinand of Aragon in 1512.

The first test of the understanding between the Habsburgs and the Valois came in January 1519 when Emperor Maximilian died, throwing open the contest for the succession to the Holy Roman Empire. Francis knew that Maximilian had wanted to be succeeded by his grandson Charles, but the seven electors were not bound to choose a member of the House of Habsburg, and Francis could not permit his rival to grow any stronger: 'If he were to succeed, seeing the extent of his kingdoms and lordship, this could do me immeasurable harm: he would always be mistrustful and suspicious, and would doubtless throw me out of Italy.'[6]

Claude de Guise was chosen as Francis's plenipotentiary in Germany. Despite his youth and inexperience, he was considered suitable because of his knowledge of matters German, his kinship ties in the Empire and the status of his family as princes of the empire. His claim on the kingdom of Jerusalem was also seen as a selling point, giving credence to French claims that they were best placed to defend Germany against Turkish invasion. Francis's extravagant promises and generous gifts were to no avail however. On 23 October 1520 Charles of Habsburg was crowned King of the Romans at Aachen. In order to become full-fledged emperor, Charles needed to receive Charlemagne's crown from the hands of the Pope in Rome. Francis's immediate objective in going to war was to keep Charles out of Italy and thus asserting his claims to Milan and Naples. He did not foresee a long campaign. In the event, the Habsburg-Valois conflict dominated European history for the next forty years.

This was a new type of war, one fought on several fronts: Picardy, Champagne, the Pyrenees, and Milan all required defence. In 1521, Guise, fighting in Navarre, led an assault on Spanish positions against the advice of his commander, the royal favourite, Admiral Bonnivet, crossing the fast-flowing Bidassoa under enemy artillery fire at the head of his landsknechts. Fuenterrabia, the key to Spanish Navarre and until then considered impregnable, fell soon after. In 1522, he served on the Flanders front under his brother-in-law, François de Bourbon, Count of Saint-Pol, raiding and skirmishing with Charles V's English allies who threatened the French interior from their possessions at Boulogne and Calais. This brought him face to face with an old adversary, the English commander, Suffolk. His growing reputation was confirmed when he took Bapaume and relieved Hesdin, harrying the retreating English force and killing 500 of them at the town of Pas in Artois.

The following year was an important one in Guise's career. The Constable of Bourbon's wife had died, causing a major crisis over her inheritance, which was claimed by the Queen Mother, Louise of Savoy. The constable refused to compromise and marry the 46-year-old widow, and as a consequence Francis, without due legal process, stripped him of the lands. He had no option but to quit France and join Charles V's formidable alliance, which included not only England and the German princes, but the Pope and most of Italy, including France's erstwhile ally, Venice. Francis moved to quell the threat of internal rebellion by showering the cadet lines of the House of Bourbon with favours. With his close ties to the Bourbon-Vendôme, Guise was in line for promotion, and on May 1524 he was named governor of the frontier province of Champagne and when, in the autumn, Francis entered the Milanese, he was promoted to the Privy Council headed by Louise of Savoy. The count, however, would have preferred a command in Italy. He wrote to his brother-in-law on the

8 June, 'I hear that the voyage to Italy is being prepared...I beg you please to send me news, and you would give me great pleasure if you were to find out whether I am among those who will go. I beg you to take the matter up with the king and with the admiral for me, for I desire that my [gendarmerie] company should come with me.'[7] Francis preferred to leave his powerful vassal at home for, once he had secured Milan, he intended to push south and conquer Naples and he did not wish to have his claim to the kingdom complicated by the presence of a direct descendant of the Angevins. Francis was particularly aware of the fragility of his rights at this time—the Constable of Bourbon, with little claim, had assumed the title of Count of Provence.

Guise's relegation to the home front soon turned to his advantage in the wake of the débâcle that then took place in Italy. Francis had unwisely divided his force and sent 6,000 men to invade Naples. Next, his army became pinned down by the main imperialist field army as he besieged Pavia. For a month (22 January–23 February 1525) the two armies, separated by only a small tributary of the Ticino river, eyed each other nervously. The French army was denuded by defections among the mercenary infantry and when the inevitable pitched battle finally came on 24 February it was clear that the lessons of Marignano about the superiority of firepower had not been learned. The charges of the French knights with the king at their head obscured the French artillery and, although they dispersed the imperial cavalry, the Spanish arquebusiers, protected by emplacements and pikemen, did terrible damage. As at Crécy and Agincourt, the French men-at-arms with their distinctive harness and plumes made easy pickings once their momentum had been stopped, and the wounded, trapped by the weight of their own armour and horses, were butchered where they lay by Spanish foot soldiers using daggers. A desperate attempt by Guise's younger brother, François, commander of the German landsknechts, to salvage the day failed; he was killed and his force practically wiped out. Pavia was the greatest slaughter of French nobles since Agincourt. Thousands were killed or captured, including the king and many princes who were led off to captivity in Spain.

Pavia's graveyard was Guise's making. Francis's captivity lasted for just over a year and during the emergency France was governed by his mother. As the king's closest adult male relative, Charles de Bourbon-Vendôme now had a much greater profile and Guise, as his brother-in-law and governor of a frontier province, likewise played an important part in the regent's defence of France and in finding the cash for the king's enormous ransom. On Francis's return in 1526 Claude was rewarded with the position of *Grand Veneur*, one of the great household offices charged with the supervision of the king's hunt. The aristocratic social calendar was organized around hunting and the post gave him close access to the king; it also gave him control of a budget and staff, and he would make many new friends among aspirants to lucrative posts, both at court and in the extensive forests reserved for the king's sport. In 1527, Claude's position in the front rank of the aristocracy was confirmed by the elevation of the county of Guise to a duchy; he thus became a peer of the realm, which gave him important rights of precedence in public life and royal ceremonial. Seniority among peers was determined by the date of their creation—only the dukes of Vendôme (1514) and Nemours (1524) preceded Guise in the hierarchy.[8]

Until his death in 1547, the principal objective of Francis's foreign policy was the recovery of Milan. To understand this in modern terms as a geo-political contest between France and Spain is anachronistic. The outlook of Charles and Francis was aristocratic, their rivalry highly personal and so bitterly contested because honour, the quality that constituted the very essence of a gentleman's being, was at stake. Francis's challenge to his foe of single combat was deadly serious; as the English ambassador put it, 'He would give his daughter to be strumpet to a bordel to be sure of the encounter.'[9] His desire to re-establish his honour and reputation was most evident in the field of arts and letters, where he projected himself as the supreme patron and connoisseur in Europe. Guise was not in the front-rank of policy-makers. From 1528 to 1541 the government was virtually run by Anne de Montmorency, another of the king's childhood companions who had briefly shared his captivity after Pavia. Montmorency collected an unprecedented array of offices. On his return to France he was made Grand Master of the king's household, which gave him effective control of court appointments, expenditure, and security and in 1538 he was named constable after successfully resisting Charles V's invasion of Provence. Guise was kept well away from Italy and relegated to the more humdrum defence of the eastern frontier. He did however make a name for himself in Paris. In 1536, while the main royal army was in the south, he, his wife, and children arrived in the city and promised to defend it when the imperialists invaded Picardy and besieged Péronne, only sixty miles away. In a daring escapade with a small force, he lifted the siege and became the toast of Parisian society.

This period was the high point of his influence. In 1538 his daughter, Marie, the widow of the Duke of Longueville, married James V of Scotland. Marie was a renowned beauty and endowed with wit and abundant charm—qualities which enabled her to shine at court after leaving the convent where she had lived with her grandmother. In order to scupper the strengthening of the Auld Alliance, Henry VIII offered his own suit when negotiations were already well advanced. It has been suggested that he was rebuffed because of his faith or because Marie was too intelligent to consider becoming his next female victim. All the evidence is to the contrary. The Guise were flattered to entertain the thought of one of their number becoming Queen of England but, in an early indication of Francis I's alarm at the prospect of over-mighty subjects, he insisted that the Scottish alliance go ahead. Guise hopes were still alive in September when an English agent and painter arrived at Joinville to cast an eye over Marie's younger sister, Louise, before setting off for Nancy to have a look at the daughter of the Duke of Lorraine.[10]

In 1542, Claude finally got his own command when he was appointed lieutenant-general and head of the military council advising the king's younger and favourite son, Charles, Duke of Orléans, who had been given 38,000 troops to command in Picardy, Flanders, and Artois. Warfare on this front consisted of many protracted sieges; a war of attrition was the result, in which victory depended on logistics. Duke Charles was only nineteen years old and surrounded by a group of young noblemen intent on winning their spurs with individual feats of arms. The arrangement which teamed the reliable old soldier and inexperienced hothead was not a happy one: there was little respect for the cautious approach and much grumbling at the sterility of the campaign. Guise had great difficulty in controlling his young charges—the generation-gap generated tensions which almost spilled over into violence when the duke indignantly challenged one of them to a duel, an increasingly fashionable way of resolving disputes.[11] Worse followed in 1544 when Charles V invaded Champagne. The rapid capitulation of the frontier town of Saint-Dizier led to recriminations between Claude and the town's captain. Showing signs that his reputation was increasingly on the line, he gave the captain the lie and 'was willing to leave aside his ranks, dignity and noble quality as a prince, in order to fight'.[12] The duke soon had other problems on his mind. The imperialists moved on to Joinville next and, in an act of spite, they burned the town, destroyed the château's landscaped garden and flowerbeds, and pillaged the church of Our Lady, carrying off a number of precious objects.

In the winter of his reign Francis, often ill and in great pain from abscesses caused by gonorrhoea, became increasingly irascible and susceptible to the whims of his mistresses, first Diane de Poitiers and then the Duchess of Etampes. Factional intrigue increased as the prospect of a succession led to much jockeying for position. In particular, the rivalry between the dauphin, Henri, and his younger brother, Charles Duke of Orléans, for whom the king displayed a clear preference, polarized political society. Claude de Guise did not suffer the disgrace that was meted out on long-serving favourites like Montmorency, but he was tainted because of the open support of his sons for the dauphin, their close friend since childhood. The king's displeasure meant that Claude was further than ever from the inner sanctums of power. In 1543, he was moved from the governorship of Champagne to that of Burgundy. Ostensibly, this was not a demotion, but he was replaced by the man with whom he had already clashed, the Duke of Orléans, and for many years there had been suspicions that Guise, whose brother had built a formidable ecclesiastical presence in the province, was using royal resources there for his own purposes.[13] In 1532, the Parlement of Paris, the senior sovereign legal and administrative court in France, had censured him for acts which were in direct contravention of royal ordinances. And there were complaints on the occasions when royal troops and resources had been employed to support the policies of his kinsmen, the dukes of Lorraine and Guelders. So when the duke went to install himself in Burgundy, the king took the opportunity to slight him, siding with a simple local gentleman in a precedence dispute, which caused much mirth among courtiers who felt the Guise were getting above themselves; and when he asked permission to keep both governorships Francis sarcastically replied, 'Conquer me new territory, and I'll give you its government along with that which you have already.'[14] The duke's political and military career had reached a ceiling and matters did not change with the palace revolution that followed the death of Francis I and the accession of the dauphin as Henry II in 1547.

* * * *

Four years younger than Francis I, Guise was, however, an altogether different personality from his master. He enjoyed hunting and music, but otherwise lacked the appetite for love and hatred on a gargantuan scale that made the king such a larger-than-life figure. Francis had had a humanist education and his interest in the arts was largely lacking in the duke, whose appetites were shaped more by the ideals of piety, duty, and discipline required of the Christian knight. As a young man he liked to perform acts of gallantry. One day in 1523, he alerted the ladies of the court of Lorraine gathered at Neufchâteau that the next morning he would give battle to the imperialists on the plain outside the town, so that 'from the windows and sheltered from all danger... they could reward with their applause and cries of joy the courage of the troops which was animated by their presence'.[15] Even in his later years he was, as we have seen, willing to challenge men of lesser status in order to uphold his honour. The duke's sexual appetites were less extrovert. He genuinely seems to have loved and respected his wife. A tale, first recorded in the middle of the seventeenth century, captures something of their relationship. On one of his visits to Joinville, a beautiful maid caught the duke's eye but, since the château overlooked the small town, Antoinette was able to spy her husband's visits to his mistress. Having identified the roof under which his infidelities were taking place, she sent the girl her best furniture, and saw that the bare walls were covered with tapestries; that upholstered armchairs replaced the stools; silver platters the earthenware bowls; and napkins of finest Flemish cloth the coarse tablecloth. When he arrived for his next assignation the duke's conscience was duly pricked, and he rushed back to his wife to ask her forgiveness. Apocryphal or not, by the standards of the time he was relatively chaste: he had one long-term mistress by whom he had at least one bastard son, but she was the daughter of a provincial judge and hardly a courtesan.

The influence of his wife and mother ensured that Claude was more devout than was usual. Philippa of Guelders was widely admired by contemporaries for her piety and by the 1620s a campaign by the Jesuits to promote her cult was underway with reports of apparitions and miracles. Her convent of Sainte-Claire at Pont-à-Mousson became an important family shrine. In 1528, her grandson, Louis, Claude de Guise's younger brother, had died from the plague while on campaign in Naples and his heart was placed in the convent 'in a casket beneath a very tall sepulchre, built in the Italian fashion, and covered in black velvet with the arms and cross of Lorraine'.[16] She too was buried there in 1547, and when her Protestant kinsman, Louis de Bourbon, Prince de Condé, was passing twenty years later he protected the convent from his troops and came to pay his respects to the memory of his 'good cousin'.

Philippa was especially troubled by the spread of heresy. The events of 1525 merely confirmed what all good Catholics knew: if the crushing defeat of Pavia was not warning enough, the elevation of a woman to the regency, in a society where misogyny was a respectable pseudo-science, confirmed the impression that the world had been turned upside down. In the absence of the king, religious conservatives in Paris were soon hunting down evangelical cells which had flourished under the patronage of his sister, Marguerite of Navarre. More serious for the Guise—and closer to home—were events in Germany, where the Peasants' War, one of the greatest popular uprisings in European history, spread panic among the ruling classes, Catholic and Lutheran alike. Fuelled by violent anticlericalism and led by millenarian preachers, peasants formed armed leagues that massacred nobles and targeted the property of the Church. In the spring of 1525 the revolt spread to Alsace and Lorraine. Under banners which proclaimed support for the holy Gospel, the word of God, and divine justice, the peasant bands seized Saverne, residence of the Bishop of Strasbourg, and set up their headquarters in the nearby abbey of Maursmünster.

It is significant that the convent of Sainte-Claire was a Franciscan establishment, for the friars would later be the order most associated, more so than the Jesuits, with the fight back against Calvinism in France, becoming celebrated and loathed in equal measure for their street rhetoric and rabble-rousing. Philippa had a particular devotion to an early Franciscan, Saint Anthony of Padua, 'hammer of the heretics', whose apparition visited the convent at her death. It was in this fiercely orthodox environment that Claude and his brother Antoine, on their way to confront the peasant hordes, visited their mother to receive her benediction: 'Do not recoil now that the occasion presents itself to die gloriously for Him, who with the infamy and opprobrium of the world upon him, died on the cross for you... Hurry yourselves... and against all who oppose you with arms strike, chop and cut... Do not fear to be cruel... heresy is of the nature of gangrene, it will spread over the whole country, if one does not confront it with fire and steel.'[17]

These chilling words were prescient. The violence and swiftness of the campaign was terrifying. Saverne was invested by the Catholics on 15 May 1525; the following day peasant relief force was defeated at Lupstein and a second band marching over from the Palatinate met the same fate at Neuwiller. The besieged peasants surrendered on 16 May and marched out unarmed under a white flag of surrender, but in consequence of a dispute between nearby mercenaries and the peasants a fight broke out, leading to a mass slaughter of the peasants. In this action alone 18,000 were slain. On his triumphal return to Nancy, the duke defeated another peasant band at Scherwiller on 20 May. During the battle, Catholic hearts were emboldened by a number of miraculous visions. Guise was himself bathed in rays of sunlight, a halo, which, with his shining sword, made him appear, so it was said, as an 'angel exterminator'.[18] Following the campaign the brothers published an account which presented their deeds as a crusade undertaken by Christian knights. Since the first crusades God had chosen the House of Lorraine to defend the Catholic Church. Antoine and his brothers were fulfilling their historic mission; the peasants, having revolted against divinely instituted order, were compared to the Philistines.[19] Propaganda was required to justify the scale of the blood-letting, for tales of the slaughter of women and children were soon current in Germany and the duke compared to Herod by the Protestants. And there was suspicion that the 'crusade' had more to do with extension of political control over the fractured lordships of Alsace. Among those who agreed that the House of Lorraine was divinely inspired, however, were the Alsatian Jews, who feared lynching at the hands of the peasants.

Much later during the Wars of Religion the events of 1525 were seen as the link between the great crusading past of the House of Lorraine and the new crusade against heresy that began with the massacre of Wassy. This view is one that modern historians have reinforced. There are reasons for being cautious about this interpretation. There is no doubt that Claude, Duke of Guise—like his elder brother and his mother—was fiercely, one might even say violently, Catholic. In a letter of 1538, he informed the constable, Montmorency, that whenever he heard rumours about 'this evil sect of heretics' in his governorship he was quick to act. Claude considered life to be like a pilgrimage, in which one was at any moment in danger of ambush. He was proud of his role at Saverne. It is the only one of his battles named on the epitaph of his magnificent tomb executed by Primataccio, the leading Italian artist in France. The figure of Justice on the tomb displays no sign of clemency and displays Claude's firmness in ordering a summary execution after the battle. But the context of Wassy was very different from that at Saverne. We should not presume that the son was impersonating the father. As we have seen, François de Guise did not evince the same moral certitude as his father, or justify himself in the same manner, although many ultra-Catholics wished him to do so, and he would later go out of his way to explain the massacre away and even apologize for it.

We should be wary of oversimplifying the religious sentiments of the Guise and of accepting ultra-Catholicism as an overriding imperative of family strategy. Marie de Guise, for example, was educated at Pont-à-Mousson under the tutelage of Philippa of Guelders and immersed in the ascetic life of a Poor Clare: cooking, cleaning, and gardening. Despite her experience there and the formidable influence that her grandmother exercised over her family, throughout her regency in Scotland she would display extraordinary tolerance towards her Protestant subjects. In France, there were many powerful vested interests which opposed not only heresy but also reform from within the Catholic Church, most notably the Sorbonne, still considered then to be the pre-eminent university in Europe. Against them were ranged those associated with the new learning, who wished to base worship and liturgy more closely on the Gospels, which had been translated into French from the Greek in the 1520s. Like many families, the Guise were divided on these issues. It would be wrong to assume that they were united as representatives of a backward-looking aesthetic resistant to change. Philippa had entrusted the education of her sons for eleven years to a theologian, Nicolas le Clerc, a man so conservative that he would be lampooned by Rabelais as one of the ignorant *Sorbonagres* and imprisoned in 1533 by the king for attacking his sister, the leading supporter of the evangelical movement. But the career of Philippa's third son, Jean, shows that an ultra-orthodox upbringing did not necessarily forge ultra-orthodox minds.

Born in Bar in 1498, Jean was the founder of the Guise ecclesiastical empire and, as such, no less important in the founding of the family fortune than his elder brother. He was an utterly different personality from the dour Claude. He was much happier at court, perhaps because he had the natural charm of a diplomat, but also because he had an eye for the ladies. It was said that whenever a new girl or lady arrived at court he would inspect them and offer 'to break them in'.[20] There was a playful side to this behaviour too. When the Duchess of Savoy haughtily offered her hand for him to kiss, instead of presenting her cheek, he grabbed her and planted one on her lips. But even a commentator favourable to the Guise could not conceal the fact that 'there was hardly a girl or lady resident at court or recently arrived who had not been debauched or ensnared by the money and largesse of the cardinal'. Jean's penchant for dressing up as a woman, though common in the macho world of the Renaissance court, was hardly becoming of a prince of the Church and is indicative of how far life in Francis's entourage differed from that at Joinville. He was also handy at tennis, falconry, and lucky at the gaming table, winning £46 12s 6d from Henry VIII at a summit in Boulogne in 1532.[21]

This sort of behaviour made him a boon companion of Francis I. Apart from feeling at home in the bar-room atmosphere of court, Jean was also known for his generosity to the poor. Every morning without fail his valet filled a bag with several hundred crowns, which would be dispersed to the poor that day. Jean could easily afford such ostentatious liberality. He was the richest prelate in France. At the age of only 3, he had been named coadjutor of the bishopric of Metz and by 20 he was a cardinal. Even by the standards of his time, his accumulation of benefices was astonishing, indicating a level of intimacy with the king that his brother never achieved. To Francis he was a 'companion of the heart', sharing the king's interest in the arts and he was admitted to the Privy Council in 1530.[22] He juggled the possession of no less than eleven dioceses throughout his life. Some were held only briefly before resigning them to men whose careers he wished to promote; others were earmarked for his nephews or administered by 'straw men' who handed over a cut of their revenue. He held on to the three wealthiest—Metz, Narbonne, and Albi—for the duration of his life. He was abbot of thirteen monasteries during his career, including some of the richest in the kingdom, such as Fécamp, Marmoutier, and Gorze. Many of these benefices owned significant property in Paris. Jean established his principal residence in the magnificent palace of his abbey of Cluny, situated on the Left Bank. Built between 1485 and 1498, it is one of the greatest examples of Parisian Renaissance architecture. In Guise possession until 1621, it was where James V lodged when he came to Paris in 1536 and it can still be visited today as the National Museum of Medieval Art. Jean had it sumptuously refurbished in the latest Renaissance style, employing Italians, like Cellini, who had worked at Fontainebleau, and filling it with *objets d'art* purchased by his agents in Rome and Venice. Its purpose was to house a salon devoted to the latest art and music.

Jean and Claude were both great music lovers. Clément Janequin, the most famous and prolific composer of popular *chansons* in Renaissance France, first composed for Claude in 1528, with his song *La Chasse*, which celebrated the duke's recent promotion to the head of the royal hunt. For the next thirty years Janequin composed several works for various members of the family, and when he died in 1558 he was chaplain of the ducal household. A family tradition of music patronage had begun which would last for another 150 years. The Guise were not just appreciative listeners: Jean's nephew, Charles, was a good lute player. When the composer of madrigals and choirmaster of the Sistine chapel, Jacques Arcadelt, quit papal service in 1553 to become choirmaster of the Guise court, it was recognition that the family ranked among the most cultured patrons in Europe. Arcadelt's popularity—his music was popular in Italy and France for more than a century and his first book of madrigals was reprinted no less than fifty-eight times—was built on his gift for marrying Italian and French styles and for writing catchy tunes which were easy to play and sing. Arcadelt's move to France has been called 'the most significant musical event of the decade'.[23] The Guise recognized the propaganda uses of music. The glorious defence of Metz (1553) by Claude's son, François, was celebrated in a composition for five voices composed by Janequin, a genre of heroic song that was reprised by Janequin's imitator Guillaume Costeley in his four-voice panegyric to the duke's capture of Calais in 1558. The Italian-style music that emanated from the Guise court in the years before the Wars of Religion had an immense influence, inspiring poets like Ronsard and du Bellay.

Thus far, Jean fits the pattern of a worldly and cultured Renaissance cardinal. What marked him out from other princes of the Church, and indeed, his own family, was that he belonged to the evangelical wing of the French, or Gallican Church.[24] He did not hide his beliefs, to the extent that for a decade the Protestants thought him a fellow traveller. In 1526 a correspondent of the Basel reformer, Guillaume Farel, reported that he often talked to the cardinal at court and found him 'certainly not unfavourable towards the Gospels'.[25] And the following year the reformer, Capito, wrote favourably to Zwingli of Jean's protection of imprisoned evangelicals and of his support for clerical marriage. In the decades before 1564, when the Council of Trent finally established the boundaries of orthodoxy in the Catholic Church, it was common for educated Catholics to hold beliefs that would later be considered dissident. The limits of Jean's tolerance were tested by people he considered sectarian riff-raff, or Anabaptists, and he assisted his brother in the campaign of 1525, raising troops and burning two heretics in Metz. But his protection of others reveals the growing polarization between Catholics in this period. In the 1520s, the Sorbonne, and in particular the fanatical Noël Beda, launched a campaign against those who sought to use the new humanist learning to translate and reinterpret the bible. One of Beda's principal targets was his former pupil at Montaigu College, Desiderius Erasmus. Erasmus turned to the Cardinal of Lorraine for help against the conservatives, dedicating his 1527 translation of the commentary on the epistles of the Galatians safe in the knowledge that 'you have always in your hands the Gospels and Saint Paul's epistles'.[26]

Psalm-singing was the classic form of worship associated with the Calvinists, and Calvin had engaged Clément Marot, a leading poet and evangelical who had composed for the cardinal until his denunciation as a heretic in 1535, to translate them into French. The Protestant hymn book was born. In 1545 the Sorbonne condemned Marot's translation. However, the psalms were not only sung by Protestants—there were many evangelical Catholics who defied the ban. And there were other vernacular translations of the psalms used by both Catholics and Protestants alike. Those of Jean de Poictevan, a humanist who based his translations on Greek and Hebrew texts, were dedicated to the Cardinal of Lorraine. In his preface, Poictevan made specific reference to the 1545 prohibition on unauthorized biblical translations, indicating that his defiance of the Sorbonne was due to the cardinal's protection. In 1548 and 1549, Louis des Masures, translator of Virgil and a friend to leading Protestant intellectuals such as Ramus and Calvin's chief lieutenant, Beza, undertook to finish off Marot's work. At this time he was the cardinal's principal secretary and councillor and had spent the previous twenty years in a circle of writers who had gathered round Jean in an atmosphere that was humanist, Erasmian, and evangelical. Towards the end of his life Francis I turned against the evangelicals and persecution of those suspected of heterodox beliefs was stepped up. The net did not only sweep up Protestants. Marot fled France in 1543, but the austere environment of Geneva was not conducive to poetry and he moved to Italy where he died in 1544. Marot's friend and fellow humanist Etienne Dolet was less fortunate; on return from Italian exile in 1546 he was condemned by the Sorbonne as a relapsed atheist and burned at the stake. Rabelais had more powerful protectors: when the *Tiers Livre* was condemned by the Sorbonne in 1546 he fled to Metz, knowing that the Cardinal of Lorraine was bishop there and that he would be unharmed.[27]

Jean's interest in and patronage of humanist learning developed alongside his diplomatic activities; his specialization in Italian affairs complementing his intellectual interests—he was a notable patron of

Italian vernacular poetry. At the age of only 17 he had been appointed French ambassador to the Holy See. In the papal conclave in 1534, he led the French delegation and successfully promoted the candidacy of Alexander Farnese, who as Paul III was more reform-minded than other candidates, but who was less compliant to French wishes than he hoped. At home, Jean posed as the protector of Italians and of Italian interests, and they in turned recognized him as the most important go-between with the king. In 1535 the papal nuncio went as far as to call him 'half of the king's soul'.[28] Visits to Italy on royal business were also an opportunity for Jean to promote his own interests and to further the careers of his own men. In Rome, he used his considerable influence to obtain the cardinal's hat for one of his own clients in 1538 over and above the king's preference.

Guise fortunes in Italy changed suddenly in 1547 when a revolt in Naples against the viceroy, Pedro of Toledo, gave hope to the pro-French faction in Rome, which included the Neapolitan exile community, the *fuorusciti*. The brilliant marriage of Claude's eldest son François in December 1548 to Anne d'Este, granddaughter of Louis XII, must be seen in this context. In his marriage contract François made mention of his Angevin heritage in a gesture to the *fuorusciti*, among whom was the Prince of Melfi, French commander of Piedmont, who assured François of his pride in being 'among the oldest servants of the House of Anjou'.[29] Another gesture—the attempt of François's younger brother Charles to take the title Anjou when he was elected cardinal—was foiled by the French ambassador. And the high point of this Italian policy was reached when, with the support of French cash, the Cardinal of Lorraine came within four votes of being elected as successor to Paul III in 1549. He was on his way back to Italy when he was seized by an apoplexy and died while dining at Nogent-sur-Loire on 10 May 1550, having laid the foundations of Guise domination of the French Church and influence in the Italian peninsula.

* * * *

Life at Joinville was more prosaic. Between 1515 and 1536 Antoinette de Bourbon gave birth every other year; of her twelve children, ten survived to adulthood: Marie (1515), François (1519), Louise (1520), Renée (1522), Charles (1524), Claude II (1526), Louis (1527), Antoinette (1531), a second François (1534) and René (1536). Antoinette's faith in the saints prepared her for the rigours of childbirth and, since in those days nearly half of new-borns did not reach the age of 10, her devotion paid dividends. Not only had she an ever-growing household to care for, but unlike her husband and brother-in-law, who were expected to live beyond their means, she was frugal. Her role went beyond the day-to-day expenditure of feeding and clothing the household at Joinville: she looked after her husband's accounts and, in conjunction with financial officials, advised him on expenditure. In 1520, Claude made her proxy for all his affairs. Two years later, she chided him for spending too much money while on campaign, on wining and dining his Swiss guard, and dressing them too extravagantly.[30] The role of financial advisor was one she would fulfil for her sons and her grandsons too.

Guise fortunes depended much on royal largesse. During the Renaissance, kings at war were always strapped for cash and commanders at the front were expected to dig deep into their own pockets and seek recompense later. Francis I was forced to resort to ever more desperate expedients to fund his wars against Charles V. In a society that was cash poor, it was easier to reward followers with offices, lands, and titles. Technically, the royal domain was sacrosanct, and the Parlement of Paris, charged with protecting its integrity, was also concerned at the practice of mortgaging royal income years in advance. In 1520, for example, Guise obtained the revenue from the royal salt depots on his lands at Mayenne, la Ferté Bernard, Guise, and Joinville.[31] The Parlement initially resisted the elevation of Guise to a duchy in 1527 on the grounds that its financial concessions were too generous. As the theatre of operations spread and the costs of war rose, so Francis became more generous: in 1541 Claude was awarded a gift of 30,000 livres, in addition to his annual pension of 16,000 livres as a provincial governor, 2,800 livres as captain of a company of one hundred men-at-arms, and 3,000 livres as *Grand Veneur*.[32]

Claude had substantial outgoings too. At this time his annual expenditure was nearly 75,000 livres but his income only just short of 65,000 livres, a shortfall of nearly 10,000 livres, which had to be met by borrowing.[33] He had a salaried household of 113 on his accounts, which included three secretaries, two physicians, a surgeon, four valets, an apothecary, nine stable-hands, three musicians, a pastry cook, a sauce-maker and a sauce-maker's assistant. One of his best-paid servants was the man who cared for his tents, a vital necessity on campaign and while out hunting.[34] Preferring life at Joinville to court, Claude indulged his passion for horses, building up one of the greatest studs in France, where there were never less than 100 or 120 horses. His position as head of the royal hunt required him to do this, but he also opened his establishment to the local squires and offered year-long riding apprenticeships at his own expense—a shrewd way of dispensing patronage and spotting the best local talent. The greatest expense was building. Little is known about the upper château, which dominated the town, since it was destroyed during the French Revolution. It was 'a magnificent structure, in front of which was a long terrace clinging to the sides of a rocky outcrop wider than seven metres supported by buttresses'.[35] Above the terrace was a ground-floor gallery with tall windows, which were decorated with cornices and columns. The upper floors were the principal living quarters, from where there were magnificent views across the hills and down into the Marne valley below. The rest of the palace was a clutter of buildings whose dimensions were determined by the rocky spur on which it was built, the entire complex being protected by a wall and tall towers. Between 1533 and 1546 Claude built himself a second palace on the banks of the Marne inspired by what he had seen at Fontainebleau and designed principally for his family's pleasure. Beautifully embellished in the latest Renaissance style, it had a grace which the older fortified palace lacked. The iconography was largely martial. Here and there on the façade, sculpted between Antoinette's and Claude's initials, was the emblem taken from his father's banner which represented an arm extending from a cloud holding a sword, but now joined by the biblical device *Fecit potentiam in bracchio suo* (He hath showed strength with his arm), signifying that political authority rests on military might. Inside there was a ballroom for receptions and festivities. The pleasure garden was watered by a canal and three fountains; it had its own little wood attached for promenades, as well as an orchard—in which grew oranges, lemons, and pomegranates—and a croquet lawn. By permission, Joinville's bourgeoisie could pass the time here and admire the latest in civilized recreation.

Amid these worldly delights Antoinette's children were not permitted to forget their devotions. The upper château had its own church, where there were a number of relics, including the belt of Saint Joseph brought back from the crusades, and the pious benefactions of successive lords allowed for an establishment of nine canons, two vicars, four choristers, and a choir master. Servants were expected to behave in a manner befitting their station, to know their catechism, and hear Mass and sermons regularly. Antoinette was much concerned with the poor, spending her leisure time stitching clothes for them while listening to pious readings. Alms were distributed regularly: 400 poor girls provided with dowries, and 100 bursaries provided to poor students. Legend has it that once, after her sons returned from a hunt, she was angered to discover that they had trampled the fields of local peasants, and so the following day she served them no bread at table: 'My children we have to save on flour, since you have destroyed next year's crop.'[36] Antoinette's daily expense account, a fragment of which survives in the British Library, gives credence to this tale. Lent was strictly enforced at home and there were doles of peas and salt for the poor. She was doubly pious: not only did she renounce the eating of meat on Fridays, but followed the same regime throughout her life on Saturdays as well. Better-quality wine and more lavish food were served when her husband or sons were in town.

Frugality did not mean that Joinville was cold and unwelcoming. On 8 September 1539 Antoinette wrote to her daughter in Scotland that her father and seven siblings had arrived 'to dance at our feast tomorrow'.[37] 'Our' feast refers to the holiday of San Gennaro (9 September according to the Julian calendar), patron saint of Naples, an indication of how family tradition kept alive the dream of the Angevin empire. Children were present at Joinville throughout her life, and the great disparity in ages between them meant that the eldest had married and on occasion moved in with their wives and children while their younger siblings were still being cared for by their mother. Particularly significant in the beginning were the children of Antoinette's eldest daughter, Marie, who were joined later by the wives and sons of François, Claude II, and René. In 1534, Marie had married Louis, Duke of Longueville, who claimed royal descent through his great-grandfather, the bastard of Orléans, heroic companion of Joan of Arc. Louis did not live to see their son's second birthday in 1537 and when Marie remarried James V and went to Scotland she left the boy, François, affectionately known as the 'little duke', with his grandmother and grandfather at Joinville. She would not see him for another twelve years. The estates which fell to the Guise as a result of this wardship, one of the greatest patrimonies in France, were a considerable boost to their income. Once again, it was Antoinette who looked after the management of the estates, keeping her daughter informed on the minutiae of administration: how much timber had been cut on one manor, which posts needed filling in another. The little duke's household was dominated by Guise servants—Jacques de la Brosse was appointed his governor. In 1547, he was briefly joined by his half-sister Mary Stuart, who had become a precious commodity on the death of her father and whose safety in Scotland could no longer be guaranteed. To protect her from English hands she was sent to her grandmother, before, as befitted royal princesses, joining the royal court. Barely 6 years old, she enchanted Antoinette: 'Our little queen is in as good spirits as possible', she wrote to her eldest son, 'and I assure you that she is the prettiest and best [girl] of her age that you've ever seen.'[38]

The letters of the little duke to his mother are touching and give us a glimpse of private life at Joinville. Claude indulged his grandson: 'he was so crazy about him that he never saw him by half'.[39] Aged 7, François wrote in a childish scrawl to his mother about how he played with his grandfather and uncles and then picnicked with them in the garden of the new château, of how every night his aunt put him to bed and how he said his 'Ave' for his mother and his aunt and for the dead and departed, of how he went pig-sticking and hawking with his grandfather. But he was a sickly child carried everywhere in a litter. He died in 1551 aged only fifteen, the only consolation for his mother being that she had briefly returned to France and was able to nurse him during his final illness.

Antoinette may have been pious and the atmosphere of Joinville austere and religiously conservative, but her attitude to heretics was more complicated than it might first appear. Marguerite of Navarre, champion of the evangelical party, visited Joinville and was on good terms with her cousin. She was, as her children would be, perfectly capable of maintaining friendly, even warm, relationships with individual Protestants. One of her closest friends, Françoise d'Amboise, Countess of Seninghem, converted to Protestantism around 1558 and corresponded with Calvin.[40] She and her sons, who also became Protestants, lived in the neighbouring château of Reynel and were frequent visitors to Joinville at this time, although out of respect for their host they did not eat meat during Lent.[41] While they may have had their differences on matters of theology, the two women were united by the depth of their piety. There are many other examples of ties of friendship and kinship cutting across the religious divide; towards their fellow princes in particular, the Guise were inclined to be indulgent. It seems that Antoinette and her children made a clear distinction between privately held beliefs and public worship, with its associations of seditious assembly. Even here they had to be pragmatic, as Marie's policy towards Protestants in Scotland shows. Likewise, during the Longueville wardship, Claude de Guise permitted the principality of Neufchâtel, which lay on the Swiss border, to maintain its religious freedoms. Ironically, Neufchâtel was to become a base for the evangelization of Champagne.

With ten children to provide for, the resources of the Catholic Church were however crucial to the maintenance of the family patrimony. The Church played as great a role as marriage in furthering the dynasty; benefices passed from generation to generation in a similar way to offices and estates, becoming virtual possessions to be handed down the generations. Not only did two of Claude and Antoinette's sons, Charles and Louis, become cardinals, but lesser benefices provided for the rest of their children. Dowries could cripple family finances and two daughters were kept out of the marriage market altogether: Renée was abbess of Saint-Pierre de Reims from 1542 until her death in 1602 and briefly of Origny and of Poulengy; Antoinette was abbess of Saint-Paul-les-Beauvais and then of Faremoutier from 1555 until her early death in 1561. Even Claude's bastard son by his mistress was provided with an abbey (Saint-Nicaise in Reims), and later the rich picking of Cluny to keep him in his old age.

* * * *

The first generation of the Guise family came to an end in 1550. On the 2 April 1550, Antoinette wrote to 'my son, my love' to hurry to Joinville because of the 'grievous illness' of his father who was 'suffering a lot'. Five doctors, one summoned from Troyes and two from Beaune, could not save him. Claude died on 12 April 1550, surrounded by his wife, his eldest son, François, now aged 31, his youngest son, René, still a teenager, and François's 3-month-old baby, Henri. Antoinette had no thoughts of following her mother into a convent. As dowager Duchess of Guise, she was guaranteed a significant income and her husband's will stipulated that she would have ownership of Joinville until her death. She would rarely leave home in future; habitually dressed in mourning clothes she dedicated herself to looking after her grandchildren and the family finances. Not only was she able to pay off her husband's debts and distribute the 10,000 livres in alms he had left in his will, but she had money left over to acquire more land and repair and expand the two palaces at Joinville.

As the son of a king, Claude required a royal funeral, and so it was delayed while preparations were made and his other sons hurried back from distant parts of Europe—his fourth son, Claude II, making the long and dangerous journey from Scotland. In the meantime, Jean, Cardinal of Lorraine, also died and his body was carried to

Saint-Laurent church in the old castle at Joinville to lie beside his brother. Every morning two high Masses were sung for them, after which the dowager duchess sprinkled them with holy water—an act she performed forty times before Jean was moved for burial with the Franciscans at Nancy. Royal burials were different from those accorded to ordinary mortals, because an effigy of the king played a prominent role. Its presence served as a reminder that the king never dies—that the state is an entity that endures despite the death of its head. So, while Claude's body lay in Saint-Laurent, a shrine was erected in the nearby convent in the suburb of Saint-Jacques, which he had founded, and his effigy, dressed in a grey doublet and grey satin breeches and draped in a huge golden cloak, was placed on a large bed, richly covered with purple velvet stitched with the eaglets and crosses of Lorraine. The effigy, whose silk-gloved hands were joined in prayer, was draped in expensive jewellery, including a golden ducal crown, studded with precious stones, estimated to be worth 80,000 crowns.

The convent was brilliantly illuminated by scores of candles, hung with rich tapestries, one of which represented the story of Esau and Jacob, and the floor covered with a Persian carpet. At the foot of the bed there was a table for the dead prince and an ornate chair and superb dais. On an empty chair was laid the duke's hat and cloak with its insignia denoting his membership of the royal Order of Saint Michel. Arranged on the altar were the precious contents of the duke's chapel: reliquaries, crucifixes of gold and silver, paintings, and other devotional objects. In the pulpit one could see the duke's book of hours open at an appropriate page, and there was a stool nearby for the almoner, who, during the funeral Mass 'presented the Bible and Pax board to the effigy, without however permitting it to kiss them'.[42] On Tuesday 25 June the strangest ritual of the ceremony took place in front of a large congregation. For the next week, at lunch and dinner, a 'royal' feast was prepared for the effigy, and once grace had been said the meat was distributed among the poor.

The following Monday the funeral began at Saint-Laurent at 8 am. It lasted for seven hours. At the church entrance hung a picture of the Passion, to its left a picture of a fierce lion confronting Claude on his knees and behind him his patron saint, Saint Claude, on which a Latin device recalled the Epistle of Saint Peter: 'Be sober, be vigilant; because your adversary the devil, as a roaring lion, walketh about, seeking whom he may devour.' On top of the funeral car there was mounted a small figure of a rhinoceros, the beast which dominates all others, carrying a large cross of Lorraine. Outside a temporary stand had been constructed so that the crowds could see the cortege, which was headed by twelve criers with bells, one hundred paupers dressed in black and a further one hundred dressed in white, followed by local dignitaries, clergy, the family itself, ducal subjects and household officers, grandees, and plenipotentiaries from France, Lorraine, Scotland, Flanders and Italy. Esquires led his finest horses, including his barded warhorse; his spurs, lance, gauntlets and harness were carried by seven gentlemen; his shield and the ensign was followed by eight banners representing his maternal and paternal ancestors. Next came the effigy on its bed of honour carried by twenty gentlemen. The rear was brought up with the kin of the Guise, many of whom will reappear in the course of our story: the Duke of Ferrara; the 20-year-old Louis de Bourbon, Prince de Condé; the Count of Brienne, representing the House of Luxembourg, who as a mark of particular respect came with twenty-five paupers dressed at his own expense; and several members of the House of Cröy.

Finally, once the body had been laid in its magnificent Italianate mausoleum in the castle chapel, the Lorraine herald called for silence in the crowd and shouted 'Claude de Lorraine, Duke of Guise and peer of France is dead! Pray for his soul.' This was a signal for onlookers to shed tears. The herald then turned towards the new Duke of Guise: 'Long live the duke! Long live milord the Duke François!' A final ritual remained. Morainville, the master of the household, summoned the staff and, taking his staff of office in both hands, raised it above his head and snapped it in two, throwing the broken ends into the throng: 'the Duke of Guise is dead, his household is broken-up, everyone for themselves!' But this scene was not the climax of the drama. While the heralds entered crying 'Largesse, largesse, largesse of the very illustrious Prince François de Lorraine, Duke of Guise', the new duke walked among his father's servants, handing each of them a silver tankard, each of which was carved with hydras' heads. 'As tall as a man's belt', the tankards were so heavy they had to be carried with both hands.

* * * *

This regal ostentation set tongues wagging. Rumour had it that Francis I would not have permitted such a claim to royalty and that as he lay dying he warned his son about the royal pretensions of the Guise:

> The former king guessed it quite right:
> That those of the House of Guise

Would leave his sons in a terrible plight,
And his subjects without a chemise.

In fact, this epigram saw the light of day thirteen years after it was supposed to have been uttered, and in very different circumstances.[43] That said, in the sixteenth-century rumours were not idle gossip but the arteries of the body politic. Francis did have his suspicions. He was reported to have dismissed claims that he did not treat the Guise as well as his favourites by reference to past injustice: 'I do not do as well for the princes of Lorraine as I should, for, when I think of how Louis XI wrested from them the duchy of Anjou and the county of Provence and other parts of their true inheritance, my conscience is clear.'[44]

What did the Guise think about these mutterings? They knew they had enemies. In April 1551, a plot to poison Mary, Queen of Scots, was uncovered. And they were convinced that Claude had been poisoned too. In the sixteenth century, almost every time an important person died suddenly the occult arts were suspected. But in this case the family went to extraordinary lengths to demonstrate their suspicions. The funeral oration for Claude alluded to his death at the hand of an 'Antichrist' and 'a minister of Satan . . . versed in the occult arts'. And the family had it printed. In 1738, when the crypt was being repaired, his lead coffin was discovered to have the following inscription: 'Here lies the high and mighty prince Claude de Lorraine, son of René of Sicily . . . who died by poisoning on 12 April 1550.' In the seventeenth century, historians with a confessional axe to grind pointed an accusing finger at treacherous heretics. But the Guise had their own theory: this was the work of the Habsburgs, their bitterest enemy, who were not only in illegal possession of Naples and Sicily, but as lords of the Sundgau in southern Alsace, of the Breisgau on the Rhine, and of Franche-Comté to the south, made for powerful and threatening neighbours. It comes as no surprise that in the following decade Claude's sons would dedicate themselves to war and the downfall of the House of Habsburg.

3

DREAMS OF EMPIRE

By the time of Francis I's death in 1547, dreams of Italy, once the ideal of every young French knight, were fading as the struggle with the Habsburg's moved to new theatres. Kings of England had never renounced their claim to the throne of France and Henry VIII's reign began with a good deal of fanfare about reviving the glorious days of Henry V. He tried, largely unsuccessfully, to profit from the Habsburg-Valois conflict, supporting now one side and now the other. Until 1525 there were serious attempts to assert his claim to the French throne. After the victory of his imperial allies at Pavia, he was disappointed not to have secured at the very least the return of the Duchy of Normandy. The opening up of the New World, the expansion of international commerce and rivalry between England and France encouraged a naval arms race, the prize for the winner being control of the Channel and the North Sea. At first, the English looked to have the upper hand, despite the capsizing of the great ship, the *Mary Rose*, in the Solent in 1545 with the loss of 500 men. The year before, in support of Charles V, the English had invaded northern France and seized the strategic port of Boulogne, to add to Calais, the last continental possession of the English crown. The death of Henry VIII did not end the policy and the 'Protector' of the new king Edward VI, the Duke of Somerset, continued to pursue aggressively the idea of Anglo-Scottish union. Further humiliation for France followed in 1547 when an English army, supported by a large fleet, invaded Scotland and crushed the Franco-Scottish forces at Pinkie.

Francis's successor, Henry II, had a vindictive streak. According to the Gascon captain Monluc, 'he never forgot a fault or injury and could not easily conquer his resentments'.[1] This was probably because, as a child, he had had to suffer regular humiliation at the hands of his father.

Aged only 6 he had been sent to Spain as a hostage in exchange for Francis; but when his father reneged on his agreement with Charles V, Henry was forced to spend three years as a prisoner in close and sometimes harsh confinement. His experience marked him for life with a loathing for the Spanish. 'As for the emperor the king hates him and declares openly his hatred. He wishes him every evil that it is possible to desire for one's mortal enemy. This virulence is so deep that death alone or the total ruin of his enemy can cure it.'[2] On his return to France he had to endure his father's indifference and, until his early death in 1545, the favouritism displayed to his younger brother, Charles. During the last years of Francis's increasingly paranoid reign, Henry gathered around him counsellors, headed by his father's disgraced favourite, Anne de Montmorency, critical of what they regarded as Francis's pusillanimity. This shadow cabinet began to prepare for power.

Henry was not yet ready to confront Spain when he ascended the throne. His energies were therefore directed at pursuing those he blamed for the fall of Boulogne, several of whom were banished; another died in prison and one, Jacques de Coucy, was beheaded and quartered. Within months the young king was reconnoitring Boulogne in person, the sight of whose strong defences reduced him to tears. Considerable sums were invested in a new navy: five new men-of-war, built in the 'English' design, were added to the Atlantic fleet in the first three years of the reign. The battle of Pinkie was dramatic reminder of the fragility of the Auld Alliance and warning that the idea of an Anglo-Scottish union, in the shape of a marriage between Mary Stuart and Edward VI, was more than just English rhetoric. Fortunately for the French, few Scots found English declarations of love and amity convincing; they saw the English occupation as one of conquest. In October 1547, Marie de Guise, Queen Regnant of Scotland since James V's premature death, made a formal appeal to the French king for support, and he responded by assembling a fleet of 130 ships to transport 5,500 foot and 1,000 horse. On 7 July 1548, a month after the arrival of reinforcements, the Treaty of Haddington was ratified by the Three Estates of Scotland, in which French responsibility for Scottish security was sealed by dynastic union: Mary Stuart was to be betrothed to the dauphin, François; and the regent of Scotland, the Earl of Arran, who became Duke of Châtellerault, was naturalized a French subject and promised the hand of a French princess. The English now found themselves fighting on two fronts. In order to defend Boulogne against French attack, they were forced to evacuate their strongholds in Scotland. Internal instability further weakened English resolve and in March she conceded terms favourable to France: ceding Boulogne in return for 400,000 crowns and recognizing the status quo in Scotland. In the treaty negotiations, Henry assumed control of Scottish diplomacy and all matters pertaining to Scotland were dealt with by French commissioners. Henry II was now the 'Protector' of Scotland. No distinction was made between his protection of the kingdom and its young queen; writing to inform the Estates of Scotland that the 'young Queen, my daughter', had arrived safely in France and was with 'her husband', Henry declared that 'in consequence, her Kingdom, her affairs and subjects are with ours the same thing, never separated'.[3] Henry's intervention in Scotland was not foreseen as a short-term commitment; rather it was the beginning of a grand project, a first step in the building of a Franco-British empire, in which the kingdoms of France and Scotland would be joined in dynastic union. As regent, Marie de Guise energetically set about establishing French power in Scotland. But the French imperial imagination went further. The Tudor dynasty in England was weak and unstable. Edward VI was a sickly 13-year-old in 1550—his potential heirs all women. Mary Tudor's claim was impeccable but she, a 34-year-old spinster, was not in rude health either. Mary Stuart was next in line to the throne: the Roman Catholic Church had never recognized Anne Boleyn as queen and in 1536 her daughter, Elizabeth, had been declared illegitimate by Parliament. The concept of a Franco-British empire, which at some future date might include the kingdom of England, was immensely attractive to Henry II, who had been schooled in classical ideas of imperial grandeur and who felt threatened by Spain's claim to world empire.

Elsewhere, French diplomacy remained cautious, its purpose to build alliances against the Habsburgs rather than to confront them openly. Its chief architect was Montmorency. Born in 1493, he possessed all the experience and gravitas that the young king lacked; he had not only been chief counsellor to Henry since he was dauphin, but filled the role that Henry's own father had failed in. An Italian ambassador described the king as trembling at the constable's approach 'as children do when they see their schoolmaster'.[4] Montmorency was made immensely rich through service to the Crown. His principal weakness was that, although he was descended from an ancient baronial house, he was not a prince and therefore lacked the pedigree of his rivals. Although they did not direct foreign policy, the Guise, with their impeccable ancestral credentials, were the principal means by which the Franco-British empire was to be forged. The themes of empire and conquest that dominated the new reign are best understood in an examination of the magnificent festival organized at Rouen in 1550 in honour of the king. All newly crowned French kings had the right to be feted during a royal entry into each of the principal towns of the kingdom, where ceremonial displays were performed, depicting such themes as loyalty, submission, and civic liberty. The Rouen entry was of a different order from royal entries before or since in its size and sophistication; it was the most spectacular event of the sixteenth century, 'a vainglorious display of [Henry's] accomplishments and a confident expression of things yet to come'.[5]

The choice of Rouen was significant in itself, a choice not predicated solely on its historic ties to the British Isles. With a population approaching 20 million France was by far the most populous state in Europe, and for the previous half-century its demographic growth had been matched by an unprecedented urban, economic, and cultural renaissance. Rouen, whose population had doubled to 75,000 during this time, was a symbol of this transformation. It was surpassed in importance only by London and Antwerp as a Channel seaport. It had a dynamic economy based on the expanding Atlantic shipping trade; a major entrepôt it was home to significant communities of English, Scottish, Spanish, and Portuguese merchants. Its geographic position, linking it to Paris via the river Seine, and its international maritime trade were crucial to fulfilling the dream of a Franco-British empire. Rouen merchants provided the capital for the trading and fishing fleets which operated out of other Norman ports, such as the new deep-water port at Le Havre, construction of which had begun in 1517. Normandy's ports sheltered the newly built navy which would protect Franco-British imperial communications. Dieppe, a significant town in its own right, larger than York, was the principal link with Scotland. It was home to a sizeable Scottish community—John Knox was among friends when he preached there in 1558.

Perhaps the most striking feature among all the cavalcades and processions was the celebration of France's contacts with the Americas. A New World-themed village was set up in a meadow beside the Seine surrounded by a make-believe tropical forest, where parrots were tethered to fake palm trees. Naked bands of Tupinamba Indians, brought from Brazil by Norman mariners who traded there, fought a mock combat in front of the king. The humanity of these 'primitive savages' was widely debated and provided the Renaissance with one of its greatest achievements in Montaigne's essay in their defence, 'On the

Cannibals'. The civilizing of these primitives was only one aspect of the benefits of an empire joined by the seas. A magnificent theatrical naval combat in which Neptune emerged from the river Seine represented the victory of Norman vessels over its two greatest sea-going rivals, the English and the Portuguese. The recovery of Boulogne was celebrated in a military parade of thousands of soldiers, as life-sized elephants made of papier-mâché ambled along in front of 'captives', representing English prisoners of war. Soldiers in Roman costume carrying banners signifying the Scottish strongholds recovered by French arms were followed by a chariot on which a winged Fortune held an imperial crown over a laurelled figure clad in armour representing Henry.

The Guise had leading parts in the production. Marie de Guise's younger brother, Charles, Cardinal of Lorraine, was heavily involved in the organization, which meant leaning on local magistrates suspicious of her right to enjoy her own royal entry. As significant landowners in the region, the Guise already had some leverage in the town, the origins of a clientele that expanded along with their ambitions for the British Isles. Several days before the festival began, Marie preceded the king to Rouen, not by horse or carriage, but on a fleet of galleys. The lavishness of Henry's entry exposed the Scots and English in attendance to the grandeur of France and, by inference, to the benefits of dynastic alliance. Mary, Queen of Scots, had a prominent part in the procession—her position alongside her future husband, the dauphin, tangible confirmation of the union of the two crowns. Henry II proudly boasted in a letter to the Sultan that:

> I have pacified the Kingdom of Scotland which I hold and possess with the same power and authority as I have in France, to which two kingdoms I have joined and united another, England, its kingship, its subjects, and its rights which, by a perpetual union, alliance and confederation, I can dispose of as my own in such a way that the said three kingdoms together can now be deemed a single monarchy.[6]

This was wishful thinking on several counts: not least the fact that the putative Franco-British empire was as much a Guise as a Valois dynastic entity.

* * * *

The rapprochement with England was the work of Anne de Montmorency. In the spring of 1551 the two kings exchanged embassies;

Henry II conferring on Edward VI the Order of Saint Michel and Edward reciprocated by sending the insignia of the Order of the Garter. Montmorency hosted the English embassy at his own château at Châteaubriant. A treaty of friendship was signed and Henry's eldest daughter, Elizabeth, betrothed to the English king. Edward VI became godfather to Henry's third son; the child, the future Henry III, being given the names Edouard-Alexandre. In recompense for his services, Montmorency's barony was raised to a duchy in July—an unprecedented step for a man of non-princely birth and an innovation which led to muttering by those of greater pedigree. As Constable of France, Grand Master of the royal household, and Governor of Languedoc, he possessed unrivalled political power and access to the king. In the earliest days of the new reign, Henry had made great display of his favouritism by permitting Montmorency the honour of sharing his bed, a practice whose indignity shocked some Italian observers. The Guise were particularly put out that the king had been present while Montmorency was having a foot bath, a moment of intimacy they could never aspire to. But Henry did not just crave paternal guidance; he needed a maternal figure too. His mistress, Diane de Poitiers, was Montmorency's only serious rival. Born in 1499, she was 46 years old when Henry became king. She took responsibility for the education of the royal children, including Mary Stuart, much to the vexation of their neglected mother, Catherine de Medici. Such was Diane's hold over her lover that the imperial ambassador, a hostile witness whose code-name for Diane was *Silvius*, reported that policymaking was done as much in the bedroom as in the council chamber:

> After having reported to her what had been negotiated all morning and since, either with ambassadors or others of importance, he sat beside her bosom with a guitar in his hands, on which he played, asking her whose opinion it was to be, the constable's or the duke of Guise's, and if *Silvius* was not watching, touching one or other of her nipples and looking at her attentively.[7]

In the palace revolution that accompanied Henry's accession to the throne, the old king's favourites—some of whom were imprisoned—and his mistress, the duchess of Etampes, were stripped of their possessions and titles at the expense of Montmorency and Diane. Montmorency was not only reinstated to his offices, but he was given the arrears of his salary for the years he had been unpaid while in disgrace, a colossal sum amounting to 100,000 crowns. The constable was in a position to favour his own clan. His brother was made Governor of

Paris and the Ile-de-France. He had a particular affection for the three Coligny brothers, the sons of his sister Louise. The eldest Odet, Cardinal de Châtillon, his most trusted counsellor, was provided with a number of new benefices, including the rich-picking of the bishopric of Beauvais. The second son, Gaspard, became colonel-general of the infantry.

Henry was equally generous to his lover: he gave her the Duchess of Etampes's jewels, including a diamond valued at 50,000 crowns and a cash gift of a further 100,000 crowns. The same year he bestowed on her Chenonceau, perhaps the most graceful of all French Renaissance châteaux, and a year later she was given a title, that of the Duchess of Valentinois, to match her new surroundings and status. Diane had once been married to a great Norman lord, Louis de Brézé, who had died as long ago as 1531. She had no sons from this marriage for whom she could sponsor a career, but she did have two daughters— Françoise, born in 1518, and Louise born in 1521. Diane was astute and ambitious and she married both to naturalized foreign princes. In 1539 Françoise married Robert de la Marck, Duke of Bouillon, a neighbour of the Guise who, like them, had interests in the Holy Roman Empire. His mother-in-law took responsibility for his career: in 1547 he was made a Marshal of France and in 1552 he became Governor of Normandy, a province where she already exercised extensive influence and, since the death of her husband, was a major landowner. The Guise too did well out of the new regime. The ageing Claude retained his governorship of Burgundy but now lived in semi-retirement at Joinville. However, his two eldest sons, François, who was confirmed as Governor of Dauphiné and whose county of Aumale was made a duchy in 1547, and Charles, who as Archbishop of Reims had the honour of crowning the new king, had long been companions of the dauphin and were now promoted to the Privy Council for the first time. From the start of their careers they were Diane's protégés. For the previous two years Charles had dined frequently with Diane, where the conversation undoubtedly turned to the future shape of the government. The burgeoning relationship was cemented in July 1546 when Diane married her younger daughter, Louise, to the third Guise brother, Claude II. This was one of the key political unions of the decade and a magnificent opportunity for a younger son whose slice of the family fortune would otherwise have made for a relatively meagre living. Diane was generous in turn with the confiscations that the king bestowed on her. It was through her favour that the Guise acquired significant properties in Paris and the Ile-de-France, a departure from their traditional landholding base and crucial to men who were now expected to attend frequently to business at court. Diane also trafficked in the profits of the royal demesne. She gave her new son-in-law Rhuys and Sucinio in Brittany. Aumale was granted the rights to administer all lands for which there was no heir and which had escheated to the Crown. In order to support better his station when he became Duke of Guise in 1550, he was awarded the revenues and rights to appoint officials in Dourdan, Provins, and Saumur. In exchange, like a commodity in a business deal, Louise left her mother and went to live at Joinville with her mother-in-law.

Duke Claude's death could easily have led to squabbling among his heirs. The complexity of inheritance laws ensured that lawyers hovered like vultures ready to feed off the carcass of any feuding family. In one respect the Guise enjoyed good fortune. Claude and Antoinette had only had one daughter (Louise) who did not take holy orders and thus required a dowry. She died within a year of marrying the great Flemish nobleman, Charles de Cröy, Duke of Aerschot, in 1541. As a consequence there were no quarrelsome brothers-in-law for the Guise siblings to contend with. Control of Church patronage, already significant in the guise of Jean, Cardinal of Lorraine, was tightened with the accession of Henry II, ensuring that of the six surviving male children only four had to be provided for. Standards of ecclesiastical propriety had recovered a little since Jean had been made a bishop at the age of 3. The second son, Charles, had to wait until 1538, when he was 14, to succeed his uncle as Archbishop of Reims, which also bestowed on him the dignity of first peer of the realm. He became cardinal in 1547. The fourth son, Louis, three years his junior, was made bishop of Troyes in 1545 at the comparatively advanced age of 18. The fifth brother, also like his eldest brother called François, was from a young age chosen to be a knight of Saint John, which meant that he, too, took holy orders and would not marry. His career was also starred. Nominally, he should not have taken his vows until he was 21 in 1555, but six years before this he was already Grand Prior of France, the head of the Order of Saint John in northern France, which had its headquarters in the sprawling Temple complex in north-east Paris. In a letter to the Pope asking for dispensation due to his youth, his brother Charles evoked the crusading mission of the order and that of his own house, as 'kings of Jerusalem and Sicily'.[8] Even before his nomination, François had gathered an impressive portfolio of estates and houses (called commanderies) owned by the knights: the commandery of Troyes alone brought him an income of 5,250 livres. As a teenager he was on the way to becoming a significant figure in his own right: a letter to his eldest sister, the queen of Scotland, written on the way to Rome on business, suggests a 15-year-old of unusual precocity.[9]

This left only three sons to share the landed inheritance, which was divided on strict geographical lines. The eldest son, François, became the second Duke of Guise and, in addition, received the marquisate of Mayenne and all the territories in the Barrois, Champagne, and Provence. The lands in Normandy were divided between the remaining two sons. The third son Claude II, was given the newly created duchy of Aumale. The reasoning behind this is clear: on his marriage to her daughter Diane de Poitiers had favoured him with a significant portion of her Norman property, and he now became one of the great magnates in a province that was crucial to the functioning of the putative Franco-British empire. The sixth son, René, was still only 14-years-old and, although the barony of Elbeuf was set aside for him, he continued to live at Joinville under the wardship of his mother.

Ambitious younger sons were thus satisfied with good marriages, generous portions, or careers in the highest echelons of the Church. As they established their own households and dynasties, their part of the bargain consisted in deferring to their eldest brother in all public affairs, as if he were their father. A letter of 25 June 1552 from Antoinette to René, who had just arrived to join the royal army, indicates how this was inculcated in each child: 'You should conduct yourself wisely and with the counsel of your brother [François]. Otherwise do not give me any cause to be displeased with you. Besides the news I get from others, write to me often. Love well your kindred and, as you are obliged, act the same towards your wife.'[10] A clan mentality was the result, a mindset that was enshrined in the ritual of everyday life in one particular ceremony, the *lever*. This ritual was usually associated with the rising and dressing of the king and was most developed by Louis XIV at Versailles, where the theatre of monarchy was most fully elaborated. For the Guise, it was a means for the younger brothers to demonstrate their respect and deference to their elder brothers, themes which are echoed in the formality of letters between the siblings. When the brothers were at court, the four younger brothers would rise earlier and then assist at Cardinal Charles's *lever*, after which they would then visit François and attend on him. When they went to meet the king they thus appeared as a group.

There is one final and simpler reason that explains family unity. The concept of 'All for One' was not imposed by discipline alone. Having grown up in a strict but loving environment at Joinville, the Guise quite simply had a great deal of love and affection for one another.

Theirs was an upbringing utterly devoid of the tribulations of, say, the king himself. Family gatherings were as frequent as matters of state permitted. In 1549 Jacques de la Brosse informed the Queen of Scotland that the Duke and Duchess of Guise, their six sons, their daughters-in-law, and the little duke of Longueville were all gathered at Reims for Easter. The crèche that Antoinette and her daughters-in-law maintained at Joinville continued to grow throughout the 1540s and 1550s. In 1553, Louise de Rieux, Countess of Harcourt—the new wife of René, the last son to marry—moved here. Such a large and vibrant household was a strong attraction, and the whole family gathered there in the same year to celebrate Christmas.

* * * *

The two eldest brothers who ran family affairs on the disappearance of the first generation of the family in 1550 complemented each other perfectly, like Castor and Pollux as their admirers had it. The Renaissance idealized the harmony between war and letters, 'these two great virtues, which your most illustrious House has in more abundance than all the other princely families of our time'.[11] François, though not uneducated—he could, for example, compose an epitaph in the style of the Ancients—was first and foremost a soldier. Whereas the king's love for his chief minister was based on respect tinged with fear of disapproval, his love for Guise was that of the favourite and evinced in masculine camaraderie. Even by the standards of French kings, Henry stood out for his love of martial sports. Upon his accession the court began to give tournaments to an extent that had not been seen since the fourteenth century, and even more unusually he refused to allow deference to his royal status, with the consequence that he was often worsted in the joust. Guise was among the most prominent knights on display and was often to be seen fighting alongside his brother-in-arms, the constable's nephew, Gaspard de Coligny, for they had 'sworn friendship together'.[12] Guise's prowess, courage, and bravery were already the stuff of legend. He was accustomed to go into battle with his visor raised. In an attack on Boulogne in 1545 he was wounded by an English lance thrust which entered above the right eye, toward the nose, and passed out on the other side between the ear and the back of the neck, with such force that the head of the lance was broken and remained embedded in his skull. Fortunately, Ambrose Paré, the greatest surgeon of his age, was on hand and with a pair of smith's pincers he drew out the object. Even so the prognosis was not initially good, given the violence of the blow and the subsequent operation. His miraculous recovery was yet another manifestation of God's special providence. Henceforth, François was nicknamed *le Balafré*, 'scar-face'. He displayed the attributes of a true Christian knight in other respects. At the siege of Metz in 1552 he refused to deliver up a slave who belonged to the commander of the imperial light cavalry, Don Luis Davila, who had fled to the French lines on a Spanish horse. Guise returned the horse as a mark of courtesy but 'could not return the slave since he became free in reaching the privileged soil of this glorious kingdom of France'.[13] He was not given to public displays of anger but showed moderation towards his enemies, even veering, as he got older, towards the sober and reserved in demeanour. The start of the battle of Renty was one of the few occasions on which he was recorded as losing his temper, striking the lieutenant of his gendarmes, Moy de Saint-Phal, on the helmet because he had broken ranks. After the battle, Moy demanded satisfaction for the offence but the duke was quick to repair their friendship, remarking in the king's tent that it was better to hit a man for being too precipitous than too cowardly and thus the 'blow carried more honour than disgrace'.[14] The duke loved camp life and esteemed soldiers even of the meanest sort, making a point of remembering their names and speaking to them familiarly. And he was tough when he needed to be: when a drunken German mercenary confronted him one day with a pistol, the duke instantly unsheathed his sword and with one stroke whipped the pistol from his hands, and placed the point of the blade against the German's throat. News of this soon spread, much to the appreciation of the other mercenaries who respected such manly bravado.

Warfare was in the process of radical change. Since the beginning of the sixteenth century fortifications had developed to deal with the advent of artillery. Sieges became longer and more complex and required more infantry and more specialists. In this respect, the duke was a very different type of general from his father: he was just as likely to be found in the trenches as cavorting with his mounted gendarmes, encouraging the ordinary foot soldiers, enquiring about their welfare and asking their opinion on tactics. The science of war now demanded much greater knowledge of logistics and attention to detail. Guise was both meticulous and, as his extensive letters to his agents and lieutenants in his governorship of Dauphiné show, a hard worker. He was interested in the minutiae of equipment and designed his own and 'gave great forethought about munitions, victuals, military discipline and all other things necessary for long sieges'.[15]

As a young man little else mattered to him beyond things martial. The duke was happiest among his soldiers, his 'compagnons' as he called them, and on getting married to Anne d'Este in 1548 he told his wife: 'Madame, there are those who marry in order to stay at home, but I am not one of those.'[16] It was a brilliant marriage. Anne d'Este received a dowry of 150,000 livres. Since she was the granddaughter of Louis XII of France through the female line, it was significantly more than a non-royal French princess could command. The wedding festivities were on a royal scale. The bride and bridegroom met each other just outside Paris in early December. In order to break the ice, Anne and her prospective father-in-law arranged for one of her ladies to disguise herself as the bride. She was presented to François and kissed him, before being unmasked to much laughter.[17] The wedding party was conducted to the Hôtel de Reims, the Cardinal of Lorraine's palace near the Place Saint-Michel, by an escort of 3,000. The wedding was followed by two weeks of festivities paid for by Henry II at a cost of 100,000 crowns. The marriage brought the Guise into the network of French alliances in Italy. The court of the bride's father, Ercole II d'Este, at Ferrara was its hub, and, as one of the most magnificent courts in Europe, was having a profound influence on French taste. Immensely rich, Ercole was a major creditor of the French Crown. In fact, Henry II agreed to pay Anne's dowry in lieu of money he owed Ercole. Anne's upbringing had been unconventional for an Italian princess. Her mother, Renée of France, was an active supporter of the Protestant cause, which eventually forced her to return to France. Born in 1531, Anne was well educated. She was a competent Latinist and had a smattering of Greek. Following the de facto separation of her mother and father when she was six, she was raised in a largely French environment and, like her younger brothers and sisters, raised as a Protestant. This did not seem to have bothered the Guise unduly. Indeed, considering Guise political interests in Scotland, England and the Empire, it may have been viewed as a positive attribute. Anne's faith was undogmatic and she adapted quickly to the demands of her new environment. Unusually for a woman, her library contained more history books than works of devotion and she seems to have been more comfortable with Herodotus, Guicciardini, Macchiavelli, and Froissart than books of hours. The mask sometimes slipped. Lent was a chore to be endured. In a letter written just after Easter 1553, Cardinal Charles gently chided his sister-in-law that her rosaries were gathering dust and that he was sending them to his sister, the abbess of Saint-Pierre de Reims, in order to give them an airing.[18] Princesses were conventionally described as beautiful, but Anne was certainly regarded as more beautiful than that other famed beauty, Mary Stuart, who was eleven years her junior. More cultivated than Mary, Anne was soon indulging her passion for the arts, patronizing Italian artists, sculptors and actors. The court allowed her a measure of freedom from her severe mother-in-law and she was on intimate terms with Diane de Poitiers, Catherine de Medici, and the many other Italians who surrounded the queen. One native humanist close to the Guise, Michel de l'Hôpital, named her Saint Venus.[19] Her husband showed less interest in the arts, though he shared her love of music, a passion he inherited from his father, and hunting. The marriage was conventionally happy: from 31 December 1549, when she gave birth to her first son, Henri, she was regularly pregnant, giving birth to five children in the next nine years. Like his father, François too seems to have been more than usually monogamous for an aristocrat, reflecting his mother's disapproval and Spartan tastes. That said, there was one bastard daughter, probably born before their marriage. She was initially cared for at court by Anne, who found her 'pretty and clever', before being dispatched to join the crèche at Joinville. François's love of crimson clothing was due to the attentions of a lady admirer, but the source of this gossip, Pierre de Brantôme, is unusually coy about her name, and since he was close to the Guise, his discretion is probably reflective of family sensibilities.

Charles, Cardinal of Lorraine was in this respect more like his brother than his uncle Jean, whose penchant for debauchery was legendary. In most other respects however Charles was different from his brother—a much more complex character, he sharply divided contemporaries. All were agreed that Charles was charming and good-looking. He had the tallness of his house, his face was long, his complexion on the dark side, and his penetrating blue eyes, set beneath a lofty forehead, indicated a quick apprehension and an acute perception. He was a highly educated and cultivated man. His memory and eloquence were proverbial. Until the age of 10 he remained with his mother and then under the tutelage of uncle Jean, he began his studies at the aristocratic college of Navarre in Paris alongside his cousin Charles, the future Cardinal of Bourbon. When he entered the college he was already Archbishop of Reims, though he could not be consecrated until 1545. Created a cardinal on 27 July 1547, he took over the ecclesiastical empire that his uncle had built when he died in 1550. It comprised some of the richest and most prestigious monasteries in Europe: Cluny, Marmoutier, Fécamp, Montier-en-Der, Saint-Urbain, Saint-Martin de Laon, Saint-Paul de Verdun and Cormoy. Charles was well versed in Greek, a language that the Sorbonne suspected of being associated with heresy; Latin; Spanish; and Italian—he even understood the fiendish Venetian dialect. His knowledge of foreign affairs was based on a network of informants: 'one of his greatest expenses was in getting news from all parts of Christendom, and besides he had paid men and pensioners who sent him news from all parts'.[20]

Plate 9 shows the portrait attributed to El Greco and which is claimed by art historians to have been painted in 1548 on his first visit to Venice. If this is so, then the cardinal looked a lot older than his 23 years. As late as 1547 he had not been able to grow a beard, so it seems more likely that it was painted on his other visits in 1556 or 1563. The parrot in the window is a reference to his eloquence, which even Protestants recognized. Calvin's chief lieutenant, Théodore Beza, is reputed to have remarked that 'if he had as much elegance as the Cardinal of Lorraine, he would hope to convert half the population of France'.[21] Unlike most of his fellow prelates he was comfortable preaching and did so regularly at Lent and Easter, although one commentator found his Easter sermons at Reims cathedral, which could last up to an hour and a half, 'were not so profound in theology as full of eloquence'.[22] This was an unfair charge, for the cardinal knew his scripture; but it points to what made the cardinal so controversial: he was too clever by half. His undoubted diplomatic skills could easily be misinterpreted as dissimulation, an attribute more commonly associated with the suave Italian than the bluff and honest Frenchman. He was portrayed as a schemer and stirrer, which fed on deep fears of Machiavellian intriguers, who were by nature cowardly and unmanly. Charles remained an enigma to contemporaries. Whereas his brother, the soldier, was expected to be affable and open, the skills required by the diplomat, courtier, and financier are very different. The former qualities were recognized in the duke even by his enemies; the latter were hardly seen as qualities at all and served to reinforce the stereotype of the worldly and unscrupulous cleric. Today, we are more likely to find the cardinal's complexity beguiling and fascinating, but for contemporaries his inconsistency and ambiguity were evidence of his hypocrisy. There are certainly grounds for these charges. In some ways the cardinal was austere. Like his mother he fasted on Saturdays as well as on Fridays and he wore a hair shirt at appropriate times. Like his fellow Christian humanists, he disdained the hunt and kept neither dogs nor horses nor birds. He did not gamble and was sober and abstemious at table. He took frequent exercise in his gardens and arcades, not merely on medical advice, to preserve his health, which was never strong, but because he liked it. But there was also something of the Epicurean about him, a man who enjoyed the benefits of his position and whose benefices and expertise in financial matters would one day make him the richest man in the kingdom. Charges of cupidity and avarice against him cannot be discounted, given his unprecedented accumulation of benefices. An inventory of 1551 shows that in two years he ordered no less than 120 exquisitely made objects for his household, such as chandeliers, a dining service, lamps, and various pieces of tableware, each one fashioned from the most sumptuous material, either silver, crystal, or gold, sometimes finished with elaborate engraving or precious jewels.[23] These commissions were ordered to augment the twenty-five chests of antiquities, which included bronze and marble statues, he had brought back from Rome the year before.

With power came arrogance. Like all princes of the Church he was highly sensitive about his dignity; but Charles's status consciousness was so extreme that it alienated his peers. Cardinal Odet de Châtillon found it 'strange' that, as the leader of the French delegation to the papal conclave of 1550, he had so little regard for his compatriots, joking at their expense that 'they were only there to make up the numbers'.[24] And this vanity was manifested in a certain vindictiveness towards those who dared challenge him or whom he felt had betrayed him. In contrast to his elder brother, he had a tendency to lose control of his temper in public—in one tantrum he tore off his red hat and stamped it on the ground.

His private life too was full of contradictions. The Venetian ambassador reported that 'he led a life that was open, honest, and suitable to his station, in contrast to other prelates of his court who were licentious by nature'.[25] Brantôme, who admitted that he was 'saintly' and 'devout', also suggested that as a young man he was something of a libertine. The man who professes to be more pious than his neighbour is always open to charges of hypocrisy. Charles's arrogance and vanity sharpened the barbs of court gossip, and few of the rumours were true. There was at least one product of his youthful indiscretion, a girl, Isabelle d'Arné, who in 1560 was sent to Spain as companion to Elizabeth of France, wife of Philip II.

Charles did not only share the financial affairs of the family with his mother. He looked after his sister Marie's interests in France. In early

1553, for example, he wrote that he was looking to invest her income in property and that he had moved her furniture and jewellery to his château of Meudon near Paris for safe keeping.[26] He was also intimately involved with the education of his younger brothers, nieces, and nephews. In particular, since Mary Stuart was at court, he had responsibility for her and he was closely involved in the establishment of her independent household in January 1554, keeping his sister informed of her progress. According to her governess, although all the brothers were fond of their niece, 'the cardinal showed her such great affection, as if she were his own'.[27] He would remain her mentor for the rest of his life. An equally important resident at court during Mary's childhood was her cousin, Charles III, Duke of Lorraine, who was two months her junior. The cardinal was appointed his tutor and kept a close eye on him, reporting to his sister in Scotland in 1553 how well he was and how much he was in the king's good graces.[28]

Differing characters though they were, the two brothers shared a strong belief in their duty of service to the king and in their joint mission to further the fortunes of their family. Charles wrote a letter to François in July 1551, consoling him on the birth of a 'mere' daughter the previous week with the knowledge that Madame de Montpensier, Madame de la Marck, and the Duke of Nevers had already offered their sons: 'if we know how to play our roles, we will have the pick of them'.[29] In the 1550s, duty to family and *patrie* were not incompatible but complementary, since royal and family policy was united against a common enemy: the House of Habsburg. Much has been made by historians of François de Lorraine's regal pretensions and the fashion in which he signed himself simply 'Francoys', like a monarch. In fact, he only did this in his capacity as royal governor and viceroy, a right that was his due as he was representing the figure of the monarch in person. The device of the cardinal (see Plate 10) reflected the binding of the dynasty to the Valois: it showed a pyramid surmounted with ivy and the motto, *Te stante virebo*, 'With you standing I shall flourish'. This was a common device throughout Europe; its symbolism was explained to Elizabeth I thus:

A mightie spyre, whose toppe dothe pierce the skie,
An ivie greene imbraceth rounde about,
And while it standes, the same doth bloome on highe,
But when it shrinkes, the ivie standes in dowt:
The Piller great, our gratious Princes is:
The braunche, the Churche: whoe speakes unto hir this.

I, that of late with stormes was almost spent,
And brused sore with Tirants bluddie bloes,
Whome fire, and sworde, with persecution rent,
Am nowe sett free, and overlooke my foes,
And whiles thow raignst, oh most renowmed Queene
By thie supporte my blossome shall bee greene.

For both Guise brothers politics came before religious scruple; they were, in contemporary parlance, *politiques* untroubled by the moderate religious line pursued by their sister in Scotland. François showed little interest in religion, theology being a matter for priests. He took part in processions and occasionally went on pilgrimage, but he seems to have shunned the ostentatious shows of piety beloved of his mother and, at times, by his father.

The eagerness to conform did not mean that tensions with the Crown or with other families were absent. In his marriage contract, François had used the vacant title, Duke of Anjou, and soon after, Charles, who was initially called the Cardinal of Saint-Urbain, had tried, at the papal conclave which met to elect a successor to Paul III, to have his title changed to Anjou. This met with opposition by the French ambassador and Charles was forced to take the title Lorraine on the death of his uncle. Their claim to the title suffered a further setback when Henry II conferred the Duchy of Anjou on his third son, Edouard-Alexandre, the future Henry III, who was born in 1551. The Guise were not yet a threat to the constable. Letters between them are full of affability and, in the early years of the reign, François and the constable's nephew, Gaspard de Coligny, continued to remain close friends. More significant in these years was the growing gap between the lofty pretensions of the House of Bourbon, as princes of the blood, and its actual political influence. Public ceremonies were a barometer of social distinction and the precedence disputes they occasioned were everyday skirmishes in the eternal struggle for recognition. On a royal visit to Chambéry in Savoy in 1548, François de Lorraine won a victory over the new head of the House of Bourbon, the uncharismatic Antoine, claiming the right to walk beside him, just behind the king. He argued that once they left the kingdom of France his descent from a sovereign house made him the equal of his cousin, who was but a simple 'subject and vassal of the Crown of France'.[30] The Guise had once traded on their close relationship to the Bourbon in order to gain influence at court; but now the position of the families was reversed. The Guise were rather snooty about Antoine's 1548 marriage to Jeanne d'Albret, heir to the kingdom of Navarre, a title which sounded grander than it was, since half of the kingdom was in Spanish hands and what was left consisted substantially of mountains populated by sheep. Jeanne d'Albret's mother, Marguerite of Navarre, was disliked by the Constable of Montmorency, and as a family they were further tainted in the eyes of the king for making secret approaches to Spain, only to have their correspondence intercepted by the constable. As a result, the new King of Navarre had to rely on the Duke of Guise, who was only a few months his senior, to offset his disadvantageous wife. Relations between him and his cousins were for the time being cordial: in letters the cardinal referred to Navarre as his 'brother' and he in turn acted as godfather to one of the duke's children. In 1548 the cardinal lobbied in Rome for the red hat for Antoine's younger brother, Charles, 'a matter which was very close to him given the proximity of their lineages'.[31] Favours from the king were harder to obtain, though the Guise did their best to secure some crumbs of patronage.

* * * *

Dreams of empire were in part responsible for the cold war between Henry II and Charles V turning hot in 1552. Renaissance humanists in both Germany and France hoped for a renewal of the ideals of the Holy Roman Empire in which the King of France would act as a reconciler of princes and a protector of German liberties. The myth of Germans and Franks united in defence of liberty against papal and Spanish despotism chimed with *Realpolitik*. Constable Montmorency had continued his successful policy of covert operations against Imperialist interests, supporting their enemies wherever possible and building up a system of alliances to counteract their domination of the continent. The treaty of alliance with England was followed by a renewal of friendship with the Ottoman Sultan; French support for the Ottoman attack on Tripoli held by the Knights of Malta causing a scandal throughout Christendom. The French also took action against the pro-imperialist Pope, Julius III, refusing to take part in the General Council called at Trent to reform the Catholic Church, seeing it as a threat to the independence of the Gallican Church. Henry II threatened to convene a national council, even to the point of considering the appointment of the Cardinal of Bourbon as Patriarch of France; he ordered that papal revenues in France should cease to be paid and sent troops to support the Duke of Parma in his dispute with the Pope. Julius was forced to capitulate in April 1552, closing down Trent and recalling his troops from Parma. The victory over Julius was widely seen as victory over his ally, Charles V. French influence in Italy was at its highest for many years.

At the same time as French and imperial forces were fighting through proxies in Italy, a new front was opening up in Germany. Crippled with gout, ageing and worn down by the burdens of running a world empire, Charles V entered his final years with the renewed hope of reuniting Catholic and Protestants in the Holy Roman Empire and of realizing the traditional Burgundian policy of controlling the Duchy of Lorraine. The work of the Council of Trent and the defeat of the German Lutheran princes at the battle of Mühlberg in 1547 suggested that the religious issues, which had troubled the whole of his reign, were finally reaching a resolution. Guided by Montmorency's cunning, Henry II had bided his time, but in 1551 his opportunity to move on to the offensive came when the German Protestant princes appealed to the French king for help and secret negotiations got under way. The treaty signed at Chambord in January 1552 was an unusual alliance. It was a confederation between the signatories, the cause of which, as set out in its articles, was to prevent the princes and towns of Germany 'from falling from their ancient *franchise* and liberty in a bestial, insupportable and perpetual servitude as has happened in Spain and elsewhere'.[32] This defence of liberty against Papal-Spanish hegemony was an idea that resonated for German Protestants and French Catholics alike, and the basis on which they had opposed Trent. Despite his persecution of their co-religionists, Protestant reformers throughout Europe still had hopes for the king of France, and Gallican writers—such as Rabelais, whose *Quart Livre* appeared in 1552—joined them in expressing strongly anti-Papal sentiments. The Cardinal of Lorraine designed the confederation's standard, on which was written the inscription 'Henricus secundus, Francorum rex, vindex libertatis germanicae et principum captivorum'. Protestant German troops adopted the white cross of France. In exchange for an initial payment of 240,000 crowns and thereafter 60,000 crowns per month to pay for the princes' army, the French were to be permitted to occupy the strategically important towns of Metz, Toul, and Verdun and to remain as 'vicars' of the emperor over the *Welcheslanden*, namely those western imperial territories which spoke non-German dialects.

There was much flummery in all this talk of liberty. Within months of signing the treaty of Chambord most of the German princes made their peace with the emperor, changing sides in return for substantial concessions—a process aided by the inconclusive break-up of Trent. The French, however, had hard-headed reasons for intervening in Germany. Montmorency was initially more cautious about risking open battle with the imperialists, but there were more bellicose counsels. The adventure appealed to Henry II personally not only because of his hatred for Charles, but because this was the emperor's twilight and Valois success would lay the ground for a future bid for the imperial crown. More immediately, the idea of a new Franco-German empire built in the ancient Merovingian lands of *Austrasia* appealed to Henry, who was represented as a new Charlemagne in French propaganda.[33] There were two families at court who had had their lands in the empire seized by Charles V and fed Henry's dreams of empire in the lands between the Moselle and the Rhine. The imperialists controlled Robert de la Marck's duchy of Bouillon and could depend on his mother-in-law, Diane de Poitiers, to press his case. The Guise too had suffered at Charles V's hands. The Cardinal of Lorraine had been prevented by the emperor from succeeding his uncle to the abbey of Gorze, which was strategically positioned on the Franco-imperial border. More seriously the Duchy of Lorraine had fallen within the imperial sphere of influence. Since the death of Duke Antoine in 1544, his widow, Christina of Denmark, had been regent and the Guise wanted her replaced by a member of their own kith and kin. In the summer of 1551 the Guise feared that the duchy would be occupied by imperial troops. They urged the king to bring the 8-year-old Charles III of Lorraine to Paris and marry him to his daughter, Claude, thereby ensuring that 'our poor house would escape from a great danger'—namely the threat of foreign domination, a threat it had faced for a century and the reason why they referred to Charles V and his family as 'Burgundians'. When imperial troops garrisoned the strategically important fortress that adjoined the abbey of Gorze, on the west bank of the Moselle between Metz and Nancy, the threat became tangible.

The imperial free city of Metz, which proclaimed its special status by sporting an imperial eagle on its coat of arms, was the strategic key to the region, threatening Lorraine and, if under French control, the Rhineland too, as well as then cutting communications between Charles V's dynastic lands in the Netherlands and south Germany. French preparations centred on its capture. The 1552 campaign was one of the most successful in French military history and one in which the Guise family played an important role. Cardinal Charles was the city's bishop but his arrival in the city would have been too conspicuous, and in any case the city was jealous of its privileges and resistant to episcopal interference. Instead, he resigned his see to one of his trusted clients, Robert de Lenoncourt, whose family seat at Vignory was close to Joinville and who was sent ahead of the French army to act as a fifth columnist, preparing the city for takeover. Montmorency's talent for organization was evident in the army that gathered in Champagne. The main force was 50,000 strong and, with the reserve and supporting units in Picardy, in all 70,000 men required feeding and supplying. It was by far the largest and best-prepared French army of the sixteenth century; its like would not be seen again until the age of Richelieu. The Guise and other magnates melted down their plate to help pay for it. Henry II declared war on 15 February and he arrived at Joinville at the end of March to review the army. The campaign was conducted at lightning speed. Montmorency, the commander-in-chief, and Guise left Joinville on 2 April and marched on Gorze, whose defenders resisted for a few days before being overrun and massacred. The constable entered Metz on 10 April without a fight. On 14 April the French army violated the neutrality of the duchy of Lorraine and marched on Nancy, where the Cardinal of Lorraine was already inside preparing for its arrival. Christina of Denmark was removed as regent and the Lorrainer nobility swore an oath of loyalty to the king of France as Protector to the young Duke Charles. Henry II announced his intention to marry his daughter to him and French garrisons were installed in the duchy's principal towns. The king retired home while his army headed east into the Vosges and then swung north before it reached the Rhine, taking town after town and restoring the duchy of Bouillon to the la Marck. At Verdun, Cardinal Charles once again preceded the main army. Following his official entry into the city as bishop, he installed a garrison of 300 men.

The imperialists were caught off guard by the speed and complete success of the French advance, which was helped less by enthusiasm for the French cause than for antipathy to the policies of Charles V and his ministers. The only obstacle to complete French victory was the behaviour of their allies. Despite his age and infirmity, Charles had responded with stoicism to defeat and invasion, swallowing his pride and meeting the rebel princes at Passau in August. He was determined to reverse the humiliation and his decision to go on to the offensive so late in the campaigning season was conditioned by the fact that communications between the Netherlands, the Franche-Comté, and his possessions in south Germany had been severed: it was imperative that Charles protect his inheritance in the region. The man who stood in his path as French commander of Metz was an old enemy, the 33-year-old François, Duke of Guise.

To undertake a siege so late in the season was a risky enterprise, but Charles's confidence was boosted by the arrival of the Spanish general, the Duke of Alva. The huge imperial army, numbering 80,000 men, moved into Lorraine in October but it was slowed by the foulness of the weather and it did not arrive at Metz until 14 October. Guise had only 6,000 men with him, but was well informed of the emperor's movements and he methodically prepared the city for a siege with the precious time he had. The city was well supplied and a scorched-earth policy was conducted in the surrounding area, denying the imperialists forage and shelter. The city's suburbs were razed to create clear fields of fire. The masses of building material that resulted in this destruction were stored in the city or used to reinforce the earthworks and build the firing platforms that the duke was constructing for cannon. Controversially, this required the demolition of several churches and monasteries. The duke made strenuous efforts to keep the population on his side. As well as maintaining strict discipline, he ordered the removal of the bones of Charlemagne's wife, Hildegard and son, Louis the pious, from the condemned monastery of Saint-Arnulf, which lay just beyond the city, with great pomp to safety inside the city. Townsfolk were drafted into digging the fortifications, but grumbling was limited by the duke's common touch; he appeared at all hours of the night and day to encourage his engineers and labourers, and even picked up a shovel himself as an encouragement to others. Realizing that the greatest siege of the age was about to take place, the French aristocracy hurried to Metz in search of glory. Educated from birth to compete with each other in acts of bravery, the arrival of these ill-disciplined hotheads might have spelt disaster for a man of lesser status and authority. But Guise knew how to channel their competitive streak. He divided the city walls into sections, each of which was assigned its own family in the knowledge that honour would ensure that no man would fail to do his duty. Among them were the greatest princes of the kingdom: the younger brothers of the King of Navarre, the Duke of Enghien and the Prince of Condé, were given the section from the Saint-Thibaut gate down to the river Seille; Charles de Bourbon-Montpensier, Prince de la Roche-sur-Yon, defended the des Barres gate and the wall up to the Charriers tower; one section of trenches and revetments was assigned to Guise's own brothers, the Grand Prior and René d'Elbeuf;

and next to them were their rivals, the eldest sons of the Constable of Montmorency, François and Henri.

As soon as the Duke of Alva appeared with his army, Guise launched sorties to disrupt the full investment of the city. His brother, the Duke of Aumale, with a force of light cavalry, operating behind enemy lines, was caught up in a skirmish just outside Nancy and captured after being wounded several times and his finger severed. Guise was proud of his brother for 'being taken while fighting to the last, not having surrendered until having been brought to the ground and having a cocked pistol put to his throat'.[34] This sort of aggressive defence would characterize Guise's tactics, constantly harrying the enemy in their trenches, disrupting and demoralizing them as the weather worsened and it began to snow. Sorties and surprise attacks in particular targeted foragers, supply columns, and the imperialist lines of communication. Charles V's arrival in a litter on 20 November was greeted with a sally which slaughtered several hundred horses and plundered the imperial mule train. Even so, the siege was not without its chivalric interludes. The monotony of hand-to-hand fighting in the besiegers' trenches was occasionally broken by challenges and jousts between Spanish and French knights.

The imperialist artillery fire maintained a furious rate of fire. By 17 December Guise estimated that the imperialists had fired 11,800 cannonballs, but even where breaches were made the defenders raised formidable earthworks eight feet high in their place and set them bristling with guns. And whereas the French were well stocked with provisions, with enough salt meat to last until Lent and flour until August, the imperialists meanwhile were starving and shivering in their bivouacs. On Christmas Day, Charles prayed for a miracle. It did not come and on 1 January he left, a broken man, his army destroyed, for Brussels. When the French moved into the abandoned positions the scene they found was pitiable; intermingled with unburied horses and many of the corpses of the 12,000 men who had died from typhus and scurvy were large numbers of sick and wounded abandoned to their fate. In the abandoned tent of the emperor the French found six magnificent tapestries, depicting significant episodes in the life of France's first king, Clovis, that had once decorated the banqueting hall for the marriage feast of Charles the Bold and Margaret of York. Their abandonment to François de Lorraine, Duke of Guise, who sent them for his brother to hang in Reims, the spiritual home of the king's of France, was symbolic. The nemesis of the Habsburgs had once again triumphed. In his retreat from Metz Charles had given up all hope of rebuilding the Burgundian dynastic empire, just as his great-grandfather's plans had been destroyed by Guise's grandfather in 1477. Guise held a solemn procession on 15 January 1553, after which the Lutheran books taken in the booty were ceremonially burnt—a sort of offering for the deliverance of the city.

In France, the response to victory was euphoric. During the siege the cardinal wrote to his brother, telling him that he was 'winning a reputation' and that 'all our affairs depend on where you are'.[35] On 20 February the king lauded the duke publicly during a full session of the Paris Parlement. Henry spoke of his 'perfect happiness' and of the 'immortal glory and honour' that was Guise's due. Public celebrations throughout the kingdom were ordered. A medal was struck. The duke had proved himself far more than a great organizer, a role which Montmorency could also perform. He had proved himself a great leader and inspirer of men. He had shown compassion too: the way he had treated the wounded and sick imperialist soldiers abandoned by Charles V was widely praised. His name and deeds spread throughout Europe: Italians took to calling him 'the great' and even Spaniards, who were harder to impress, often referred to him as 'el gran ducque de Guysa' or 'el gran capitan di Guysa'.

* * * *

Success bred jealousy. Constable Montmorency noticed that the king kissed the duke and called him his 'brother' on his return to court, a level of familiarity that was alarming. The hatred that divided the Houses of Guise and Montmorency and that would dominate politics for a decade had yet to germinate, but the first seeds had been planted. Despite his elevation to a dukedom the year before, Montmorency was not a prince; he was however a true-born Frenchmen. Though the Guise felt themselves far superior to a man whose father had been a mere baron, they too were sensitive to quips about their 'foreignness' and the ammunition it provided to their enemies. In April 1552 Henry II had taken the unusual step of raising the barony of Joinville to a principality, so that the Guise were not simply naturalized foreigners but princes *in* France. This did not put an end to malicious gossip. One purpose behind the projected marriages of both Mary Stuart and the Duke of Lorraine to royal children was to end such talk. After the marriages took place, the Cardinal of Lorraine was not only delighted that the 'head of his House' could quarter his arms with those of France, but henceforth no one would be able to claim that they were 'foreign princes'.[36]

Having failed at Metz, Charles V moved his field of operations onto French territory. In April 1553 his army invested the small fortified town of Thérouanne, an isolated French enclave surrounded by the emperor's Burgundian inheritance. Thérouanne was well provisioned and garrisoned but it fell in June and the constable's eldest son, François was captured. The fall of Thérouanne was a great shock to the French. The king was dismayed and, it was reported, blamed the constable. Worse followed when Hesdin, which had not been repaired since a French assault six months earlier, fell on 19 July. Guise made no attempt to profit from the constable's discomfort publicly, for he had no need. The constable's caution in the field contrasted to the youthful vigour of his rival and it was compounded by a serious illness in the autumn, which left him and his army debilitated. He was the object of derision and lampoons. To make matters worse, his foreign policy was unravelling. The final illness of Edward VI placed the Franco-British project in grave jeopardy. Charles V's goal was to ensure the succession of his cousin, Mary Tudor. The French, in turn, supported the Protestant candidate, Lady Jane Grey. The French were genuinely surprised and deeply disappointed when word came in mid-July that Mary had been acclaimed queen. The gloom deepened with news of her betrothal to Philip of Spain and the prospect that the first son of the union would add England to the Burgundian territories of the Netherlands and the Franche-Comté. Henry II was left speechless, conversing with the English ambassador on 18 December 1553 he 'showed by his gestures and drawling half-swallowed words that he was so exceedingly put out [by the marriage] that he could not frame a reply or finish his sentences'.[37]

These setbacks were the origins of the rivalry between the Guise and the Montmorency. In January 1554 the Cardinal of Lorraine had to send one of his servants to Scotland because the man had stood up for the Duke of Bouillon, who had been taken prisoner at Hesdin, against slurs on his honour made by Gaspard de Coligny. The cardinal told his sister that 'if he remained here, he would be killed' and he told her to keep the matter quiet.[38] But the mistrust soon became public knowledge in the most dramatic fashion. Despite his limitations as a field commander, the constable continued to enjoy the king's confidence and he led the armies that counter-attacked in the spring of 1554 in Artois, Hainault, and Luxembourg. The two sides were evenly matched with about 45,000 men each. On the French side, the campaign proved a huge disappointment and once again the constable's over-cautious approach was criticized—some suggesting that he was more interested in ransoming his son, others that he did not want to engage the enemy lest Guise, who took the field as a simple captain of gendarmes, be given the chance to win more glory. The desultory war of position was not the way of war for French aristocrats and once again it was Guise who lifted morale. He had been detailed to shadow the enemy, but on 13 August he suddenly found himself facing the entire imperial army. By a clever ruse, using forest cover and well supported by the infantry under their colonel-general, Coligny, he inflicted a sharp reverse on the enemy, capturing twenty ensigns, killing 500 imperialists, and taking 300 prisoners. The victory celebrations were marred that evening by the quarrel between the two captains over the responsibility for the victory. They were at the point of drawing swords. The king hastily made them exchange the kiss of peace, but their close friendship, already under strain, was at an end.

The failure to follow up Renty and French setbacks in Italy, especially the fall of Siena, made Henry willing to discuss peace. Montmorency and the Cardinal of Lorraine were delegated to meet the imperial representatives in the Pale of Calais on 23 May 1555. The Guise were less interested in peace than Montmorency, and not simply because of François's growing reputation. Claude d'Aumale had been released from captivity in 1554 for 60,000 crowns paid by his mother-in-law Diane de Poitiers, his mother, and his brother Charles, and had resumed his post as captain of the royal light cavalry and dragoons. Among the setbacks in Italy, the capture of Corsica, involving the two youngest Guise brothers, the Grand Prior, and René d'Elbeuf, stood out as a solitary French success. The latter was rewarded with appointment as commander of the Mediterranean galley fleet; based at Toulon and Marseilles it had considerably increased since the beginning of the reign and comprised forty-two galleys. The constable had nothing to gain from further campaigning, and much to lose. He wanted to hold on to what he had and reunite his family—his son François was still in captivity, along with his nephew, Andelot, who had been captured in 1551. The constable's desire for peace was evident to one of the imperial negotiators, Cardinal Granvelle. Montmorency was effusive in his praise for the emperor. 'He knew that in your majesty he had to do with a person who knows what is what. At this point the Cardinal [Lorraine] cast a glance at the constable, who reddened a little, and added "after my master".'[39] The negotiations were inconclusive, but so was the fighting that ensued. The abdication of Charles V and the division of his titles between his brother Ferdinand and son Philip eased French fears that the latter intended to become a universal emperor in the mould of his father. The breakthrough was made by the delicate diplomacy of Coligny. He was emerging as a major figure in the regime; his rapid rise making him enemies in the process. The favourite nephew of the constable, in 1551 he was made Governor of Paris and the Ile de France, a key post which was becoming a Montmorency fief, and a year later he became Admiral of France, an office that had little to do with naval affairs but which was immensely lucrative and in prestige ranked only second to that of the constable. In an exceptional display of favour, he was awarded a second governorship in June 1555, that of the strategically important province of Picardy, against strong opposition from the princes, especially the man whom he replaced, Antoine de Bourbon. Coligny used his new position on the frontier to maintain discreet contacts with the imperialists and in February 1556 at Vaucelles, with the backing of his uncle, the king was persuaded to accept a five-year truce. This seriously jeopardized Guise plans. French fortunes in Italy had recently been boosted by the election of the anti-Spanish Pope Paul IV. While Coligny was negotiating peace in the north, the Cardinal of Lorraine had been dispatched to Rome in October 1555 to negotiate a league with Paul. The pact that resulted, promising the Pope a monthly subsidy of 350,000 crowns and an army of 12,000 men, was secret and not known to the Habsburgs until the middle of 1556. According to the Venetian ambassador in France, the court was divided between the peace faction and the war faction: 'the adherents of the constable together with the public, being desirous of its conclusion; whilst on the other hand, the dependants both of the Queen and the house of Guise, together with those of Madame de Valentinois, demonstrate openly that for the benefit of his affairs his most Christian Majesty ought not to come to this agreement, but pursue the execution of the League'.[40] Montmorency continued to dominate policymaking and the fact that the war had already cost Henry 45 million crowns also figured large in the decision to make peace. The opposition of the Guise to the peace was a matter of policy and not personality—their enmity was reserved for the Habsburgs. Six weeks before the signing of Vaucelles the duke had written to the cardinal, 'The Constable and I, we are getting on well together; he always shows me some sign of friendship as he did before your departure [to Rome]'.[41]

* * * *

As the man who established the Roman inquisition; who sponsored the first index of prohibited books; and who persecuted evangelical

Catholics, Protestants, and Jews alike; the ascetic, nepotistic, and volatile 79-year-old Paul IV must be the sixteenth century's most unappealing Pope. But his chief attributes in the eyes of Cardinal Charles was that he was a Neapolitan patriot, a supporter of the exile cause who desired nothing more than to drive the hated Spanish from Italy. In Paul IV's twisted view of the world, Charles V was a friend to schismatics and heretics; Spaniards a blend of Jews and Moors. In return for French support, the Pope consented to the transference of Naples and Milan to the younger sons of Henry II. As soon as the Pope was engaged in hostilities—he excommunicated both Charles V and Philip II for good measure—the Guise pressed the king to honour his commitments. Montmorency, on the other hand, was reluctant to commit himself to further his rivals' Italian ambitions and the royal council remained deadlocked for months. Finally, on 23 September 1556, the king agreed to send an army, emphasizing that in doing so he was aiding the Pope and not violating his truce with Philip II. Having lost the argument, Montmorency was said to have remarked that 'we shall all ride across the Alps but come back on foot'. The Duke of Ferrara was made commander-in-chief and Guise received the grandiose title of 'Lieutenant of His Holiness and of the Most Christian King, Captain-General in the army of the Holy League'. His standard sported the papal keys surmounted by the fleur de lys. His orders stated that once he had reconquered Naples he would be made viceroy. The army itself was not large—11,000 foot and 1,800 horse—but it was battle-hardened. The choice of officers was an *affaire de famille*. As well as his brothers, Aumale and Elbeuf, the army consisted of a host of friends, followers and volunteers eager to share in the glory. The captain of the French infantry, Jacques de Savoie, Duke of Nemours, one of Guise's closest companions, had come to escape the wrath of the King of Navarre, who had sworn to kill him and all his friends for making his niece pregnant. Guise promised to marry Nemours to his sister-in-law, Lucrecia d'Este.

The campaign was wholly misconceived, largely because the duke had been totally unprepared by his brother for the viperous labyrinth of Italian politics. Charles could do little to influence events from Paris and displayed a wholly unrealistic grasp of military logic. François received his baton as field commander of the allied army from his father-in-law on 16 February 1557. Ercole, wearing a helmet inlaid with jewels valued at a million crowns, staged a magnificent welcome. But this was just for show; he had no interest in his son-in-law's southern adventure and his logistical help was derisory. The duke's magnificent entry into Rome also masked tensions between the allies. There were vast differences between the Pope and his nephews—who dominated policy-making at the Vatican—French diplomats, and the duke on how to proceed. The spring invasion of Naples was a lamentable failure. Guise knew his best strategy was to force a quick 'day of splendour' with his veterans, but his experienced Spanish adversary, the Duke of Alva, had no intention of fighting on his enemy's terms, opting for a war of attrition. The French were at a serious manpower disadvantage and sickness soon began to take its toll. The duke himself was often ill from fevers contracted in the malaria-infested countryside around Rome. Lack of money was another problem. The campaign cost a staggering 1.8 million livres during the months of March, April, and May 1557. The failure of the Duke of Ferrara to provide the necessary funds led to some sharp exchanges between son and father-in-law. Ercole complained that he would not be treated as a banker. Relations with the splenetic and unpredictable Paul IV were even worse. In his final interview with the Pope the duke lost his habitual sang-froid, venting his frustration on the Pope's beloved nephews. As early as May, it was clear that retreat was necessary and the duke delayed only for fear of leaving the Pope at Alva's mercy. Revealing his ignorance of field operations, the Cardinal of Lorraine maintained his optimism in the face of reality and was alone among the king's ministers in wanting to continue the campaign.

Guise's poor progress was music to Montmorency's ears at court. Charles wrote to his brother in mid-January that he had to spend every hour with the king in order to balance the constable's hostility to the project. Anne d'Este's complexion went sallow from stress, a consequence of everyone at court telling her that her husband was 'lost'.[42] One summer's day Guise fortunes changed forever. Ironically, it was Montmorency who was the author both of his own downfall and his rival's rehabilitation. Over Christmas 1556, he had suddenly changed his mind and counselled the king to resume the war with Spain, either because he considered it inevitable or because, with the campaign in Italy yet to run into problems, he feared that Guise would steal the glory. Hostilities recommenced in January when Coligny, himself eager to enhance his reputation, launched an abortive surprise attack on Douai. Montmorency's previous performance in the field did not augur well for the summer campaign and the gloom was worsened when England declared war on 7 June. The campaign was incompetently handled from the start and it ended disastrously on 10 August near Saint-Quentin. So one-sided was the encounter, it is hard to characterize the rout followed by a massacre as a battle at all. Saint-Quentin was a worse defeat than Pavia; for whereas Pavia had been a glorious chapter in the annals of chivalry, the poor knights who survived Saint-Quentin would recover their reputations from the ignominy and shame they had incurred with great difficulty. The French army lost all but one of its fifty-seven standards, at least 2,500 dead, and 7,000 prisoners, which included a roll-call of great aristocrats. Montmorency's army was also an *affaire de famille*: several of his closest kinsmen were killed; others were captured along with the constable himself. Worse was to follow a few days later with the fall of Saint-Quentin and the capture of Coligny.

The effect of the defeat on morale was crushing. Utterly dependent on his 'father' for counsel and emotional support, the king was lost as to what to do next. In Paris and at court panic set in and was mixed with recriminations towards Montmorency. As architect of the Neapolitan folly, the Cardinal of Lorraine was not spared either. François's failure was all but forgotten. 'For my part', wrote a Parisian banker, 'I wished that Monsieur de Guise had been over here! And God willing all would have been well conducted.'[43] On 23 August the duke was at Spoleto when a courier arrived summoning him home to defend the kingdom from invasion. Delayed by illness, he arrived at Saint-Germain-en-Laye on 6 October accompanied by 400 gentlemen. Those courtiers who watched their saviour arrive would have found the motto displayed on his banner, *Chacun à son tour* ('To each his turn') particularly apt. The wheel of fortune had spun once again; his turn had come.

4

CHACUN À SON TOUR

The Venetian ambassador watched as Guise arrived at court and threw himself at the king's feet. 'It may be credited that his Majesty felt very great joy at his arrival, and principally from now having a companion for his business and his toils, he alone having hitherto despatched the numberless affairs of recent urgency, rarely employing the Cardinal of Lorraine in military matters.'[1] On 20 October 1557 François, Duke of Guise, was made lieutenant-general of the kingdom, conferring on him vice-regal powers. Cardinal Charles had already been entrusted with the royal signet and taken responsibility of civil and financial matters. A week later they were joined by their brothers, the Duke of Aumale, the Marquis of Elbeuf, and the Grand Prior.

Henry believed that an attack on Calais, the plan for which had been in long gestation, was the surest way to restore French honour. Guise was initially sceptical. In English hands since 1347, Calais was protected by a formidable system of outlying forts which had been modernized during the reign of Henry VIII. Moreover, the campaigning season was late and the Calais pale was dreadfully inhospitable terrain; its marshy and windswept flatlands presented a formidable challenge to supplying an army during the worst months of the year in a country that had recently suffered one of the great military disasters of the sixteenth century. Despite his misgivings, Guise had been presented with the opportunity of posing as the saviour of the country and he seized it with alacrity. The campaign exemplifies how the Guise brothers worked together as a team, or as 'two heads in one hood' as a contemporary put it.[2] Charles and François left nothing to chance. The final months of the year were dedicated to meticulous planning. An old-fashioned captain in the army, Blaise de Monluc, was astonished that a soldier like François should spend so much time on paper work: 'The devil take all these writings for me, it seems he has a mind to save his secretaries labour.' The logistical problems of supplying an army of 30–36,000 men throughout the winter in country suffering from war fatigue cannot be underestimated. Cardinal Charles busied himself with feeding Mars, using expedients to screw cash from taxpayers and reluctant lenders. 'I do not cease day and night', he replied to his brother's urgent demands, 'to torment myself to advance your money and to pick all the purses I can find to help you.' Squeezing them until their pips squeaked did nothing for his popularity among the common people.

Calais's dozen or so outlying forts amounted to a formidable obstacle. Above the town's main gate was the inscription 'Then shall the Frenchmen Calais win; when iron and lead like cork shall swim'. Its main weakness was its old-fashioned castle, which had been overlooked by Henry VIII's engineers. The English were caught off guard by an attack outside the campaigning season. The suddenness of the attack on 1 January allowed the French to capture a number of outlying forts and bring the town within cannon range. The French were thoroughly prepared for the terrain, to the point of having made pitch-covered mats to serve as artillery platforms on the marshes. They were helped by the cold weather which froze the shallower marshes, enabling their guns and equipment to cross the treacherous ground easily. After two days of bombardment from across the river Hames a breach was made in the castle walls. The river was fordable at low tide and the duke advanced, waist-deep in the water, at the head of several companies, while diversionary attacks elsewhere drew off the defenders. His troops took the castle with ease and put the garrison to the sword. He retired to camp, leaving his brothers, Aumale and Elbeuf, to hold the castle against two bloody English counter-attacks. On 8 January Lord Wentworth sued for terms. He and several English lords were held for ransom (though they were eventually released) and the rest of the garrison and all those inhabitants who wished to leave were given safe passage to the Flemish border. Guise captured a significant quantity of military supplies and commercial goods, which he shared among his captains. The constable's nephew, François d'Andelot, the colonel-general of the infantry, who had done much to rehabilitate his family's reputation, was given a share of wool valued at 25–30,000 crowns.

* * * *

The fall of Calais shocked Europe in its daring and its challenge to the traditional ways of war. Guise retained his habitual modesty when writing to his mother: 'Since all things come from God...it must be recognized...that this enterprise was ordained by Him alone, and that it was not a thing...in the power of men. I also wish to attribute the glory to Him and not myself.'[3] This did not mean that he was awaiting his reward in heaven. Good service demanded recognition and that the king fulfil his promise to marry the dauphin, Francis, to Mary Stuart. The king had reiterated his promise as recently as December, but there were powerful objectors. From his captivity Montmorency desperately tried to stop it, sending a Spanish agent to propose the dauphin's marriage to the sister of Philip II as part of a more general peace. Henry listened and postponed the betrothal. Calais changed everything. The marriage festivities were arranged with the same meticulous attention to detail as the war. Mary knew her husband intimately; she had been raised with the dauphin. Cardinal Charles was already calling him 'l'Amoureux' when he was just 5 years old. On Tuesday 19 April 1558 Charles joined the betrothed's hands together in the new wing of the Louvre. The contrast between the two was stark. Aged 15, Mary was distinctively a Guise; she was tall at around 5 feet 11 inches and had blond hair. She was vivacious and had received the same humanist education as her future husband. She owned a copy of Erasmus's *In Praise of Folly* and his *Colloquies*. Two years before her marriage she had given an oration as part of her studies, defending women's rights to study. A year younger than his bride, Francis profited little from his education, showing an interest only in hunting. He idolized his new uncle, watching him in tourneys with an admiration reserved today for sporting idols. In 1551 he wrote that he was practising so that he too could 'fight one to one and hope to win the favour of a beautiful and honest lady like your niece'.[4] The trouble with the dauphin was that as he reached adolescence his physical and mental capacities halted abruptly. He was weedy, intellectually limited, and debilitated by frequent attacks of illness.

The wedding that took place the Sunday following the betrothal was one of the most magnificent public occasions seen in sixteenth-century Paris.[5] Everything possible was done to increase the visibility of the occasion for onlookers. A gallery or temporary covered walkway, twelve feet high, connected the starting point of the wedding procession, the nearby palace of the Bishop of Paris, to a stage built in the main square in front of the cathedral, surmounted by a canopy of azure-blue silk embossed with gold fleur de lys. It continued along the nave to the chancel, where the couple would hear Mass after the ceremony had been completed in the open air. Dignitaries were seated around the stage, but the sides of the gallery were open so that everyone could watch the procession. Festivities began at 10 am when the Swiss guard arrived, leading a troop of musicians dressed in the yellow and red livery of the House of Guise. They entertained the crowd for half an hour before Duke François arrived to be welcomed by the Bishop of Paris. The duke was master of ceremonies and onlookers noticed that he carried the staff of the Grand Master of the King's Household in the constable's absence. While the wedding was performed on the stage, the duke busied himself clearing interlopers off the stage, so that the people who were crammed into the surrounding streets and hanging out of neighbouring windows could see. But the people were not just there for the spectacle. Once the ceremony was finished two heralds, crying 'largesse', threw handfuls of gold and silver coins into the throng. The wedding party turned its back on the scrimmage that followed, as people dived for the coins, pushing and elbowing their neighbours, to enter the cathedral and hear the wedding Mass. During the offertory the heralds threw another shower of coins in the cathedral.

To loud cheers the wedding party returned to the bishop's palace for the private banquet. At 5 pm there was a new procession to the Palais, official residence of the Parlement of Paris, a few hundred yards from the cathedral at the opposite end of the Ile de la Cité. In order to maximize the drama, Guise chose a route which wound its way indirectly, crossing the Pont Notre-Dame into the heart of business and residential districts of the Right Bank before returning across the Pont au Change, which was lined with shops and houses. The state banquet organized by the duke and his cousin the Prince of Condé was accompanied by entertainments on a vast scale to impress foreign ambassadors and the city's dignitaries. The theme was the triple monarchy of the Franco-British empire. Six giant mechanical ships were constructed, as if to emphasize this was a seaborne empire. Ronsard, the star of the Pléaide, the most fashionable collective of poets in France, began the festivities with an epic poem in honour of the Guise. He was followed by a panegyric from Michel de l'Hôpital, president of the Court of Accounts, that boasted of how Mary's marriage would subjugate England 'without murder and war'. The underlying message was that the marriage would make Scotland and England provinces of the French empire, a dream that was made tangible by the secret clauses of the marriage treaty. Under the influence of her uncles, Mary passed her rights to Scotland and her claim to the throne of England to her husband should she die without posterity. The Cardinal of Lorraine even proposed that the crown of Scotland be removed to Saint-Denis for safekeeping. Later that year Henry issued a law granting letters of French citizenship to all Scots and thereby extending his sovereignty over them. It was the first step towards incorporating Scotland into an 'imperial' monarchy modelled on the example of the Roman Empire.

Anyone who has organized a wedding will know that the seating arrangements for dinner are the most likely to cause friction among the guests. Happily, the awkward conundrum of where to seat the king's mistress does not arise today. Mary Stuart's wedding planners were fortunate in that they had the largest and most magnificent table in Europe at their disposal. The Table of Marble was mainly used in the Palais for legal and administrative business, but it could also double up as a stage for theatrical performances. Members of the lesser aristocracy and the Parisian civic elite sat further away according to their rank. The top table was a microcosm of the ideal social hierarchy as conceived by the Guise. There was no member of the Montmorency family among the thirty-five people on the top table, except Odet de Châtillon, who took his place alongside three other cardinals. The other members of the wider Guise family were all princes: the Houses of Bourbon, the la Marck, the Clèves-Nevers and the Orléans-Longueville were all represented. And the king's mistress was here too, seated between her daughters. The composition of the table also pointed to future family tensions. Leaving aside the king and queen, the bride and groom, and the papal legate, twelve of the remaining thirty guests were either practising Protestants already or soon to convert.

Their fellow princes' private beliefs were a relatively unimportant matter for the Guise. They had reached the height of their influence and power, and had every interest in maintaining the status quo and turning a blind eye to things which did not perturb it. During this period the distinction between royal power and Guise power became blurred. Contemporary estimates which put the Guise fortune in this period at around 600,000 livres per annum are almost certainly too low. We can put this figure in context by comparing it to the annual income of Elizabeth I in the first decade of her reign, which was in the region of 200,000 pounds sterling. Since the English pound was usually reckoned to be just over ten times the value of the French pound, the Guise were worth more than 25 per cent of the Crown of England. But this seriously underestimates the reach of their power, because the King of France enjoyed powers of patronage that were unequalled by all but the Habsburgs. And in Montmorency's absence the Guise came close to its total control, the duke being responsible for military posts and the cardinal for civil offices. He already controlled ecclesiastical appointments. In 1554 he wrote to his 'sister', Marguerite of Bourbon, Duchess of Nevers, that he would ensure that the abbey of Notre-Dame-de-Nevers would not be given to anyone she did not approve of, and in his own hand he added: 'watch that you do not go and have yourself a daughter, but give us a little priest and I'll help you turn him into an honest man'.[6] Every day the brothers had to deal with requests for favours from all over France. Pierre Rémon, a magistrate of the Parlement of Rouen, wrote to the Duke of Guise in favour of a nephew's promotion to the royal falconers, which would 'increase and augment his wages ... so that he has better means of doing good service to the king and also to you'. When Rémon himself died in 1553 the Cardinal of Lorraine was pitted against his brother and mother in supporting rival candidates to the post. The seigneur of Escavolles, whom the king had awarded a meagre pension, wrote from Toul to request an office in Burgundy, which he could resell for 1,400 or 1,500 crowns. On a different level, the war disrupted trade and created all sorts of shortages, so that certain luxuries could only be obtained through influence. In 1558 the Princess of la Roche-sur-Yon wrote to the duke, her cousin, to complain about the difficulty of obtaining good claret. Her request for a permit to ship 100 tons was sweetened by the prospect that she 'would be better able to treat M. the marquis [of Elbeuf] your brother with my niece his wife, whom we are expecting in these parts this spring'.

Charles, Cardinal of Lorraine, accounted for half the family's income. In the era before Trent, bishops were regarded primarily as administrators of their temporal lands. Spiritual leadership was left to others. Charles had brushed aside opposition from the constable to inherit part of his uncle's portfolio. During his career Charles held twenty-four or so abbeys at one time or another, only four of which had been inherited from his uncle; it was his political ascendancy in the 1550s that allowed him to collect what benefices he pleased.[7] The major prize in his collection was Saint-Denis, the spiritual home of the kings of France and the richest monastery in France. As abbot *in commendam*, he took the income from his abbeys and made appointments, but left the praying to others. The treasurers of each abbey sent annual accounts, which were checked by his secretaries and then signed by the cardinal himself. This fiscal regime could stretch the monastic ideal of poverty to its limits: the monks of Bec in Normandy complained that the stewards responsible for the abbey's administration left them so little they barely had enough to eat. Abbots and bishops were significant lords in their own right. As abbot of Fécamp, for example, the cardinal had the right to appoint the town captain of this port on the English Channel. Influence reached far into the rural hinterland as the petty gentry competed for minor benefices and to place their younger sons and daughters into monasteries. Charles d'Aubourg from Normandy had nine sisters. He offset this misfortune by becoming an esquire in the Duke of Guise's household, enabling him to get seven of them into convents!

The power that control of the Church gave to the Guise can be seen in the career of the fourth Guise brother, Louis, who became cardinal in 1555. In one sense Louis was a nonentity. Pamphlets denouncing him as the 'cardinal of the bottles' were more than Protestant propaganda. Charles complained to François in 1556 that their brother was 'always lazing about. He acts like a king and there is no order to guard him'. Louis did not need to exert himself. At the age of 18 in 1545 he was Bishop of Troyes. He inherited Albi from his uncle in 1550 but resigned it to become Archbishop of Sens in 1560; two years later he turned Sens over to a family servant. He then retained only Metz, which had been given by his brother in 1551 and which afforded an income of 80,000 livres per annum. Louis may have been overshadowed by his elder brother, but he was an extremely resourceful benefice hunter too. He inherited none of his uncle's monasteries, but traded in thirteen abbeys during his lifetime; the greatest, which included St Victor in Paris—home to one of Europe's largest libraries—he kept for most of his life.

Households displayed the grandeur and generosity of the prince. Duke François supported a household of 156 persons in 1556 rising to 164 in 1561. At this time his wife's household contained fifty-five people at a cost of 4,435 livres per annum. The Cardinal of Lorraine supported 129 persons, including no less than seven secretaries, at a cost of 16,510 livres. These people did not simply perform duties and receive wages; they had the right to be clothed and fed and sheltered. It was estimated in 1576 that each of the duke's twenty-one pages, seven lackeys and three chantry priests cost 180 livres to clothe.[8] Those who had no official position had dining rights. The cardinal described his diplomatic agents as being men 'of my table'. Service with the Guise led to some starry careers. The cardinal's chief counsellor, Nicolas de Pellevé, began life as a lawyer, but through his 'servile devotion' became Bishop of Amiens in 1559, counsellor to the regent of Scotland in 1559, Archbishop of Sens in 1563 on the resignation of the Cardinal of Guise, and cardinal in 1570. Jacques de la Brosse, one of the principal authors of the massacre of Wassy, began his career with the Guise in the 1540s as the governor of the 'little' Duke of Longueville, for which he was paid 600 livres and had the services of four valets. On the death of the 'little duke' in 1551 he performed the same role for the 9-year-old Duke of Lorraine. When the Duke of Guise became lieutenant-general in 1557, he appointed la Brosse *père* as one of his *maîtres de camp* and had him made a knight of the Order of Saint Michel. He was chosen to be co-governor of the dauphin in 1559, which gave him control of a staff of 300 people and budget of 68,000 livres, before being sent with Pellevé to Scotland. Service was a family affair and passed through the generations, and so in 1555 his son Gaston was appointed as the duke's standard-bearer.

Mary Stuart's household was more problematic. Proposals had first been mooted in February 1553 when, in a letter to his sister, Charles expressed the opinion that, since the king was establishing a household for the dauphin, it was time for Mary to have hers. Even at this stage it was clear that a royal household was going to be expensive. Charles calculated that, if it was to be done properly, it would cost 24,000 livres, a sum equivalent to half the regular income of the Crown of Scotland. Added to this was the news that the Guise could expect no assistance from the king, who had other priorities. The haggling lasted for months and the new household was not inaugurated until 1 January 1554. Mary of Guise shouldered most of the burden, sacrificing her French pension and her dower from the Longueville estates; the remainder came from the Crown revenues of Scotland. Even so, money was short, wages often in arrears and the organization chaotic in the first two years. The money was not wasted, however. It provided a good living for the Guise and their servants: half of the best-paid ladies' positions were reserved for the family. Lords were expected to provide protection for their men and to further their marriage prospects and those of their children. The Cardinal of Lorraine was not just the family diplomat and financial wizard, he dedicated a significant amount of time to managing the affairs of his brothers' and sisters' servants. Like the godfather of some mafia family he was constantly expected by 'his people' to patch up quarrels, help out with dowries, sort out wardships and find them jobs. The cardinal even arranged the marriage of his illegitimate daughter to a German servant, Johann von Janowitz, a man who will reappear in our story during the Saint Bartholomew's Day

Massacre. What distinguished the Guise from other patrons was that the clan mentality that the family had developed was replicated among their servants. The households of the Guise brothers were not separate entities: they complemented each other with different members of the same families appearing in the household roles or in the musters of their gendarmes, a corporate identity that was reinforced by intermarriage among serving families. The replication of this clan mentality can be seen in operation in 1555 when the last of the Guise brothers, René, made a marriage far beyond the expectations of anything most younger sons could hope for. Rumours about Louise de Rieux's Protestant inclinations did not put the Guise off because she was co-heiress to one of the great inheritances of the sixteenth century. Better to support his new status, Henry II raised the barony of Elbeuf to a marquisate. The dowry comprised the county of Harcourt in Normandy. The 19-year-old marquis had became a great Norman magnate, part of a deliberate strategy by the Guise to control a province crucial to the functioning of the Franco-British empire. Success was shared among the brothers: René received a pension from his brother Charles of 2,000 livres per annum and in the wake of the fall of Calais the king granted him a gift of 12,000 livres. René's part of the bargain was to show obedience to his brothers and his mother in matters of policy and to let them choose his household and recruit his gendarmerie company—one of the precious sixty in existence. Antoinette filled the posts with long-standing clients, many of whom can be traced as family servants over several generations. Continuity of service and loyalty to the family thus fostered a sense of group solidarity.

The 1550s did not just see dramatic changes in the political and religious landscape of Europe; it marked a fundamental shift in Guise policy in France. Hitherto, the family had been content with its landed interest in the northern and eastern peripheries of the kingdom, its provincial governorships, and commissions in the army. Henry II's generosity and the profits from the ecclesiastical empire-building were ploughed into the purchase of land. From the beginning of the decade they embarked on the voracious acquisition of real estate in the vicinity of Paris. In 1552 the cardinal purchased for 50,000 crowns the duchy of Chevreuse to the south of the city, to which he added the nearby château of Dampierre for a further 40,000 livres, and which was soon renovated in an Italianate style and hung with pictures celebrating his diplomatic career. Not content with one palace in the region, the cardinal soon added another, the château of Meudon, on the southern outskirts of the city; it was renovated by Primataccio, the family's favourite artist, who had worked on Fontainebleau, and its gardens were landscaped according to the latest fashion. A third palace at Marchais, to the east of the city, was purchased at the same time and augmented with new parks and gardens. The duke competed with his brother, purchasing the counties of Joigny and Nesle in Champagne in 1553, and more significantly two years later the county of Nanteuil, a day's ride from Paris, for 260,000 livres. In Paris itself, the family bought not one, but two residences, the adjoining hôtels de Clisson and Laval, which were amalgamated into a vast palace covering two hectares of the Marais. Above the main door were two monograms: a pun on the duke's device *chacun A son Tour* (which can be read as every A has its circle). Primataccio's renovation was inspired by his visits to the north Italian *palazzi*. Particularly remarkable was the chapel, whose frescoes depicting the procession of the *Magi* and the *Adoration* had political overtones. Not only would the attentive visitor have recognized various members of the Guise family impersonating actors in the story of Jesus' birth, they would have identified the *Magi* en route for Bethlehem with the Guise's own claims to the throne of Jerusalem.

The new family seat augmented the existing foothold in the most fashionable quarter of the Right Bank. Just a few streets away was the vast fortress cum monastery of the Temple, originally built for the Knights Templar but now the headquarters of the Grand Prior and his knights of Malta. The Guise had long been a more significant presence on the Left Bank: all the major benefices they controlled owned property and often palaces, such as the Hôtel de Cluny, in this part of the city. The land-grab is partly explained by the convenience of having residences closer to court and of being able to receive the court more often on its peregrinations. But in a society where landowning was politics, its implications were immense and long-lasting. The Montmorency had long seen themselves as the power in this region and the purchase of Nanteuil made the Duke of Guise an uncomfortable neighbour of the Montmorency heartlands to the north of the city. It is tempting to see the constable's frenetic activity in the land market in the three years before his captivity as a response to this threat. Matters came to a head over the county of Dammartin, which was disputed between the heirs of Françoise d'Anjou. In 1554, Montmorency bought the rights of one of the claimants for 192,000 livres, a price that was over the odds for a property that had revenues of only 5,750 livres per annum. In the summer of 1559 the opposing claimant opened negotiations with the Guise, who coveted Dammartin because it was contiguous with Nanteuil, and they bought out the claim for a sum which the Cardinal of Lorraine estimated would exceed 200,000 livres when legal fees were taken into account. From this moment, what had begun as a petty quarrel within the provincial gentry, became a battle royal between France's two most powerful aristocratic houses. In sixteenth-century France, protracted lawsuits were often the product of feuds and the Dammartin case, which was not settled until 1572, was one skirmish among many in the greater struggle for power.

Despite Montmorency's captivity, he and his family continued to hold the upper hand in the late 1550s because of their dominance of offices in the court and in the army, while the Guise had the edge of their rivals in the Church. Future promotions for the Guise were also unlikely because Montmorency intended to pass his own offices on to his sons. The policy of permitting a family to pass down offices through the generations like a piece of property was to prove extremely damaging to royal authority. To be fair to Henry II, he had not invented the practice. The post of Chamberlain in the Royal Household (*Grand Chambellan*) had long been considered a hereditary post of the dukes of Longueville, until the Guise had wrested control of it during their guardianship of the 'little duke'. Henry turned a practice into a policy. The Duke of Aumale was not only permitted to inherit his father's governorship of Burgundy on his death in 1550, but also his father's position as head of the royal hunt. But these positions did not fulfil the ambitions of the Guise to control the court and the army. The Duke of Guise's appetite for the power he had fleetingly wielded as the Grand Master at Mary Stuart's wedding had been whetted, and when he returned to the front for the campaigning season he felt that his achievements required more permanent recognition. Guise was heavily outnumbered by Philip II, whose superiority rested on the seemingly limitless resources of the New World silver mines. So Guise chose to remain on the defensive in Picardy and strike through the Ardennes. At Thionville, a heavily defended town situated on the Moselle and surrounded by bogs, which was invested on 3 June, the duke once more displayed the skill and bravery which made him the most celebrated general in Europe. He spent days and nights in the trenches, sleeping there if necessary, supervising the mines dug by the English miners he brought with him. It was highly dangerous work: on 20 June he was inspecting a gun emplacement with Piero Strozzi. While chatting away, he placed his hand on Strozzi's shoulder who in the same instant collapsed, mortally wounded by a musket ball fired by a sniper. Despite the loss of his friend and the final bloody assault, in which 800 defenders gave their lives, Guise exercised his customary generosity towards the vanquished. He then pushed deeper into Burgundian territory until he was halted by news of another crushing French defeat at Gravelines in Picardy on 13 July. Once again the French interior was exposed and the duke had to conduct a forced march to Picardy. Twice within a year he had been required to repair a disastrous defeat. But even before the battle of Gravelines, the king, concerned about the dominance of the Guise faction, had already resolved to make peace.

* * * *

All empires eventually overreach themselves and self-destruct. The Franco-British empire had hardly been founded before cracks began to appear caused by unrelenting royal fiscal pressure and the disruption of trade. In Rouen, hub of the new empire, peasants in the surrounding region were fleeing their homes to escape the new impositions ordered in the wake of the constable's defeat. It was at sea that the French could not compete. They were no match for the combined Anglo-Spanish navy. France itself was invaded in 1557 when a Spanish force landed in Brittany and the English sailed the Channel with impunity, burning the flagship of the French fleet at Cherbourg. At Gravelines terrible casualties had been inflicted by English ships which had come close to the shore and fired broadsides.

But it was religion that would end dreams of a Franco-British empire, and it was at the heart of this project that the Reformation rebellion would strike first. Protestantism had been harshly persecuted at the end of the reign of Francis I and it was a policy that his son had maintained during the first years of his reign. By the mid-1550s however heretic-hunting had slackened. In 1555—the year that Paul IV accelerated the prosecution of heretics in Italy and Mary Tudor began persecution in England—the Parlement of Paris, whose jurisdiction covered one third of the kingdom, executed no one for heresy. Elsewhere in France executions were sporadic. There were many reasons for this. Partly, it was an expression of the growing numbers, organization, and confidence of the Protestant movement in France. Growth was stunningly swift. Just four years after the first two churches were founded in 1555, seventy-two churches sent delegates to the first national synod. By 1562, there were upwards of 1,000 congregations, with a total membership in the region of 1.5 to 2 million people. Suspects were now better able to resist arrest, the forces of law and order wary of causing a disturbance. But partly, too, there were many Erasmian Catholics, especially among the civic elites and the judiciary, who abhorred the practice of burning people for their beliefs and who blamed the failings of the Catholic Church for the schism.

Then in the summer of 1557 the court was stunned by an assassination attempt on Henry II. The culprit, Caboche, was a respectable chancery clerk and thus unlikely to have been a madman. Some witnesses claim that they heard him shout 'King, I have been sent by God to kill you'. His two brothers, who were from Meaux, the longest-established centre of French Protestantism, had recently been tried for 'atrocious insults, defamatory libels and blasphemy' against the Catholic Church, and Caboche wanted his revenge. For at the heart of Calvin's theology was a revolutionary radicalism. It did not just reject the structures, traditions, and rituals of the Catholic Church. Calvin reserved his bitterest bile for the Nicodemites, those hypocrites who secretly believed in the new religion but maintained a mask of outward conformity to the established Church. The true believer testified to the Truth. The psychology of Calvinism, rooted in biblical fundamentalism, gave a movement born in adversity immense strength and boldness. Persecution was a trial sent from God and martyrdom the ultimate test and expression of faith. Calvin stressed the need to obey the duly constituted authorities, but he found it difficult to control his followers from faraway Geneva. Protestants were both instruments of God's will and behaved in accordance with demands of conscience. God's Commandments summoned them to disrupt blasphemous rituals, destroy profane relics, and tear down abominable images. The Old Testament in particular gave succour to the idea of divine vengeance that would strike down the wicked and impious. Assassination of the godless by religious fanatics, both Catholic and Protestant, was to be a particular feature of the French Wars of Religion, distinguishing it from the later religious conflicts in England and Germany. In France, traditional politics, based on the struggle between rival factions, was about to be overturned by a new politics shaped by conflicting religious ideologies.

The assassination attempt on Henry failed and the culprit was hastily executed without a trial—at a moment of national crisis any division that gave succour to the enemy was to be hushed up. But the size of the Protestant Church in Paris and its growing audacity could not be ignored altogether. To many Catholics, the disaster at Saint-Quentin was evidence of divine disapproval at the spread of heresy in their midst. On 4 September, a Protestant service was held in a house in the rue Saint-Jacques. The house backed on to the Sorbonne and, although the meeting took place at night, it was difficult to keep the arrival of hundreds of people secret. Rumours of acts of debauchery and even child sacrifice roused the ire of local Catholics. Priests from the Sorbonne alerted the watch, the gentlemen in the congregation drew their swords and permitted many to get away, but 130 were arrested. Coming just three weeks after the battle of Saint-Quentin, there was strong pressure for exemplary punishment. Calvin wrote to the Duke of Württemberg to intercede on behalf of the prisoners and complained that all authority had been given to the cardinal, 'who only asks to exterminate them all'.[9] There were reasons for this suspicion: that year the cardinal had been made an Inquisitor of the Faith in France. But there are good reasons for thinking that Calvin was wholly wrong about the Cardinal of Lorraine. The role of chief architect of repression had to be invented; conveniently it was one that avoided implicating the king directly. Later, when the first Protestant histories were written, the cardinal's role became embroidered into their story of resistance to persecution and formed an essential part of the black legend of the Guise.

In fact the creation of the office of Inquisitor of the Faith is a red herring. Two other cardinals—Bourbon and Châtillon—were also entrusted with the position. But even if Lorraine had had the time and inclination to fulfill his duties, the idea of an Inquisition was a dead letter in a country where the secular law courts had little truck for such Roman and Spanish practices. But the failure of the Inquisition in France was not simply due to a lack of will and a desire to protect cherished liberties. There were Catholics who accused the Guise of openly favouring heretics, and not just in Scotland. The radical Catholic priest Claude Haton, who knew the Guise far better than Calvin, wrote in his diary that during the period of their ascendancy at court 'they were renowned for belonging to the party of the heretics'.[10] And there is evidence to support this claim. Many magistrates turned a blind eye to Protestant assemblies. The arrest of those involved in the rue Saint-Jacques affair was the work of the lieutenant of the Paris

Provost, Jacques Meusnier. Like many Parisian officers, Meusnier was a creature of the Montmorency and a bitter enemy of the Guise. Before the Saint-Jacques affair, Meusnier had been charged with the pursuit of Françoise d'Amboise, Countess of Seninghem, whom the constable accused of abetting the escape of his prisoner of war, the Duke of Aerschot, who was worth a fat ransom. The countess was imprisoned, but as we have seen, although she was a Protestant, she was a kinswoman of the Guise and one of the dowager duchess's closest companions. The Cardinal of Lorraine intervened on her behalf, launching a counter-suit against Meusnier, who was eventually stripped of his position and banished to the Ile de Ré for the subornation of witnesses.

To argue that the Guise were either 'for' or 'against' heresy during their ascendancy following the battle of Saint-Quentin is to overestimate the role played by religion in their thinking. In a time of war and crisis it was not a significant issue. When his sister, the abbess of Faremoutier, wrote to complain that their own lands in Saumur were so infected with heresy that it had become a second Geneva, the cardinal did nothing. Of the 173 letters of his that survive in this period only one mentioned the subject. He wrote to the Bishop of Verdun in June 1558 to advise caution in dealing with heretics: 'you must look on it in the gentlest and most prudent way that you can, until we are out of the troubles and wars that occupy us, when we will have the means to deal with it carefully and more according to its merits'.[11] These were private sentiments. As leader of the Church in France the cardinal was expected to take a public stance against heresy. His public opinions were also shaped by the attitude of the king and his mistress who were both violently opposed to heresy and demanded exemplary punishment for those arrested. Henry talked of finishing off the 'Lutheran scum' for good, revealing his ignorance of some of the basic theological issues. The problem faced by the authorities in Paris was that many of those arrested in the rue Saint-Jacques were high-born; they did not fit the stereotype of heresy as the preserve of the seditious rabble. The criminal prosecution of the blue-blooded was a sensitive matter and always involved questions of politics. The case was taken away from the zealot Meusnier and handed over to the judges of the Parlement and they opted for a classic compromise, executing eight of the suspects between the end of September and the end of October, but only one of them was of high status. The victim was Damoiselle Philippe de Luns, a petty noblewoman from Périgord and widow without heirs. She had no one to intercede for her. All the others refused to recant, but were permitted to dissimulate or were better connected politically. The Dame de Rentigny heard Mass in prison and was released. After all, her husband was a zealous Catholic and ensign of the Duke of Guise's gendarmes. She soon returned to the Paris Protestant Church. There was another reason for limiting the number of executions in Paris: although it appeased the Catholic masses at home, it did not play well with France's allies abroad. The disaster at Saint-Quentin had left huge gaps in the French army and the Guise brothers dedicated a huge amount of time to wooing the German Protestant princes, sending agents to raise fresh levies in the Empire. The Duke of Guise wrote to his old friend and comrade the Lutheran Duke of Württemburg to reassure him that those executed were not 'Lutherans', whom he was very careful to distinguish from 'sacramentarians' who denied the miracle of the Mass.[12] The contrast of the approach of the Cardinal of Lorraine to Cardinal Pole, another Erasmian faced with schism and foreign war, is highly revealing. Pole shares responsibility for the execution of over 300 people in England—a state with a fraction of the population of France—between 1555 and 1558.

Guise moderation was politically motivated. When there was political capital to be made they did not shrink from making accusations. At the beginning of 1558, the Reform movement in France planned a carefully prepared series of demonstrations to show its strength. During Lent, the King of Navarre began to show an interest in Reformed ideas, listening to Protestant sermons among other things. This raised some eyebrows at court, where Antoine was better known for his love of dancing. His new interest in morality happened to coincide with the launch of his suit against the Duke of Nemours for the seduction of his niece. He was also increasingly preoccupied by the recovery of his kingdom from the Spanish. Most people were tiring of war and Antoine reckoned that any deal would leave his claim unrecognized. Like the Protestants, who had much to fear from a Habsburg-Valois rapprochement, he too feared a general peace. Navarre joined the 5,000 to 6,000 people who met throughout May, hearing sermons and singing psalms on the Pré aux Clercs, waste ground just beyond the city walls. These were carefully organized to coincide with the high point of the festal calendar in Paris. The period of festivities between Rogationtide and Ascension was particularly important to Parisians. It was the time of year for planting maypoles, the most important of which was that set up by the *bazoche*, the confraternity of the clerks, ushers, and other petty officials who serviced the law courts and which played a significant role in Parisian popular life. There was much feasting and merrymaking and not a little of the disorder commonly associated with gangs of drunken young men. It was precisely the sort of ungodly profanity that the Calvinists gathered to protest against.

Henry II was furious at the Protestant assemblies, but the Guise were too busy to be directly involved in the investigation. Henry disliked his total reliance on them and began to tire of their haughtiness. He flatly refused the duke's request for the office of Grand Master on a permanent basis. He was missing his alter ego, Montmorency, and inclined to make sacrifices in order to secure his return. During May the cardinal was dispatched to negotiate. Although he did not openly sabotage the talks, like the Protestants, he had nothing to gain from peace and much to lose. Cardinal Granvelle, Philip II's plenipotentiary, was angered by his counterpart's attitude. But the Spanish had a cunning plan up their sleeves to increase divisions in the French camp. Granvelle told Lorraine that intercepted correspondence between Admiral Coligny, currently languishing in a Spanish prison, and his brother Andelot, proved that they were Protestants. Without asking for proof Lorraine hurried back to Paris to hammer another nail into the political fortunes of the Montmorency.

The king's suspicion had already fallen on Andelot: on his travels to Brittany and the Loire valley at Easter Andelot had promoted open-air preaching. And on his return to Paris he was one of the organizers of the rallies in the Pré aux Clercs. On 22 May Henry summoned Andelot to answer to the cardinal's charges; the principal one being that he refused to attend Mass. Andelot replied that his goods and life were at the king's service, but he could not retreat from his refusal to attend Mass. Henry became so angry that he could barely refrain from striking him; but instead hurling a plate which only succeeded in hitting the dauphin. Andelot was clapped in prison, stripped of his post of colonel-general of the infantry and Protestant meetings in Paris were prohibited on pain of death. Andelot's fall was planned by the Guise because they knew it would be popular among a group with whom they were always keen to curry favour: the princes. Andelot was viewed as an arrogant upstart; he had a reputation as a hot-head who was keen to dispute his status at the point of a sword. He had already killed one man when, in 1548, he fought a duel with Charles de Bourbon-Montpensier, Prince of la Roche-sur-Yon, in which both were wounded. Charles was, like most of the princes, a religious moderate, but like most of the princes, too, he developed a deep aversion for the constable, who would give him no satisfaction and fully supported his nephew. The feud that resulted was so serious that one contemporary thought it 'the preamble and first strike in our civil wars'.[13]

Victory over the Montmorency was shortlived. The cardinal was forced to admit that he had been duped and Andelot was released in July after he made a garbled promise to attend Mass. The Saints expected to suffer for a just cause and Andelot emerged from captivity wrapped in a cloak of of righteousness. Ironically, the Guise remained the best hope of the Protestants. Peace would allow both the Valois and the Habsburgs to turn their full attention to the war on heresy. But even before news arrived of defeat at Gravelines, Henry's patience with the Guise was at an end. Crucially they had lost the support of Diane de Poitiers, who resented their move from her shadow into the spotlight. She made a rapprochement with the constable which was sealed in October by the betrothal of her granddaughter to his second son. At court only Catherine de Medici, champion of French intervention in Italy, could now be counted on for support.

The constable did his best to undermine the Guise from his prison cell, and in October Philip II took the gamble to parole him for several days in order to break the king's resolve: 'if he returns to France the Guise will not have so much power as now...whereas if the Constable be there the war matters will be in his care...which will be good for our affairs'.[14] 'Nothing in the world can turn me from the love I have for you', wrote the king in his own hand after their meeting. Word of their mutual recriminations against the Guise soon got back to François who, almost exactly a year to the day that the king had welcomed him as a saviour, quit the court. Although the Cardinal of Lorraine was included in the French negotiating team that met Philip's representatives on the Flemish border, the constable was clearly in charge. On 29 October Henry dramatically announced that he was resolved to make peace and in order to do so was willing to renounce the territories in Italy. Guise was enraged: only the day before Henry had sworn that he would never surrender Piedmont. He told the king that those behind these plans had lost their heads. The duke's mood blackened further when the king announced he would pay the 200,000 crowns demanded as ransom for the constable. Montmorency arrived at the court at Saint-Germain on 21 December; that evening the Cardinal of Lorraine returned the signet ring, which he had been given in 1557, without any order from the king. When the king asked him why he and his brother no longer attended the council, the cardinal replied that he did not wish 'to pass for Montmorency's valet'.[15] Within a few days fortune's wheel spun quickly once again. Pensions and offices awarded by the Guise were revoked, Montmorency's nephews were reinstated in their commands, and the king promised him that the office of Grand Master would pass to his eldest son. In the narrow corridors of the royal apartments the air bristled with hatred between the two clans. On Christmas Eve the Duke of Guise challenged Montmorency's eldest son to a duel. The constable was easily able to laugh off his rival's indiscretion; he now had tighter control of affairs than ever before.

The death of Mary Tudor in November had already removed one of the main stumbling blocks to peace, namely Calais. The Treaty of Cateau-Cambrésis, signed on 2 April between France and England and on the following day between France and Spain, was one of the most controversial in European history. It established the legal and political framework of Western European affairs and marked the beginnings of nearly a century of Spanish preponderance on the continent. Italy was abandoned by the French, who kept Calais and the three bishoprics of Metz, Toul, and Verdun. The veterans of Italy in particular were furious at what they considered a dishonourable peace. According to them, the king had ceded lands that cost 40 million crowns and 100,000 lives to win. Guise became a spokesman for their discontent. The princes too felt they had been sold out. Neither the King of Navarre nor the Duke of Bouillon gained compensation for the loss of their lands in the Treaty. The Duke of Longueville got no financial help with his crippling ransom, probably because he was a member of the Guise faction (he was betrothed to the Duke of Guise's eldest daughter on 23 January). Guise had made it clear that peace was an affront to his honour, for which he got widespread sympathy at court. He became the focus for those dissatisfied with the partisan rule of the man they snobbishly referred to as the 'little baron from the Ile de France'.

* * * *

There were, however, good dynastic reasons why Henry could not afford to let the Guise fall too far into disfavour. Their prominence at the marriage festivities of their cousin, the Duke of Lorraine, to Henry's daughter, Claude de France, during eight days in February 1559 was a sign that they could not be ignored. During the marriage the English ambassador was infuriated to find that the dauphin and the dauphiness—who as early as 16 January had styled themselves 'Mary and François, King and Queen Dauphins of Scotland, England and France'—appeared with a new set of arms which quartered their British titles with the arms of France. Having decided to cut his losses in Italy, Henry's support for the Franco-British empire was crucial to his reputation. Peace with England did not preclude the future possibility of the Pope excommunicating the 'bastard' Elizabeth. Henry had already sounded out the Pope about such a possibility. But promoting Mary Stuart's Catholic credentials over her dynastic rights was to prove disastrous. In May 1559, iconoclastic riots and violence, stirred by Knox's thunderous sermons, signalled a full-scale rebellion against her mother in Scotland. On 29 June Henry wrote to the Pope that he was resolved to send an army to crush it. Meanwhile the peace with Spain was being celebrated with a magnificent tourney in Paris. It was a return to the good old days. The king, now in his fortieth year, appeared in the lists wearing the black and white of his mistress, Diane de Poitiers. He rode well against the Duke of Guise who was wearing his customary crimson. But on the 1 July the king felt slighted by the Count of Montgommery, a younger man, who had dislodged him from his stirrups. The count reluctantly agreed to a second run. His lance shattered on Henry's visor, sending a large sliver through his eye. Henry's end was slow and agonizing. He died on 10 July.

CONGREGATIONS, CONSPIRACIES, AND COUPS

Henry II's death is conventionally seen as the end of an era, in which glory and strong rule was overnight replaced by the divisive and chaotic rule of the Guise. The accession of his son, Francis II, is the starting point of the black legend of his Guise uncles. According to this legend, their rise to the pinnacle of power was the result of a Machiavellian plot to sideline the princes of the blood, in the process of which they acted as bloodthirsty tyrants. In truth, there is little to be said in favour of Francis himself: he was a physically and emotionally stunted fifteen-year-old. In terms of policy, if not personality, however, the two reigns were characterized by continuity. Father and son faced the same problems and at first the Guise, well aware of their precarious hold on power, continued the old king's policies. What was new was the level of opposition: those who under Henry could only mutter under their breath were now inclined to speak out openly. Many in the Protestant leadership rejoiced at Henry's death— their prayers had been answered, divine justice had delivered them. But we should be wary of interpreting events through Protestant eyes alone. Often written a decade or more after the events they purport to describe, the purpose of their accounts was to scapegoat the Guise and heap the blame for France's descent into civil war and chaos on their shoulders. The most frequently consulted source claims that the Cardinal of Lorraine procured children's blood for the sickly king to quaff (a crime more commonly associated at the time with Jews). Other sources, such as the dispatches of the Spanish ambassador, Chantonnay, shed a different light on affairs.

The slow agony of Henry's death was shared by all those close to him as their futures waxed and waned with every fading breath. There was feverish wheeler-dealing around the deathbed. The role of Catherine de Medici, hitherto neglected by her husband, was paramount. She prevented Diane de Poitiers from entering the king's bedchamber; she never saw her lover again. When the king was unconscious she would keep Montmorency, whom she also disliked, at bay. When he was conscious the king would call for his old friend. While others had ignored the indignities that she had been forced to endure, the Guise had always accorded Catherine the respect that she craved. They also shared many of the same views, placing a high priority on conquest in Italy and a low priority on religious persecution. She offered her support to them in return for the humbling and banishment of Diane de Poitiers. But a Guise takeover was not inevitable: even though the new king was beyond the legal age of minority, his faculties were such that a regency was a possibility. Montmorency looked to the King of Navarre as the senior prince of the blood to do something to stop his rivals taking control. Further support came from Chantonnay, the representative of Europe's only superpower. Spain, 'the arbiter of Europe' according to the Venetians, was a new and significant presence in French internal affairs. Philip's impending marriage to Henry II's daughter, Elisabeth, would seal the peace and unite the two royal families. Montmorency was the architect of this policy and Spain's chief ally at court. The day before he died Henry II wrote a letter to Philip II, surely inspired by the constable, urging him to protect the faith and support his brother-in-law. It was too late. As soon as Henry II died the Guise pounced: the new king and his mother were surrounded by Guise loyalists and escorted to the Louvre, leaving the constable in possession of the corpse.

One of the many myths about the new regime was that it introduced all sorts of innovations that made it extremely unpopular. In fact, there was no repeat of the palace revolution that greeted the accession of Henry II; rather the Guise brothers wished to turn the clock back to 1557–8. The cardinal, now aged 34, was the dominant figure in the partnership: 'He is both Pope and King', wrote the Tuscan ambassador.[1] He took responsibility for diplomacy, finance, and the administration of civil and religious affairs, while his brother, François, was given control of the army. When he was snubbed by the new king and told that he was too old, the constable realized which way the wind was blowing and retired to his château at Chantilly. Within weeks, at the request of Catherine, he resigned the office of Grand Master: François had the office he had long craved. But the Guise were careful not to push the constable into opposition, and so his sons and nephews were retained in their offices. François's magnanimity and courtesy helped the transition: unlike the young king he treated his old enemy with respect and continued to write him affable letters that kept him abreast of events. On the whole, governors were retained in their posts, even those whose religious disposition was the object of suspicion. As friends and kinsmen of the Guise they were trusted; their private beliefs of little significance. The greatest change at the centre was the role of the Queen Mother: all key decisions were now discussed with her in her chambers after lunch.

This does not mean there was no opposition to the new axis: everything depended on the House of Bourbon. The constable urged the head of the House, Antoine, King of Navarre, to stake his claim to a role in the government as a prince of the blood. In late July representatives of the two clans met at Vendôme in the company of two pastors from the Paris Congregation and an agent of the English ambassador, Sir Nicholas Throckmorton: on one side sat Navarre, his younger brothers, and his Montpensier cousins; and on the other sat Montmorency's beloved nephews, Admiral Coligny and Andelot. As a group they were riven by religious differences and personal animosities: all they could agree on was an end to the feud between the Montpensier and Montmorency which had soured relations for a decade. The Guise handled relations with the princes of the blood with skill and delicacy—on the day after Henry II's death the cardinal of Lorraine wrote Navarre a warm letter.[2] Dealing with him was made easier by the fact that the Guise had their own spies in his council who reported to the Duke of Guise how:

> The king of Navarre ... had resolved to be entirely in friendship with him and Monseigneur the cardinal of Lorraine, not only as a cousin, but as a friend ... Although Monsieur the Constable has written several letters, nevertheless he always tells me that he would never trust him, knowing that the friendship he feigns him is to attract him to his side, in order to ruin his cousins.[3]

In return the Guise promised to add Poitou to his governorship of Gascony, giving him control of the entire south-west. When Francis II was crowned by Cardinal Charles at Reims on 18 September 1559 Navarre took precedence over all other peers. For the first time in his life, he was centre stage and he had no intention of putting it at risk: promises to the Protestants to pose as their protector were conveniently dropped. Condé was more troublesome. But since he was poor and had never held significant office a cash gift of 70,000 livres and the promise of the governorship of Picardy, which his family claimed as a hereditary right, were felt enough to secure his loyalty. By the time of the coronation, the cardinal was able to write that 'It is impossible to see things more tranquil and quiet than they are, with every demonstration and observation of fidelity, obedience and devotion from everyone towards the new king.'⁴ This was the quiet before the storm. Although the Guise had proved themselves supremely adept and clever players of the traditional game of faction, politics was about to change forever: Europe was being swept by a religious revolution that would overthrow regimes, and the cities and towns of France would seethe with popular discontent as ordinary people mobilized for and against the Reformation.

* * * *

In the last months of his life Henry had mapped out the broad parameters of policy—the implementation of the Treaty of Cateau-Cambrésis and peace with Spain, the extermination of heresy at home, military intervention in Scotland—and the Guise immediately set about putting these policies into practice. All these issues were interdependent and complex and would have presented formidable challenges to a strong and experienced man like Henry II; for his uncharismatic and puerile son they would prove insurmountable.

Peace should have brought France dividends. She lacked the resources of Spain's world empire and had paid for the war by using the tax receipts derived from an essentially agricultural economy as collateral in order to borrow money on the international money market. The Crown was bankrupt and the peace of Cateau-Cambrésis did not come cheap. On top of the ransoms Henry had agreed to pay for those grandees captured at Saint-Quentin, he also had to provide his daughter with a dowry of 1 million livres. Confidence in the Crown was buoyant while Henry lived. Although he was beginning to experience some trouble in borrowing money and found that rates of interest became exorbitant as the war dragged on, this was nothing compared to the collapse of confidence that occurred after his death. Michel de l'Hôpital, President of the Court of Accounts, the cardinal's chief financial advisor, proposed radical reforms. The rescheduling of loans, the raising of taxes, and financial cutbacks amounted to a form of Thatcherism *avant la lettre*. The rapidity with which this shock treatment was applied to a weak and fragile body politic did not make them any more palatable. There was resistance to tax increases. In the richest province, Normandy, a forced loan of 800,000 livres demanded by Henry II remained unpaid. Twenty years later people recalled vividly the hardships that this particular tax caused. In the fertile countryside around Rouen peasants fled their villages in order to escape payment. Cardinal Charles did not have to pay the new taxes: his many benefices were exempted by royal decree. In November he introduced fiscal reforms and rescheduled repayments on loans that had been contracted by the previous regime. Royal officials, who were among the most significant creditors, now found themselves out of pocket. Bankers lost confidence and refused to lend. The new regime would soon find itself seriously short of specie. Another apparently sensible financial reform was the resumption of Crown lands. Henry II had rewarded his favourites generously with grants of royal demesne—a practice that was both harmful to royal income and technically illegal. The manner in which the resumption was handled was, however, openly partisan. While the constable was stripped of his grants, the Duke of Guise was reconfirmed in possession of the royal lands of Saumur, Provins, and Dourdan. Cutbacks at court, the cancellation of grants, and the suppression of venal office—the insidious practice by which positions were sold and then traded on as a form of private property—alienated those who lost out. Some observers were as delighted as the accountants in the manner which the cardinal's reforms cut bureaucracy 'reducing all offices and positions to the [levels] of the time of Good King Louis XII'.[5] The office-holders themselves were less enthusiastic at losing their investment.

The size of the army was slashed. But the cancellation of promises made by the previous regime and the failure to pay arrears left many soldiers seriously out of pocket and they swelled the ranks of the discontented who flocked to court in anger to petition for redress. The treatment of these veterans, who were ordered to leave the environs under pain of death, was odious even to supporters of the Guise. Where the sinews of power were lacking, the Crown should have awed its subjects into submission. Monarchy demands magnificence in order to work its magic. But the accountants demanded cutbacks. Penny-pinching meant that even Francis II's royal entries were scaled down to a minimum: France had come a long way since the Rouen festivities of 1550.

Historians today are wary of attributing religious change to social and economic factors. Contemporaries were less reticent. They saw the problems that confronted them—political, social or economic— and their solutions in moral terms. The idea of a godly Reformation that returned the world to its pristine state gave fresh meaning to all manner of discontents. The way in which the ideal of divine justice lent legitimacy to acts of resistance to the new regime can be seen in one small corner of France. Lower Normandy was already a hotbed of Protestant activity centred on the prosperous city of Caen, where a third of the city's population of 15,000 was Protestant by 1562. For thirty years the revenues of the region and the right to nominate to all royal offices there had been granted to one of the monarchy's biggest creditors, the Duke of Ferrara. As confidence in the new regime collapsed elsewhere, the Guise turned to their kinsman for help; he advanced them 600,000 livres and they in turn exempted him from the resumption of Crown lands. Tax collectors are never popular, but the administration of the Ferrarese was especially resented. In 1560 a Falaise tax collector and the king's lieutenant in Orbec were murdered. Italians, without sympathy for local hardships, were a particular target: the murder of Giulio Ravilio Rosso, chief agent of the Ferrarese in the region, by Protestants two years later was a populist act, widely supported. Protestants were not only highly organized and well armed, but their strong sense of moral righteousness behoved them to act and their deeds struck a chord among those in the wider community fed up with corrupt exploitation by outsiders.

In Scotland, too, religious revolt challenged the political status quo. The Lords of the Congregation fumed 'against the fury and rage of the tyrants of this world; and especially from the insatiable covetousness of the Guisians' generation'. Their programme of a return to a purer faith was mirrored by calls for a return to 'the ancient laws of the kingdom'.[6] Since the interests of the great powers of England and Spain were also at stake, events in Scotland threatened the tenuous European peace. Both Elizabeth and Philip were keen to see the Franco-British empire scuppered for good. Henry II had dismissed English complaints when Mary Stuart insisted on quartering her arms with those of England, retorting that she had the right to do so since Elizabeth had not renounced her claims on France.[7] The Cardinal of Lorraine wrote to his sister in Scotland that Henry would punish these 'wicked Lutherans' and that their younger brother, the Marquis of Elbeuf, would be sent with a force of 200 gendarmes and 20 ensigns of foot.

Henry II's death jeopardized these plans and seriously weakened the Guise room for manoeuvre in Scotland. The cardinal was worried about the financial implications of war. He also had to take account of Philip II's suspicion of Guise ambitions; he left the cardinal with no illusions that the peace was fragile. Marie de Guise survived largely thanks to her formidable diplomatic skills and charisma, managing to stall the Congregation with promises of her good intentions before they overwhelmed her. Charles's initial instructions to his sister were to settle the rebellion with promises and cash and he sent Jacques la Brosse and Nicolas Pellevé, Bishop of Amiens, with a token reinforcement. The decision to use force had not yet been made. But the Congregation viewed the arrival of French troops at Leith as a breach of Marie's promises. It made for good propaganda, allowing them to play on Scots' xenophobia and fear of conquest by foreigners. The Lords of the Congregation transformed themselves from sectarian rebels into a patriotic resistance movement against Guise dynasticism and French domination. Only when she wrote to Charles in desperation on 22 September 1559 that 'she did not have a bean' did the full extent of her plight become apparent. Preparations got under way in the Channel ports for reinforcements to prevent her being toppled and replaced by a candidate from among the Congregation. But there were continual delays. Only at the beginning of November did Elbeuf receive his commission replacing his elder sister as 'viceroy' of Scotland. Finally, on 6 December, the relief force set sail but the North Sea at this time of year is perilous and it was driven onto the sand banks of Zeeland in a storm. Out of thirty or forty ships, only a few survived. Elbeuf left Calais on the 21st but could make no headway against the northerly winds and had to put in at Dieppe, though eleven transports carrying 900 men did reach their destination.

Further military aid to Marie would depend on the attitude of England. At the beginning of January 1560 a new ambassador, Michel de Seure, a gentleman of the privy chamber, was sent to London to ensure English neutrality. But his mission was compromised by the arrogance of his masters. While the Guise were cautious and penny-pinching in most areas of domestic policy, honour and reputation required that they proudly display their dynastic rights. At the accession of the new reign the heraldic arms of Francis and Mary were emblazoned with those of England wherever the court came to rest. At Amboise in December 1559, Chantonnay noted down the Latin inscription that accompanied them:

Gaul and warlike Britain were in perpetual hostility—At that time they fought amongst themselves with equal hatred—Now the Gauls and the distant Britons are in a single territory—Mary's dowry gathers them together in one Empire—Because of this you will keep your weapons under a French peace—Your forefathers could not achieve this for a thousand years.

Throckmorton, the English ambassador, was shocked to discover that the design for a new great seal of Scotland showed Francis and Mary seated in 'imperial' majesty above the legend 'Francis and Mary, By the Grace of God, King and Queen of France, Scotland, England and Ireland'. After Francis's coronation these claims were embossed on the plate and carved on the furniture with which Mary's household was newly equipped as Queen of France. In a crass diplomatic blunder Throckmorton was invited to dinner and then forced to eat his meal off silver dishes bearing the offending insignia.

Though Elizabeth disliked the idea of supporting rebels, the French ambassador in London was clear why she had little choice: 'being informed that the marquis of Elbeuf had been created and named in his letters of power the King's Lieutenant-General in Scotland, England and Ireland was sufficient argument to push her to defend herself'.[8] English ships blockaded Leith and a formal alliance was concluded with the Lords of the Congregation at Berwick on 27 February 1560. Elizabeth became a protector of Scotland's 'freedoms and liberties' and of the Protestant faith against foreign tyranny. Three weeks later the Guise regime in France was rocked to its very foundations by an attempted coup, whose inspiration owed much to events in Scotland.

* * * *

The most serious accusation against the Guise, and the one that has been an enduring image of their legend, is that they pursued a consistent line towards and instituted a bloody persecution of Protestantism. According to this reading of the events the Saint Bartholomew's Day Massacre and of Wassy had their origins in the policies developed during the reign of Francis II, whose genesis can in turn be traced even further back to the butchery of the Alsatian peasants in 1525. In later decades when the Guise wished to pose as the champions of Catholicism this was not an accusation they were disposed to contradict; on the contrary it was an image they encouraged. But in the age before civil war and the formation of religious parties the Guise attitude to heresy was complex and more tentative than either they or their opponents were later prepared to admit.

It hardly needs repeating that Henry II's agreement with Philip II to make the fight against heresy a priority of the new European order was not in accordance with Guise interests. Henry was highly conservative on matters of faith. And the return of the constable to power and his new friendship with Diane de Poitiers made for a court in the final months of the reign that was opposed even to the most moderate evangelical innovations in worship. The Cardinal of Lorraine, in contrast, was criticized both inside and outside France for being too soft on heresy. One unfortunate priest who had the temerity to accuse the cardinal of being 'affiliated' to heresy was himself executed on the orders of Antoinette de Bourbon.[9] Paul IV also accused him of 'favouring' heresy. Although this opinion was hardly the product of a balanced mind, it does indicate the sort of pressure that the de facto head of the French Church was under from the ultras. The failure to establish the Inquisition was one case in point. The reasons for this were partly to do with the cardinal's own Erasmian inclinations, in which heresy was better fought on the spiritual front unless some crime had been committed. Unlike Cardinal Pole, the contemporary he most resembled, he was sceptical about the efficacy of mass burnings. In April 1559 he told the Venetian ambassador that two-thirds of the kingdom were 'Lutheran', an early indication of his belief that only reform from within the Church would bring them back.

Rather like his uncle Jean before him, Charles did not permit private sentiments to impinge on political realities. All the evidence suggests that the war on heresy was very much Henry II's initiative. And it was one area in which the Guise could insinuate their way back into royal favour. In a grovelling letter to the royal mistress Cardinal Charles wrote that 'God be praised for the means I have to do the services which you deserve, to give the appearance in the light of my actions of my profound gratitude, and to be able to have greater effect in helping the entire re-establishment of his holy religion.'[10] The cardinal was not present on 2 June 1559 when a new tougher law against heresy was signed at Montmorency's château at Ecouen. Ironically, just three days before, Montmorency had been conducted to Notre-Dame in Paris by Coligny, who had slipped away without hearing Mass. Montmorency must have been aware that at the very least his nephews were sympathetic to Protestantism. But to argue that those leading the war on heresy were hypocrites is to misunderstand its purpose and remit. No one seriously expected it to target members of the social elite. So long as they outwardly conformed, what aristocrats did or did not do in their private chapels was of no public concern; this had been the lesson of Andelot's rehabilitation. This distinction between public conformity and private faith lay behind the good relationships that the Guise enjoyed with the Calvinist princes. On 23 January 1559 the Duke of Guise betrothed his daughter Catherine, then only 6 years old, to Léonor d'Orléans, Duke of Longueville, twelve years her senior; the dowry being offset by their assistance with the duke's hefty Spanish ransom. If Longueville's correspondence with Calvin was a secret, that of his mother, Jacqueline de Rohan, was certainly not. Jacqueline was a zealous Protestant and her desire to contract a union with the Guise would surprise us if we did not know that they were happy to entertain Protestants in their home and were not yet exclusively identified as enemies of the Reform. Many people seriously believed and hoped in these years that Europe's religious differences were soon to be solved by a meeting of the General Council of the Church, whose reforms would restore the unity of Christendom.

The target of the war on heresy were the 'seditious'. In the sixteenth century, heresy and sedition were synonymous and, like all other members of the social elite, the Guise believed that the seditious were by nature riff-raff from the lower orders. As a result, they found it very difficult to conceive of their fellow princes as heretics. The war on heresy was essentially about the re-establishment of social and political order. In France, the king was the embodiment of the mystical union of the kingdom under One King, One Faith, One Law. His authority derived from the sacred powers he claimed on being anointed by God, a power most clearly evident in his ability to heal the sick. While the dominant voices of French Protestantism were replete with discourses about the need for passive obedience to the powers that be, the actions of their followers was often in stark contrast. In the civil wars of the 1560s the tombs, effigies, and monuments of the kings of France were the object of systematic iconoclastic destruction—at Cléry, the most important shrine devoted to the Valois, the effigy of Louis XII, kneeling in prayer, was treated to the charade of a mock execution before being smashed.[11] The threat to the normal conventions of kinship and hierarchy was evident in the shocking practice by which the elect saw themselves as equals in the eyes of God and referred to each other as 'brothers' and 'sisters'. If kings were not sacred it followed that they were mere mortals subject to God's retribution like us. John Foxe's Latin martyrology, which was translated into French in 1561, reinforced this point in its preface by explaining that God uses the most insignificant individuals to exemplify his glory. Kings may come and go; political empires will decay. The only enduring empire is that of the 'captain-general of God's elect'. These ideas quickly reached down into society: summoned to surrender in the name of the king in February 1562 Jehan du Verdier, king's advocate in the seneschal court of Armagnac, replied 'What king? We are the kings, he that you speak of is a little turdy kinglet; we'll whip his breech and set him to a trade, to teach him to get his living as others do.'

Not all Catholics believed that heresy and sedition were one and the same thing. Many magistrates, whose humanist education rendered them sceptical of the infallibility of much of Catholic dogma, were unwilling or unable to enforce the existing legislation, which accounts for the very low number of heresy trials in France at the end of the 1550s. The edict of Ecouen therefore proposed to dispatch special commissioners into each province who would take cognizance of heresy cases from local courts. The laxity of the Parlement of Paris, the senior law court in the kingdom, was of particular concern. The cardinal had already intervened significantly in its affairs once before, though not to recommend more burnings. Quite the opposite: he procured the dismissal of the most notorious persecutor, President Pierre Lizet, head of the 'Burning Chamber', which until January 1550 had specialized in mass *autos da fé*, the like of which were not seen in France again. Because this was the work of the cardinal, the Protestant historian Regnier de la Planche, writing in the 1570s, could not resist the temptation to condemn the manner in which poor Lizet was 'disgraced and forced out'![12] Most of the court's judges were moderate Catholics whose consciences were troubled by the difficulty of establishing the boundary between the orthodox and the unorthodox. The vast majority were opposed to projects for an Inquisition, fearing that it would cede too much sovereignty to the Church. In the opinion of one of them, 'the record of the medieval Inquisition did not inspire confidence . . . [it was] marked by savage brutality and gross errors of judgement'.[13] Judges were adept at using Fabian tactics to scupper legislation they disapproved of and by 1559 the prosecution of heretics had all but ceased. However, the court's unity was by now seriously compromised by the existence of a small Protestant cell within it and the polarization of opinion it caused between moderate and ultra-Catholics. In violation of the confidentiality of its deliberations, informers among the judges passed a list of names to the king identifying the suspects. The session of the court on 10 June 1559 was surely one of the most dramatic in its history. Henry II, accompanied by an armed escort, the cardinals of Lorraine, Sens, and Guise, the constable, the Duke of Guise, the Duke of Montpensier, and the Prince de la Roche-sur-Yon, interrupted the deliberations, announced his dissatisfaction with the pursuit of heresy and his determination to stamp it out. He then ordered them to continue with their deliberations.

It was then that two of the councillors made bold attacks on the king. Many of the magistrates criticized the abuses of the Church and called for a free general council—but this was hardly controversial. The tension was raised when Louis du Faur was bold enough to challenge the king directly, recalling the words of the prophet Elijah to King Ahab: 'It is you who trouble Israel.' (1 Kings 18:17–8). Judge Anne du Bourg was bolder, commenting on the contrast between the flourishing and prosperous condition of blasphemers and adulterers, and the persecution of those who led pure lives, whose only crime was to demand the reform of a corrupt Church. A furious Henry took the attack on adulterers as an attack on himself, a remark that constituted lèse-majesté. Along with six others, du Bourg was arrested and imprisoned in the Bastille. On 19 June Henry appointed a special commission to try them. Exactly one month after he had sworn 'to see [du Bourg] burn with his own eyes', Henry was dead. The fact that his mortal wound was caused by a thrust through his eye did not escape the attention of Protestant pamphleteers who were quick see the hand of God smite the persecutor of the righteous. Du Bourg's arrest and trial were to have enormous repercussions for the new regime.

Events in Scotland were a clear indication of what would happen if the war on heresy was not stepped up. Stability depended on its success. In the autumn of 1559 four new laws were added to the judges' armoury, ordering the demolition of meeting houses and the prosecution of any landlord harbouring Protestants. An order to arrest those who threatened and intimidated witnesses, judges, and officers of the law also revealed the obstacles to enforcement. The cardinal recommended these measures to the aldermen of Metz 'for the love and repose of your patrie, which, if this contagion of evil is not rapidly purged, I see it will soon be threatened by ruin and perdition, letting you judge if a town where there is a diversity of religion can long remain united'.[14] The cardinal's fresh zeal can be explained by the fact that the Protestants represented a political threat to the regime. In house raids in Paris at the end of September, pamphlets were discovered mocking both the Guise and the Queen Mother. Libels and placards were posted in the streets. One memoir accused the Guise of planning to usurp the House of Valois, in proof of which it cited their claim to descend from Charlemagne, their supposed designs on the duchy of Anjou and county of Provence, and the war for the kingdom of Naples conducted against the best interests of France. As an antidote to their 'tyranny', it made a novel appeal to the sovereignty of the people (a theme that Protestant thinkers would develop more fully after the Saint Bartholomew's Day Massacre) and called for the convocation of the Estates-General, a body that had not met since 1484. The Guise took these attacks seriously. On 15 November the English ambassador reported how the king had abandoned the hunt for fear of some conspiracy and that his Scots Guard had been issued with mail coats and pistols.[15]

To Protestant eyes these months were characterized by a persecution in which 'Satan's rage went beyond all excess'.[16] The archives suggest that this is hyberbole. In the outlying provinces the heresy laws remained a dead letter, either ignored or unenforced. Only in Paris did the cycle of death sentences against heretics outlast Henry's death and accelerate under his son. The Parlement confirmed three death sentences in July, four more in August (two of whom escaped), one in September, five in December, and four more in January 1560. Henry II's extraordinary visit in June cowed the judges into curbing their lenient inclinations. Even so, this handful of executions was not systematic enough to stop a movement that was developing into by far the largest unofficial Protestant Church in Europe. There was another option available. In Spain, Italy, and the Low Countries the Inquisition had stepped up its bloody business. The Habsburgs had already shown what might be achieved in northern Europe. In the Low Countries, with its much smaller population, there were 1,300 executions for heresy between 1523 and 1565. A further thousand would follow during the bloody repression of 1567–9. In early December 1559 the Spanish ambassador complained about the low number of French executions and their quality—there was little value in burning people of 'simple and base' condition. He made it known to the Guise in the strongest terms that he 'was not happy with the manner in which they were proceeding'.[17]

However ghastly and abhorrent the sight of people being burnt may appear to us, in the sixteenth century most of these burnings were hardly newsworthy. The lives of the socially inferior were worth much less than their betters. Literally so: the French criminal justice system continued to operate on the concept of blood-money, which was paid according to the status of the injured party; the lives of the labouring classes were valued in *sous*, the lives of aristocrats in tens of thousands of pounds. This is precisely why the trial of the five judges arrested in June caused so much consternation and public debate—its like had not been seen before. The Guise regime too was also being put on trial. In 1559 there was a new medium that hitherto had played little role in the old-fashioned game of court politics: public opinion, which was stirred by the unprecedented number of cheap pamphlets rolling off printing presses across Europe. Paris was gripped by the trial and divided between those who were horrified to see judges put on trial for holding opinions that did not appear unorthodox, and others who argued that the gangrene of heresy had penetrated so far into the body politic that only some drastic surgery could save it.

To their fellow judges the very idea of executing a member of their own body was repugnant. The interrogations were conducted in such a fashion as to give the accused every opportunity to get themselves off the hook. They revealed little about their true beliefs, confining themselves to adherence to the Bible and the Athanasian Creed. In the main, they supported the death penalty for those they called 'sacramentarians', who denied the real presence in the Mass, making a distinction between them and 'Lutherans', who retained elements of the Mass. Punishments were mild. The harshest, a fine and five years' suspension, was reserved for the judge who had uniquely called for a national council of the Church and a suspension of persecution. There is no reason to believe that the Guise were disappointed at these verdicts. A senior judge, Christophe de Thou, who intervened on the accused men's behalf, was the Guise's chief client in the Parlement. 'I can never adequately repay what I owe to your house', he wrote to the Duke of Guise.[18]

What was required from the judges was outward conformity. But one of the accused, Anne du Bourg, refused to play the game. Unlike his co-defendants this young judge (he was 37) not only admitted to attending Reformed services and buying their books, but taking their communion at a recent Easter service. Most shockingly of all he denied the miracle of the Mass. In early December there were desperate last-minute efforts to avoid the scandal of public execution by coming up with an ambiguously worded confession of faith that would satisfy both du Bourg and his moderate colleagues. During these delicate negotiations events took a dramatic turn. Protestants had not stood idly by during the trial: in October and again in early December there were attempts to rescue him from prison. On 12 December an ultra-Catholic judge, President Minard, was gunned down by masked assassins outside his home in the rue Vieille du Temple, not far from the Hôtel de Guise—it was almost as if they wished to scupper the compromise. The following day, before the final judgment had been made, du Bourg signed the compromise. But the pressure not to be another Nicodemite was immense. Six days later du Bourg formally repudiated it. Under such circumstances the Parlement had no alternative but to order his execution; he was garrotted and his corpse publicly burned on 23 December. French Protestantism gained its supreme martyr; the tyranny of the Guise regime had been laid bare.

The Cardinal of Lorraine wrote to the ambassador in Rome that it would act as a deterrent, and he probably also hoped that it would end calls from Rome and Madrid for more of the same. The du Bourg affair was a call to arms for French Protestants: resistance to tyrants was not only legitimate, it was necessary for the good of the commonwealth. Du Bourg's trial was responsible for two more sinister developments, which were to have immense consequences for France over the next three decades. First, the use of assassination as a legitimate tool of resistance made its first appearance; its origins lay in Protestant psychology, which construed the individual as an instrument of divine vengeance. Second, during the last tense days of du Bourg's ordeal, there was an outbreak of sectarian violence in Paris. In the week leading up to Christmas there were clashes between Catholics and Protestants, who had taken to meeting in a house next door to the parish church of Saint-Médard. At least two Protestants were killed and on Christmas Day the priest saying Mass was stabbed and mortally wounded.[19] The parish was to become a byword for sectarian violence in the city. Du Bourg's death was divisive and counterproductive. Opponents of the Guise were filled with a renewed sense of purpose and energy. A conspiracy was underway that would not only rock the regime on its foundations but would put the lives of the Guise brothers in mortal danger.

* * *

During that Christmas and New Year, rumours of a conspiracy were circulating abroad, and they reached the ears of the Guise. Cardinal Charles was right to fear for his life. When one of his servants was murdered, a law banning the wearing of masks and long coats that might conceal pistols was issued. On the 12 February the court left the château of Marchenoir, where the Duke of Guise's prospective son-in-law, Longueville, had entertained Francis II with a strenuous bout of hunting and games, to make the short journey to the royal residence at Amboise on the Loire. On route they were overtaken by the duke's secretary, Millet, who had raced from Paris. With him he had a man called Pierre des Avenelles, a lawyer in the Parlement from a well-to-do and cultured family. Avenelles was apparently a sincere Protestant, whose Paris home was being used as a safe house. He said that the conversations he overheard there made him feel uneasy and afraid, although the gift of 10,000 livres he was soon to receive suggests other motives. He told of a conspiracy to seize the king while he was at Amboise and present him with a request demanding liberty of conscience. The cardinal and the duke were to be arrested in the name of the three Estates and killed at the first sign of resistance. He named the leader as Jean du Barry, seigneur de la Renaudie—it was a name the Guise knew well.

The Conspiracy of Amboise was the culmination of events that were European in dimension. French Protestants were impressed at how rapidly popery had been overturned in the British Isles. They heard the call of John Knox 'to take the sweard of just defence agains all that should persew us for the mater of religioun'. The initial rejoicing at the death of Henry II had given way to despair when it was clear that the new regime would continue his policies. Throughout France and among Protestant exiles in Geneva and Strasbourg there was vigorous debate about whether it was legitimate to resist an anointed king. Out of these debates was developed a theory of just resistance to 'foreigners' and tyrants', as the Guise were called. It was a proposition that attracted disgruntled Catholics too. Its major failing was that it rested on the claim of the princes of the blood to rule as regents in the name of the king, and Francis II, idiot though he may have been, was three years past his thirteenth birthday, the legal age when French kings reached their majority. Antoine de Navarre was branded a 'coward' by the minister of the Paris Congregation when he refused to oppose the new regime. In Scotland the Calvinist rebellion was sanctified by its aristocratic leadership. Calvin was wary of proceeding without them in France, prophetically warning that 'If a single drop of blood was spilt, the rivers of Europe would run with it.'[20] But there were other less cautious voices who had read in their Bibles that 'Whoso sheddeth man's blood, by man shall his blood be shed' (Gen. 9: 6)—these men had no need of the princes. Calvin was distant from the congregation in Paris, which was embattled and endangered.

Since the princes did not see fit to protect the 'constitution', the role devolved to the lesser nobility. La Renaudie had more personal reasons for involvement. He moved in the Guise orbit in the 1540s and it was probably through their favour that he escaped imprisonment for fraud and fled justice in 1546. La Renaudie converted to Calvinism during exile in Switzerland and saw the Conspiracy as an opportunity to defend the faith and recover his status in France.

Above all he craved vengeance: he blamed the Cardinal of Lorraine for the execution of his brother-in-law, a leading member of the reform movement at Metz. La Renaudie's protectors had now become his persecutors. The men whom he inducted into his plot from September 1559 were inspired by more noble sentiments. The oath they swore was to 'liberty'. They were drawn from the ranks of the well-connected provincial gentry and captains were appointed to lead bands recruited in every province of France. Most of their support derived from local Protestant churches: in Provence representatives of sixty congregations came together and pledged to raise a force of 2,000 men. And there was a vast pool of poverty-stricken soldiers willing to take the daily wage of eighteen sous for a cavalryman or ten sous for a foot soldier that la Renaudie was offering. On 1 February 1560 the plotters held a 'parliament' at Nantes in order to put the finishing touches to their plan. The Baron de Raunay offered his château two miles from Amboise as a rendezvous; other units were to seize towns and disrupt the movement of royalist reinforcements.

Were the plotters acting alone? The involvement of Elizabeth is unlikely, though the Guise suspected her. They feared an English descent into Gascony, a province where Protestantism was well entrenched and whose historic ties to England gave substance to their suspicions. Among those arrested in the wake of President Minard's assassination were two Scots, Robert Stuart and the Earl of Arran's younger brother, and a French Protestant who had emigrated to England only to return to France to escape the reign of Bloody Mary. Financial support from Germany and Switzerland is a possibility. More certain are the negotiations with Louis de Bourbon, Prince of Condé. The twelfth-born of his family, Condé was a 29-year-old political nonentity. He was even less well regarded by Henry II than his brothers; he had no military reputation and little money. According to the Venetian ambassador, 'He was a man of a quick and unquiet temper, very different from his brother, who was of a most amiable and easy character.'[21] There was little else to admire: he had to walk with his head held high in order to hide his stoop and had a voracious sexual appetite that relied as much on force as seduction for its fulfilment. His wife Eléonore de Roye, was made of steelier material; she was highly intelligent and made up for her husband's absence of true piety. But this unlikely Protestant hero had one crucial qualification: he was a prince of the blood. Condé gave his blessing to the enterprise but he was careful to leave no trace of direct involvement and worked through his many servants who signed up. Even so, the Guise already had their suspicions: the 70,000 livres he had been promised went unpaid and he was passed over for the governorship of Picardy in January 1560.

The *putsch* was planned for mid-March. It was at this time that the word 'Huguenot' first entered widespread usage. A corruption of the word *Eidgenossen*, the members of the Swiss confederation, it had overtones of communalism and republicanism totally at odds with the traditions of the French monarchy. It became a popular term of abuse because 'le roi Huguet' was a ghost who visited the Loire Valley at night, a time when the Protestants held their secret services. As bands of conspirators, or liberators, depending on one's point of view, moved to take up their positions around Amboise they had no idea they had been discovered and were walking into a trap. Many Huguenots agreed with Calvin that violence would only increase their suffering. Coligny for one had sunk his differences with the Guise—he had even stayed at the duke's palace at Nanteuil in the autumn—and he was hastily summoned to Amboise on 21 February along with the rest of the aristocracy, including Condé. With each day that passed the tension mounted in expectation of an attack. The Cardinal of Lorraine took to wearing a mail coat. The Scots suspects were brought, in disguise, from Paris and tortured to see if they would reveal the precise date. Caches of weapons were discovered. Most of the insurgent units did not get within sight of the château before they were rounded up in the woods by heavily armed patrols. It was said they surrendered 'like sheep'. A general pardon was issued on 8 March which contributed to the ease with which they laid down their arms. When thirty or so of the ringleaders were picked up at the château of Noizay on the morning of the 15th it looked as if the danger was over. But two days later, at dawn, the Guise brothers were woken by shouts from down below. Boatmen plying their trade on the Loire, swollen by winter rains, had spotted 200 heavy cavalry on the Blois road, sporting distinctive white sashes. White was the symbol of purity in the Christian faith: it was the first appearance of the colour adopted by the Protestants to symbolize their cause. The Prince de Condé could only watch from the battlements, as after a confused two-hour fight in the suburbs, his co-conspirators were forced to flee. In the aftermath, la Renaudie was hunted down in the woods and killed. His corpse was taken back to Amboise and hung from a gibbet just outside the château gates with a placard around it: 'La Renaudie, also known as la Forest, author of the conspiracy, chief and leader of the rebels.'

The aftermath caused more controversy than the conspiracy. The captured papers and interrogations of the prisoners made for good propaganda: the rebels were represented as regicides. The Parlement of Paris conferred on the duke the title of *conservateur de la patrie*. But his actions did not meet with universal approval. What shocked contemporaries most was not so much the numbers of executions—these were wildly exaggerated—but the quality of these men and the summary fashion in which it was done. Dozens were hanged from the battlements for all to see, others were drowned in the Loire. There were about twenty beheadings, the spectacle of which was quickly turned into anti-Guise propaganda. Even the Duchess of Guise was appalled by the extent of the blood-letting. She pleaded for the life of the Baron de Castelnau, who had surrendered on condition that no harm would come to him. Though her husband's conduct was usually governed by chivalrous convention, in this case he refused to budge and the baron was executed.

Meanwhile, Condé kept up appearances so as not to arouse suspicion. Remaining at Amboise, where the mutilated and stinking cadavers of his accomplices had been exposed, he denounced in front of the whole court the 'scum' who accused him of complicity. When the court moved to the Queen Mother's château at Chenonceau he called the rumour-mongers 'liars', the worst insult a gentlemen could proffer, and challenged anyone who accused him to single combat. The king and his mother accepted his denials. The Duke of Guise supported him too—for good soldiers never reveal themselves to their enemies. The Cardinal of Lorraine was unable to hide his feelings; standing behind the throne, he kept his eyes fixed to the ground 'without making the slightest sign of agreement with what they said'.[22] They were certain of his guilt, but lacked proof. On 18 April, while he was present at the king's *lever*, the Queen Mother had a thorough search of his apartments conducted. Nothing was found. A few days later he slipped away from court and headed south to join his brother at Bordeaux.

* * * *

The Guise controlled the court and they were safe here, but the Conspiracy of Amboise seriously weakened their control in many provinces. The final eight months of Francis II's sickly existence were to witness desperate attempts to reimpose authority in those parts of the kingdom where conspiracy and sectarian clashes were taking place in an atmosphere of increasing paranoia. The threat to stability was not only internal. Spain sought to take advantage of their troubles to rid them once and for all from the international scene. The Queen Mother was urged to take power. The brothers were so incensed at the intrigues of Chantonnay that they lodged a formal complaint. Elizabeth too wanted rid of them and she did little to disabuse their suspicions that she had bankrolled the Conspiracy. Shortly after she issued a proclamation simultaneously in English and French urging their overthrow.

The deepening crisis in France and Scotland created tensions between the Guise brothers. As a soldier, François's solution was simple: force had to met with force. At Amboise he had revealed his ruthlessness. Charles, the diplomat and scholar, disagreed. Since the beginning of the year he had had his doubts about the policy of repression and argued that dialogue and temporization were a better means of achieving their political objectives. Family disagreements were kept behind closed doors and the brothers were careful to maintain a united front in public. Mary Stuart complained to her uncles that their policy was responsible for the loss of Scotland. The brothers wrote to their sister Mary explaining that the insurgents in France were using the cloak of religion as mask for political ends 'almost in the same fashion as your rebels'.[23] The cardinal's reasoning was that if the religious pretext for sedition were removed order would be restored. Already, during the height of the Conspiracy, the decision was taken to treat religious and political dissidents as distinct categories. The general pardon issued on 8 March was a remarkable document. The king stated baldly that the policy of persecution had been a gross mistake, which caused 'a marvellous shedding of the blood of men, women, girls and boys, a thing which comes as a perpetual regret, is against our nature and not appropriate to our [young] age'.[24] Henceforth Huguenots were tolerated if they worshipped 'secretly and without scandal'. Only preachers and conspirators were exempt. The distinction between matters of faith, which required Christian understanding, debate, and even compromise; and sedition, which required punishment, remained the cornerstone of policy for the second half of Francis II's reign. The new policy was most immediately felt in Scotland. On 2 April 1560 the cardinal wrote to his sister to commend it, distinguishing between political (bad) dissidents and religious (reasonable) dissidents: 'the best way to break this fury is to come to an agreement with the rebels letting them live as they are, so long as they remain in the obedience of the king and the queen your daughter'.[25]

This essentially *politique* view of religion was in most respects wishful thinking. The difference between religion and sedition depended on one's point of view: the Calvinist who sang psalms and listened to sermons did not consider himself or herself a rebel, while the Catholic viewed these acts as challenge to his or her precious notion of a universal Church and the sacredness of the community united under one faith. The Conspiracy of Amboise had thrown policymaking into confusion: even the Spanish were approached for assistance in Scotland, but Philip II persisted in his view that Scotland should be ruled by the Scots. Marie de Guise complained at the lack of consistency and clarity: 'they were so diverted over there at that time that did not know what they were doing'.[26] The debate between moderates and hardliners among the Guise and their counsellors was continued in the British Isles. In April, the Cardinal of Lorraine sent one of his most trusted counsellors and a leading moderate, Jean de Monluc, Bishop of Valence, to negotiate a peaceful end to the rebellion in Scotland. But his announcement in London that Mary Stuart was prepared to renounce her claim to England came too late. The arrival of 6,000 English troops bolstered the Lords of the Congregation in their belief that their cause was a matter of conscience and they were in no mood to compromise. They demanded the evacuation of all French troops, leaving Marie under their control. Ultra-Catholic opinion was represented by Jacques de la Brosse, the man the Earl of Arran, leader of the Congregation, called the 'throat cutter'. La Brosse wanted action not dialogue. He knew Scotland well, having first campaigned there in 1543. He was shocked to see on his arrival that churches and monasteries burned during his previous visit remained destroyed, 'acts so notorious', he wrote, 'that it is not possible [to do] worse'.[27] Since his arrival he had set about compiling reports of iconolasm and a dossier of treasonable acts committed by the Congregation. Following the failure of Monluc's mission he had to endure a renewed Anglo-Scots bombardment with little prospect of help: by June the Leith garrison was reduced to eating rats. It is hard not to feel that la Brosse's humiliation at the hands of heretics in Scotland was at the back of his mind on the road to Wassy eighteen months later.

Reinforcements were hurriedly prepared and, in the need to confront the Royal Navy, financial caution thrown to the wind: 500,000 livres was placed at the disposal of the Channel fleet.[28] In a clear signal that the Guise would henceforth distinguish between 'religious' and 'political' Huguenots, Admiral Coligny, who had remained loyal during the Conspiracy, was sent to Normandy to prepare twenty-four vessels and gather victuals for 10,000 men. Ten galleys from the Mediterranean fleet, under the command of the Grand Prior, were ordered to sail to the Channel. The English knew all about these preparations because, with the aid of local Protestant sympathizers, they were building a formidable network of informants to keep them informed of affairs on the Channel coast. This spy network was unprecedented in its sophistication and over the next thirty years would give Elizabeth's ministers a better knowledge of events in Normandy than the French government itself. Their agent in Dieppe reported in March 1560 that the town had passed over to the Reform and was uneasy about the presence of the Marquis of Elbeuf and his troops: 'the Captain of Dieppe . . . proclaimed that no one should call the people there Lutherans on pain of death. The people of Dieppe every night in the market-place and afterwards, going through the streets, sing the Psalms of David and some days have sermons preached to them in the fields.'[29] Protestants articulated opposition to the war openly and the Governor of Normandy, a Protestant loyalist, the Duke of Bouillon, was sent to put their minds at rest. Protestants drew sympathy from their Catholic neighbours worried about the disruption to trade and resentful of having rowdy soldiers billeted on them: an English spy wrote with satisfaction that 'the people and the mariners are so evil satisfied that the [Guise] dare not trust them'. Even worse for the Guise: the English spymasters had cracked their codes and they knew that there was no possibility of any reinforcement before August. The death of Marie de Guise on 10 June 1560, undoubtedly weakened by the isolation she felt and the immense pressure she was under, signalled the end of French resistance. In death, her brother Charles showed more attentiveness: he arranged for the transfer of her remains to their sister Renée's convent of Saint-Pierre in Reims, where they were interred beneath a magnificent tomb in the middle of the nave of the church. By the treaty of Edinburgh, signed on 6 July, Mary Stuart renounced her coat of arms officially and French and English troops withdrew from Scotland. The French commissioners had left Mary and Francis with only nominal sovereignty. Cardinal Charles was furious and accepted it 'only in order to get them out of the wolf's mouth'. The treaty was never ratified in France. The Guise did not give up their dynastic claims in the British Isles. Within three years Duke François was full of 'beautiful plans' for an invasion of England. But before the Guise definitively replaced Philip II with Elizabeth I as their chief external enemy, they faced one more challenge at home.

* * * *

The crushing of the Conspiracy of Amboise and the de facto end of persecution did not bring an end to opposition. In the aftermath of the Conspiracy, the brothers continued to be assassination targets. For the rest of his life the cardinal would everywhere be escorted by a squadron of dragoons. Arsonists targeted Guise properties in the vicinity of Paris. In the city itself an effigy of the cardinal was hung in broad daylight and there were arson attacks on four of his Paris residences. An attack on the Hôtel de Guise was repulsed with musketry which left two dead. No doubt these attacks were inspired by the various pamphlets, of which there were more than a score, denouncing their tyrannical rule.

In many provinces order collapsed completely in the wake of the Conspiracy. In the south-east in particular—Dauphiné, Provence, the Lyonnais—forces raised by the Protestants were never intended to go to Amboise and they now formed the nucleus of a highly effective guerrilla army. Order also collapsed because of the incertitude created by the new policy. Many Catholics agreed with Philip II that no distinction between heresy and sedition could be made; they were one and the same thing. The new policy relied much on the discretion and common sense of local officials, who were often simply confused and lacking in resources. They found the distinction between 'religious' and 'political' dissent almost impossible to make. Many simply preferred to turn a blind eye with the result that the Protestant movement, which had no intention of worshipping in secret like the detested Nicodemites, grew at a faster rate than ever and became ever bolder. From all over France in the summer of 1560 reports flooded in of Protestants worshipping openly under the protection of armed guards. And they did not stop there. Normandy was said to resemble a 'mini-Germany'. During the great summer horse fair near Falaise, excited crowds proclaimed the abolition of the Mass and conducted their own popular reformation, running priests, sellers of papal indulgences, and prostitutes out of town. In Montauban the church of Saint-Jacques and in Montpellier the church of Saint-Mathieu were seized, their interiors cleansed of the trappings of popery ready for services on the Genevan model. Catholics who tried to stem the tide received little assistance from the centre. In Rouen, the governor drew up a list of those who had failed to do their Easter observances and when he attempted to make participation in the June Corpus Christi processions compulsory there were riots and a demonstration against him by 2,000 citizens. The Cardinal of Lorraine wrote to the governor to complain 'accusing him of too much zeal and inquisitiveness in having thus caused such great turmoil, and that he ought rather to have dissembled and pretended not to see what did not please him, than to proceed to such extremities for the discovery of what was kept hidden, whereby he has done nothing but place all his Majesty's ministers in danger and anxiety'.[30] One accusation levelled at the cardinal by his detractors was that he was a coward. The similarities with the situation in Scotland were obvious to contemporaries, where the absence of a clear and consistent policy, either for toleration or for outright repression, had spelt failure in the face of a determined and well-organized movement.

* * * *

Historians and contemporaries rarely have a good word to say about Antoine de Navarre. The Venetian ambassador complained that he was 'very weak', a dilettante who had spent too much time in pleasure and comfort; a man who was easily led by the opinions of others and, even worse, listened to the opinions of his wife, Jeanne Albret, such that he attached 'himself now to one party, now to another, favouring today the Catholics, in order to court the pope, and tomorrow the Huguenots to be assured of their support'.[31] In fact, we should consider his flexibility shrewd politics: the ability to change religion when necessary was something he transmitted to his son Henry—it was a lesson that would eventually help Henry win the French crown. Initially, Antoine had cooperated with the Guise regime and was chosen to conduct the king's sister to Madrid for her marriage to Philip II. He had gone with unrealistic expectations of receiving compensation for the loss of Navarre. He was disillusioned by Philip's attitude and on his return home was prepared to listen to the Protestants once more. In the summer of 1560, at the request of him and his wife, Calvin sent François Hotman, who had already made his name as a political propagandist, and Théodore Beza, his most trusted theological lieutenant, to the Bourbon court at Nérac in the Pyrenees 'to teach them the word of God'.

The success of the Congregation in Scotland had given the French Protestants fresh heart. They viewed their plight in identical terms to their Scottish brethren: they were patriots resisting foreigners, who had usurped the ancient laws and custom of the kingdom and were preventing a return to a purer form of religion. In order to enlist Navarre as the French leader of a Congregation, Hotman deployed arguments using a new science developed by the humanists: History. He compared the genealogy and history of the Guise family unfavourably with that of the Bourbon. But the most serious charges he made were racial in origin: the Guise were simply not French. It was said that Claude, Duke of Guise spoke 'French with a German accent'.[32] The duchy of Lorraine was just a lot of forest whose princes 'told Germans they were great in France and the French that they were great in Germany'. The Guise were tin-pot German princes who had usurped the rights of the true-born French princes of the blood.

Navarre listened and revelled in being compared to a new Gideon or Samson who would lead the Israelists out of bondage. Certainly, the Calvinist leadership was given to believe that he would support resistance. Navarre's direct involvement in the next challenge to the Guise is shadowy, since he was far too smart to commit anything to paper. He would not do anything openly without support from Elizabeth or the German princes; they were strong on moral support but less forthcoming with cash. His hot-headed brother was more precipitous. He sent an agent, la Sague, to the Constable of Montmorency with letters written in invisible ink. Condé planned to infiltrate 1,200 men into Lyon, France's second city, supported by an uprising of 500 of its citizens. The coup would be supported by forces from Dauphiné and Geneva. The insurgents would call for an immediate summoning of the Estates-General to press the claims of the Bourbon and call the Guise to account. Unfortunately for the plotters, la Sague was arrested and tortured. The plot and the names of the conspirators were divulged to the Guise.

Armed with this information the brothers were able to outmanoeuvre their opponents. In August, they summoned an assembly of notables from all over France to meet at Fontainebleau. Only Navarre and Condé failed to appear. Forty grandees, ministers, and men of letters deliberated for several days and agreed on a thorough-going reformation of the state and of religion. The calling of the Estates-General and preparations for a National Council of the Church was announced. The impression was given, to the delight of the English ambassador, and to the fury of the Spanish ambassador, that a tacit Interim was now in force in which Protestants were free to worship until the calling of the Council, so long as they did not cause a public scandal.[33] In order to isolate the House of Bourbon-Vendôme further and keep the rest of the princes of the blood onside, the interior provinces of the kingdom were consolidated under two super-governorships. Louis de Bourbon-Montpensier, was charged with order across the entire Loire Valley: Anjou, Touraine, Maine, Perche, Vendômois, Loudunois, Blois, Laval, and Amboise. His brother, Charles Prince de la Roche-sur-Yon, took control of the Orléanais, Berry, Beauce, Montargis, and the Chartrain. The Bourbon-Vendôme had been utterly outsmarted.

On 31 August the Guise openly denounced the plots against them, warned Navarre that the royalists had 40,000 troops at the ready and summoned him and his brother to account for their conduct. Two days before it was due to begin Navarre made desperate efforts to halt the Lyon coup, but it was too late and royal forces dispersed the insurgents and captured some of the ringleaders, whose testimony under torture implicated Condé. In the autumn, civil war seemed a distinct possibility as royal troops, under the command of the Duke of Guise, were sent into the provinces to restore order. In Nîmes and Montpellier, with cries of 'Navarre! Navarre! Liberty! Liberty!', Protestants ran the Catholic magistrates out of town. But this was not yet a religious war, as the Venetian ambassador was well aware: 'in the whole kingdom one finds not a single man . . . who is not impassioned, possessed by a political rage on his own account or for his friends: these hatreds among the grandees [do] more harm to the king than the arms of the Huguenots'.[34] The war on heresy was not revived—the Guise did not use this word; they stood firm on the policy of distinguishing between malicious and peaceable Protestants. Cardinal Charles made it clear that though 'rebels'—which included Protestant ministers—must be subject to martial law, as for the rest who were baptized or took the sacraments in the 'Genevan fashion' restraint was to be exercised.[35] In the event, civil war was avoided. The Bourbon, backed by 700–800 horse and 6,000 foot, were vastly outnumbered, and when Spain promised to send troops to the Pyrenees it was clear the game was up. Navarre and Condé could not stay away from court any longer. They thought they would be safe at Orléans where the Estates-General was soon about to open and which they expected would provide support for their cause. They had not however reckoned on a new political figure: the 16-year-old king. The phoney war roused Francis II from his pre-pubescent torpor. Rebels were supposed to be riff-raff and his anger at the betrayal by men of royal blood was noted by several eyewitnesses. If there was a proof against Navarre he threatened that 'he would make him feel who was king'. He made all the nobles present at Orléans re-pledge their allegiance to him. As soon as the brothers arrived on 31 October Condé was arrested.

* * * *

As the opening of the first Estates-General to meet in seventy-five years approached and as the king began to act in manner befitting his dignity, the regime seemed to have turned the corner and finally achieved a measure of stability. Chantonnay announced to Philip II that troops had been disbanded since 'the altercations in this realm have ceased'.[36] The trial and conviction of Condé would set an example and seal the beginning of the new order. The Guise remained aloof from the process; they did not sign the arrest warrant. They had no need to: the king was so incensed at the rebellion that he took a close personal interest in the prosecution. Condé filibustered, refusing to recognize the competence of the commission gathered to try him and demanded a trial by his peers. He was eventually tried and found guilty, but there was no consensus about what to do with him. There is no evidence that the Guise wished to see their first cousin beheaded. The execution of a prince of the blood would have been unprecedented and politically dangerous. The Venetian ambassador thought the worst that could happen was imprisonment in the notorious dungeons in Loches castle. In the event, the Guise victory was fleeting. Within days Condé was free.

At the beginning of November the king had taken advantage of the unseasonably warm weather to indulge his passion for hunting. But there was a sudden change of weather and it became excessively cold. On Sunday 17 November Francis was seized with a severe shivering fit and fever. A build up of catarrh led to swelling the size of a nut appearing behind his left ear; it caused severe pain in his teeth and jaws and catarrh oozed out of the ear. Francis was probably suffering from mastoiditis—an infection of the mastoid bone at the back of the ear—induced by chronic catarrh. The prognosis was not good: astrologers had predicted he would die before the age of eighteen. As their nephew lie dying in great pain, the Guise regime began to unravel. With tears in his eyes the cardinal had a very frank interview with Chantonnay on the 3 December—all the more surprising since the Spanish ambassador was already manoeuvring to return the constable to power. He told Chantonnay that there was no hope and that, since Francis's younger brother Charles was only 10 years old, a regency headed by the Queen Mother had been agreed between all the factions at court. The cardinal poured out his heart and told Chantonnay that he and his family were 'lost'. The death of Francis II before midnight on 5 December left the Guise exposed to their enemies: the Montmorency, the Habsburgs, and the Tudors. Calvin wrote to Jacob Sturm triumphantly: 'Did you ever read or hear of anything more timely than the death of the little King? There was no remedy for the worst evils when God suddenly revealed himself from Heaven, and He who had pierced the father's eye struck off the ear of the son.'[37]

The reaction of the Duke of Guise to the fall was entirely different from his brother's lachrymose despair. In the first Privy Council meeting of the new regency on 8 December he crossed words with Admiral Coligny over the issue of Protestant assemblies. Coligny could hardly contain his elation at the impending fall of the Guise. The duke said afterwards that if it had not been for the dignity of the place he would have stabbed the admiral. With so many enemies the Guise would need to find new friends. He and his brother were divided about how to achieve this. Five days later the duke went on pilgrimage on foot to the royal shrine of Notre-Dame de Cléry. The duke was not known for his piety. But this was no ordinary pilgrimage: he was accompanied by 500 men in a show of strength. The duke came under pressure from senior counsellors and, if we believe Brantôme, his brother, to undertake a putsch, arrest his rivals and declare himself regent. Their reasoning was that Guise still had control of the royal apartments and the army and could coerce the Estates-General into accepting his candidature. The clergy, so the argument went, would also provide support. Guise, however, would not countenance violence 'saying that it was neither God's [will] nor reasonable to usurp the authority of another. But in a matter of such importance it should be done justly.'[38] Like the good soldier he was, he had undoubtedly also weighed the risks and considered the likelihood of civil war too great.

In Orléans fears of a coup were widespread and, despite the duke's support for the constitution, the oft-heard accusation that the Guise were over-mighty subjects was given fresh impetus. In contrast to her uncles, the fate of Mary Stuart aroused some sympathy. Catherine de Medici had endured insults from Mary about her lowly origins and demanded the return of the crown jewels with indecent haste, the day after Francis died. As the Venetian ambassador commented: 'Soon the death of the late King will be forgotten by all except his little wife, who has been widowed, has lost France, and has little hope of Scotland...her unhappiness and incessant tears call forth general compassion.'[39]

6

THE CARDINAL'S COMPROMISE

Fiendish tiger! Poisonous snake! Sepulchre of abomination! Spectacle of wretchedness! How long will you abuse the youth of our king? Will you ever make an end of your unbridled ambition, your pretences and thefts?

The Antichrist is a shape-shifter. His power lies in his cunning: he does not announce himself with horns like the devil, but is more likely to appear in the form of a friend, cloaking himself in holiness and mingling falsehood with truth in order to tempt and trap the unwary. The *Tigre*, François Hotman's seven-page diatribe against Charles, Cardinal of Lorraine, set new standards in European political discourse, outdoing even the splenetic John Knox. It stood out from the score of other pamphlets denouncing the Guise in the wake of the Conspiracy of Amboise. So explosive were its contents that anyone found in possession was liable to hanging. It represented the cardinal not only as a shape-shifting monster from hell, but also as a 'villainous sodomite' and 'bugger' (for the denizens of Gomorrah only celestial punishment will suffice). Hotman's vitriol transformed the lexicon of European political discourse in other ways too. Drawing on Cicero, he justified tyrannicide and reminded the citizen of his duty to defend the Commonwealth against tyrants. Those who read this pamphlet had not heard this sort of political language before—Brantôme recalled that he was 'gutted' when he first read it.

Protestant hatred for the leader of the Catholic Church in France seems at first glance to be so obvious as to be barely worth investigation—that is until we recognize that the cardinal was similarly vilified by Catholics, and that his brother was never subjected to the same level of abuse. In fact, though the duke had more Protestant blood on his hands than his brother, his affability and modesty left his reputation intact. On the death of Francis II, the Venetian ambassador reported that 'although the Duke of Guise is popular, and above all with the nobility, everybody so detests the Cardinal of Lorraine that, if the matter depended upon universal suffrage, not only would he have no part in the Government, but perhaps not in this world'.[1] The cardinal responded by asking Ronsard, the most fashionable poet of the day, to give his image a makeover:

> His name shall be the prelate of Lorraine
> Charles de Guise, and then the Virtue Sovereign,
> Justice herself, shall pass into his form,
> The vicious ways of mankind to reform
> And his body metamorphosed be.

The cardinal was an intellectual and statesman, whose humanist education inspired him with grand ideas for the reform of Church and State. Objections to him and his programme were partly based on personality. Intelligent and able, he was also a difficult man. He could be charming and suave but also haughty and irascible, and vindictive towards those that he considered had betrayed him. But there was another more serious charge made by contemporaries: he was, in the words of one Protestant, simply a 'hypocrite'.[2] The 'pretence' that the *Tigre* refers to was a charge made more explicitly by Andelot at the time of his arrest on heresy charges in 1558:

> I am very certain of my doctrine and you know better than you are letting on, Monsieur le Cardinal; I call upon your conscience as witness, whether you did not once favour this holy doctrine, but honours and ambition have since deflected you, indeed even to persecute the followers of Jesus Christ.[3]

Protestants were not the only ones to charge Charles with being a Nicodemite. Catholic hardliners had their suspicions too. One of these was Paul IV; and the Pope who succeeded him, Pius IV, referred ironically to another aspect of his hypocrisy: 'the Cardinal of Lorraine is a second pope with 300,000 livres of revenue who has taken the opportunity to remonstrate to the Council [of Trent] against the plurality of benefices'.[4] What people distrusted about Lorraine was the impression that his theological position might be flexible, his approach to matters of faith shaped by contingency. In fact, the cardinal's theological position was largely consistent: thoroughgoing reform was needed within the Catholic Church in order to bring back the souls it had lost. His tactics, dictated by the double hostility to his position of both ultra-Catholic conservatives on the one hand and Calvinists on the other, would lead to charges of dissimulation and pretence. In order to understand the genesis of his compromise, the reasons for its failure and the tragic consequences of that failure we need to return to his childhood.

* * * *

In 1535, at the age of 10, Charles began his studies at Navarre College under the aegis of François le Picart. An inspiration for the early Jesuits, Picart was the leading preacher of his day and a celebrity—when he died in 1556 it was said that 20,000 people attended his funeral in Paris. He was also a leading opponent of heresy: in 1533 he was exiled from Paris after accusing the king's sister of unorthodox opinions. But Picart was different from other conservative Sorbonne theologians, who thought it was simply enough to denounce heretics in lurid tones. The funeral sermon for Claude, the first Duke of Guise, in 1550, was an example of this old-fashioned approach, which contrasted the subject's piety with:

> The Lutherans, who believed in sexual freedom and hold all in common, are now expanding everywhere, just like the Goths, the Gepids, the Vandals, the Ostrogoths, and other barbarians, in order to ruin Christendom.[5]

Such firebrand rhetoric may have stirred the hearts of the uneducated listener, but the precocious Charles de Guise was different. Navarre College was the leading centre of humanism in Paris and Picart taught his pupil that the new learning was the best way to combat heresy. Picart was not afraid to read Protestant works in order to refute them with reference to the scriptures. The result, as the more conservative preachers pointed out, was more akin to debate than denunciation. He was also prepared to admit that the Protestants might have a point: in contrast to many of his colleagues he was prepared to denounce clerical abuses. In stark contrast to the wrathful and vengeful deity portrayed by other preachers, who warned that heresy was a sign of the coming of the end of the world, Picart had an optimistic message; his God was good, loving, compassionate, and merciful. Love would reconcile lost souls. God was so good he even wanted Martin Luther to be saved![6] The important role he attached to scripture, to preaching, and to reform of the clergy had a profound influence on the young Charles. One of his first acts on becoming Archbishop of Reims was to found a university there.

He was deeply touched by humanism. But humanist learning was much more controversial in France—where it was accused of promoting paganism, relativism, and immorality—than it was in Italy. By the time he had succeeded his uncle as head of the Catholic Church in France, humanists were under attack from both Protestants and conservative Catholics alike. The godly on both sides were wary of learning they associated with impiety. In his youth the greatest opponent of Catholic Reform remained the Sorbonne. When François Rabelais' *Tiers Livre* was condemned in 1546 Charles rushed immediately to his defence and provided him with the living of Meudon. In gratitude Rabelais dedicated his next work, *Le Sciomachie*, to the young cardinal.

Charles's other mentor at Navarre College was a considerably more radical figure than Picart. Ten years older than his pupil, Pierre Ramus was from a poor background. He achieved notoriety for his attacks on the outdated medieval syllabus taught at the Sorbonne. In 1544 he was banned from lecturing on Aristotle and Plato; his books were burned and he was condemned to a year in the galleys. Lorraine was present in the Parlement when the sentence was quashed in 1546, and as soon as he came to power in the palace revolution of 1547 he had the ban on Ramus's lectures lifted. When Ramus was condemned once more in 1551, the cardinal again oversaw his defence and afterwards, in order to give him more freedom, procured him a professorship at the Collège Royal. Ramus was grateful, dedicating twenty works to his patron and in 1555 praised 'the splendour of your very noble race, first issued from the Great Emperor Charlemagne, which has since bound together the crowns of Austrasia, Aragon, Sicily and Jerusalem'.

For his platonic salon, which emerged in the early 1550s, the cardinal created an idyll at Meudon on the fringes of Paris. It was arguably the most important non-royal commission of the French Renaissance and served as a museum to display the antiquities that the cardinal had brought from Rome. Busts were chosen and juxtaposed with care: Cicero and Demosthenes alluded to the cardinal's own eloquence. Perseus, representing the Duke of Guise, is paired with Mercury, representing the cardinal at the capture of Calais; for it is Mercury who arms and counsels Perseus before his battle with the Medusa. The high moral tone imparted by the gallery dedicated to busts of Roman emperors was offset by the representation of Bacchus in the entry to the pavilion, reminding the visitor of the ancient proverb that 'good wine makes for a good mind', and reassuring Rabelais, whose *Tiers Livre* begins with a eulogy to the inspirational powers of wine.

The extensive gardens were laid out under the cardinal's direction. The sculptor Jean le Roux built a grotto in 1556–7, which long remained a marvel to sightseers, on whom hidden fountains would playfully turn unsuspected sprays of cold water. Above the grotto were busts of Plato and Aristotle beneath which poets like Ronsard and thinkers like Ramus could escape from the thought-police operating on the Left Bank. Ramus's increasingly heretical beliefs could not have escaped his patron. The salon was a broad church, an irenic academy, where free thinking was permitted, as long as public conformity to the Catholic Church was maintained. Ramus's break with the cardinal came only at the end of 1561 with (the *sine qua non* for all Catholics) refusal to attend Mass. During the 1550s, however, it was the existence of the salon that gave the Protestants the impression that the cardinal was a fellow traveller. In reality, he was nothing of the sort. He enjoyed the latest taste in art—he had met Titian in 1547—and music, whether it was secular or religious in tone. He played the lute and Protestants later sneered at him for putting the lascivious and corrupting verses of Horace to music. Though he knew his scriptures, the letters he wrote are very different from those of his Protestant contemporaries. Scripture is largely absent. In contrast to the godly, he was an Epicurean, happy to discuss the latest court gossip, make jokes, and discuss matters of faith in earthy and simple language.

The liberal atmosphere of Meudon can be resurrected from the surviving rolls of the cardinal's household. Many of his staff were gentlemen whose families are more usually associated with the Protestant cause. His closest advisor, referred to as his 'great governor', was Gabriel de la Vallée. A Catholic, la Vallée rarely left his master's side and slept in the cardinal's chambers for his security. His wife however was described as a woman 'who mixes freely with the '"Huguenotical", "Calvininian" and Lutheran' religion. His stepdaughters were raised as Protestants. One of them, Marie, has a significant role to play later in our story. For she was at the heart of the Protestant network in the Brie, a tightly knit group whose internal disagreements shed light on the conspiracy that sparked the Saint Bartholomew's Day Massacre.[7] Among the prelates in the household there were some ultra-Catholics, but there were many more evangelicals such as the Guillart brothers, respectively bishops of Senlis and Chartres, who became notorious for their unorthodox views. In 1561 they were cited by the Roman Inquisition. The Bishop of Chartres's indulgence towards heretics made him the target of fanatics. During the Saint Bartholomew's Day Massacre a Catholic mob went in search of him but, unable to find him, had to be satisfied with ransacking his palace.

What was discussed in the grotto of Meudon can be deduced from the writings of the two leading thinkers surrounding the cardinal, the chief theologian in his household, Claude d'Espence and his friend, the humanist Michel de l'Hôpital. Michel de l'Hôpital was born into the Guise orbit in 1506 as the son of the Duchess of Lorraine's physician. He became a lawyer and entered the cardinal's service in 1553, emerging as the Guise's chief polemicist. He poured scorn on claims that they were foreigners, arguing that France extended to the Rhine and calling the Cardinal of Lorraine 'the hope of the French race'.[8] It was he who first developed the concept that religion was being used as a cloak for sedition, and that a distinction needed to be made between faith and politics. D'Espence was five years younger and another product of Navarre College in the 1530s. In 1543 he was forced to retract some of the propositions made in his Lenten sermons and is said to have remarked of his conservative opponents that 'to know anything of Greek made man suspected, to know anything of Hebrew almost made him a heretic'. He was widely admired and visited Geneva for an interview with Calvin in 1548.

The friendships that developed at Meudon were based on a shared admiration for Erasmus. There was a shared commitment to the evangelical attack on the cupidity and absenteeism of the clergy and to calls for returning the Church to its ancient purity; rejecting outright those innovations, such as purgatory, which had commercialized the road to salvation. As an alternative, the Meudon circle promoted a Christocentric piety that required the believer to imitate Christ. Most were also hostile to the Protestants: d'Espence wrote a thesis attacking predestination and upholding the role of free will in grace. But, they argued, heresy could only be defeated by reform within the Church and by showing charity to those separated from it. It was these voices that the cardinal listened to as he decriminalized heresy in the spring of 1560.

These men considered themselves to be orthodox; none repudiated the miracle of the Mass. The most outspoken of them was Jean de Monluc, who had served as chief minister in Scotland in 1548 before being summoned by his patron to join the caucus of reform-minded progressives on the Privy Council. In the intervening years his evangelical experiment in his bishopric of Valence, which included offering the chalice to the laity, had proved highly controversial, not least with the Duke of Guise, governor of the province in which the see was located. Ultra-Catholics ascribed the rapid spread of the reform there and the breakdown of order to the temperance of mealy-mouthed moderates. Consequently, there were limits on what could be said in public. The household of the Duchess of Guise, another space in which heterodox ideas were welcomed, came under renewed scrutiny in 1554 when her Italian almoner, Boturnus, was accused of preaching heresy. Otherwise light was made of the duchess's devotional shortcomings. It was only when the Duke of Guise visited Rome in 1557 and Paul IV fulminated that Boturnus 'was one of the greatest and most wicked heretics in Christendom' that the matter became politically sensitive.[9] Boturnus was dismissed and retired to Geneva. With every new crisis, Protestant servants of the Guise were forced to make the difficult choice, either to quit their service or maintain a stricter outward conformity. The most serious defection occurred in the wake of the Conspiracy of Amboise when the master of the ducal household, François de Hangest, left after a decade of service. Until then, his well-known closeness to Calvin—Calvin himself was raised and educated with the Hangest family and his early career owed much to their patronage—had not hindered his career. Despite his departure, strenuous efforts were made to keep him in the fold with cash and gifts and the conferral of the Order of Saint Michel in September 1560. On the eve of his arrest, Condé had recourse to Hangest to intercede for him, knowing that his fellow Protestant was still 'an especial servant' of the Guise.[10]

While the Protestants left, their moderate Catholic colleagues prospered. Despite the breakdown of order, civil war did not yet appear inevitable and there was genuine cause for optimism among those who favoured compromise. Following the Conspiracy of Amboise, the team of humanists and progressive Catholic theologians that the cardinal had groomed at Meudon was brought into the Privy Council with the intention of beginning a thoroughgoing reform of Church and State.

* * * *

In the early months of Francis II's reign, the reforming impulse was initially felt only in the realm of finances. The cardinal had deeply disappointed his supporters among the Protestants by continuing the religious policies of the previous regime, limiting himself to scripture classes for the young king. The controversy caused by du Bourg's execution and President Minard's murder made the dangers of continuing this policy plain. Within days of these events, and in the wake of the election of Pius IV, the cardinal urged Philip II to join him in reviving the idea of a General Council of the Church, and, in a revealing glimpse of his arrogance, claimed that together 'they could make the rest of Christianity go where they wanted'.[11] Even before the Conspiracy of Amboise, his mood had changed. At the end of February he complained bitterly about the abuses in the Church as the cause of the current unrest. During Lent, at the height of the Conspiracy, he joked 'that those who chose to eat meat could do so'.[12] For the next two years he would wage a struggle for a free and general council that included the Protestants, opposing the 'Popish' Council of Trent, whose continuation he correctly foresaw would make the current schism in Christendom permanent.

After Amboise, Michel de l'Hôpital entered the Privy Council as chancellor along with the Bishop of Valence, who was dispatched to explain the new moderate line in Scotland. Bishops were ordered to return to their dioceses. Catherine de Medici has long been credited with the change of policy and personnel, but this not the case. The 41-year-old Queen Mother emerged from the Conspiracy as a more significant figure, but she had no political experience, no provincial power base and no faction behind her: the new men on the council were the cardinal's protégés, not hers. Her religious position was always dominated by political considerations, which meant the security of her children. She had been crucial to the Guise regime from the beginning, supporting the policy of repression, but was just as happy to support the decriminalization of heresy if it improved the security situation. Fellow Italians found her shallow. 'Religion did not enter her soul. Neither gratitude nor love seems to have prompted her prayers but rather a desire to placate His wrath.'[13] Catherine had a vested interest in promoting as many factions as possible so that she could play the arbiter. To this end she arranged for the return of an old Guise enemy from Rome: the papal legate, Cardinal Tournon. A spokesman for the Pope and Philip II, he quickly emerged as the leader of the ultra-Catholic faction at court. She had no antipathy to Protestants, however, and heterodox beliefs were rampant in her household. Catherine was to emerge as a brilliant player of the dangerous game of faction politics. But her inability or unwillingness to grasp fully the subtle issues of dogma that divided Frenchmen was to have serious consequences for the kingdom. Typically, she preferred the dashing Duke François, for whom she had a 'profound veneration, founded on his personal merit', to the cardinal, who made her feel socially and intellectually inferior.

The cardinal's Easter sermons that year, 'of incomparable eloquence' were a call to arms for the evangelical cause. On 22 March he announced to the Pope plans for a National Council of the Gallican Church, which would return the Church to its primitive beauty. It was his initiative. Others on the Privy Council still preferred to wait for a General Council, until which time, as Chancellor l'Hôpital explained in July, Frenchmen 'would have to attempt to live in quietness'. Rome and Madrid were horrified at the prospect of some form of Gallican compromise, leading to the establishment of a local variant of Catholicism independent of Rome. Philip II sent an envoy to press for a return to persecution. Pius IV accused Lorraine of being a schismatic. The severity of their response was an indication of how carefully he would have to tread. The Calvinists were suspicious too. As early as 1549 Calvin had denounced those he disparagingly called *Moyenneurs*, or 'Mediators', who thought they could find a third way between the confessions. Calvin and his followers had little interest in compromise: the Truth was revealed in scripture. They demanded liberty of worship. They were right not to trust the cardinal; he was still intent on their destruction, but this time his weapons would be compromise and reform. Rumours began to circulate that the cardinal favoured a princely style Gallican reformation and that he would take the title of Patriarch of France. Certainly, he was a keen student of the confessional situation in the Holy Roman Empire, where the 1555 Religious Peace of Augsburg had devolved the issue of religious allegiance to the imperial cities and the territorial princes. He made it clear that he wanted any future General Council to include the Lutherans, and preferred a German venue over Trent. But he also realized that the solution in the Empire, with its decentralized and heterogeneous political structure, could have no application in France if the monarchy was to be preserved. England was a more promising model: the Elizabethan *via media* was providing a measure of stability for a kingdom similarly plagued by religious division and dynastic weakness.

On the 21 August 1560, fifty-five grandees and men of letters met at Fontainebleau to discuss the current crisis. It was a stage-managed event, in which the evangelicals would triumph over their internal and external enemies. Proceedings started well when a caucus of *Moyenneur* prelates close to Lorraine denounced the abuses of the Church. In proposing the motion for Gallican reform, Jean de Monluc argued that it was a patriotic duty: as Paris burned it was absurd to look to the Tiber to douse its flames when there was plenty of water flowing in the Marne and the Seine. Cardinal Tournon was not amused. But, just as things were going according to plan, an unexpected and unwelcome intervention upset the proceedings. Admiral Coligny took the floor and proposed a different solution to the religious troubles: pacific coexistence between the two confessions. He presented a petition with 50,000 signatures calling for liberty of worship. There was a sharp intake of breath among the audience as he did so; it was the first time that the Protestants had dared to petition the king in such a fashion. Coligny had hijacked the conference and the Guise brothers were furious at his audacity. Old animosities were rekindled, for vital questions of etiquette, honour, and reputation were at stake. Coligny would not be forgiven. The agenda had called for the Guise to give an account of the kingdom's affairs under their tutelage. Quite unexpectedly, they were now forced to confront the admiral on the issue of religious reform, a matter that they had intended to leave to the bishops. Their differing responses revealed for the first time the divisions within the Guise family itself. The duke straightforwardly told Coligny to keep his nose out of Church business; he for one:

> would leave it to those who were more learned than him on matters of theology; though he was sure that all the councils in the world would not happen to divert him or make him change the ancient ways of his predecessors, principally regarding the Holy Sacrament.[14]

The cardinal spoke for much longer and with more subtlety; he opposed the simple certainties represented by his brother and Coligny, both men, incidentally, who would be martyred for their beliefs. The cardinal conceded that the petitioners were obedient subjects. But in a famous quip he said he could oppose the 50,000 signatures gathered by Coligny with a million of his own. Liberty of worship was impossible because it would show 'approval of their idolatry, and the king could not conceive of it without being perpetually damned'. Less well reported is what he said next:

> He was of the opinion that [as regards] those who went to services without arms, who sang psalms and who didn't go to Mass, and other things they observed, since the penalties had served no good until now, the king must forbid that they should be troubled by judicial punishment. He being very upset that they had carried out heretofore such grievous punishments...That

the bishops and other persons must labour to win them over and correct [abuses] according to the Bible.

This passage reveals Lorraine's caution and moderation. Its contrition for the failed war on heresy and acknowledgement that, contrary to what he was telling Rome and Madrid, an Interim was in force, was followed, as the cardinal was increasingly moved to do, with a passage from the Gospels. 'Moreover if thy brother shall trespass against thee, go and tell him his fault between thee and him alone: if he shall hear thee, thou hast gained thy brother' (Matt. 18: 15). This was a call for dialogue. Within days preliminary talks to discuss the idea of a National Council were announced. To Philip II this was backsliding, and it redoubled his hatred for the Guise. Rome and Madrid vowed they would do everything to stop it happening. The Guise had to write reassuring letters and dispatch envoys to explain themselves.

Coligny emerged from the Fontainebleau conference as the most eloquent and most convincing leader of the French Protestant movement. But in the rich religious soup that was France in 1560 there was one ingredient that historians, often with a confessional axe to grind, have neglected—the 'Protestant loyalists'. These were aristocrats who, while embracing the Reformed faith, despised the militancy of the urban congregations, whose popular reformation displayed worrying signs of Swiss-style communalism. The 'Protestant loyalists' had their private chapels and, with their deep sense of loyalty to the king, were hostile to the plots and conspiracies of the House of Bourbon. They were on the whole better disposed to the Guise. Indeed many of them were kinsmen or neighbours of the Guise in Champagne. Some were, like them, princes in the Holy Roman Empire and impressed by the way in which divisions in Germany had been resolved by the 1555 Religious Peace. The loyalists shared many of the social attitudes of their elitist Catholic evangelical friends, despising the vulgar and ignorant devotional practices of the masses. And they would later see the Massacre of Wassy in class terms—as an affair between a lord and his subjects—and in the ensuing civil war side with the Crown against their co-religionists. Following the Fontainebleau conference, Cardinal Charles made a bold attempt to include this group in a *Moyenneur* or Middle Party.

He spent the summer of 1560 matchmaking, obtaining the appropriate papal dispensations and planning the most glittering social occasion of the year. In the first week of October all the French princes, bar the House of Bourbon-Vendôme, gathered at the Queen Mother's château at Saint-Germain-en-Laye, to witness multiple exchanges of vows. An old Guise friend, the 44-year-old François de Clèves, Duke of Nevers, Governor of Champagne, was getting remarried. At the same time his 12-year-old daughter Catherine, married Antoine de Cröy, Prince de Porcien. Catholic ritual was followed, which was ironic since many of those gathered with the Guise family for the festivities were Protestants. But whether they were Catholic or Protestant mattered little: the wedding guests were overwhelmingly *Moyenneurs*. The event reunited many of those who had sat at the top table at Mary Stuart's wedding. We know that Catherine de Clèves was not yet a Protestant because, after the death of her mother, she had been raised at Joinville by the dowager Duchess of Guise. Her father and brothers oscillated between Rome and Geneva, but, as their loyalism during the civil wars would later attest, they backed the Cardinal of Lorraine's search for a compromise. Porcien was more open about his faith and kept Protestants for company, but his mother Françoise d'Amboise, whose conversion in 1558 had not disrupted her close friendship with the Duchess of Guise, believed that outward conformity was a price worth paying for maintaining the friendship of her Catholic neighbours. Approval of these marriages came from the aristocratic Protestant women who were so numerous in the household of the Queen Mother. These courtly ladies disapproved of the dangerous and dissolute rabble-rouser, Condé. They were charmed by Lorraine's suaveness and his talk of concord and dialogue.

The betrothals were the most exclusive of social occasions: the rarefied company was distinguished by their pedigree and their kinship ties to each other and their roots in the Champagne region. The snobbery of the princes extended to the Montmorency, whom they considered social upstarts. French Protestant princes, such as the Longueville, the la Marck, and the Clèves, had little taste for rebellion; they possessed lands in the Empire and looked with envy at the German princes who controlled religious matters. As well as organizing the weddings, the Cardinal of Lorraine had also been discussing and thinking about the Eucharist, the most divisive issue between Protestants and Catholics. He had found a creed whose conservative reformism and obeisance to social hierarchy appealed to aristocrats in particular. The cardinal was becoming intrigued by the possibilities of a French compromise based on the Lutheran Confession of Augsburg.

* * * *

Hoc est corpus meum. Rarely in history has the interpretation of so few words led to so much death and destruction. The Eucharist had been divinely instituted as a bond and token of union; it had now become the chief source of discord and strife. What did Christ's words at the Last Supper mean? Was the substance of the bread and wine converted into Christ's body and blood during the miracle of the Mass, or was 'this is my body' to be taken figuratively? Calvin argued that Christ's body was not 'physically' present in a gross sense. The Eucharist was spiritual sustenance in which Christ's presence penetrated the marrow of the true believer. For Calvinists, the Catholic Mass was an abomination, more akin to a pagan sacrifice, with overtones of idolatry and superstition. But to Catholics the Mass was more than a rite: it symbolized the unity of the community; participation was a social obligation in which the power of the body of Christ, 'one bread and one body', united the disparate parts of society into a body social. The Mass did not just give spiritual sustenance; it was vital to social and political order. The Calvinist interpretation of the Eucharist threatened to break the body social apart.

For Catholics religious unity was also essential to personal and collective salvation; it was prized as a manifestation of the Spirit; division was the work of Satan. Erasmus, the greatest irenical figure of Renaissance Europe, argued for reform, reconciliation, and reunion *within* the Catholic tradition. And the French *Moyenneurs'* proposals for reform in the Catholic Church—the suppression of exorcism at baptism, communion in both kinds, the abolition of private Masses and feast days and cults which lacked due reverence and solemnity, the singing of psalms in the vernacular—were largely inspired by Erasmus. However, they wished to leave the Mass largely intact. Even these modest reforms were controversial and they were being overtaken by events, as Protestants at court and conservative Catholics in the country began to assert themselves in the early months of 1561.

An early indication of the growing controversy over the Mass came just before Francis II's death when the English ambassador, Sir Nicolas Throckmorton, caused a scandal by refusing to stand during the Elevation of the Host. Protestants no longer had to show restraint. Throckmorton became a considerable factor in the emergence of a Protestant party at court under Charles IX. Coligny could not hide his satisfaction as Catherine took over the regency 'without using any dissimulation, praising and thanking God' for the fall of the Guise.[15]

He even went to Catherine to offer evidence that would incriminate them and bring them to justice. But Catherine needed the Guise, as they had once needed her: to check the pretensions of the King of Navarre, the first prince of the blood, to the regency. Catherine proved herself to be a shrewd and clever manipulator of men and, though she lacked a power base herself, deftly played off the Guise, the Montmorency, and the Bourbon against each other. Compromise was in the air too. Guise retained the office of Grand Master but rendered the keys to the royal apartments to the Queen Mother in February. The following month Navarre took Guise's title of lieutenant-general of the kingdom, but crucially the royal seals remained in Catherine's hands. Satisfied by his promotion, Navarre no longer had to play to the Calvinist gallery. While at court his ostentatious appearance at Mass and abstinence during fasts were noted. Calvinists noted disapprovingly that, away from his devout wife, the temptations of court life were too great and his behaviour was more befitting a libertine gallant than a member of the godly. As his support for the reformers waxed and waned, leadership of the Protestant movement devolved more and more on Coligny.

Another source of contention at court was more easily dealt with. Hatred of the Cardinal of Lorraine was the one thing that both Catholics and Protestants could agree on. As the Venetian ambassador noted, this had less to do with his policies than his overbearing personality: 'his desire was to appear that he was the person who knew everything and did everything'. In this atmosphere, he feared for his safety and retired to his diocese at Reims, where he would preach and set an example to others by administering to what he termed 'his little flock'. His retirement allowed his brother greater freedom of movement. While the cardinal had little faith in Philip II's commitment to reform of the Church, his brother's thinking was more straightforward: since the family had so few friends it was time to cultivate the Habsburg enemy. Though Philip continued to mistrust the Guise and continued to place more faith in Montmorency, his ambassador, Chantonnay, in competition with Throckmorton, did his best to bring Catholics at court together and form a united front.

In the cardinal's absence it was the Protestant party that gained the upper hand. Under Coligny's protection Protestant preachers held Lenten sermons at court, testing the tacit acceptance of Protestant worship behind closed doors. Catherine continued the religious policy of the previous regime. But the law remained ambiguous and difficult to enforce, and the Protestants determined to test her resolve. Coligny had the backing of Elizabeth I who assured the admiral that he could 'boldly make record of her constancy and determination to advance the work of Almighty God by maintaining the truth of the Gospel'.[16] As the climax to the religious year approached, tensions reached breaking point. On Palm Sunday, Coligny opened the doors to his apartments, permitting anyone to hear the service, which was attended by Condé and 500 supporters. Chantonnay was scandalized. But it was the news that the Queen Mother and her young son had heard the sermon that brought matters to a head—Protestants hoped and Catholics feared that the king of France was about to convert.

The counterpart of Calvinist self-confidence was Catholic resignation. Defeatism and opportunism swept through the ruling elites. Among the educated, in particular, there was little stomach for a fight and Protestantism was in fashion. But just when the elites seemed ready to give in to the Protestant tide, a vigorous and popular Catholic reaction occurred. Since their rulers seemed unable or unwilling to defend the cause, the people themselves would have to take responsibility. Violent riots—virtual pogroms—erupted in Provence, Angers, Pontoise, Le Mans, Toulouse, Lyon, and Beauvais in the spring and early summer of 1561. Clustered around the chief moments of the Church calendar, they targeted those who failed to take Easter communion or failed to pay due reverence to the elevation of the Holy Sacrament in processions. These incidents were not entirely spontaneous. Especially noteworthy was the role in the violence played by new confraternities that were springing up all over France. They were very different organizations from the traditional boozy social clubs associated with the guilds. The new brotherhoods were characterized by their piety and by their devotion to the Holy Sacrament, an institutional rebuttal of the heretics' denial of the Real Presence. Cutting across traditional trade and class boundaries, they called for a militant and united response to heresy. By publicly parading and venerating the sacred Host and proclaiming the miracle of the Mass, they would confront Protestants openly and directly. The confreres were inspired and motivated by doom-mongering preachers whose sermons the people now flocked to hear. And Catholic printers showed that Protestantism was not the only religion of the book: in the years before 1562 there were as many as 70,000 copies of anti-Protestant sermons, libels, and tracts circulating in France. Dominican and Franciscan preachers did not confine their vitriol to heretics; they denounced the Erasmians as fellow travellers of heretics.

The Crown made desperate attempts to halt the cycle of sectarian violence. Insults, such as 'Huguenot' and 'Papist', were made a punishable offence. But it could do little to stem the torrent of abuse that streamed from the pulpit. The printed sermons of one of the most notorious preachers, Artus Desiré, reveal 'the narrowness of his intellectual range and the lengths he was willing to go to achieve his violent ends'.[17] Desiré's sermons were a call to arms in order to preempt God's wrath: 'when the [Holy Sacrament] is put down and Mass no longer said in the world, when the dissolute prevent the sacrifice, God will come to judgement and the world will come to an end'. And the preachers were not afraid to call their betters to account. Desiré was arrested in April on his way to Spain to exhort Philip II to intervene in France. As the Protestants at court gathered for Communion on Palm Sunday, a Paris preacher identified the enemy: 'It is this [House] of Coligny that is against you and will ruin you.'[18]

Paris's resolute ultra-Catholicism was in contrast to the liberal atmosphere at Fontainebleau. It was the Constable Montmorency who made the first break with the consensus at court. He and his wife were deeply conservative and he now had to choose between his faith and his beloved nephews. He told Coligny he wanted unity and could not tolerate a repeat of the Palm Sunday events. But it was not just the Protestants that led the constable to revolt. Jean de Monluc had become the Queen Mother's favourite preacher at court, and the constable no longer wished to hear sermons that criticized the Church and denounced deeply cherished practices, such as the cult of images and the invocation of the saints. Easter Sunday, 6 April 1561, was a day of mounting drama. It began when the constable and the Duke of Guise heard that Monluc was to preach the Easter Sunday sermon. The old enemies met and agreed not to attend. Next, Guise went to Catherine de Medici, who was out walking in the gardens, and told her that she must stop 'drinking from two fountains'. The two former enemies followed by a host of other Catholic grandees then descended into the servants' quarters to hear an obscure friar. Quite deliberately they shunned the intellectual and elitist *Moyenneurs* and joined the humble people. Cardinal Tournon stood godfather to the reconciliation, which Protestants denounced as the 'Triumvirate', a conspiracy against the state. Guise and Montmorency received Holy Communion from the cardinal's own hands after exchanging the kiss of peace. Montmorency left court the next day followed by the duke twenty-four hours later—Catherine was left isolated. Since Guise now had new Catholic friends, he publicly repudiated some of his Protestant ones. He summarily broke off the engagement of his daughter to the Duke of Longueville, citing the latter's refusal to attend Mass and snapping that he would 'rather marry his daughter to a poor gentleman than to the duke'.

After Easter, public order began to break down and the prospect of civil war loomed once more. Nowhere was the breakdown more in evidence than the capital. At the end of April, 2,000 Catholics in Paris attacked a Protestant meeting house on the outskirts of the city which was stoutly defended by its occupants and several of the assailants were killed. Catherine came under intense pressure from both sides. On 11 May the Parlement of Paris issued a stern remonstrance against the policy of tacit toleration, arguing that the only way to stop sedition 'was to cut the root, which is religious division'.

* * * *

In the summer of 1561, the moderate Flemish theologian, George Cassander wrote that there were three parties in France: 'the Papists' led by the Cardinal of Tournon, the Huguenots led by Coligny, and another party called the Third or Middle Party, which consisted of the Queen Mother, Chancellor l'Hôpital, Monluc, the King of Navarre, and the Cardinal of Lorraine. Historians invariably disagree with this. To them, the Guise, as chief architects of Catholic reaction, must belong to the 'Papist' party. But this was not so: in the years immediately preceding the outbreak of civil war in 1562, politics was in a state of flux and uncertainty. We should avoid the temptation to interpret the events of 1561 through the prism of later events. For there is good reason to believe that François, Duke of Guise, too, was behind his brother's efforts to find a middle way in the summer and autumn of 1561. All too often the story of France's troubles concentrates exclusively on the clash between two opposing religious parties to the detriment of those who were yet undecided, or caught in the middle. It would be the split in the Middle Party and the falling away of the middle ground that led France to fall into the abyss.

In the mounting chaos after Easter, Catherine once more turned to the Guise. As late as May, Cardinal Charles remained exiled from court because of the animosity towards him, and he was now joined by his brother. And yet only a month later the Guise were back at the centre of power and the English Ambassador Throckmorton was singing the Duke of Guise's praises. The Triumvirate was forgotten: 'The like hope there is by some good arguments [Guise] will become an earnest Protestant.'[19] Had even the English ambassador, whose despatches had hitherto rarely arrived in London without containing some diatribe against the Guise brothers, been duped by François's famous courtesy and affability? Protestant historians have always thought so: the Guise were laying smokescreens while they secretly directed the Triumvirate conspiracy. But there is not a shred of evidence that a cunning plot was being masterminded. Although the Protestants wished it otherwise, the Triumvirate remained only a loose agreement to drop old antagonisms during the current crisis. Throckmorton may have been naïve but he was no fool. In order to understand what was really going on in the summer of 1561 we need to lay aside confessional bias, and to consider what solutions to the crisis were on offer.

Initially, it was the fear of a breakdown of order in Paris that led to the duke's recall. Catherine feared that the processing of the Host at Corpus Christi would lead to riots, and so just two days before the feast she hastily ordered the duke to come and maintain the peace. As he passed through the city dressed in his favourite crimson, he was welcomed as a saviour:

> The press of people filling the streets was such a crowd that it took him an hour to reach the King's lodgings, and the joyous clamour of the voice of the people applauded his arrival, demonstrating the confidence and assurance they had in him.

The queen not only noticed that the duke was popular and able to maintain order in a way that the commander of the army, Navarre, had been unable to do, she saw that the duke's retinue of 400 men was twice as large as Navarre's. But Guise did not consider exploiting his popularity with the Catholic mob for political ends. As a prince, the only constituency he wished to appeal to were his peers. The duke ignored appeals from Rome and Madrid and pledged his support to his brother and the Middle Party, joining his brother in a dialogue with Lutherans and 'Anglicans' (a term which was coined at this time in France to denote the Church of England, although its use in English is not recorded until 1635). Guise wrote of his hopes that a National Council would solve religious divisions and start a 'good Reformation'.[20] Calvinists denounced his letters as a ploy to split the reform movement. True, the Elector Palatine was sceptical and the Landgrave of Hesse cautious. But the Duke of Württemberg was convinced, because Guise spoke with frankness. He had, he wrote, no intention of 'embracing any religion, other than that which he had been brought up in', but he then went on to condemn the 'blindness and idolatry' into which the Catholic Church had sunk; he looked back not to Catholic tradition but to the scriptures as the basis for concord. Württemberg had greater reason than his fellow Lutherans to trust the duke. He was an old friend and had served under him in Italy. Having been raised at the French court, he was a product of the same evangelical milieu as Anne Boleyn and the Cardinal of Lorraine, whose interest in the Confession of Augsburg was in the French evangelical tradition of working with Lutherans. The conservative princes, German or French, shared more in common with each other than with the plebian ultra-Catholics and Calvinists confronting each other in the streets. Soon envoys were shuttling between Joinville and Stuttgart; Württemberg, cautioning his friend against coercion, sent him a copy of the Augsburg Confession.

Antoine de Navarre was also reading the Augsburg Confession. Historians, echoing Calvinist despair, have been unimpressed at his 'vacillation' and 'weak will'. On the contrary, Navarre's reverence for both the Mass and the cause of the Gospels is indicative of growing conviction. Lutherans' reverence for a truncated version of the Mass seemed to offer the best hope of compromise; its conservative reformism the best antidote to the growing political disorder. Navarre's reconciliation with the Guise was more than opportunism; it was built on a realization that they shared similar beliefs. Crucially, the Duke of Guise would be able to rely on Navarre's support in the dark days after Wassy.

The renewed impetus behind the search for a *via media* was partly due to the decision made to return Mary Stuart to Scotland. Her faith was also inspired by Erasmus and she agreed with her uncle Charles on the need to make a deal with the Protestants, rebuffing a delegation of Scots Catholics. While she could not embrace Protestantism she promised to respect it, as long as she was free to have a private chapel. Following these successful negotiations she and her uncle returned to court on 10 June. The revival of Guise fortunes in Scotland would require the support of England and the family now moved to repair its relations with Elizabeth. As soon as the cardinal returned to court, he had an interview with Throckmorton at which the issue of Church reform was raised. When an ultra-Catholic pamphlet was published in Lyon denouncing Elizabeth I as a bastard and her mother, Anne Boleyn, as Jezebel, Throckmorton was grateful to the

Guise for their attempts to suppress it and arrest the culprit. Throckmorton's *rapprochement* with the Guise suggests that he had seen the memorandum, drawn up at the behest of the cardinal, principally with the Lutherans in mind. It outlined the major points of controversy that needed to be resolved, including the issue of the Real Presence.

Throckmorton reciprocated these overtures: he told his masters that all the French Catholics he met were for some sort of Reformation; all that each man desired was 'to make his bargain as honourably and profitably as he can', and of how they looked with envy across the Channel at the way order had been maintained. They feared the Calvinists because they were Levellers, who wished 'to pluck down an old building which consists of good and bad stuff'. With the Guise apparently leaning towards the Confession of Augsburg, Throckmorton sent off hurried appeals for a French or Latin translation of the English Prayer Book; he told William Cecil that an explanation of the English *via media* was urgent: 'a modestie in the Apologie will commende it greatlye, and to avoyde as may be to irritate anye partie'.[21]

What the Guise were offering was not toleration—an idea abhorrent to the vast majority of Europeans. The word toleration lacked the positive connotations it has today. In the sixteenth century it meant putting up with something one did not like. They could not countenance liberty of worship and wished above all to preserve the unity of the Church, the foundation of social order. Their proposal was to make a pragmatic distinction between public worship and private conscience. This was very different from the violent solution demanded by the preachers in the towns and the Spanish ambassador at court, a solution which the confraternities devoted to the Holy Sacrament were already fighting for. Lorraine's proposal was a Gallican version of the *via media* that was being tried in England and that would later come to pass in the Dutch Republic. It reconciled social order with a limited degree of liberty of conscience.

While his brother kept the peace in Paris, Cardinal Charles made a triumphant return to the Privy Council. The enforced sabbatical spent in his diocese, devoted to preaching, pastoral care, and spiritual reading, was one of the happiest periods of his life, one in which he had felt a sense of freedom he had rarely known before. His depression of the previous winter had lifted and he returned to politics with renewed vigour and energy. He talked excitedly about the necessity of returning to the practices of the primitive Church as a preliminary step to healing division. The breakdown of order he argued was due to the fact that the law was ambiguous and each side interpreted it as it saw fit. What was required was both an 'inviolable law', which was clear to everyone and which would maintain peace in preparation for the summoning of a National Council of the Church, which Catherine had announced on June 12. The Calvinists too stepped up the pressure for an unambiguous law: the day before they had presented a request for liberty of worship. From 23 June to 17 July 150 grandees and magistrates debated the two proposals. The cardinal's persuasive eloquence was much in evidence. He 'listened to almost every hour [of the debates] and his interventions were accorded much attention and admiration, even from his enemies'.[22] The Duke of Guise was frank; if toleration was accorded 'he would not keep his sword sheathed forever'.[23] But the Guise proposals were also heavily opposed, and not only by Protestants. Chancellor l'Hôpital, now convinced of the need to accommodate the Protestants, clashed with his former patrons and argued eloquently that attempts to outlaw Protestant worship were absurd and unworkable. Cardinal Tournon, whom Pius IV referred to as the only good Catholic in France, opposed the summoning of a National Council, calling it 'the greatest evil that had ever been pursued in France'. Senile and in fragile health, he lacked the charisma of his opponents and the Guise proposals were accepted by a majority of Catholics present. The resulting edict of July outlawed Protestant worship. At the same time, it ended corporal punishment for heresy and 'prohibited all men to investigate what is going on in the house of his neighbour'.[24] 'Unity with reform': the pragmatists had triumphed over the dogmatists. Guise statecraft owed more to Elizabeth I than to Philip II.

It was now that Catherine dropped her bombshell. On 25 July, less than a week before the French clergy were due to meet at Poissy, where they had been detached from the other delegates of the Estates-General because Pontoise was too small, Catherine made it clear that the assembly was not to be one of prelates alone; 'subjects' who desired to be heard were welcome too. When it became known that safe conducts were to be issued to Protestants there was an outcry. Pius IV demanded that heretics be met with 'fire and sword', and he despatched the Cardinal of Ferrara and Lainez, the General of the Jesuits, to France; their aim to oppose the Cardinal of Lorraine, whose eagerness to debate on the issue of the Real Presence was well known. Dialogue with the Protestants was all the more important since the Guise now had a Protestant kingdom to rule. Mary

Stuart embodied their commitment to upholding the distinction between public conformity and private belief. Hope abounded that the Auld Alliance was being renewed and revived, as one of her supporters put it, 'as it has been between their predecessors, by most ancient band and league, inviolably in all times past'. On the day that the National Council was announced she left Paris, accompanied by five of her uncles, heading for the cardinal's great Benedictine abbey at Fécamp on the Channel coast. From here she set sail for Scotland. She would never see her uncles or France again.

* * * *

Perched on a bluff which nestles in a loop in the Seine, the royal château of Saint-Germain-en-Laye has extensive views to Paris fourteen miles to the east. Three miles to the north, the river, which has come round a loop flung several miles to the east, is met and spanned at Poissy by one of the finest of French medieval bridges. Convalescing after an illness, the Cardinal of Lorraine arrived at the great Dominican convent there in a litter on 29 July. He was among forty-six bishops and archbishops, including six cardinals, who convened to debate a panoply of ecclesiastical matters, of which the meeting with the Protestants—the Colloquy of Poissy—was only a subsidiary event. Even so, more than half the complement of French bishops did not attend. For the Doctors of the Sorbonne, Chantonnay, the Pope, and perhaps a majority of the French bishops, the mere presence of the Huguenots was in itself an abominable scandal, but that they should be allowed to detail their heretical opinions in front of the young king was outrageous. The General of the Jesuits summed up the ultra-Catholic sentiments when he referred to the Calvinist delegation as consisting of 'wolves, foxes, serpents, [and] assassins'.

The captain of the Genevan delegation was Calvin's second-in-command, Théodore Beza. Six years older than Cardinal Charles, he shared the same humanist background—he was a fine Latin poet and professor of Greek—as well as the refinement, good looks, and aristocratic background of his enemy. Beza arrived at Saint-Germain-en-Laye on 23 August, where he was assured that a formidable array of support awaited him: a crack team of a dozen Calvinist ministers and theologians provided theological expertise and sixteen laymen, most of them nobles, provided moral support. Catholics complained that the Protestant delegation was better received at court than 'would have been the Pope'.[25]

On the day after his arrival Beza was called into the chambers of the King of Navarre, where he found not only Antoine, but Catherine herself, Condé, and the cardinals of Bourbon and Lorraine. The meeting between Beza and Lorraine must rank as one of the most extraordinary of the Reformation age. There was a moment of tension as they confronted each other for the first time. Lorraine started icily: 'Hitherto you have been known to me only through your books, which in your absence abroad have occasioned the greatest disturbances in France. Now that you are here in person, I trust you will show a spirit of peace and goodwill and lend us your aid in suppressing these disturbances.'[26] Beza denied that he had written the *Tigre* and replied modestly that he was too unimportant a person to possess the wide influence with which the cardinal credited him; moreover he had always condemned violence. Lorraine then steered the conversation onto the terrain on which he wished to fight: the Real Presence. Had not, he asked, Beza written that 'Christ is no more in the Eucharist than in the mud'—words offensive to the queen and rest of the company present. Beza dismissed the notion as 'absurd and full of blasphemy' and went on to advance the Calvinist interpretation. The cardinal then made an oblique reference to the Lutheran interpretation. At the first mention of Lutheranism Beza was on the alert. Calvin had warned him that at all costs the cardinal must not be able to make capital out of Lutheran-Calvinist dissensions and drive a wedge into the reformed edifice. But this was not the cardinal's principal intention: with a mixture of arrogance and *folie de grandeur* he believed that he could save the whole of Christendom if agreement on the Real Presence was found. 'Do you confess then that we communicate truly and substantially the body and blood of Jesus Christ?' The cardinal was taken aback when Beza answered in the affirmative that he did so 'spiritually and by faith'. The cardinal did not pursue this important qualification but replied positively: 'This also I do believe.' On parting both men embraced and the cardinal in particular was heartened by the meeting. 'You will find that I am not as black as they make me out to be.'

It was a distinguished company that on Tuesday 9 September 1561 made the short journey to the convent at Poissy. The twenty-two Huguenot ministers and lay deputies were ushered into the great refectory by the Duke of Guise, fulfilling the office of Grand Master. They were placed behind a barrier erected at one end (Plate 16), where they were expected to stand throughout. Charles IX was already in place at the other end of the hall, surrounded by his mother, the princes of the blood, and other courtiers, among them the cardinal's protégés Ramus and Ronsard. Chancellor l'Hôpital started the proceedings, addressing the bishops seated behind Lorraine, urging them to listen to the Huguenots with charity in the general interests of peace and harmony. Then Beza rose to deliver the first full-length oration of the Colloquy. It was important because it would set the tone for the course of the whole assembly. It was a polished and refined performance. Beza set out to woo the royal family, pledging himself to concord and sounding an ecumenical note. He avoided the complexities of the doctrine of predestination and accentuated, without exaggerating, the not inconsiderable common elements that united the two confessions. He then spelled out the orthodox Calvinist position on the Eucharist, stressing several times that the Calvinists believed in the Real Presence. It was at this point that he made an immense tactical blunder. He affirmed that the reformed doctrine did not render Christ absent from the Eucharist, but added that this was not a corporeal presence: 'We say that His body is as far removed from the bread and wine as is heaven from earth.'[27] This was too much for the prelates sitting opposite who had hitherto listened in polite silence. Cries of 'Blasphemavit!' were followed by murmuring and hissing as some of the prelates made as if to walk out. Even Coligny covered his face with his hands. Cardinal Tournon, trembling with wrath, stood up and asked how Catherine could permit 'to hear these horrible blasphemies, in the presence of the King'. Beza tried to explain his analogy, noting that the glorified body of Christ can now only be in heaven and not elsewhere, but the damage had been done. Catherine had found the blunder offensive too. She assured Tournon, who was by now in tears, that she and her son would live and die in the Catholic faith.

The morning after Beza's speech Lorraine was elected as the unanimous choice of the bishops to reply—Beza's horrible blasphemies must not be permitted to pass unchallenged. The commuters from Saint-Germain took their seats again on 16 September. As an orator he was Beza's superior, choosing to fight the Protestants on their own ground—scripture—and eschewing the impenetrable scholastic terminology favoured by the doctors of the Sorbonne. The longest part of his one-and-a-half-hour speech consisted of an exposition of the Real Presence in the Eucharist. He regretted most that what had been given as a 'bond of union and peace' had become a bone of contention. By concentrating on the Real Presence he was able to show the substantial agreement between Greek Orthodox, Catholic, and

Lutheran confessions and isolate the Calvinists. Reactions to the oration did not divide, as one might expect, the audience on confessional lines. His defence of orthodoxy naturally got him golden opinions from his Catholic hearers. But others noted the rapprochement with Lutheranism: Condé was impressed and so too Hubert Languet, representing the Elector of Saxony. Beza saw the danger and poured scorn on it: 'Never in all my life', he wrote to Calvin, 'have I heard a greater display of ineptitude and imbecility.' What the Calvinists most feared was that the cardinal's speech opened up the possibility of reaching an agreement with the Lutherans.

Lorraine's commitment to the Colloquy's continuation in the face of Catholics who wished to call a halt to the proceedings swelled the ranks of his enemies. In order to reduce tensions, the second part of the Colloquy between two teams of twelve theologians took place in private and would focus upon trying to find a compromise on the Lord's Supper. Interest in Lutheranism was not restricted to Lorraine. The court, in particular, was humming with talk of the Confession of Augsburg. The political axis on which it was based was the revival of the Guise-Bourbon friendship of old, which had been formally sealed by the public reconciliation of the Duke of Guise and Condé on 24 August. Antoine de Navarre's suggestion that the invitations to the Colloquy be extended to the German Lutheran princes was warmly approved. They arrived too late, however, to save it from the disaster that was about to occur.

After more fruitless debate, on 24 September Lorraine tried to cut the Gordian knot by stating that the time had come for an agreement, failing which the conference could not continue. He produced the Confession of Augbsurg and demanded that Beza sign it as a condition of continuance. Historians of a Protestant bent accused Lorraine of a ploy to publicize the Calvinist-Lutheran schism, and to play one confession off against another. In actual fact, his sole purpose was to get Beza to admit the Real Presence without having to submit completely to Catholic terms. Calvin had warned his team about precisely this sort of eventuality and Beza was prepared. He responded by asking if Lorraine would volunteer to subscribe first. The atmosphere between Beza and Lorraine was becoming increasingly acrimonious. Beza retorted, 'since you yourself do not want to subscribe to the confession, it is unreasonable to ask that we subscribe to it'.[28]

The cardinal has borne a large share of the onus for the failure of the Colloquy. Certainly, his ultimatum destroyed the last chances of maintaining a dialogue on the principle of persuasion. But to further argue that his injection of Lutheranism was a masterstroke of deceit is based on ignorance of what he was trying to achieve. Protestants viewed the compromise as a trick, as part of a wider conspiracy to divide and destroy them, a stratagem that led inevitably to the Massacre of Wassy. But all the evidence points in another direction. There was nothing conspiratorial about Lorraine's desire to defeat heresy, and he was no Lutheran. What he sincerely believed was that the Lutheran position on the Real Presence was the first step in building a Gallican variant of Catholicism. At first he thought that the Calvinists might be persuaded; if only he could get the Calvinists to accept the Lutheran Confession of Augsburg he would eventually convert them to his position. He now realized that agreement with the ministers was impossible: 'They don't want to hear; but to be heard.'[29] After Poissy he turned his back on them forever. But he had also cut his ties with the ultra-Catholics and, though it seemed to matter little at the time, he had no faith in the Council of Trent. For him the Gallican Middle Way remained the only option.

Turning his back on Geneva and Rome meant stepping up the dialogue with the Anglicans and Lutherans. In doing so he ran the risk of becoming dangerously isolated. Catherine was disappointed in him as he had promised her victory, and she now looked elsewhere for counsel. She was now considering a new and more controversial solution: toleration. He was caught between her and her Protestant allies on the one hand and the ultra-Catholics on the other. His liberalism had offended his own bishops and laymen like the Constable of Montmorency, who had, as long ago as 1532, denounced communion in both kinds. The cardinal's relationship with the papal legate, Ferrara, broke down altogether and the two men (much to the glee of the Spanish ambassador) became 'declared enemies'. Lainez, the General of the Jesuits, launched a furious attack on the Colloquy and on conferences of any kind with heretics. Ultra-Catholics agreed with the Calvinists that one could not compromise with Error, that the Truth could not be pared and pruned to fit political circumstance. Time was running out for the cardinal's compromise.

* * * *

Lorraine was morose and depressed in defeat. There is some evidence to suggest that the failure of the Colloquy placed great strains on the rest of the Guise family too, as hard-line counsellors opposed continuing the moderate policy. Some of these men went as far as to hatch a plot to seize the king's younger brother and heir to the throne, Henri, though nothing came of it. As usual, internal divisions were kept behind closed doors. Though it was decided they could no longer remain at court, there was to be no change in policy. The Duke of Guise departed on good terms with Navarre and Catherine; his retreat from court was not a declaration of war but a realization that his influence was ebbing and that Catherine had no intention of enforcing the edict of July. He would, as he had done in May, await the inevitable recall. The barometer of his intentions as he departed on 19 October was his relationship not with the Triumvirate but the Protestant loyalists. The presence of the Protestant Duke of Long-ueville in his retinue, his rehabilitation, and return to the family fold suggests that Guise was still behind his brother's compromise.

The situation the brothers found on their return home to Joinville was far worse than they expected. At Wassy, heresy had reached the gates of the Guise domain. Across France the Protestant Reformation gathered pace and strength: churches were seized, cleansed of their Popish trappings, and friars and priests threatened or run out of town. In some southern towns, such as Montpellier, Catholic worship ceased altogether. In Gascony the cause of the Gospels was sharpened by grievances against landlords; guerrilla attacks on the nobility and the refusal to pay the tithe culminated in the savage murder of the Catholic Baron de Fumel by an army of 2,000 commoners, who stormed his château on 23 November 1561. All across the south-west, local Catholic leagues had sprung up to defend the Mass and churches against the iconoclastic tide. In Paris, the Catholic preachers accused the Crown openly of complicity, and sectarian violence reached a new pitch of intensity as winter approached. On 27 December Saint-Médard was once more the scene of serious rioting. Though he was concerned about events in Dauphiné where the situation was critical, Guise rebuffed Spanish requests to lead the Catholic faction at court. He spent his time hunting and visiting friends—this was the first holiday he had had in many years. Amicable relations with Catherine were maintained via a weekly correspondence.

Meanwhile, the cardinal returned to his diocese, where he preached sermons whose Lutheran tone—an attempt to stem the tide of apostasy—were widely noted. Rumours of his admiration for the Book of Common Prayer even reached Scotland, where Scottish Catholics were roused to indignation over his flirtation with Anglicanism. A direct correspondence was opened with Elizabeth I who now wished 'to gratify the duke and the rest of the House of Guise'.[30] But it was their old friend, the Duke of Württemberg, who offered the best hope. He agreed to meet them at Saverne, halfway between Joinville and Stuttgart. So sensitive was this meeting that Rome had to be deceived about its true intent. On the morning of the 16 February 1562 the cardinal preached on Justification by Faith, a message which went down well with the Lutherans among the audience of 200. In the afternoon, the two dukes met to discuss the political and religious situation in France. Württemberg's record of this interview provides our best guide to Guise's state of mind in the weeks before Wassy. He admitted that, as a soldier since his youth, he was ignorant of religious matters, but as he began to talk he revealed evangelical inclinations close to his brother: 'I know that I cannot be saved by my good works, but only by the merits of Jesus Christ.'³¹ What Guise craved above all else was unity over the Eucharist, for without it 'everything was false'. Württemberg was certain that Guise was being frank and he pressed him hard on his responsibility for the execution of heretics, prophetically warning him to beware of spilling innocent blood. Guise's conscience was so troubled by this conversation that he could not sleep that night.

The next day the cardinal preached against the cult of the saints and later Württemberg and his theologian, Brentius, sat down with four of the Guise brothers: the duke, the Cardinal of Lorraine, the Cardinal of Guise, and the Grand Prior. It was almost as if Lorraine was trying to convert his other three brothers. And it was now that he made the big leap: since there could be no hope from the Calvinists or the Council of Trent, he put his faith in changes both in the liturgy of the Mass and in the ecclesiastical hierarchy—if he had to wear a black robe instead of his red one, then so be it. He said that he approved entirely of the Confession of Augsburg. Then, on their word of honour and on their souls, the Guise promised not to persecute the partisans of the 'new doctrine'. The meeting of Saverne was not a Guise deception to neutralize the German princes in preparation for the coming civil war, for there was no question of their conversion to Lutheranism. Instead, they foresaw the eventual conversion of the Lutherans. The success of the policy depended entirely on their ability to show good faith. The new order would last only weeks; it was smothered in its infancy at Wassy. Guise had promised restraint and, even if we accept his protestations of provocation, he could not deliver. He had committed the worst evil a knight could do: he had broken his word of honour. It was something that later tormented him on his deathbed.

Wassy changed France forever but it did not change Guise policy. News of the Edict of Toleration had come at the end of February—they had long opposed it and their opposition was inevitable. Yet it was not the ultra-Catholics who summoned them to Paris. Catherine would hardly have summoned them if she feared a plot. Lorraine had nothing to hide; he wrote to her without 'flattery' that toleration would 'set up the Ministers of Antichrist . . . who are against God and the King'.[32] But he had not given up hope that she would still listen to the Guise solution; his brother would come with news of the meeting at Saverne. Antoine de Navarre, now the leader of the crypto-Lutherans at court, urged the duke to Paris to come to his aid. When Condé raised his standard in defence of the Edict of Toleration on 2 April 1562 France stood on the brink of civil war. Even so, desperate attempts to find a peaceful solution to the crisis continued. Catherine thought she had reached an agreement in the summer. The Guise, joined by the King of Navarre, maintained their search for doctrinal compromise and embassies to Germany continued for the rest of the year. Finally, in the summer, delayed by his appointment to head the financing of the royal cause, the cardinal produced a Gallican confession. So explosive were its contents that it was top secret and would later be systematically suppressed. It has only recently been discovered.[33] Lorraine proposed that the Mass be cleansed of its sacrificial elements and spoken in the vernacular, that communion be taken in both kinds, that idolatrous images be removed from churches, and that priests preach the Gospels daily. The proposals were broadly in the line with the Lutheran Confession and were the culmination of more than a year's study of the Augsburg Confession and discussion with Lutheran theologians. But the summer peace talks stalled: France was about to enter a thirty-six year civil war. The cardinal's proposal for an inter-confessional colloquy between Catholics, Anglicans, and Lutherans was impractical. Wassy had been a huge propaganda coup for the Calvinists and the Guise were no longer trusted in England and Germany. The Cardinal's compromise was in ruins; his struggle to include the Protestants in a General Council had failed. The only possible way left forward for a reformer like himself was to go to Trent and triumph over the Papal party.

* * * *

Plate 17 shows an enamel, a fashionable and expensive medium, by Léonard Limousin, which was commissioned to represent the Guise triumph over heresy. Art historians have conventionally viewed the composition as representing the historic mission of the House of

Guise as the scourge of heretics. Antoinette de Bourbon, with a cross surmounted by a victory wreath in her right hand, raises the chalice and Host, symbols of Christ's body and blood, for all to see, while her triumphal golden chariot, drawn by doves of peace, crushes the bodies of heretics, ancient and modern. To the left is her eldest son Duke François, guiding the chariot. In the centre stands her deceased husband Claude, with her fourth son, Louis, Cardinal of Guise. To the right is Cardinal Charles, bending down to offer his parents and brothers a copy of his reply to Beza at Poissy.

The central theme of the unity of two generations of the Guise in defence of the Real Presence is clear from the prominence accorded to Duke Claude, who had been dead for a decade at the time of composition—his spirit enduring as paterfamilias and moral compass of the family. Nevertheless, the enamel was for private viewing and there are clues to suggest that it may have meant different things to each member of the family, revealing the subtle tensions between them. The presence of the Cardinal of Lorraine's climbing ivy badge and his device, *Te Stante Virebo*, suggests that it was his commission, and that he ordered it the year between the end of the Colloquy of Poissy in 1561 and his departure for Trent in September 1562. A date coterminous with the Saverne interview is possible. A further clue to its date is the motley crew of heretics it depicts. There are several medieval sectaries, the Anabaptists, as well as Hus, Calvin, and Beza. But there is one notable absentee: Martin Luther. For the enamel defends not only the Real Presence but also the cardinal's compromise with Lutherans. Some family members, Antoinette in particular, were no doubt uncomfortable with the policy, and the enamel thus provided a comforting idealization of family unity. It could be interpreted both as a statement of rapprochement and as a reaffirmation of the family's commitment to the war on heresy. It is further proof that before he left for Trent, Lorraine believed that the true allies of the Gallican reformers were Lutherans rather than the Pope.

When he left Paris on 19 September 1562, at the head of more than sixty bishops and over a dozen doctors, there were widespread fears among the Italians and Spaniards that Trent's conservative direction would be diluted by so many heterodox Frenchmen. And they were right to be alarmed. Not only did Lorraine travel with his putative Gallican confession, he was also ordered to address a long list of clerical abuses and explosive issues such as clerical marriage. Lorraine's arrival at Trent provoked panic among the Pope and his entourage. This was the man who had talked to heretics! Some of the Pope's counsellors urged him to punish him and in doing so 'reduce this proud House [of Guise], the cause of so much evil'.[34] He quickly emerged at Trent as the leader of the opposition to the Papal party. Throughout November and December Lorraine took the fight to the dogmatists, arguing that the priority must be a reform of morals, which would bring heretics back into the fold, and not the establishment of Roman Catholic orthodoxy. He had not yet given up the hope that the Lutherans and Anglicans would be able to participate in the Council. The Spanish, in particular, poured scorn on his crypto-Lutheranism. The Council had reached an impasse; he could not even get the Spanish to agree on episcopal residence. By Christmas, exasperated by the sterility of the proceedings, he was desperate to return home to France, where the first civil war had reached a critical phase. In the New Year he denounced Rome as the source of all woe and he vainly explored the possibility of transferring the Council to Germany, farther from the influence of Rome and Madrid.

And then over the summer of 1563 relations with Pius IV thawed. As he wrote to the Bishop of Rennes, the Pope's letters were now 'full of honest and gracious words, of demonstrations of friendship'.[35] He was summoned to Rome at the end of September for a personal audience and lodged in the pontifical palace in apartments adjoining the Pope's. His gradual conversion to the Tridentine project was not due to Pius's flattery and bribery—though the offer to make cardinals of Lorraine's choosing was no doubt welcome. Lorraine put it down to the Pope's 'great desire to see a good reformation done'. The journey was made easier as a consequence of a genuine spiritual conversion. Had this been solely the result of his visit to Rome, sceptics would be right in claiming him to be perhaps the first person converted by a city that was a byword for corruption and vice—it usually had the opposite effect on visitors. In fact, his conversion had a long gestation: the journey from Gallican to Roman Catholicism was helped by his affinity for Italian culture. His long sojourn in Italy had put him in touch with the dynamism of the Catholic revival in southern Europe, introducing him to a spirituality that confronted him with the narrowness of the north European evangelical tradition and its fixation with scripture. He came into contact with once worldly prelates like Cardinal Farnese, who had undergone a similar conversion experience, recalling their meeting in Rome when 'he was able to open his soul [to Farnese] better than in letters or other means'.[36] During his stay he would have observed the shoots of the

Catholic revival in Rome too. As a music connoisseur he was surely intrigued by the novel ways in which the Oratory, founded by Filippo Neri in the 1550s, used the power of music to inspire devotion in the laity, a form which later became known as the oratorio. More importantly, his conversion was politically motivated; he was isolated and weak. One of the liberal French bishops captured Lorraine's utter sense of isolation: 'how the poor lord is treated by all sides. The Huguenots take him for their greatest enemy, and he will be no less odious to the Pope if he continues to speak of Reformation.'[37] Reconciliation with Rome was the only way to escape his sense of isolation, to break the impasse and salvage something from the wreckage of his reform ideals. Abandoning the Gallican third way was a price worth paying for maintaining Catholic unity and achieving serious reform of the Church Universal.

His role in the making of the Council of Trent, which remained the basis for Catholic dogma until the middle of the nineteenth century, turned Lorraine from a model Gallican into defender of *Roman* Catholicism. It was a turning point in the story of the Guise family and in the history of France: his championing of *Roman* Catholicism placed him and his family on a collision course with the monarchy. But the need to break out of the isolation into which he had led his family and forge new alliances was imperative; on 8 March 1563 he received the news that his brother had been shot and killed by a Huguenot assassin. The fortunes of the family had changed forever.

7

BLOODFEUD

Shortly after daybreak on the 19 December 1562, scouts in the royalist army, which was drawn up in line of battle just south of the town of Dreux, between the villages of Nuisement and Le Lucate, reported hearing the drums of the Protestant army as it approached the village of Imberdais two miles to the south. A brief council was held by the three royalist commanders. They were men long used to campaigning together, though not always happily so. As Constable of France, Anne de Montmorency was the senior commander. Second-in-command was Marshal Saint-André, like his comrades, a former favourite of Henry II and a founding member of the Triumvirate. Also present was the Duke of Guise, though he had no formal rank beyond command of a 200-strong gendarmerie company and an equal number of gentlemen volunteers—an indication of his huge popularity among the nobility. Together the Triumvirs resolved to force the enemy to give battle and, leaving its baggage at Nuisement, the royal army advanced about three-quarters of a mile further south to a position between the villages of Epinay and Blainville.

The royalist battle line extended across a front of slightly more than a mile. The 20,000-strong army was particularly well provided with infantry, but had only 3,000 horse. In order to minimize its inferiority in this arm, a strong defensive position was adopted and the cavalry interspersed with the foot. The right flank, anchored on Epinay, was nominally under the command of Saint-André; it comprised first the Spanish infantry, then Guise with his gendarmes and volunteers, followed by a block of veteran French infantry, then came Saint-André himself with more heavy cavalry, a regiment of German landsknecht infantry and gendarmerie units under Guise's brother, Aumale and the constable's second son, Henri de Montmorency,

Duke of Damville. The centre of the royalist position was occupied by the largest unit on the field, a phalanx of Swiss pikemen, whose reputation as crack troops was expected to inspire the regiments from Picardy and Brittany, which were designated by the grandiose title of legions, though in reality they were composed largely of half-trained peasants. Their flank was protected by the dragoons under Sansac and the rest of the gendarmerie stationed in front of the village of Blainville, which were commanded by Montmorency in person.

The Protestants, led by Coligny and Condé, had not sought a battle and had not expected the royalists, whom they knew to be deficient in cavalry, to offer it. They were on the retreat from a failed attack on Paris and were heading towards Normandy, where they intended to join with their English allies, under the command of the Earl of Warwick, and use English subsidies to pay their mutinous mercenaries, who made up more than half their 13,000-strong army. Despite their inferior numbers, the battlefield, which sloped gently down from the royalist position, suited cavalry and gave the Protestants the chance of making their considerable superiority in this arm count. With only about a mile of open plain separating them from the royalist's defensive line, it was still uncertain if the Protestants would commit themselves to a risky pitched battle. The Huguenot leaders hurriedly formed a line of battle in front of the village of Imberdais and immediately to the south of the hamlet of Maumasset. It was drawn up in two lines, the first of which comprised most of their 4,500 cavalry, anchored on its left by two regiments of German pistoliers, or *reiters*, followed by Condé's gendarme regiment, then two more gendarme regiments, one behind the other, a unit of light cavalry, then a regiment of gendarmes under Coligny and, protecting the right flank, two more regiments of *reiters*. The second line contained all the Protestant infantry—a large block of volunteer French infantry flanked on either side by two regiments of German landsknechts—and on the extreme right a reserve regiment of *reiters*. The Protestants were more innovative than their opponents. In contrast to the dazzling confusion of colours that made up the royalist lines, the Protestants were distinguished by their white surcoats and sashes. Like their royal counterparts, the Huguenot infantry regiments were in rectangular blocks about ten deep, and the heavily armoured gendarmes in a single rank formation, ready for the shock charge with the lance. The *reiters*, however, were organized in massive columns sixteen ranks deep, a formation dictated by their tactic, the caracole—a demanding manoeuvre which called for each line in succession to discharge its pistols into the enemy before peeling away towards the rear in order to reload.

The journey to Dreux had begun eight months before. Catherine and her ministers knew that the Edict of Toleration would be controversial, and so most of its provisions were leavened with sweeteners for the Catholics, requiring Huguenots to restore all Church property, from buildings to relics, and forbidding them to build churches or hold assemblies inside the limits of any town. Even so, the opposition of the Parlement of Paris was inevitable—it only registered the edict under extreme duress and then immediately disclaimed it in a secret register. But it was the volte-face of Antoine de Navarre which significantly tipped the scales in favour of a united opposition: he pleaded with the Duke of Guise to come to Paris and join him. Protestants denounced Navarre as 'Julian the Apostate' and accused him of accepting Spanish bribes. But opposition to the edict was not the work of fanatics. The prospect of toleration forced moderate Catholics to make a choice—the Middle Party was itself split down the middle. The moderates were not opposed to the edict on the grounds of bigotry; as one liberal judge put it prophetically, far from re-establishing unity in the body politic, toleration would create 'two diverse commonwealths each opposed facing one another', which would inevitably fight and destroy royal authority.[1] Another moderate Catholic, Etienne Pasquier, went even further and described the Edict as stillborn: 'it was, so to speak an abortion suffered by France . . . [like a dead child] that will cause many tears in the entrails of the mother who produced it'.[2]

Paris learned of the Massacre of Wassy within forty-eight hours. The pulpits and the Catholic press praised their Moses, their Jehu, who by spilling the blood of the infidels had consecrated his hands and avenged the Lord. The Protestants demanded justice and Catherine summoned the duke to her residence at Monceaux to answer for his actions. Navarre promised to stand side-by-side with his 'brother'. What would Guise do? On 12 March he arrived at his château of Nanteuil, only fifteen miles to the north-west of Monceaux, where he met his fellow Triumvirs, Saint-André and Montmorency. In agreement with Navarre, they urged him to ignore Catherine and march on Paris. On 16 March the duke and three of his brothers, escorted by over 1,000 horse, entered the city through the Porte Saint-Denis to a rapturous reception from a welcoming committee of nobles, city officials, and bourgeois. The crowds that lined the street to view his entry shouted their joy—and their hatred of the Huguenots. The city council pledged him 20,000 men and 2 million crowns if he would assume the title of 'defender of the faith'. On his journey through the city he met Condé, accompanied by 500 horsemen, returning from a service in the suburbs. He could afford to be courteous to his rival, the Protestant being so heavily outnumbered. In the words of the Protestant captain, la Noue, it was an elephant against a mouse. Violence seemed inevitable as Easter approached. A bloody riot took place on 20 March when a Catholic crowd attempted to disinter a corpse that had been buried according to the Reformed rites in the Cemetery of the Innocents. Palm Sunday processions two days later were the signal for clashes between the factions as they criss-crossed the city. One observer noted 'that one heard so often the retort of firearms that it seemed that Paris was a frontier town'.[3] Eventually both sides were persuaded to remove their soldiers from the city in order to avoid further bloodshed. The Triumvirs headed to Fontainebleau and effectively placed Catherine and the king under house arrest. Condé rode to Orléans and raised his standard on 2 April. He and seventy-three others signed an association 'to maintain the honour of God and to defend liberty and the kingdom'. It was the first of many such leagues which over the next thirty-six years would promise to defend the Commonwealth against tyranny.

The Huguenots had been preparing for this eventuality since the previous summer and the rapidity with which they mobilized and struck with a largely volunteer army stunned the royalists. During the whirlwind months of April and May many of France's principal towns fell. From the outset the fighting was characterized by its savagery, vindictiveness, and pogroms carried out by the majority Catholic population against their Protestant neighbours. In Toulouse, the one great provincial city the insurgents failed to take, days of bloody street-fighting between makeshift militias left 500 people dead. Thousands more Protestants were butchered after their defeat, many of them lynched by vengeful peasants as they sought refuge in the countryside. The Catholic captain and memoirist, Blaise de Monluc, brother of the Bishop of Valence, explained that desperate times required desperate measures: 'I found it necessary, against my inclinations to use not only severity, but cruelty.'[4] Protestants did not always limit themselves to iconoclasm and priest killing; their successes at Beaugency in the Loire and Mornas in Provence were followed by massacres of the defenders.

The Duke of Guise remained aloof from the destruction. Perhaps he had seen enough at Wassy. He took no part in the levelling of the two principal sites of reformed worship in Paris, which was personally overseen by the constable. Even though Guise was the best and most popular general in France, status dictated that the King of Navarre should command the royal army. In the autumn, during the siege of Rouen, talent and luck combined to propel him once more to the fore. The failure of the English, who had entered the war with the hope of regaining Calais, to send more than 200 reinforcements condemned the beleaguered Protestant garrison. Catherine, whose return to power rested on her ability to arbitrate between the factions, had no interest in the outright victory of either side and pressed for a negotiated surrender. Meanwhile, during an inspection of the front-line trenches on 13 October, Antoine de Navarre was mortally wounded by a musket shot in the shoulder. Despite the attentions of the great surgeon Ambrose Paré, who had saved Guise's life at Boulogne, there was no hope and he died, apparently according to Lutheran rites. A week after taking command Guise began an all-out assault; within five days the walls were breached and the city fell. He tried to save the Norman capital from the customary fate of a captured city by announcing a bonus to his troops, but they were not about to be bought off so cheaply and three days of looting, in which not even its churches were spared. The booty was sold off at bargain rates by the soldiers as far away as Paris, where the poor victims had to travel to repurchase their property.

As the Protestant and royalist armies faced each other two months later at Dreux, the savagery of the past months was momentarily forgotten. The Protestants reconnoitred the royalist position and considered it too strong to attack. For about two hours the two armies remained standing facing each other. Thirty thousand men were crowded into an area about a mile wide and half a mile deep; many were facing kinsmen and neighbours and, in the case of the Protestant loyalists serving in the royal army, their co-religionists. The constable was directly opposite his nephews. La Noue described his emotions during these moments:

> Each one braced himself for battle, contemplating that the men he saw coming were neither Spanish, English, nor Italians, but French, indeed the bravest of them, among whom could be found his own comrades, relatives and friends, and that within the hour it would be necessary to start killing one another. This added some horror to the scene.

He himself had a dozen friends in the Catholic ranks, but 'honour and conscience' dictated that neither one side nor the other would show mercy. Untouched by religious division, the remarkable solidarity of his family meant that Guise faced the prospect of battle with less trepidation. Three of his younger brothers, Aumale, Elbeuf, and the Grand Prior were present in the Catholic ranks. Even the Duke of Nevers was here. After an initial flirtation with Condé, the Protestant loyalist was now in Guise's unit, though we do not know if he joined his cousin in hearing Mass and taking communion on the eve of battle.[5]

The Catholic position was a strong one, but to the Protestants it looked more tempting than it actually was because they could not see its right flank, obscured by trees and the houses of the village of Epinay. Guise himself could barely see from this position and had to stand in his stirrups. The Protestant first line attacked what they considered to be the main Catholic force at 11 am. The constable's cavalry moved down from the hill to meet it and were hit by Coligny's gendarmes in front and by the *reiters* in the side. A terrible swirling melee ensued, but the Catholics were outnumbered and routed—some did not stop until they reached Paris, where they spread news of a calamitous defeat, whereupon Catherine is reported to have observed, 'In that case we shall have to learn to say our prayers in French.' The constable, his horse killed from under him and missing two teeth from a pistol shot, was taken prisoner. The next phase of the battle was the most crucial. If the infantry in the centre could not hold, the Catholic army would be annihilated. The French legionnaires were easily dispersed but the Swiss, who lived up to their reputation as the best soldiers in Europe, repulsed charge after charge by the Protestant cavalry. When the Protestants sent their German landsknechts against them they not only held firm but at the push of pike forced their traditional enemy to take refuge in the village of Blainville. The price was heavy: the Swiss lost their colonel and about half their men. But they could not be broken.

Saint-André was impatient to attack, but he was in only nominal command of the Catholic right and could do nothing without the Duke of Guise's assent. Guise's judgement that they should bide their time, even though the left flank was crumbling, was to be the source of much criticism. Before his capture the constable had requested assistance. Guise, however, remained impassive. When the constable's youngest son was killed, his brother, Damville, rode over to the duke to beg him to avenge his death. He was dismissed: 'We will have revenge, but now is not the time.' Guise was too good a general to be swayed by sentiment. He was waiting until the Protestant horse was thoroughly disordered and dispersed—many *reiters* had headed towards the Catholic baggage train in search of pillage. When he judged the moment right the attack was launched with the words

'Allons, mes compagnons, la bataille est gagnée.' Condé and Andelot rallied their men and swung round to meet the charge and the two lines of heavily armoured gendarmes crashed into each other with tremendous force. Condé, his horse wounded, was dismounted and taken prisoner. After taking a fresh horse, Guise then charged his old enemy Coligny, who had managed to scrape together 1,200 exhausted horsemen. Catholic losses were heavy: the Duke of Nevers, Marshal Saint-André, and the perpetrators of Wassy, Jacques and Gaston de la Brosse, Guise's standard-bearer, were killed as the Protestants put up fierce resistance. With night approaching and his men exhausted after five hours on the field, Coligny finally signalled his horse to retire, leaving the battlefield to Guise and 8,000 corpses, two-thirds of them royalists.

The battle of Dreux was a disaster for all the major protagonists, except Guise. The Protestants had been defeated and Condé captured, but the royalist casualties were much heavier. The slaughter of so many gentlemen—the royalists lost more than 500—had swept aside any remaining chivalrous hesitations about the killing of other Frenchmen. Civil war had been normalized. Montmorency's capture for the third time in a less than distinguished military career was a disaster for the Queen Mother too for it left her totally reliant on Guise. Just three days after the battle the duke was once more made lieutenant-general of the kingdom. Dreux confirmed what people already knew—the Duke of Guise was the greatest captain of his age. His treatment of Condé enhanced his reputation further. Ignoring the fact that Condé had once sponsored a plot to kill him, Guise courteously invited his first cousin to share his table and even his bed. His generosity was a sign that chivalry was not altogether dead. Even Protestants, like la Noue, exhorted 'all those who make a profession of arms to study and imitate [him] in order to distance themselves from the cruelties and unworthy things which are often permitted to pass in these civil wars'.[6] But this was a war about salvation, not honour, and few were listening.

Of all the protagonists only Guise had anything to gain from the continuation of the war. While Montmorency and Condé now joined Catherine in calls for a negotiated settlement, Guise pressed home his advantage. On 5 February 1563 he invested the remnants of the Protestant army at Orléans. Coligny was able to slip out and head for the safety of Normandy, but the situation of the defenders was desperate. On 18 February, Guise announced its certain submission and ordered the assault for the following evening. He did not live to see it.

The assassination was planned well. Poltrot de Méré, a 26-year-old petty gentleman insinuated himself into the duke's household and discovered that for the duke to reach his lodgings from the siege trenches he had to cross a river by a small ferry, which could carry only two others. Pistols were useless at more than a few feet, but there were bushes in which to hide and he succeeded in shooting the duke in the back. At first, the doctors did not consider the wound life-threatening, as the bullets seemed to have passed through his body. However, on 22 February, with the duke in the grip of fever, they performed an excruciating operation, making a cross-like incision in the wound and inserting their fingers to look for a foreign body; they found nothing except an abscess. They cleaned the wound as best they could and cauterized it with a red-hot silver iron. To no avail; four days later, on Ash Wednesday, at the age of 44 the duke died. Did Poltrot act alone? Under torture he unravelled a conspiracy and implicated Coligny. What is certain is that the assassin was burning with the desire to avenge his kinsmen killed at Amboise. Poltrot's deposition was sent to the admiral, who admitted paying him 120 crowns to spy on Guise's camp but he furiously denied that he suggested the murder. By removing the main stumbling block to peace, the duke's murder was a godsend to Catherine. The day after Poltrot's execution the Peace of Amboise, negotiated between Condé and Montmorency, brought the first civil war to an end. The belief that the duke's murder would restore stability was illusory. His murder radically altered the political situation; having already broken from the Middle Party, the Guise henceforth severed their links altogether with their former allies. For the next decade politics would be dominated by their quest for blood revenge.

* * * *

As the contemporary historian Jacques-Auguste de Thou put it, the Duke of Guise 'was, even by the admission of his enemies, the greatest man of his century'.[7] Tears were shed in the Catholic courts of Europe. In Holyrood palace they fell 'lyke showers of rayne'.[8] As the duke drifted in and out of consciousness in the last week of his life the struggle over his legacy had already begun. His deeds passed into myth as they were recast by Catholic propaganda, which identified the duke as a martyr for the Catholic cause and his heirs as the champions of orthodoxy. The death of a prince was a public drama, in which themes of serenity, redemption and suffering were embroidered by poets, preachers, and pamphleteers to edify the masses. As he lay dying, listening to the Gospels, in imitation of Christ he forgave his murderer and requested that he be pardoned. He spoke of his desire for a 'good Reformation of the Church' and begged forgiveness for the events of Wassy, which had happened against his will.

Had his brother Charles, who received news of the death at Trent with Christian resignation, been present things would have been handled differently. The duke's widow, Anne d'Este, and 12-year-old son, Henri, were inconsolable and craved vengeance. Anne intoned, 'God, if fair you are, as you must be, avenge this.'⁹ It seems unlikely, however, given what we know of her crypto-Protestantism, that Anne was behind the orchestration of her husband's last hours. For the hawks, Claude d'Aumale and Cardinal Louis, it was imperative that the rumours of unorthodoxy that had accompanied the death of Antoine de Navarre be avoided. As he lay dying, the duke reverted to a deeply traditional and conservative creed. His reassertion of Roman orthodoxy was significant because his deathbed words and deeds, reported by his confessor, the Bishop of Riez, were soon circulating in cheap print. Riez, confessor to Henry II and Catherine de Medici, was a convenient choice, but in other respects a rather unusual one. He was a deeply conservative polemicist opposed to the evangelical traditions of the Guise family and to the Colloquy of Poissy who had translated the works of the Polish Cardinal Hosius, Rome's leading apologist and the main opponent of the Cardinal of Lorraine at Trent. Conservatives like Riez and Hosius acidly rejected even the most limited reforms—demands for communion under both kinds were described as 'satanic'—and savaged the idea of any compromise with Lutherans; heretics were to be rebuked and not talked to. Others who were present at the deathbed accused the bishop of changing the emphasis of the duke's last words and in particular of playing down his repentance for Wassy. According to Riez, the duke defended the Real Presence, in which Christ is 'present in reality and in essence'. In his last hours he enjoyed listening to the epistle of Saint James, a controversial choice from the biblical canon, since it had been condemned by Luther as an 'epistle of straw' for its teaching that faith alone was not enough for salvation. The duke spurned food for he had celestial nourishment: 'I was killed for my support of the Church and the quarrel of my God.' Guise's death was represented as an explicit rejection of his and his brother's flirtation with Lutheranism.

How far the duke himself was consciously engaged in reshaping his image in a reactionary mould we are unaware. His brothers did not

1. Portrait ou Plan de la Ville de Wassy. The Protestant meeting house was situated between the church (A) and the castle (D, E).

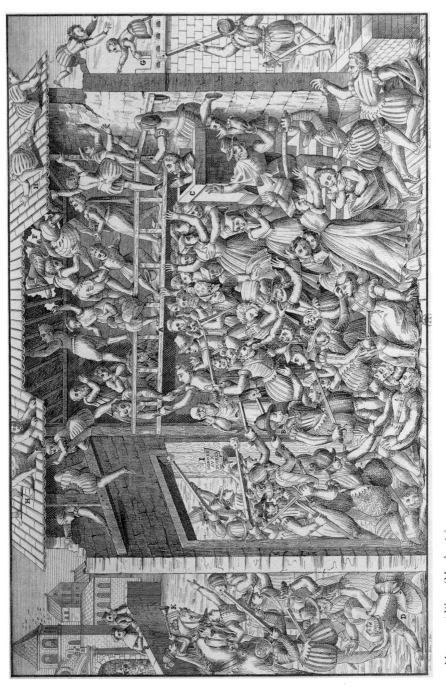

2. Massacre at Wassy (March 1562).

3. Jean Clouet (or Cloet), Portrait of Claude de Lorraine, 1st Duke of Guise (Galleria Palatina, Palazzo Pitti, Florence).

4. Antoinette de Bourbon, Duchess of Guise.

5. Mary of Guise and King James V.

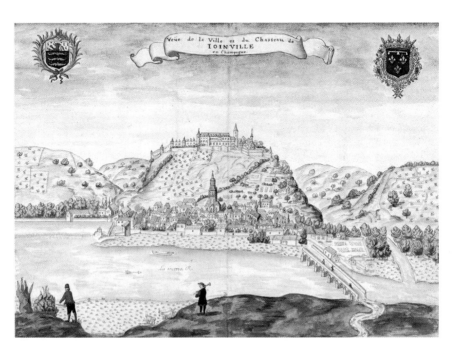

6. Joinville.

7. The Italian garden and new palace at Joinville.

8. Anne, Duke of Montmorency.

9. El Greco, Cardinal Charles of Lorraine.

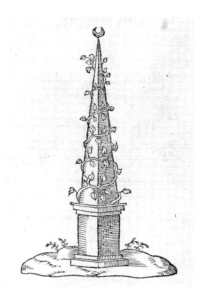

10. The Cardinal of Lorraine's device.

11. François de Lorraine, Duke of Guise.

12. Catherine de Medici.

13. Arms of Mary Stuart, Queen of France,
England, Scotland and Ireland.

14. The executions at Amboise, 15 March 1560.

15. View of the grotto of Meudon.

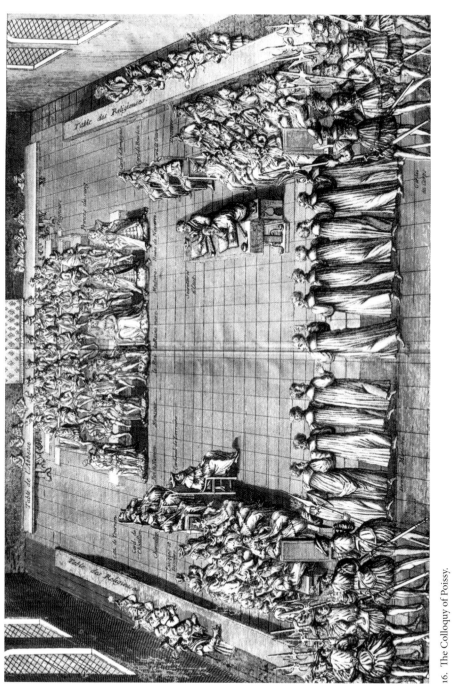

16. The Colloquy of Poissy.

17. Leonard Limousin, Triumph of the Eucharist, c.1562.

18. The Duke of Guise is mortally wounded.

19. The three Coligny brothers, from the left Odet, Gaspard, and François.

21. Francois Quesnel the elder, Henri III.

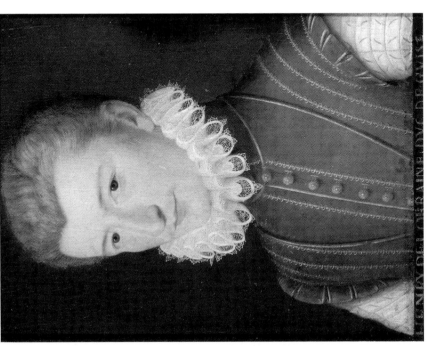

20. Henri de Lorraine, Duke of Guise, aged sixteen.

22. Francois Dubois, The Massacre of Saint Bartholomew's Day. Coligny's body is first pushed out of the first floor window on the right, Guise then stands over the corpse.

23. Portraits of the three Guise brothers, from the left Charles de Mayenne, Henri de Guise, and Louis Cardinal de Lorraine.

24. Ball at the court of Henri III.

25. Façade of the château of Eu.

26. Richard Verstegan, *Briefve description of divers cruelties.*

27. The assassination of Henri de Lorraine, Duke of Guise

need to orchestrate the extraordinary scenes that attended the procession of his corpse to its final resting place at Joinville. The Parisian authorities in particular cited the duke's protection of their city from heresy as their reason for mounting a special funeral procession: twice before to popular acclaim he had come to save them. The procession of the funeral cortege across France was unique for a sixteenth-century French prince; it was the occasion for a spontaneous response by Catholics to the death of a great military hero, a public display of gratitude and grief for a martyr who had sacrificed himself in order to protect them and their faith. He was their Hector and Achilles, their Machabee, their Gideon and Samson. The body lay in state for three days in camp so that the army and the local population could come and pay their respects. Once it had been embalmed it was placed in a coffin and moved downriver along the Loire to Blois in preparation for its arrival in Paris. On 8 March the judges of the Parlement of Paris and the municipal officers attended a service in Notre-Dame in which the cathedral was everywhere bedecked with the arms of the House of Lorraine. The bells of every parish church in the city sounded all day in his memory. In the early hours of the 18th the duke's coffin arrived at the monastery of Chartreux on the outskirts of the city. The drama was heightened later that day by the extraordinary fate that was visited on Poltrot's corpse: in front of the packed crowds outside the city hall he was tortured; while still alive each of his limbs was tied to a horse and pulled apart, his body was burned and his severed head mounted on a post.

On the day after Poltrot's execution, all the city's gates were shut except the porte Saint-Michel, through which the funeral cortege would pass on its way to Notre-Dame; here the duke's heart was to be buried before he was carried to Joinville to lie beside his father. First came the twenty-two criers, calling on Parisians to pray for their hero; they rang bells and were dressed in mourning clothes, on the front of which were emblazoned the city arms and on the back those of the House of Lorraine. Representatives of the mendicant orders of Paris and the vicars and curés of each parish, holding crosses aloft, followed them. Two hundred representatives of the best Parisian families carried torches emblazoned with their arms. But this was a martial as well as a solemn event. There was a silent file-past of 6,000 infantry with their drums silenced and their banners lowered. The twenty-four flags, behind which marched the city militia, were of 'black taffeta, trailing on the ground and emblazoned on the right-hand side with the arms of the city and on the other side with the arms of the deceased seigneur de

Guise'.[10] Nothing symbolized better the common cause of the House of the Guise and the city, whose population was overwhelmingly Catholic, than the union of their coats of arms.

There was yet no talk in the family of exploiting this association politically, nor could they have done so for the family was in turmoil: the duke's death was compounded a week later by the death of natural causes of the Grand Prior, who many considered to be the ablest of the younger siblings. The impact of these deaths can be measured by the reaction of the Cardinal Charles who, according to Montaigne, bore the news of both these deaths at Trent with exemplary fortitude. Yet when one of his menial servants happened to die a few days later 'he let himself be carried away...he abandoned his resolute calm and gave himself to grief and sorrow...The truth is that he was already brimful of sadness, so the least extra burden broke down the barriers of endurance'.[11]

The duke's son, Henri, was confirmed in his father's offices as Grand Master of the Household and as Governor of Champagne, but he was only twelve years old and leadership devolved to the third and fourth brothers, Claude, Duke of Aumale and Louis, Cardinal of Guise. Both men were hawkish and happy to connive in François's staged ultra-Catholic exit. Though a competent soldier, Claude lacked charisma, and Louis, though rich, was best known for his playboy image.

The family council that met at Joinville at the end of March 1563 was a bitter occasion, the stoicism demanded by Charles absent. Offers of support came from all over Catholic Europe. But words were cheap and resources otherwise lacking: the duke had left debts in the region of 200,000 crowns, much of it contracted in the defence of the faith. Meanwhile, the constable told his fellow privy councillors that he 'would support his nephews as if they were his own children and to that effect would employ all the power of his kinsmen, friends and servants' against the Guise.[12] The dominance of the Montmorency on the council was painful enough and then Coligny rubbed salt into the wound: 'This death is the greatest good which could have happened to this kingdom and to God's Church, and particularly to me and my entire house.'[13] His gloating made what became known as 'a public feud' inevitable. For the widow there was 'only one solace; that is to make sure that his friends will remember one day at the right time to avenge her injury'. For their part, Protestants sang songs in praise of Poltrot, 'the sweetest word in the French tongue', and read pamphlets that referred to him as 'the hand of God'. But the feud cut across religious lines: Coligny could rely on the support of his uncle and his uncle's eldest son, François de Montmorency, who as Governor of Paris kept an eye open for signs of support for the Guise in the city.

The family council, in which the dowager duchess took a leading role, developed a dual strategy.[14] Public armed demonstrations pressured the Crown towards effective legal action against the admiral. Meanwhile, in an effort to limit the protection the constable offered to his nephew, public opinion was bombarded with propaganda vilifying the Montmorency. They replied in kind, defending themselves as upholders of the monarchy and of the Peace of Amboise. The Guise launched a private suit against Coligny (26 April 1563) supported by demonstrations of force in the capital. The conflict soon centred on who would conduct the judicial investigation. Anne d'Este moved the king to tears when she made a dramatic personal appeal, prostrating herself before him after Mass in Meulan church on 26 September. The drama moved to Paris four days later when Anne, who was dressed in mourning, the Ferrarese ambassador, and Cardinal Louis gathered with their lawyers and 200 supporters outside the Sainte-Chapelle and, two by two, made the short walk to the law courts of the Parlement of Paris. They packed the chamber in closed session, and despite the objections of the attorney general, their menace ensured that the judges proceeded to name commissioners to begin the investigation. The Guise were followed everywhere by a large retinue and every session of the Parlement attracted excited crowds. But victory was short lived. Within weeks the king evoked the case to the royal council. Tensions increased on 23 November when the admiral and his supporters arrived in the city in a magnificent show of force. The Venetian ambassador, estimating the numbers at 8–10,000 men, feared 'that any little accident might unleash a great scandal'. While the factions roamed the streets, the Guise withdrew from the royal apartments in the Louvre to their own stronghold in the Marais.

Fearing the outbreak of civil war in the capital Catherine summoned the parties to the Louvre on 6 December to try to broker a peace settlement, but events on the streets upset the plans of the policy-makers. Soon after the abortive peace conference Condé's chaplain was attacked by the members of the congregation of Saint-Germain de l'Auxerrois and saved only by the intervention of Huguenot soldiers. More seriously on 22 December a man attacked the priest of Saint-Séverin during Mass, wrestling him to the ground as he raised the Host. The royal family led the public reparation for this act eight days later, in a procession through the streets from the Sainte-Chapelle to Saint-Séverin on the Left Bank, in which the

Venetian ambassador recorded the prominent role of the Guise. Along the route the people complied enthusiastically with orders to cover their houses with hangings and mount lighted torches. Rumours of conspiracy fuelled the combustible atmosphere, and they were not without foundation: handbills posted around the city threatened the life of the Queen Mother and her chief councillors.

Public enmity between the parties and their supporters was displayed day in day out through taunts, challenges, and insults. Gangs of liveried lackeys roamed the streets looking for trouble. Gradually the Protestants and their Montmorency allies gained the upper hand. Their demand that Catherine remove Guisards from key positions was backed up by force: on New Year's Eve a captain of the royal guard was assassinated in cold blood. The Guise were unable to counter the ascendancy of their enemies on the regency council, causing the Spanish ambassador to despair that 'the Guise and the Catholics act so meekly and [are so] defeatist, as if there was no remembrance of the death of M. de Guise nor of the Catholic Religion'. Finally, on 5 January 1564, the king issued a decree, suspending judgment on the murder for three years, during which time the parties agreed to desist from attacks on each other. When he returned from his thirteen-month sojourn at Trent, the welcome extended to the Cardinal of Lorraine at court was cold to the point of rudeness—he was even searched for concealed weapons. The Privy Council dismissed his demands for the implementation of the Tridentine decrees and, in a clear illustration of the tip in the balance of factions, the meeting ended in angry uproar. Until then, Chancellor l'Hôpital had displayed deep affection for the cardinal, his former patron and godfather to his grandson, but their differences now spilled over into personal animosity. Faced with the chancellor's contention that the Tridentine decrees were prejudicial to the independence of the Gallican Church, the cardinal shouted in exasperation that he did not know what religion the chancellor was of. The argument became so fierce that the Cardinal of Lorraine called l'Hôpital an 'ingrate', who was trying to harm the cardinal and his family despite all that he owed them. L'Hôpital replied that he remained grateful and would risk his life to repay his debts, but he declared that he would not do so at the expense of the honour and profit of the king. He would remain loyal to his office, to the Queen Mother, and to the policy of toleration of which he was the principal architect. He reminded the cardinal that it was the Guise who had trampled on the Edict of January in Wassy, a violation that had caused so many troubles in the kingdom.[15] Lent 1564 saw Guise fortunes reach their lowest ebb. Cardinal Charles was invited to open the season with a sermon to the royal family at Fontainebleau. The night before some Huguenots stole into the chapel and 'did a great stinking shit on the seat of his ceremonial chair'.[16] This was one humiliation too many and the family quit court in haste.

A new strategy was called for. The cardinal spent the rest of the year building a wider, non-confessional, base of support by attracting their cousin Condé to their cause. The death of his wife in July 1564 had severed his kinship ties to the Montmorency and removed a godly influence from his life. The two men had a genial meeting at Soissons, where the cardinal offered him a Guise princess: Anne d'Este or Mary Stuart. The dowager Duchess of Guise, in particular, was keen to revive the old alliance with the House of Bourbon. Assured of Condé's goodwill, the next move was to build on the popular support that the family had attracted in Paris, and challenge the traditional Montmorency power base there. To this end, the cardinal planned a sort of triumphal entry into the city with his nephew, Henri. Fearing for his life, the cardinal was accompanied by a retinue of fifty men, even when he sang Mass and preached in church. On the pretext that he had the royal consent, he ignored warnings from the governor, François de Montmorency, that arms were forbidden in the city. A showdown was inevitable. It proved to be yet another humiliation. The two retinues clashed in the rue Saint-Denis on 8 January 1565. At least two men were killed and the Guise men scattered: the cardinal and his nephew, pistols in each hand, were forced to take ignominious refuge in the house of a rope-maker. At nightfall they stole across the river to the safety of the Hôtel de Cluny on the Left Bank, where Aumale joined him. Their dishonour was compounded by their failure to rouse the Parisians. For the next two days the cardinal was trapped in his residence surrounded by hostile troops. The only Parisians who turned up came to poke fun: even among Catholics, anti-clerical feelings were strong. Both sides began to gather forces in the vicinity of the city which cut across confessional lines: Montmorency was supported by Coligny; the Guise by Condé.

Both sides took the fight to the public in an exchange of vicious libels. At stake was the claim to be the greater lineage. The Guise appealed to the other princes, and Condé in particular, to unite against the Montmorency, 'for the princes should not easily permit that any of their rank be outraged by people of inferior condition'; they were no better than levellers who wished to overturn the traditional hierarchy. As for the Montmorency, to the traditional complaints about the Cardinal of Lorraine—he was accused of hypocrisy, buggery, and incest and of being the Antichrist—was joined a new strain of anti-Guise propaganda, which mocked their royal origins and pretensions to be the heirs to the Angevin empire. Rather, they were descended from the counts of Vaudémont—foreigners and simple gentlemen. They were the real parvenus, ruthlessly usurping the traditional role of the Montmorency as protectors of Paris.

In the provinces, too, the Guise tried to build an anti-Montmorency coalition, tapping into local Catholic discontent with the Peace of Amboise. They elicited terrifying oaths, such as the one sworn by the seigneur de Sansac: 'I promise to use all my strength up to the last breath to expel from this kingdom or kill those who have made peace without punishing the murder, and to inflict a shameful death on those who shared in the homicide, and I swear also to use all my strength in exterminating those of the new religion.' Guy de Daillon pledged 'to avenge the death of the said duke up to the fourth generation of those who committed the said homicide or connived at it and of those who are yet defending the culprits'. Chilling though these documents are they proved to be of little practical value in the pursuit of Coligny; these men were offering moral rather than material support. Daillon's promise to serve the Guise up to the fourth generation is a biblical convention (Exodus, 20: 5) that had no legal force. He would never support the Guise with arms and always remained a loyal servant of the Crown.

Neither was sympathy for the Guise translated into support on the streets of Paris. Over the next couple of years the family presented its interest as a public cause and tried to broaden its base of support, but the people remained aloof. During the Guise-Montmorency clash in Paris in 1565, attempts to rekindle memories of Parisian solidarity for the Guise backfired, allowing Protestant pamphlets to demonstrate the shallowness of Guise influence among the people. After quitting the city, Aumale toured neighbouring provinces hurriedly trying to form an association. A letter to his brother, the Marquis of Elbeuf, was intercepted and published by the Protestants. It not only publicized the names of his co-conspirators but revealed his disillusion with the Catholic populace: 'I find it good that the said lords wish to take heed leaving aside the towns, all the more since there is no assurance to be had in the people, as I have lately seen once again. But with the nobility, for my part I am firmly resolved and prepared.' This association also came to nothing. Support for the Guise in the provinces was fickle. Their weakness was vividly exposed on 12 January

1566 when the cardinal journeyed to Moulins and, employing all his powers of eloquence, in front of the royal council and princes implored them to open judicial proceedings against Coligny. He appealed to the princes to uphold his family's honour 'which is yours as well'. The Cardinal appealed to their sense of gratitude—for a decade or more, the Guise liked to fashion themselves as protectors of the princes against Montmorency preponderance. But this idea no longer had any credibility. The overwhelming majority of the princes voted against the motion. The Bourbon-Vendôme had first shown the way in 1560 and over the next decade or so, as Guise power at the centre waned, the other princes followed suit, aligning themselves with the Crown's toleration policy, which offered the best hope for stability. With support for the Guise waning, the Crown was able to impose a settlement at Moulins. Coligny swore publicly that he was not responsible for the murder of François de Guise. He and the cardinal then exchanged a kiss of peace.

The cardinal had one more trick up his sleeve. He shifted the focus of his opposition, posing as the defender of the Catholics in the council. On 16 March he presented a petition from the judges of the Parlement of Dijon protesting against a royal amendment to the Peace of Amboise which allowed ministers of the Reformed religion to visit and console the dying and to instruct the young. This was an extension of the original peace which had allowed Protestant worship in only one designated town in each baillage or seneschalsy and Lorraine claimed that it was a covert means of proselytizing. The petition caused a stir in the council because it was apparent that the amendment had not been discussed in the council, but issued on the sole authority of the chancellor. L'Hôpital turned to the cardinal and remarked drily 'Monsieur, you already came back to trouble us.' The cardinal exploded: 'You, who enjoy your position today, thanks to me, dare tell me that I came to trouble you.'[17] Council members leapt up and the meeting was plunged into uproar. Order was only restored when the Queen Mother intervened. She ordered that the offending edict be burned, that the teaching of the Protestant catechism be strictly prohibited and that the chancellor be forbidden from sealing edicts without the consent of the royal council. Lorraine's tactical victory was undermined by his arrogance, which alienated even those who agreed with his principles. He accused the chancellor of always wanting to be 'cock of the dunghill', and declared that he would attend no more councils in the chancellor's presence. L'Hôpital retorted that they could manage quite well without him. A dangerous precedent was thus set: any recall of the cardinal to the council would be widely interpreted as heralding an alteration to the Peace.

* * * *

For the first time since the early 1520s the Guise found they had minimal influence at the centre of power. Any sympathy for the widowed duchess was offset by the loathing everyone on the Privy Council had for the cardinal: 'It is an infallible maxim that the queen hates the Cardinal of Lorraine as much as any man living.' The papal nuncio added that 'those that remained of their party were not loved for their personal merits but out of consideration for the duke they had lost'.[18] Only Cardinal Louis remained at court for any length of time. From the spring of 1564 to the summer of 1565 during its tour of the war-ravaged kingdom—an attempt by Catherine to show the king to his people and to impose the Peace of Amboise on his divided sub-jects—his presence as an emissary was endured. Cardinal Charles had returned from Trent with his spirits raised; the sense of spiritual renewal is betrayed by the religious paintings and objects he brought back from Italy, including a Tintoretto and a Titian, to embellish Reims cathedral, and by the frequency with which his letters now contained passages of scripture. In constant fear for his life, he took to reciting psalm 30 with its theme of deliverance: 'Thou hast turned for me my mourning into dancing; thou hast loosed my sackcloth and girded me with gladness.'[19] Before Trent, bishops had been regarded primarily as administrators of the temporalities. The cardinal now threw himself into the missionary role that Trent had set out for bishops. He sum-moned a provincial synod at Reims on the 25 November 1564 and urged the clergy to reform themselves before they reformed the Church. Within three years he had established a seminary in Reims—the first of its kind in France. He became a leading patron of the new religious orders, arranging for Jesuits to preach at court and in his dioceses, and establishing a Capuchin community at Meudon—another first. Stung by Trent's opposition, he and Louis ceased to be episcopal pluralists, although political and ecclesiastical control was maintained by resign-ing sees they once occupied to their clients. Tentative reforms in some of the many monasteries they controlled were also begun. He set the standard in pastoral care, serving dinner to the poor at Reims hospital during the Easter, Pentecost, and Christmas holidays.

The poet Remy Belleau described family life during the retreat from court in the mid-1560s. Belleau arrived at Joinville in 1563 to take charge of the crèche, and in particular the education of the 7-year-old son of René d'Elbeuf. Belleau was inspired by the charms of Joinville's gardens to put on summer festivities of music, dancing, and poetry in the grounds of the new château. His pastoral *bergerie*, a mixture of prose and poetry first performed in 1565, centres on the upper château of Joinville, a household ruled meticulously by Antoinette de Bourbon. Belleau describes many works of art in detail which explore the prestige and misfortunes of the Guise family. The Guise fondness for music was also evoked in the tapestries depicting shepherds and shepherdesses dancing and singing. Three shepherdesses dressed as the three Fates sang in honour of the eldest son of the Duke of Lorraine, Henri Marquis du Pont, who was born in 1563. In Belleau's poetry Joinville is represented as arcadia, but melancholia was not far away. At dawn every morning Antoinette de Bourbon awaited a troop of young girls in the gloomy old castle, she then processed across the main hall, to the gallery in which stood her open coffin and thence to the chapel. Awaiting her were her chaplains and six burning candles, four in front of a portrait of her husband at the foot of an immense cross and two in front of his tomb. The daily prayer she said for her husband for fourteen years, followed by the *Dulcissme Jesu* and the ringing of bells, was now joined by prayers for her murdered son, whose magnificent mausoleum placed beside his father was inscribed with the words *Laus Deo*, 'To the Glory of God'. The mood at Joinville darkened further in 1566 with the death of René d'Elbeuf and his wife Louise de Rieux in Provence, where he had recently been installed as commander of the Mediterranean galley fleet. Belleau returned to Paris soon after. The shadow of death that hung over Joinville encouraged Henri, Duke of Guise and his younger brother, who were not welcome at court, to leave France and try their hand crusading against the Turks in Hungary in the summer of 1566.

Just as the family reached the nadir of its fortunes, the domestic and international situation suddenly turned in its favour. Catholics everywhere began to reassert themselves, providing the Guise with an opportunity to rally the cause and set out on the road to political rehabilitation. The religious provisions of the Peace of Amboise were so complex it would have proved devilishly difficult to enforce them even if there had been goodwill on both sides. Protestant noblemen took advantage of the rights it gave them to multiply the sites of worship on their property much to the annoyance of Catholics, who formed local defence leagues and associations to oppose its provisions. Every burial, prayer meeting, and procession was a potential flashpoint. And there was a subtle shift at court too where the atmosphere slowly became less welcoming to the Protestants. The moderates continued to dominate the Privy Council, but Catherine de Medici was raising new men; wholly dependent on her favour, their careers did not rely on the success of the toleration policy. Many were Italians with Catholic sentiments more Roman than Gallican. And as the balance in her entourage shifted, so the interpretation of the articles of the peace by the Crown and its officials began to go against the Protestants. Nothing captures the change in mood better than the demeanour of Charles IX himself and more especially his younger brother, Henri, Duke of Anjou. Born in 1551, it is easy to see why Henri was Catherine's favourite son: he had all the qualities to rule—true piety, charm, and intelligence—that his other siblings so palpably lacked. Henri could do no wrong in the eyes of his mother and she indulged his sometimes outrageous behaviour: in April he tempted the king into a game in which they mocked the Protestants in the presence of the whole court; it ended with them tearing up a book of psalms and a Protestant catechism and showering each other with bits of paper. The Protestant leaders ground their teeth as they looked on. Anjou's youthful irreverence, so in contrast to the dourness of his mother's counsellors, was immensely attractive to young courtiers. He quickly became the darling of the ultra-Catholics.

These changes alone would not have conspired to undermine peace had it not been for the revolutionary events that were taking place in the Low Countries. In the summer of 1566 Habsburg authority broke down and the spread of Protestant worship and iconoclastic fury seemed to presage a repeat of the Calvinist revolts in Scotland in 1559 and France in 1560. Philip II was not prepared to make the same mistakes the Guise had made. He possessed not only the means of repression—the most formidable army in Europe—but was prepared to unleash it with as much cruelty as it would take to stamp out heresy. On 29 November 1566, the Duke Alva, the former foe of François de Guise, now sixty and crippled by gout, was appointed captain-general of an army with a projected strength of 70,000 men. The attempt to re-establish Habsburg hegemony in the Low Countries by force was a Rubicon for Spanish imperialism: a threshold which, once crossed, would transform the political situation in northern Europe. French Protestants trembled at the prospect. They feared a wider conspiracy to suppress the Reformed faith and felt with some justification that the fate of their co-religionists in the Low Countries was tied to their own. There were strong kinship and cultural ties between the Confederate nobility in the Low Countries, which was French-speaking, and the nobility of north-eastern France. The House of Montmorency straddled both sides of the porous border, and the constable and his nephews were soon in secret discussions about mutual aid with the Confederates. The tension increased in the summer of 1567 as Alva's army marched north close to the French border, through Savoy, Lorraine, and Luxembourg. The Huguenots' loss of influence and fears that at any moment the Peace of Amboise would be revoked was confirmed in August 1567: after more than a year's absence, Catherine summoned the Cardinal of Lorraine back to the Privy Council.

At the same moment several hundred miles to the north, events in Scotland took a dramatic turn, which would push the Guise irrevocably into the arms of the old Habsburg enemy. The stability of Mary Stuart's regime was based ultimately on the pursuit of détente with England. Scots and English alike assumed that an unmarried Elizabeth had to name a successor, and Guise policy was to ensure it would be Mary. For a time the cardinal even foresaw the possibility of her conversion or marriage to a Protestant prince, such as Condé. She had not liked this. 'Truly I am beholding to my uncle; so it be well with him he cares not what becomes of me.'[20] Though he did not care for her choice, her cousin, Lord Darnley, whom he termed an 'agreeable nincompoop', he reluctantly set about obtaining the appropriate papal dispensation. This disastrous marriage set in train events in which Scottish affairs would spiral out of Guise control once and for all. Darnley was vain, foolish, idle, and violent, and he had a habit of offending people. His murder in February 1567 was followed by Mary's overthrow, imprisonment, and abdication. Within a year she had fled to England and perpetual captivity. Until then relations between the Cardinal of Lorraine and Philip II had remained cool. Hostility ran deep—unusually for French princes in this period the Guise did not write letters grovelling for Spanish pensions. Spain was deeply hostile to the crypto-Lutheran proposals that Lorraine had carried with him to Trent. Following the assassination of François de Guise, the Emperor Ferdinand had required no prompting to write to the cardinal and offer his condolences and support. Philip II, in contrast, had to be reminded of his duty by Ambassador Chantonnay. He eventually did so on the 9 June, just as the cardinal was shifting his position at Trent. But the main reason for their mutual suspicion is made clear from the letter's opening flourish: 'Don Phelippe, por la gracia de Dios Rey de Espana, de las Dos Sicilias, de Hierusalem'.

Friendship with Spain meant privileging matters of faith over lineage and would require the Guise to deny (at least temporarily) their Angevin heritage. Events in France, Scotland, and the Low Countries in 1567 clarified the relationship as the mutual dynastic and religious interests of Habsburg and Guise coalesced. From the beginning of 1568 the Cardinal of Lorraine would maintain a regular correspondence with Philip II and his advisors, whose warmth could not hide Guise subservience to Habsburg power and its pursuit of hegemony in northern Europe: 'There is no family', he wrote in November, 'more devoted and dedicated to Your Majesty's service than ours.'

The Huguenot answer to the defeat of the Confederates in the Low Countries and the return of the cardinal to the council was a desperate gamble. The attempt to seize the king and his mother at Meaux on 26 September was a watershed, altering for good the precarious balance of politics at the court. It was a disaster for the Protestants on two fronts. In the first place the king escaped and made for Paris. Secondly, their repeated claims to be acting virtuously in defence of the common weal sounded hollow. A secondary objective had been to purge the Privy Council of their opponents. There is little doubting what would have befallen Charles had he fallen into their hands. He wrote with relief from Reims that 'The Huguenots narrowly missed cutting [him] to pieces en route.' He escaped on a swift Spanish mount, but had to abandon all his baggage and silver and gold plate to his pursuers. One of his servants was killed.[21] Despite the death of the Constable of Montmorency at the battle of Saint-Denis in December, the second civil war resolved little. The six months of uneasy truce that followed the Peace of Longjumeau in May 1568 resolved even less. The cardinal did not have a good war. He spent the winter of 1567 in Champagne organizing the eastern army, but when he was ordered by Charles IX to the frontier itself he was indignant, judging that at his age such a journey 'would in no way be worthy of service to you'.[22] Catherine was trying to keep him out of the way while she negotiated. In January 1568 he could not prevent German Protestant mercenaries from systematically destroying the family estates. Though he disliked the idea of peace and feared that it would put his life in danger, he also recognized how destructive the war was proving.

In the meantime, Philip II showed that there was an alternative, Spanish solution to the problem of heresy, entirely at odds with the French experiment. A special tribunal, the Council of Troubles, was established in September 1567; it eventually tried 12,000 people, 9,000 of whom, including the Confederate leader, William of Orange, were judged *in absentia* and had their property confiscated; more than 1,000 were executed, including two magnates—the counts of Egmont and Horne, who were kinsmen of the Montmorency. French Protestants could not remain on the sidelines and they took part in the disastrous campaign against Alva in the summer of 1568. In August Condé, Coligny, and Orange formed a united front and the black image of the Cardinal of Lorraine was at the heart of their propaganda campaign. When the Protestants took up arms again in September they blamed him for conspiring against the peace and plotting to kill them. In order to link events on the continent with those in England and draw Elizabeth I into the conflict, they claimed that following the imprisonment on Mary Stuart in May 1568 she was also the target of an elimination plot. Some historians have taken these claims at face value. But while fears of a Catholic conspiracy may have been genuine, it does not mean that such a conspiracy existed. Nicola Sutherland has even suggested that in the course of the summer of 1568 a plot to eliminate every leading Protestant in Europe was in the making, a forerunner to the Saint Bartholomew's Day Massacre.

The image of the cardinal as the evil mastermind of a vast international Catholic plot was a figment of the Protestant imagination. The cardinal's letters show that if any such conspiracy existed it was an aspiration rather than fully operational. The Protestants were well aware of his rapprochement with Philip II because they were intercepting his correspondence. His language was now not dissimilar to Calvinist rhetoric, calling on Philip in January 1568 to come north and take 'vengeance for all the heresies and blasphemies against [God's] name against the precious sacraments'.[23] When one of his valets was murdered soon after, he was more careful about committing things to paper. In private he tended to be more ambivalent about the war: while he told Philip that he would give his life in the fight against heresy, he was himself prone to melancholia and tired of the fighting—'better a good peace than a bad war like this'.[24]

There were many other factors in the failure of the Peace of Longjumeau. In many localities of France there was no peace at all but an armed truce and the internationalization of the Protestant-Catholic schism had left both sides looking nervously at events abroad. Protestant fears of impending persecution were heightened by the dismal failure of their invasion of the Low Countries. Alva had protested strongly to Charles IX about their incursions into Habsburg territory. There can be no doubt the decision of the Protestant leaders to take up arms again on 23 September was precipitated by their irrevocable loss of influence at court: they were now completely eclipsed at court by the Duke of Anjou, whose rivalry with Condé was particularly poisonous. The chancellor's influence at court was in rapid decline. The conciliatory line he had taken after the Meaux coup doubled the hostility of the ultra-Catholics, who accused him of conniving with the Huguenots. He had lost the confidence of Catherine and, though she refused to accept his resignation, he ceased to appear on the council in late June 1568. This paved the way for the cardinal to return. One of the first matters that he attended to was the suppression of Huguenot corsairs operating out of La Rochelle against Spanish shipping.

Catherine recalled the cardinal partly to appease Spain, but also because the Crown was desperately short of cash. The cardinal had shown in the 1550s that his financial acumen was unsurpassed and in the winter of 1567–8 he advanced money to keep the royal army on the eastern frontier in the field. His solution was to place the enormous revenues of the Church at the Crown's disposal. On 1 August Pius V issued a bull allowing the King of France to alienate Church properties up to an annual revenue of 150,000 crowns. But there was a catch: the Pope dictated that this money be used only to suppress 'the uprisings of heretical and rebellious Huguenots'.[25] The council was sharply divided over the offer and l'Hôpital made a dramatic return to court to oppose its acceptance and save the toleration policy. On 19 September 1568, in the presence of Catherine, he argued that the bull was an infringement of the Gallican Church and that in time of need the king had the right to close churches and use the income without permission from the Pope. According to the English ambassador:

> the cardinal being herewith much stirred reproached him to be a hypocrite, and that his wife and daughter were Calvinists, and that he was not the first of his race that had deserved evil of the king. The chancellor replied that he was as honest a race as he, whereupon the cardinal gave him the lie, and rising incontinently out of his chair to take him by the beard, the Marshal Montmorency stepped between them. The Cardinal in great choler turned to the Queen and said that he was the only cause of the troubles in the realm, and that if he were in the hands of the parlement his head should not tarry on his shoulder twenty-four hours. The Chancellor said contrariwise that the Cardinal was the original cause of the mischiefs that had chanced as well to France within these eight years as to the rest of Christendom.[26]

Despite l'Hôpital's efforts, the king issued letters patent confirming the content of the papal bull. Realizing that he no longer exerted any influence on royal policy, he asked to be relieved of his office. His place on the Council went to one of Catherine's hawkish Italian protégés, Birague. L'Hôpital's final intervention had already come too late: the return of the Cardinal of Lorraine to power had been the last straw for the Protestants and they had already taken up arms again.

The cardinal was now responsible for financing the royal war effort. He used the sale of Church property to raise loans, thereby making the Crown financially dependent on the Catholic Church. For the first time in nearly a decade, his time was absorbed with war and diplomacy, except that instead of opposing the Habsburgs he was now their ally. For dynastic reasons he wished to internationalize the war on heresy further. In his letters to Alva and Philip II, he talked of Elizabeth as their mutual enemy and pressed for military intervention to free Mary Stuart.

During the third civil war the cruelty that characterizes sectarian violence reached a new peak. The royal army, commanded by the dashing 17-year-old Duke of Anjou, initially carried all before it on the battlefield. Nothing better encapsulates the collapse of traditional chivalric values in this period than what followed when, at the battle of Jarnac in 1569, Condé was again taken prisoner. This time there was no prospect of honourable captivity or ransom. He had the misfortune to fall into the hands of the captain of Anjou's guard who promptly shot him through the head. Anjou then permitted the corpse of his cousin to be paraded around the camp on a mule as a sign of mockery. The Cardinal of Lorraine's change in mood also catches the new uncompromising zeitgeist. His transformation into a Counter-Reformation warrior revealed the darker side of his personality; his vindictiveness grew at the expense of his wit and charm. The proposition of his 1569 Lenten sermon in front of the king was that 'heretics were more wicked than the devil'. The spite that had marred his political struggle with the chancellor was on display again when Ramus wrote to him in October 1570, reminding him of their thirty-five-year friendship and requesting his support in regaining his professorial chairs in Paris, from which non-Catholics had been removed. The cardinal's reply accused Ramus of ingratitude, impiety, and rebellion.

The royal army was unable to follow up its battlefield victories. Despite the cardinal's financial expertise, it lacked the logistical wherewithal to reduce the Huguenot heartlands in the south. Huguenot cavalry forces excelled in guerrilla tactics, which not only slowed the royalists' progress but, in ravaging the countryside and terrorizing the population, sapped the will of the Catholics to fight. Catherine, realizing that civil war was seriously undermining the power and prestige of the monarchy, made tentative peace moves. Charles IX was emerging from his mother's shadow and jealous that any glory to be won had gone to his younger brother. Courtiers began to whisper that the only people who profited from the war were the Guise. In the spring of 1570 Coligny, who was now the undisputed leader of the Protestants, began a spectacular march across France. He marched from Nîmes across the Vivarais and into Burgundy. On 18 June his men sacked the great abbey of Cluny. He avoided the royalist field army near Autun and, after picking up reinforcements at Sancerre and La Charité-sur-Loire, he moved on Paris in the hope of securing a speedy and advantageous peace. Lorraine's opposition to concessions were backed by Spain and the Pope, but by now nearly all the king's council wanted a settlement. On 8 August 1570 Catherine made peace with the Huguenots at Saint-Germain-en-Laye. Its terms were so favourable to them that it has been called a 'Calvinist charter'. This is an exaggeration: Protestantism was still banned at court and in Paris. Nevertheless, freedom of conscience was allowed throughout the kingdom and freedom of worship where it had taken place before the war, and the edict marked a distinct departure in providing the Protestants with four security towns—La Rochelle, Montauban, La Charité and Cognac—for two years. The edict baffled many Catholics, who did not think the Huguenots were in a sufficiently strong position to exact such favourable terms. Monluc complained that they had gained 'by writings' what they had lost by fighting.

The Cardinal of Lorraine was utterly defeated; he wrote to his client, the Bishop of Verdun, that as 'for the peace, the articles in it are bad and pernicious, but what is still more annoying is the despair'. He called for patience.[27] During the peace negotiations he had fallen seriously ill. In part, this was induced by the pressure of the work and the fear of assassination, no doubt made worse by the bouts of melancholy to which he was subject during his later years. But it was also aggravated by the anxiety of having to run his nephew's affairs. Henri, Duke of Guise, was proving an exasperating and taxing ward.

INTERLUDE: PRINCESS MARGOT AND THE 'NEGRESS'

Born at Joinville on New Year's Eve, 1549, the life of Henri, third Duke of Guise, was forever scarred by one harrowing event. At the age of twelve he had been forced to watch his father die in agony. The letters he wrote as a 7-year-old to the father, who was away on campaign, reveal a precocious intelligence. Henri idolized his father. When his uncle suggested that he would make a good priest he wrote to his father: 'I would rather be next to you breaking a lance or a sword on some brave Spaniard or Burgundian to show that I like much better to fence and joust than to be always shut up in an abbey dressed in a gown.' His formal education was, however, brief. At the age of 7 he was sent to Navarre College with the two other Henris, who would one day be his rivals: Henri, the son of Antoine, King of Navarre, and Henri, Duke of Anjou. But it was barely a year before the Prince of Joinville, as he was styled, was summoned by his father to learn the profession of arms. He was soon joined by his younger brother, Charles, (born in 1554), while his youngest brother, Louis, born in 1555, was destined to inherit his uncles' ecclesiastical empire. Henri was not interested in letters and, in spite of the close attention of his uncle and his grandmother, his knowledge of matters theological was superficial: 'I heard the beautiful sermons that my uncle gave at Reims but I promise you,' he wrote to his father, 'that I will not be about to recite them because they were so long I can only remember half of them.' Like his father and grandfather, he was more interested in traditional aristocratic pursuits and his letters resound with the themes of horses, hunting, and war.

In an age when looks and demeanour were thought to herald majesty, the beauty of the House of Guise was renowned. It contrasted with the ugliness that afflicted most of their Habsburg, Valois, and Bourbon contemporaries. And the portraits of the new duke support the contention of observers that Henri—as 'beautiful as an angel', according to the Venetian ambassador—surpassed even his cousin, Mary Stuart, in looks. He had the trademark pale visage and curly, strawberry blond hair. He was tall too and had a good physique shaped by the usual martial sports and tennis and, more unusually, swimming—he could, it was said, swim across a river in armour. He inherited both his father's charm and common touch: his immense attractiveness to women and affability with commoners would later be major political assets. If Henri had an Achilles heel it was hubris. In his father, the inbred pride of the aristocrat had been tempered by reserve and modesty, which charmed even his enemies. Henri, in contrast, inherited some of his uncle's arrogance. A story told by Marguerite de Valois about the young duke is instructive. Asked by her father, Henry II, which prince she preferred, Guise or the Marquis of Beaupréau, son of the Prince of la Roche-sur-Yon, she agreed that Guise was without doubt the better looking but she preferred the other because 'every day the duke does something bad to someone and always wants to be master'.[1] The story is probably apocryphal but it stood the test of time because it captured something essential. It is borne out by an event which took place over a decade later. During a solemn religious procession in Paris led by the king, there was a scuffle between one of the duke's pages and a royal archer. Alerted to this, the duke walked over to the archer and in the middle of the street ordered the man to kneel while his page administered two small slaps. For good measure Guise then struck the poor man with his own gloves, 'which several people, including the king, found very strange'.[2] This exaggerated sense of his own reputation extended to the hatred which consumed him. Brantôme, a confidant of the young duke, was convinced that others carried more guilt than Coligny, but Guise would have no truck with the small fry: 'he only had ill-will for a great captain like him, because the others were not worthy of his hatred, anger and revenge'.[3]

Living in his father's shadow was a great burden. His juvenile *entrée* into politics was disastrous. In the autumn of 1561 he became involved in a plot to encourage his friend, Anjou, the king's brother and heir, to run away from court and spearhead the Catholic opposition to Catherine. His father and uncle were furious at him for undermining their rapprochement with the Lutherans. The 11-year-old Henri had been led into this folly by Jacques de Savoie, Duke of Nemours. The most hawkish of his father's friends, the debonair 30-year-old

Nemours was something of a role model for the young man, and in 1566 Nemours became his stepfather when he married Guise's widowed mother. Guise's prowess in tournaments was already a matter of record 'not yet fifteen, but yet very adroit, and already then very sharp in combat, as much as those much older than him'.[4] But the triumph of his enemies made the daily humiliations of court life unbearable. Coligny and Marshal Montmorency ignored the challenges to personal combat that he issued; he in turn refused to appear at Moulins with his uncle or sign any document of reconciliation. In order to restore his honour he sought to emulate his father, even to the point of being wounded, for, as he himself remarked, 'there is more honour to be had in receiving a wound than in giving one'. In May 1566 he and his brother Charles, accompanied by a retinue of 350 men, left France to fight the Turks in Hungary under the command of their uncle, Alfonso d'Este. However, it was during the third civil war, when he was made colonel-general of dragoons, that he began to show that he was a cut above the other ultra-Catholic gallants who had gathered around the Duke of Anjou.

In the wake of the royalist victory at Jarnac he would finally confront Coligny on the field of battle. The royal army was so mutinous for want of pay and so ravaged by sickness that it had been unable to follow up its victory. On 19 July 1569 Henri de Guise, who was in the Limousin, received news that Coligny and the main Protestant army was heading north. Spurred on by his vow of revenge he and his brother Charles quickly mustered a force of 1,200 horse and made rapidly for Poitiers, where they arrived on the 22nd to reinforce the weak garrison. Coligny invested the city three days later with 30,000 men and, knowing that he had his principal enemy in his grasp, began a fierce cannonade. On one day alone 800 shots were fired into the city. Like his father at Metz, Guise did not shirk from the mundane tasks of siege life, such as supervising trench diggers. On the 24 August a breach was effected and the situation became so critical that the wives of the gentlemen were armed should the Protestants break into the city. For the next week the duke figured prominently in the defence of the breach against enemy assaults and was lightly wounded in the foot. Having repulsed the final assault on 3 September, he assisted at a procession of the Holy Sacrament around Poitiers as one of the bearers of the monstrance. Coligny raised the siege on 7 September. In seven weeks the garrison had lost a third of its effectives; the Huguenots about 2,000 men. Five days later Coligny was declared a rebel and the price of 50,000 crowns put on his head.

The duke's victory celebrations were short-lived. Peace feelers were already being extended. Worse still, a dynastic marriage between the duke's childhood playmates, Marguerite de Valois and Henri de Navarre, who had been raised a Protestant by his mother Jeanne d'Albret, was being mooted as a means of reconciling the religious factions. During the negotiations Cardinal Charles's melancholia returned: 'I am in extreme need of rest and cannot recuperate.'[5] When peace was signed on 8 August 1570 he had come down with a fever and was seriously ill. But it was not only his failure to influence the talks and the ease with which the Protestants were intercepting his letters that laid him low. Like any other teenager, Henri de Guise was difficult to handle. First, there was his profligacy. Though his father had left huge debts, the son had appearances to keep up. His uncle did his best to stave off the creditors. Henri's majority in September 1568 improved matters for a time, and the cardinal hoped that the war would mean a suspension of lawsuits. But in March 1569 the duchy of Chevreuse, which the cardinal had given to his nephew, was seized by creditors. The demands of Henri's younger brother, Charles, the 15-year-old Marquis of Mayenne, were no less irksome. The cardinal wrote to his sister-in-law in May 1570 moaning that these days 'everyone wants to be an inhabitant of Paris'.[6] Mayenne had found a house in the city he wanted to buy. More worryingly, he had taken to wearing green, a dangerous choice because it was the colour of the House of Anjou, a title that was currently occupied by the heir to the throne.

But a much more serious challenge to the Crown, one that put Henri de Guise's life in danger, came as a result of the other major cause of angst for the parents of teenage children: sex. Henri was beginning to discover just how attractive he was to women. He later confided to Brantôme that when it came to the opposite sex his aristocratic nonchalance deserted him; he became something of a 'tyrant', and when one caught his eye he would have to have her by 'love or by force'.[7] As the finishing touches were being put to the Peace of Saint-Germain en Laye, the young duke threatened one of its key elements—he had fallen in love with the king's sister, Marguerite. It was a matter of the utmost significance; the future of France and the European balance of power depended on it. Within a week of signing the peace accords, Catherine de Medici wrote that she had hurried to Paris 'to see the Cardinal of Lorraine in his house where he has been ill for the last 2 or 3 weeks'; they discussed 'the rumour circulating for some while among several persons of the proposed marriage of my daughter and the Duke of Guise'.[8] The cardinal had long been aware that his nephew was up to something, and at first he may have even encouraged him, as a means of stalling Marguerite's betrothal. From Marguerite's point of view there was no comparison between Guise and the 17-year-old Navarre, who was not only a heretic but short, ugly, and coarse. But in April the cardinal wrote with alarm to his sister-in-law: 'The ladies at court are real stirrers and mixers. The poor little [Marguerite] and your son are riding luck in such a way that it is very bad.' The most worrying aspect of the affair was the attitude of Marguerite's brothers. At first, Anjou, who displayed a morbid fascination for his sister, encouraged the duke; it seemed a bit of harmless fun. But he was too much under the influence of his mother to resist her will for long. Court gossip became so pernicious that by May the royal family was refusing to talk to the Guise. When proof of the illicit affair came to light in the form of an intercepted letter between the lovers, Anjou was furious and refused to leave his rooms. When he reappeared he had taken violently against his former friend, and urged his brother to punish Guise's impudence. Charles IX, the same age as Guise, though physically fragile and less able, was beginning to emerge from his younger brother's shadow; he felt strongly that *his* peace treaty was being undermined. Matters came to a head on 26 June at Gaillon in Normandy, where Marguerite was berated for fifteen minutes by her mother and brothers, and the king hit her and tore her clothes. Guise's murder was discussed and their bastard brother, the Duke of Angou-lême, approached—bastards being traditionally employed in aristo-cratic families to protect female honour. The cardinal had 'never seen such a long and cruel anger'. In the end, the king limited himself to banishment; when the duke dared to approach him during a ball he was brusquely dismissed: 'I no longer have need of your service.'[9] Relations were so bad that the cardinal dared not commit the events to paper, fearing that letters to his sister-in-law would fall into the wrong hands. There were strong words too between nephew and uncle, following which the latter was able to report to Anne that if her son 'wishes to follow [good] council and be wise, there will be nothing else except good news'. So when the Queen Mother visited the cardinal in Paris he was able to announce that the matter was now closed and his nephew was betrothed to someone else.

* * * *

By September the cardinal's melancholy had lifted and he was once more enjoying his daily stroll in one or other of his residences around

Paris. On 3 October, Henri de Guise married Catherine de Clèves, Countess of Eu. Henri's hurried engagement was not initially to his liking. He is purported to have turned up his nose at Catherine de Clèves as a 'negress', either because he wished to marry royalty or in reference to her Protestantism. But there were compelling reasons for the match beyond the need to placate the royal family. The Clèves, like the Guise, hailed from the marches of the Franco-Imperial border, and the families had long been allies. Indeed, Catherine had been raised at Joinville. The sovereign principality of Château-Regnault, which she brought to the marriage, strengthened Guise's position on the borders of the Holy Roman Empire. The most significant and valuable part of the inheritance was however the county of Eu in Upper Normandy; comprising 270 fiefs and manors this consolidated bloc of territory sealed Guise dominance in the region. Facing England on the Channel coast, it would prove to be an acquisition of the utmost strategic importance. The dowry of 100,000 livres, paid by the king, eased the duke's financial problems and the marriage was celebrated with three days of tourneys in Paris. For the marriage feast, the banquet table in the Hôtel de Guise was covered with vases of gold, crystal, and silver gilt valued at 100,000 crowns and the ambassadors of Scotland, Spain, Venice, and Ferrara invited. The English ambassador, Walsingham, was diplomatically excluded on the pretext that he would otherwise have had to acquiesce to the precedence of the Scottish ambassador, the Archbishop of Glasgow.

Although one crisis had been averted, the coming of peace had left the Guise once more in the political wilderness. The duke's friendship with Anjou would never heal properly and the heir to the throne, with the sort of melodramatic flourish that he was fond of, declared that 'If the duke of Guise after his marriage lays eyes on [Margot] again, he who would not drive a dagger through his heart, in such a way as to make him bite the earth, would be declared a renegade and miscreant.'[10] The 1560s had seen a dramatic alteration in the fortunes of the Guise family; they turned their back on compromise with the Protestants and emerged as the leading champions of the Counter-Reformation. The lessons of the battle of Dreux were clear. Conflict with the Habsburgs had made the Guise fortune, whereas the Peace of Cateau-Cambrésis had favoured their enemies. The return of war once again ensured their ascendancy. To be associated with civil war was, however, fraught with dangers for it left the family open to accusations that they were perpetuating confessional conflict for their own ends. A self-fulfilling pattern was established: since their political fortunes depended on the continuation of the war on heresy, they became identified exclusively as the 'war party'; consequently the main guarantor of peace was their disgrace. By the end of the decade it had become abundantly clear to Catherine, her ministers, and to her sons that the Protestants could not be defeated militarily, and that civil war served only to reduce the power of the monarchy. This left the Guise with a paradox. They owed their rise to pre-eminence to the Valois and without royal favour would remain impotent; their already serious financial difficulties worsened. Therefore they had looked elsewhere. In the event, the princes and the people had proved either fickle or indifferent. Charles IX heralded the arrival of peace in 1570 with an impressive cycle of festivities that had not been seen in France since the reign of his father. The theme of his reign would henceforth be *Concordia*. Guise influence had reached a new low. Events in the Low Countries would soon change all that.

8

A WEDDING AND FOUR
THOUSAND FUNERALS

Paris was not only sixteenth-century Europe's largest city; it was its first metropolis. To wander the warren of streets behind its medieval walls was to experience such a bustle, noise and stench that it was compared to an entire province. Everywhere the visitor was reminded of its extraordinary Catholic heritage: its 300,000 souls were crammed into nearly 300 streets, divided into 39 parishes and served by 104 churches and monasteries; its conservative and celebrated university was spread over 49 colleges on the city's Left Bank.

As he left the Louvre at 11 am on Friday 22 August 1572, Gaspard de Coligny paid little attention to his surroundings. He had just attended a council meeting, chaired in the absence of the king and the Queen Mother by the Duke of Anjou, and as he walked along was absorbed in reading an important piece of business. He did not return the hostile looks of the locals. At 55 he was the kingdom's most experienced politician and soldier and used to the menacing gazes of Catholics. The curious were kept at a distance by a dozen body-guards. His serious expression, penetrating gaze and white beard lent him a gravity that was out of place amid the gaiety of a rejuvenated court. Even his enemies respected his courage and piety. He was often compared to his contemporary, François de Guise—France's 'two shining diamonds'. Better educated than the friend who became his bitterest enemy, he was a good Latinist and maintained a journal (since lost) for posterity. Like Guise, the admiral spread fear among his enemies. There was an uncompromising element in his character which suited him well to Calvinist discipline. In war he knew the value of cruelty and terror as a weapon. To the Protestants this made him a hero, and the leadership was in awe of him. That morning he was making the short walk to his lodgings in the rue de Béthisy. Soon after he turned into the rue des Poulies a single shot rang out from a hundred feet away. Protestants placed their trust in providence for good reason: at the very same moment the shot was fired Coligny stopped and turned suddenly, and the shot missed his vitals, fracturing his left forearm and taking off an index finger. His men immediately rushed to the house from where the shot had been fired and tried to force the door, but the assassin had planned well. The house had a rear door that opened onto the square in front of Saint-Germain l'Auxerrois church, where a horse was awaiting him.

Coligny was not killed by the bullet; he would have lived. And yet within forty-eight hours he was murdered. Several days of anarchy followed in which between at least 2,000, and perhaps as many as 6,000, Protestants were butchered. Upwards of 600 houses were pillaged. The Saint Bartholomew's Day Massacre is the greatest imponderable of sixteenth-century history. The barbarity with which defenceless women and children were massacred has echoes of the horrors of the twentieth century—horrors that were literally unspeakable: such was the cruelty and terror of those August days that very few were ever able to set down in words what they had seen or experienced. The task of the historian is made all the more difficult because the sources that survive, written amid the confusion or put together much later in an attempt to shift the blame, are even more than usually partial and suspect. Over the centuries a plethora of suspects and motives have been put forward. Older interpretations rested on Catherine's reputation as a wicked Italian Queen schooled in the dark political arts of Machiavelli. Coligny's assassination, it is claimed, had been planned years before and was the signal for a premeditated programme of extermination. Catherine, it is claimed, was driven insane by maternal jealousy. Coligny was increasingly powerful at court and threatened to supplant her in her son's affections, and so she employed the Guise to eliminate the admiral. This conjecture relies more on xenophobia and misogyny than hard evidence. In fact, the evidence for Coligny's preeminence is rather thin: in the year before his death he was at court for a total of only five weeks. In a major reinterpretation in 1973, Nicola Sutherland argued that an assassination was inconsistent with Catherine's larger political aims.[1] Catherine had spent more than ten years trying to preserve the peace by balancing the Catholic and Protestant factions, and there is little reason to believe that she would suddenly abandon these consistently held policies and order the death of the Protestant leader, let alone a more general policy of extermination. If not Catherine, then who? Sutherland claimed to have uncovered an international Catholic conspiracy, involving Spain, the Papacy, and the Guise. The Spanish scenario is plausible. In the summer of 1572 Coligny was pressing for immediate intervention in the Low Countries. Philip II of Spain and the Duke of Alva wished him dead. Once again, however, the evidence is flimsy. Spanish policy was tempered by *real-politik*, recognizing that the admiral was a force for division and therefore contributed to France's present weakness. There are other suspects and motives: the Duke of Anjou, the Italians on the council, or a combination of the two—all have their accusers. Charles IX has recently been rehabilitated as an idealistic philosopher-king who, fearing that his dream of concord was about to be shattered, played a decisive role in planning Coligny's murder. Fresh clues have been gleaned from the prosaic (rising grain prices) to the esoteric (the neo-platonic environment of the court). One benefit of recent research has been to uncouple the plot to kill Coligny from the general massacre that followed. Few historians would now argue that the plotters had a premeditated plan to murder thousands. In order to understand the Massacre we must first answer the riddle of Coligny's death. Only then will we begin to uncover the link between aristocratic conspiracy and mob violence.

* * * *

Despite the recent research, much that surrounds the death of Coligny continues to remain the stuff of myth and legend. But the historian is no ordinary storyteller. Solving his murder is not substantially different from any other puzzle half a millennium old. The sources may be partial and the interpretations of the events will vary depending on which sources one places most trust in—but this is always the case in historical reconstruction. In fact, the historian of the Massacre is blessed with a great deal more evidence than is usual for the sixteenth century. We are not like the detective left bemused by the absence of a body, a suspect, and a motive. The most glaring omission in the investigation so far has been the absence of serious analysis of the principal suspects: the Guise family. Although most are now agreed that the Guise were responsible for the assassination of Coligny, the gaze of the historian continues to fall principally on Philip II, Catherine de Medici, or Charles IX: getting the Guise wrong means getting the Saint Bartholomew's Day Massacre wrong. Reconsidering the political events of the period 1570–2 from their perspective gives a very different impression of events at the centre than is usual. We shall find that there are as many myths about the background to the Massacre as there are about the events of 22–24 August itself. Not only will we find that we have a body and weapon; but that we have a motive and conspiracy to kill too.

The first myth about the months preceding the Massacre is that there was a united ultra-Catholic faction in France. Certainly, there were many Catholics, probably a majority, opposed to the Peace of Saint-Germain, and the Guise were their principal hope. But in Paris, while the people were happy to invent rousing songs in their honour, they were more reticent about showing armed support. Calls to support the family in its feud with the Montmorency had fallen on deaf ears. What made the Protestants such a formidable threat, despite their numerical inferiority, was their relative unity. Catholics, in contrast, were bitterly divided by personality and policy. Nowhere was this more evident than in the royal council itself. The overwhelming majority of councillors who signed the Peace of Saint-Germain shared the same ultra-Catholic sensibilities as the Guise and the same distaste for heresy. But what these councillors shared too was a dislike for the Guise. Peacemaking was self-interested, enabling its sponsors to consolidate their grip on power. A renewal of civil war would only rejuvenate the Guise. Since these councillors played a crucial role in the Massacre it is worth briefly sketching out who they were.

Ironically, the only councillor personally well disposed to the Guise was the one man who opposed them on ideological grounds. Jean de Morvilliers, Bishop of Orléans, was the last surviving member of the Cardinal of Lorraine's evangelical circle still on the council. He was widely respected for his opinions and often presided over the council in the absence of the king. A key architect of the toleration policy, he had negotiated the Peace of Saint-Germain and wished to maintain it at all costs. Though his and Morvilliers' paths had long since diverged, Lorraine still wrote warm and affectionate letters which recalled 'the liberty of our ancient and firm friendship'.[2] The same could not be said of the other religious moderate on the council. The religious peace had allowed the Montmorency to reassert themselves. Following the death of the constable in 1567, leadership of the family passed to his eldest son, the Marshal of France, François, who entered his fortieth year in 1570. François was utterly unlike his religiously conservative father; suspected of being a Nicodemite, he now emerged as the champion of the free Gallican Church, which would be the natural ally of Anglicans and Lutherans. A fierce opponent of the Guise, he was very close to his cousin Coligny. Coligny had no need to visit the court to make his influence felt: his cousin acted for him. Montmorency's influence on the council was reinforced by the fact that his brother-in-law, Marshal Cossé, had control of the finances. François quickly emerged as the strong man of the peace party. Just like his father, he dealt with any signs of popular sedition with exemplary brutality. On 18 March 1571 the Protestant congregation in Rouen was attacked after some of them had failed to remove their hats as the Host passed them in the street. The fighting left forty dead. Montmorency's role in condemning sixty-six suspects to death, levying swingeing fines, and removing others from office left Catholics bemused. One eyewitness thought he and his men 'were of the colour of Calvinists'.[3] Even more controversial was his role in the Cross of Gastines Affair in Paris. This cross had been erected by Catholics to celebrate the execution of three Protestants during the recent civil war. Article 32 of the Edict of Saint-Germain demanded the suppression of all such reminders of sectarian hatred. Catholics were outraged and tried to prevent it being pulled down on 29 December 1571. In his capacity as city governor he quickly nipped sedition in the bud, immediately hanging one rioter; others were severely punished. With the Protestants under his protection Parisians turned their sights elsewhere. The fevered religious atmosphere was conducive to witch-hunting and there were several burnings in the city. In June 1572 there were anti-Italian riots caused by tax hikes. The marshal and his substantial following in and around Paris were the only counterweights to the seething discontent.

Otherwise the council was dominated by Catherine de Medici's protégés. In the main they were Italians with ultra-Catholic inclinations but, in the short term, took a pragmatic view of the peace and shared Montmorency hostility to the Guise. At 33, Louis Gonzaga was the youngest and most intelligent of them and, as the highest born, their natural leader. Catherine had carefully managed his career since his arrival from Italy, bending the law in order to permit him to inherit the duchy of Nevers, the greatest landed fortune of the age, when the last male of the House of Clèves died, leaving three daughters. Louis was a new type of Catholic: a man of intense piety, he was an early promoter of the Counter-Reformation sensibility emanating from Italy. A serious leg wound received in 1568 effectively ended his military career, and his energies were directed into matters of state, in which he had pretensions to be something of a controversialist and thinker. He emerged as the chief mentor of the Duke of Anjou, shaping the heir to the throne's intellectual and devotional interests and encouraged the young duke to distance himself from the Guise. It was Nevers who articulated the inchoate animosities of Catherine's faction. In a memoir on the state of the realm written for Anjou in 1573 he argued that one of the principal causes of the weakness of the monarchy was the monopoly of royal offices that the Guise family had built up over the generations, such that they held 'half of the principal honours, estates and emoluments'.[4] Whereas the grandfather had been worth only 30,000 to 40,000 livres a year, his grandchildren were now worth 500,000 to 600,000 livres per year. They were over-mighty subjects. He disparaged Louis, Cardinal of Guise—with some justification—as lacking the capacity and intelligence for affairs of state, and did not believe Duke Henri was fit to sit on the Privy Council. This was all the more surprising because Henri de Guise was his brother-in-law. Nevers had married Henriette, the eldest of the three Clèves heiresses in 1566 and Guise married Catherine in October 1570. Temperamentally they were very different. Guise was primarily a soldier who displayed little interest in the finer matters of theology; he must have appeared shallow to the more mature and more cerebral Nevers. And their personality clash was exacerbated by their wives, who did not see eye to eye. There was an almighty squabble over the partition of the Clèves estate and the debts that had accrued. Henriette does not seem to have been a Protestant, while Catherine renounced her faith only shortly before marrying Guise.

The final actor in the drama was the king himself. Charles IX had recently emerged as a political figure in his own right and, though he despised heresy, invested much energy in the success of the peace. He was not without intelligence and could speak with passion, if not much art, on subjects as diverse as theology, poetry, architecture, and military strategy. Recent attempts to rehabilitate him as a philosopher-king, however, surely go too far—this is a more apt description of his more intelligent and able younger brother. Charles was happier outdoors. His frenetic dedication to hunting, even by the standards of the time, was obsessive. His fondness for metal-working—he had a forge installed in the Louvre—was even more unkingly. Though his tutor, Amyot, the translator of Plutarch, had proscribed the reading of Rabelais, Charles had an earthy sense of humour. Some of his jokes, though lacking in wit, were relatively harmless. When Guise's only sister, Catherine, who at the age of 17 was already noted for her independent spirit, married the widower, Louis de Bourbon, Duke of Montpensier, then forty years her senior, Charles quipped that her blood 'so fiery and vivacious would turn as cold as a fish's on contact with the creeping coldness of the Duke of Montpensier'.[5] Other 'jokes' reveal the crassness behind the civilized veneer. Charles gloated that the scene after the consummation of his marriage to Elizabeth of Austria resembled a 'German corset bloodied by a pistol shot'.[6] Charles may have been wedded to peace for the moment, but he had been raised in an environment in which political assassination was common currency. He was a man of his age and gave his blessing to political murder: on 10 December 1571 a group of assassins murdered Lignerolles, favourite of the Duke of Anjou, whose crime had been to intrigue against royal policy.

* * * *

Marriages were among the few occasions that the Guise were able to attend at court in the two years before the Massacre, otherwise they were not welcome. The Montpensier marriage in February 1570 had been under negotiation for a year and was crucial for rebuilding ties with the other princes, which had been lately under strain. Catherine de Guise was the only daughter of Anne d'Este and Duke François. As a descendant of French royalty through her mother, she commanded a huge dowry—200,000 livres—of which the Crown agreed to pay half. But the marriage was not a happy one, and with his brother-in-law soon in deep trouble for his pursuit of Princess Margot, Montpensier found it expedient to feign that he was 'no longer a friend to the Guise'. Duke Henri's hurriedly arranged marriage in October permitted him to return to court and he resumed the duties of the Grand Master of the Royal Household. On 25 March 1571 the Cardinal of Lorraine officiated at the coronation of Queen Elizabeth and he and his nephews figured prominently in her triumphal entry in Paris. And then suddenly royal favour was removed. There was not, complained the Spanish ambassador, a 'spoonful' to be had. Power was passing once again to the old Montmorency enemy. Just a few weeks after the coronation, tensions exploded in the king's chamber itself, and Guise and Méru, Marshal Montmorency's younger brother, gave each other the lie. Once more, the duke, his brothers, and uncles had no alternative but to leave.

'The Cardinal of Lorraine is no longer spoken of, except as if he was dead, nor any of the Guise, about whom nothing is known.' The words of the Spanish ambassador hardly suggest that the retirement from court was the cue for the start of a conspiracy with Philip II and Alva. The family gathering which took place in the summer of 1571 had a sinister purpose for some historians. In fact, it was to celebrate the birth of the duke and duchess's first born, Charles, Prince of Joinville, on 20 August. Philip II still considered the Guise his chief ally and told his ambassador to help them; but they were of little use to him in disgrace. The amicable correspondence between the Cardinal of Lorraine and Philip II and Alva ceased. If there was a Guise-Habsburg plot to overturn the peace in France it was kept remarkably well hidden. Cardinal Charles accepted his fall stoically and busied himself with visitations of his diocese and the reform of the breviary. He lamented to the Duke of Ferrara that 'the court had changed greatly since the time when he was raised there. Now they seek to discriminate against the old servants of the Crown, never telling the truth in an attempt to create division among the great and, if possible, break good alliances and friendships, in order to put everyone at odds with his peers.'[7] Things got worse in September when Coligny reappeared at court. The warmth with which he was received could not have been in more contrast to the way in which the king treated the Cardinal of Guise, who remained near the court in his customary role as envoy; 'hardly remembered by their majesties' the king did not bother to summon him.[8] Coligny was rewarded with a gift of 100,000 livres and the revenues of the benefices of his recently deceased brother, the Cardinal of Châtillon. He was welcomed back to his seat on the Privy Council and permitted the quasi-princely honour of being surrounded by a retinue of fifty gentlemen everywhere he went.

With Coligny on board the council could now press ahead with its plans to heal the religious divide. Future stability would be achieved by two dynastic marriages and one reconciliation. In the first instance an anti-Spanish alliance with England would be concluded and sealed by the marriage of Elizabeth I and the Duke of Anjou. Secondly, negotiations for the marriage of Henri de Navarre and Marguerite de Valois were to be finalized. The final piece in the jigsaw would be the reconciliation of Guise and Coligny. These policies were strongly supported by the Montmorency. Catherine could count on her creatures to fall into line. Opposition came over matters of conscience. Anjou flatly refused to marry a heretic. The council was however united in its desire to see the end of the poisonous Guise-Montmorency feud. In October 1571 Guise was ordered to court to make his peace. He was to come only with his ordinary retinue.

Guise found himself cornered: to renounce his enmity while the Montmorency were in such a position of ascendancy would be yet another humiliation. His uncle urged caution, but at the age of 20

Henri was less inclined to accept fate. The cardinal's letters are filled with world-weary resignation rather than Machiavellian scheming. An experienced politician, he knew the values of patience and forbearance. He had made peace with Coligny once before, only for civil war to alter that within eighteen months. He assured Charles IX of his 'entire obedience and fidelity' and promised 'charity towards his neighbour and the forgetting of past injuries. He placed in the hands of the king, who has the power of the sword, all the justice he could wish for and in the hands of God all his revenge.'[9] His nephew had other ideas. He went to Paris to show his solidarity with the oppressed Catholics.

The city was in turmoil over the Cross of Gastines Affair, symbol of its resistance. Mounting anger at its impending removal was fuelled from the pulpits, and especially that of Simon Vigor, the king's own stipendiary preacher. Vigor, whom the Protestants referred to as 'the bellows of Satan', pleaded with Governor Montmorency to leave the cross and delivered a fiery sermon on 4 November full of menace. Vigor's sermons were popular because of their simple and uncompromising language, insisting that the king annul 'the damnable edict that allows [the Huguenots] freedom of conscience, and constrain [them] to return to the Catholic Church by depriving them of their properties and reinstituting the punishment of execution by burning'.[10] Montmorency maintained order with difficulty following the 20 December riots. He reported to the king 'that in Paris there are a growing number of gentlemen friends of the lords of Guise, and they have rented rooms in various quarters, plotting nightly something between them...and that among the plans they have one will go and kill the admiral in his house'.[11] Since Coligny was in Burgundy this was highly unlikely. This was yet another trial of strength, as had occurred in 1565. Montmorency warned the Crown that in any confrontation he would be obliged to support his cousin. Coligny issued orders for his men to be ready to mobilize. The dukes of Guise and Aumale and the Marquis of Mayenne entered Paris on 14 January with a retinue of 500 men, about the same number that Montmorency commanded.

Their presence gave succour to the malcontents. Two houses on the Pont Notre-Dame, occupied by suspected Protestants, were the object of continual intimidation; their walls defaced with mud and filth. We do not know where the duke heard Mass on Ash Wednesday 1572. If he had gone to Notre-Dame he would have been subjected to an extraordinary political sermon by Vigor, denouncing the hypocrisy of the peace edict and challenging the Crown. Citing Saint Augustine, he argued that it was permitted to kill only at the king's command, but that the moment the king gave his order, it was sinful not to obey it. To illustrate the point he said that 'if the king ordered the Admiral [Coligny] killed, it would be wicked not to kill him'.[12] Had the Duke of Guise been present, or read the version that was hurriedly printed, he would have taken this as a sign to be patient. In any case, Guise's motives in coming to Paris had less to do with religion than with the restoration of his damaged honour. There was more bluster about him than menace. In requesting leave from the king to fight Coligny in single combat, he was trying to put off the inevitable. Cardinal Charles would have none of this foolishness and left for Reims at the onset of Lent. In April the Marquis of Mayenne quit France altogether to go on crusade. If Guise was plotting to restart the civil war beginning with a strike on Coligny it is inconceivable that he would have permitted his brother, Mayenne, to depart with 200 family retainers, or that his cousins, the young Marquis of Elbeuf and the eldest son of the Duke of Aumale, should go to Rome in the train of their uncle, Cardinal Charles. Henri de Guise's show of strength in the city had achieved his purpose; his challenge to Coligny had shown that he was not coming to the peace table defeated. On the 12 May 1572 he bowed to the inevitable and arrived at court to make his peace. Guise agreed to abide by the terms of the 1566 Moulins accords, at which the 'king was overjoyed, and wishes that, under grave penalties, no more mention is made of things past'.[13] As a gentleman Guise was bound by his word of honour—that is until such time as the king said otherwise.

Things were going well for Catherine and she moved on to her next objective. Within a month she struck a deal with Jeanne d'Albret, Henri de Navarre's mother, on the matter of the great Bourbon-Valois dynastic alliance. Navarre's uncle, Cardinal Bourbon, would perform the service in the square in front of Notre-Dame, but without wearing a surplice. Navarre would escort his bride into the cathedral, retiring before Mass. The marriage contract, signed on 11 April, was followed a few days later by the signing of the Treaty of Blois, a defensive alliance between England and France. Catholics opposed on grounds of conscience could do little about either. It is commonly asserted that the Guise did everything they could to oppose royal policy. But things were not as simple as that. Immediately after the reconciliation with Coligny, Cardinal Charles left for Rome for the papal conclave to elect a successor to Pius V. Catherine charged him with obtaining the appropriate dispensation for her daughter's marriage. Already in disgrace, the cardinal was under pressure to deliver. His predicament was made worse by Mayenne's departure from France without royal dispensation. The depth to which stock in the Guise had plunged is revealed by the grovelling letters the cardinal wrote in order to placate the king's displeasure. He himself was angry at his nephew's folly and pleaded with the king to 'have pity on a poor, hopeless and debauched boy'.[14] Mayenne was forced to seek the king's pardon. Once in Rome, the cardinal had to appear, at the very least, not to be subverting royal policy. He swore on the damnation of his soul that he was doing all he could, but despite twisting arms and greasing palms, there was a stumbling block which even his powers of persuasion were unable to overcome. As he wrote to Catherine on 28 July, the issue was not one of consanguinity, but the 'difficulty is in the religion of the King of Navarre and in his person. It is of public notoriety that he acts against the Catholics in his lands'.[15] The marriage, delayed by the death of Jeanne d'Albert and rescheduled for 18 August, would have to proceed without the cardinal or the dispensation. Just as the final touches to the peace and reconciliation project were being finalized, a political earthquake occurred in the Netherlands that would change the balance of power in northern Europe forever. The artfully constructed peace edifice began to crack and totter.

* * * *

The repression and exploitation of Alva's regime had led to widespread revulsion in the Netherlands and elsewhere in Europe. Protestant pirates, known as the Sea Beggars were a serious menace, but they had confined themselves to raids on the coast and attacks on Spanish shipping from their bases in La Rochelle, Emden, and the English Channel ports. When Elizabeth I, who was always cautious in her relations with Philip II, expelled 600 Beggars from England they seized the small, unimportant port of Brill. This time the Beggars stayed and held out: the revolt of the Netherlands had begun. By early July the whole of north Holland, except Amsterdam, was in rebel hands. The States of Holland recognized William of Orange as 'Protector' of the Netherlands in flagrant defiance of Alva's commission from Philip II. For Protestants everywhere the liberation of the Netherlands was the great cause of the age, and since the end of the third civil war in France the French Protestant leadership had tried to persuade Catherine and her ministers that intervention in the Netherlands was in the national interest, uniting Frenchmen against the old enemy.

William of Orange's younger brother, Count Louis of Nassau, was the rebel's chief envoy in France. He had fought valiantly with the Huguenots in the third civil war and Coligny had given his word that he could count on them during his hour of need. He also told Count Louis that he could persuade Charles IX to help. As soon as Brill had fallen, Nassau had rushed troops and supplies from Huguenot-controlled La Rochelle. He then embarked on a bold plan in the southern Netherlands in support of his brother in the north. On 24 May he seized the town of Mons by stealth and garrisoned it with 1,500 men. At the same time another force of exiles and Huguenots under the command of François de la Noue crossed the frontier farther west and captured Valenciennes. Then they launched an audacious raid on Brussels to capture the Duke of Alva himself by surprise.

Alva was convinced of Charles IX's complicity and that France would soon declare war. Fearing the French more than the Sea Beggars, he concentrated his efforts on Mons. Just before the Spanish managed to surround the city, Count Louis sent a messenger to beg Coligny to fulfil his promise and mount an invasion of the Netherlands in the name of Charles IX. The messenger, Genlis, was a cousin of Coligny as well as of the late Egmont and Hornes. Arriving in Paris on 23 June he set out to persuade Coligny and King Charles to send immediate relief to Mons, arguing that it did not mean a total break with Spain. In this limited objective he was successful and he left Paris with 6,000 men on 12 July. According to the Spanish ambassador, Diego de Zuñiga, Charles secretly gave him 60,000 livres.[16] Seven days later Genlis marched straight into a Spanish ambush at Saint-Ghislain about six miles south of Mons: the French were wiped out, Genlis was taken prisoner, tortured, and strangled. Papers captured by the Spanish confirmed Alva's suspicions that Charles IX was himself aware of the Orangist invasion. Charles protested his innocence but was aware he had been seriously compromised. On 12 August, just six days before his sister's wedding, he wrote to his ambassador in Brussels: 'The papers found on those captured with Genlis [show]...everything done by Genlis to have been committed with my consent...Nevertheless, [you will tell the Duke of Alva] these are lies invented to excite suspicion against me. He must not attach any credence to them.'[17]

The precise level of Charles IX's involvement in the invasion is difficult to gauge. Twice in July 1571, he and his mother had met Louis of Nassau in secret. No doubt he dreamed of emulating his father and grandfather and of regaining the ancient French lands in

Flanders and Artois that had been usurped by the Habsburgs. Charles wrote to Nassau on 27 April 1572 in support of the liberation of the Low Countries from Spanish 'oppression'. 'All my fancies are bound up', he wrote a month later, 'with opposing the grandeur of the Spaniards and I am determined to conduct myself as subtly as possible.'[18] Zuñiga, the Spanish ambassador, was well aware of Charles's game and of his limited room for manoeuvre. In a letter of 1 June Philip II ordered him to play along: 'as long as [France] does not lower its mask, we shall not lower ours, but give them to understand that we believe them'; and more explicit instructions were issued a month later: 'it is necessary that they believe that we believe their external appearances'.[19] In this context, the attitude of England was crucial. There was some misplaced hope that England could be persuaded to act as France's proxy. But the failure of the English marriage and Elizabeth's flat refusal—fearing French hegemony as much as Spanish—to sign anything more than a defensive alliance made Catherine, in particular, resistant to an adventurous foreign policy that threatened the fragile peace at home. The overwhelming majority of Frenchmen shared the Cardinal of Lorraine's assessment that summer: 'If France enters the war, all is ruined.'[20]

In the hot and humid summer of 1572, the Privy Council was dangerously divided on the matter of intervention. Coligny returned to the Council on 6 June. His familiarity with the king raised eyebrows and rumours spread about his influence on policy. His chief ally, Marshal Montmorency, was sent to England, where he arrived on 10th to ratify the Treaty of Blois. More than protocol was at stake: a man of high status was required to impress upon Elizabeth and her ministers the benefits of an Anglo-French invasion. He was empowered by Catherine to make another marriage offer, this time in the shape of Charles IX's youngest brother, the Duke of Alençon. Elizabeth made it clear that she found the idea of marrying a man twenty-two years her junior ridiculous and restated her desire to remain on friendly terms with Spain. Catherine refused to countenance taking risks without the English and her opposition to intervention was hardening. On his return Montmorency put a favourable gloss on his mission and convinced Charles, in a meeting on 20 July that, notwithstanding the Saint-Ghislain debacle, all was not lost and the prospect of the English marriage and an Anglo-French offensive still alive. The court then dispersed for three weeks: the king went to the Loire and the Queen Mother went to Châlons to visit her daughter Claude, Duchess of Lorraine. When the Privy Council reconvened in

Paris on 6 August 1572 the tensions that had been simmering that summer exploded in two stormy meetings.

The various ambassadors found it difficult to glean what went on. The ambassador of the Grand Duke of Tuscany reported that all was in 'confusion'; Walsingham told Elizabeth that Paris was in a state of 'suspense'. However, the basic positions are not difficult to ascertain from the memoranda which survive. Coligny put his case for war with an undercurrent of menace: 'The war is not only just, it is necessary if we wish to avoid a more dangerous one in the future.'[21] The ultra-Catholics objected to the king supporting a military adventure in favour of heretics and rebels. The Duke of Anjou was at their head, the Duke of Nevers his most eloquent mouthpiece. Nevers was not only opposed to war on grounds of conscience, but against all forms of covert operations too: to provoke Philip II was to run the risk of an invasion of the south from Philip's bases in Italy and across the Pyrenees. Since the spring he had argued that a pre-emptive strike on the Protestant leadership was necessary and justified. But it was not the ultras who swung the day. The key intervention came from the ageing Jean de Morvilliers, who had been summoned from semi-retirement. Despite his antipathy to the ultras and his closeness to Montmorency, he came down firmly against war. 'Truly', he wrote, 'it must be confessed that the conquest of the Low Countries would be the finest and the most suitable that the King could accomplish. I do not say it is impossible but I cannot imagine it being done.'[22] What concerned Morvilliers was the failure of Elizabeth and the German Princes to commit themselves to an offensive alliance. Coligny lost the day.

Though open war was out of the question, the king did not cease to continue with covert encouragement for the rebels. Agents in England and Germany were secretly instructed to do everything they could to get Elizabeth and the German princes to break with Spain, thus creating the preconditions for an immediate French attack. But Coligny would wait no longer. French volunteers, not all of them Protestants, had already departed without encouragement. He was also driven by a sense of divine mission. In a letter to lord Burghley he saw himself as 'God's warrior' about to go into battle against the 'servants of Satan'.[23] Just as Guise had found himself cornered months previously, so Coligny was now trapped: honour required that he fulfil his pledge to the House of Orange; conscience that he follow the path of Truth; and the youthful entourage of Protestant captains gathering in Paris for the royal wedding were impatient for action. With or without royal dispensation, he resolved to go to the

Netherlands. In a letter to Orange on 9 August he announced that he would bring 12,000 foot and 3,000 horse with him, and the following day he walked out of a council meeting without promising to desist. The date of his departure was fixed for the 25 August.

Historians remain divided over whether the failed assassination on 22 August was carried out on Guise's orders. He had a motive and there is evidence that links him with the assassin. But he vigorously denied involvement and the evidence pointing to him is circumstantial. It is at this point, as myth and legend becomes entangled with fact, that the conspiracy theories take over. In the absence of evidence we are reduced to conjectures about motive. Was the duke the scapegoat for a wider conspiracy? Did Catherine, motivated by insane jealousy at her son's newly won independence, want Coligny dead? The conceit is seductively Shakespearean. Despite recent attempts to restore her image, Catherine remains the prime suspect. Charles IX was in awe of Coligny, perhaps even a little frightened by his cold conviction, and had taken to referring to him as 'father'. The date of the assassination—22 August—is surely significant in establishing a motive. Those hostile to the Guise claim that they had been plotting for months to undermine the peace and stop the marriage. But if the Duke of Guise was the lone conspirator why did he wait until after Henri de Navarre's and Marguerite's marriage, which took place on the 18th, to do the killing? No: whoever wished Coligny dead also wished the marriage to go ahead. The assassination was not designed to end the peace; nor was it a pre-emptive strike in the next civil war. In fact, the opposite was imperative: that Coligny be stopped from beginning a foreign war and threatening internal peace. This can be shown by subsequent events: as Paris descended into chaos the king issued several orders from 24 to 28 August upholding the edict of pacification. There is a more fundamental objection to considering the failed assassination as a Guise plot. The duke had made his peace with Coligny. To break his word after only three months would have been a flagrant challenge to royal authority, for which 'grave penalties' had been threatened. Guise was young and inexperienced, but he was no fool. Most of his family were in Italy, leaving himself and his uncle, the Duke of Aumale, to face the inevitable judicial and political backlash. The Spanish conspiracy theory is at its weakest here. The success of the revolt in the Netherlands meant they had little more to offer the Guise than moral support. If the Spanish were sending him money it was pitiful: the duke continued to be plagued by creditors and in September was forced to make his first sale of property (the barony of Cuverville for 18,000 livres) in order to keep them at bay. More crucial to the duke's calculations were local circumstances, especially the attitude of Paris's Catholic governor, Marshal Montmorency, who had already faced him down twice. Montmorency's absence from the city in August is a conundrum; it has received scant attention, but was crucial to the chain of events. The marshal was still working for the English alliance early in the month but fell ill and retired to his estates at Chantilly to the north of Paris, and was unable to attend the royal wedding. But Guise could not have known that the marshal would not return to the city at any moment. The absence of a man with a large retinue, who had recent experience of and an aptitude for quelling Catholic sedition, remains a mystery. It was one of the reasons why events in the streets would get out of control so quickly.

If Guise was involved then it is most likely that he was in collusion with someone in authority; that he was given the nod to assassinate Coligny by one or more members of the royal council in the week that followed 10 August. In Guise's mind, this was less murder than the justice he had been searching for a decade. And he was surely provided with assurances of a royal safeguard when the inevitable response, judicial or otherwise, from the Protestants and their Montmorency allies came. In such a scenario, Catherine's involvement is likely. The Spanish ambassador certainly thought she was implicated. Her motives were twofold: to maintain the peace and to remove a man she despised. She had never forgiven the Protestant leaders for their treachery at Meaux in 1567 and now she believed that Coligny was about to do the same again and start another civil war. Catherine was a woman who bore a grudge. In particular, she had long wished the death of the Count of Montgomméry, the unfortunate who had killed her husband in the fateful joust in June 1559. Although it was an accident, Montgomméry was a marked man. He was stripped of his post in the Scots Guard, banished from court, and went into exile where he converted to Protestantism. Finally, in 1574 she had him cornered in Lower Normandy and personally attended to his trial and execution in Paris. In a show of petty vindictiveness his descendants were degraded of their nobility. She was not alone on the council in wanting Coligny dead; but only she could have given Guise the guarantees he needed. Her faction in the Privy Council may have been in on the plot, but Guise would not have trusted the word of men he considered to be his social inferiors and whom he blamed for usurping his rightful position in government. The only other person he trusted was the Duke of Anjou. All the sources suggest that the duke would play a crucial role in the days that followed the assassination. Did the duke egg on his one-time boon companion, in the same way that he had once encouraged him to flirt with his sister? Intelligence and cultivated manners are not barriers to murder, and Henri, Duke of Anjou, was also an accomplished intriguer and dissimulator who placed great store in the powers of manipulation. Deeply pious he may have been, but murder and assassination did not trouble his conscience: he had used them before to remove his enemies and when he ascended the throne as Henry III he would use them again. The assassination appealed to the plotters in the council because it was the perfect political murder. The Crown would get rid of one enemy and the blame would fall entirely on another. It could be represented to the world as a private affair—as the Massacre initially would be—that left the Guise dependent on royal grace.

* * * *

There is another intriguing possibility (one first put forward by Denis Crouzet in 1994) that the gunman was not part of a conspiracy at all; that he had a different motive for wanting Coligny dead, one that was rooted in parochial, not national or international, events.[24] Three documents, until now hidden in the archives, lend credence to this conjecture. The Guise family papers record that on 25 September 1573, a year and a day after Coligny's death, Duke Henri promised to pay annually Charles de Louviers, lord of Maurevert, near Chaumes-en-Brie, who had been raised as a page in his father's household, the sum of 2,000 livres until such time that the king provided him with an equivalent pension.[25] Another document in the Parisian notarial archives is a receipt signed by Guise and Maurevert on 23 May 1581, which attested the latter had received 2,000 livres on 22 August 1575, three years to the day after the attempted assassination took place.[26] By this date Maurevert was already in receipt of a smaller royal pension, amounting to 650 livres. Presumably, it was necessary to get the receipt notarized in the hope that the difference could be claimed from the royal treasury. Two thousand French pounds was a large sum of money—it was a much larger sum than the best-salaried ducal man received—and the fact that Maurevert was paid on the anniversary of the assassination is surely significant. Maurevert is the man that most contemporaries accused of pulling the trigger on 22 August, and his nickname *Tueur du Roi* (King's Killer) takes on a more sinister tone now we know that Henri d'Anjou was happy to award him a pension when he became king. When Coligny was finally killed on 24 August, a reliable commentator says that it was on the express orders of Anjou 'to have the Admiral killed at whatever price it took'.[27] It is entirely proper to speculate that Anjou and Guise were involved in the initial plot and that Anjou agreed to fund the operation, and also that the intrigue cast a shadow over their future relations, which were to have such enormous repercussions for the kingdom. This leaves the question of why the Duke of Guise waited over a year to promise Maurevert his money. Surely an assassin carrying out such a dangerous mission would have expected something sooner, or at least something up front? After all, those who finally killed Coligny were gratified much sooner. This raises the possibility that Maurevert was not contracted to kill, but played the role of minion to Guise's Henry II of England and Coligny's Thomas Becket. One of the most considered accounts of the Massacre, that of the secret agent, Tomasso Sassetti, says that news of the shooting came to the Duke of Guise when he was playing tennis with the king, 'who was very shaken and very angry with the arquebusier and his accomplices. And because the common talk was that Guise had had the shot fired out of his old enmity, His Majesty turning round to him . . . asked him if what was being said was true. [Guise] denied knowing anything.'[28] The Venetian ambassador also thought that Guise was innocent; his reasoning being that the duke:

> would never have had the audacity to go to such extremes in the king's presence, because it would have been an affront to the king; and even if the latter had feigned not to be displeased at the time, he would have remembered later to the great shame of Guise and his House, excluding him from his service and depriving him of favour.[29]

Guise himself pointed the finger at his father's old foe, the Duke of Alva. Was Maurevert ingratiating himself rather than executing a direct order?

Maurevert's story is worth telling because it answers the question why so many Frenchmen wanted Coligny dead. It begins in the Brie, a region whose proximity to the city and fertile pastures made it particularly attractive to Paris's nouveaux riches. There were social tensions as the wealthy newcomers jostled with established families for power. More significantly, the local gentry were strongly attracted to Protestantism. Their high profile in the cause can be gauged by the trip made by Charles IX in July 1571 to the château of Lumigny in the

Brie for a secret meeting with the Protestants. The hostess, a rich widow called Marie de Luzé, was a senior figure in the Protestant leadership and had only just returned from England, where she had been kept hostage as security for money borrowed by the Huguenots. But being a Protestant in the Brie was not like being a Protestant elsewhere in France. Many were servants of the Guise and traditional family and neighbourhood ties were thrown into confusion by the high rate of conversion, causing a large number of internecine family feuds. The civil war in the Brie had a particularly brutal character. Marie de Luzé personified these conflicts. Marie's step-father was a senior Guise counsellor. But she was a Protestant and her husband was a senior Protestant captain during the civil wars. In 1569 Maurevert was serving as an officer in his cavalry company. One day on campaign, the captain had to dismount in order to do 'his necessities' and he wandered off from his troop. Maurevert followed him and shot him in the back. He rode off with the body to the Catholic camp. His motive for treachery was money: a price had recently been put on the heads of the Protestant leadership. The Duke of Anjou gave him 2,000 crowns and, in an act that showed chivalry to have become utterly debased, the collar of the Order of Saint Michel.

Maurevert therefore already had one paid assassination under his belt when he took it upon himself, or was contracted, to kill Coligny. He was descended from a wealthy Parisian family and had been raised as a page in the household of François, Duke of Guise. He was probably still in Guise service in September 1561, because he made a great marriage to Marguerite Acquino, the daughter of Neapolitan exiles and supporters of the Angevin cause, soon after which he converted to Protestantism. The marriage was childless and at her death in 1579 she bequeathed her property and titles in France to Henri de Guise.[30] This may have been gratitude for longstanding protection: at the time of her marriage not only was her husband already in trouble with the law but her uncle, the Bishop of Troyes, had been forced to resign his see after presenting himself to the Reformed Church in the town and asking to be its Pastor. The subsequent investigation by the Roman Inquisition was a serious affair for a family with interests in Naples.

Even by the standards of the age, Maurevert was a violent man. He murdered one of his cousins in 1574 and lost an arm in an encounter with a nephew in 1579. He knew that he was a marked man and was accompanied everywhere by armed heavies and took to wearing chain mail under his clothes in case of attack. He needed protection and this came in the form of the Guise. In April 1571 he signed over all his goods to his half-brother, Pierre de Foissy. By cutting out the lawful heirs of his inheritance Maurevert was announcing a break with the rest of his family—no wonder he soon came under attack from his cousin and his nephew. Maurevert was making a statement the implications of which could only be fully understood by people from the Brie: the Foissy were the most important of all Guise servants in the region. But even Guise protection was not enough. His past caught up with him on 14 April 1583 when Marie de Luzé's son finally cornered him in Paris and had his revenge. Maurevert died 'regretted by none, hated by all'.

To sum up: by 1572 Maurevert was an outsider, who severed ties to one side of the family only to betray the other side when he returned to the Catholic fold. His marginal status made him the perfect assassin. After Coligny's murder he became a pariah. Wherever he turned up people scattered, according to Brantôme, as if the arrival of the plague had been announced. Maurevert pulled the trigger; but he was not alone. He was a desperate, hunted man, whose sole prospect of a career depended on his ability to kill before he was killed. Maurevert relied on the Guise for protection, but this did not come without favours in return, and meant he could never speak out or tell the truth about the conspiracy to kill Coligny. Maurevert was the perfect patsy.

But here the evidence of a lone desperado, driven to kill for existential or financial reasons breaks down. The investigation that followed the attempted assassination revealed that the plot went to the heart of the Guise inner sanctum. The house from which the arquebus was fired was owned by a Parisian servant of the Guise, François de Pilla, whose career really took off *after* the assassination. In early 1574 'he had charge of the affairs of Monseigneur the Duke of Guise and by 1580 was superintendent of the ducal finances'.[31] Evidence for his involvement is however circumstantial. After all, in August 1572 he was out of town and the house was being used by the servants of Anne d'Este. More significantly Maurevert had accomplices who helped him to plan the operation. A lookout post was prepared: the trellised window overlooking the rue des Poulies was hung with garments in order to obscure those watching Coligny's movements. The getaway was well planned. Two of Coligny's men gave hot pursuit, but the assassin changed mounts at Charenton, crossed the river Seine and made for the château of Chailly, near Fontainebleau, where his pursuers had to give up chase. 'The drawbridge being raised and the walls filled with arquebuses.' The château belonged to Jean de la Boissière.[32] La Boissière was the most important man in our story and has good claim to be the mastermind behind the assassination. He had been a senior counsellor since at least 1550, when he was master of François de Guise's household. In 1556, Guise procured him a post in the royal household and he also became *grand louvetier de France*, Master of the Royal Wolf Hunt. Like Pilla, he was now a senior counsellor to Henri de Guise.[33] The counsel they gave to their young charge was informed by their own experience of civil war: many of the colleagues, kinsmen and friends who had shared with them the successes of the 1550s had betrayed the family and its followers in joining the Protestant cause.[34] The current state of research does not permit us to state with any certainty whether Henri de Guise had ultimate responsibility for ordering Coligny's assassination. His retinue was full of retainers who had a motive, thought the risks acceptable, and were willing to do the dirty work themselves. No orders were necessary. Civil war had overturned old certainties and hierarchy and lesser gentlemen could act autonomously: faith required them to do so. Maurevert and his accomplices were quite capable of destroying the hated peace of their own volition. They were fulfilling their duty to the memory of the dead duke, but their motives were also personal. By killing Coligny they were taking revenge on those who had betrayed them and done wrong to their families.

* * * *

Coligny's political position, which had become so precarious since his determination to march on Brussels, was given an immense boost by the shooting. This was why he was determined to remain in the city, despite pleas from his supporters to retire to safety. At 2 pm Charles IX hurried to see the admiral in his bed and promised that the investigation would leave no stone unturned. Anjou's guard were stationed around the admiral's lodging. The investigation could only work to the advantage of Coligny: it would unmask his enemies and advance his plans for an invasion of the Low Countries. He demanded that Guise be arrested. Charles's verbal assurances were not enough for many around the admiral. They were angry and they were frightened. Some of the language used when addressing the king was threatening; some hotheads went as far as giving the king an ultimatum. Many Catholics feared Protestant reprisals. On the afternoon of Saturday, 23 August, an informal meeting of Catherine's faction was held at which Anjou was also present. The talk was of impending civil war, since the current investigation was likely to implicate any privy councillors involved in a conspiracy. It was suggested that now, while the Protestant leadership was gathered together, was the time to strike. A quick strike would entail a minimum of violence and obviate the need for civil war. For Louis Gonzaga, Duke of Nevers, it was not a matter of faith, but rather about curbing Coligny's ambition. All that was required was a list of targets and a coordinated plan of attack.

At around 11 pm a second meeting took place, this time with the king present, in which the urgent need to slay the hydra of civil war was put to him. It was agreed to proceed. We cannot be sure that Henri de Guise was present. At midday the duke and his uncle, Claude d'Aumale, had been preparing to leave the city as tensions mounted. They did not do so. To leave would have been an admission of guilt. It is possible they were summoned to remain. The duke was certainly present at the third and final meeting of the day which took place in the Louvre at around midnight—he did not have to walk far from the Hôtel d'Aumale, which was round the corner. This was a council of war at which the dukes of Guise, Aumale, Angoulême, Anjou, and Montpensier drew up the definitive list of targets—about seventy men in all—and divided up their men into assassination squads. Guise would take care of Coligny before crossing over to the Left Bank and striking at targets in the faubourg Saint-Germain. Another detachment was earmarked for the rue Saint-Honoré. The Duke of Montpensier would proceed with the killing in the Louvre and be responsible for the task of forcing Navarre and Condé to attend Mass on pain of death. At this juncture a fateful decision was made, which would send the clinical strike spiralling of control. The former and current mayors of the city were summoned and told that the city militia was to be mobilized to maintain order. It was a highly risky policy. The rationale among the military men was simple: Paris and its 300,000 citizens were notoriously difficult to control. But the militia was a recent creation, formed during the tumultuous days after the Massacre of Wassy. It had never proved an unqualified success as a peacekeeping force. Many of the 30,000 militiamen were ordinary folk who begrudged bearing arms, and this allowed the fanatics to take the lead. The Paris militia had always been keener on hunting heretics than on repressing Catholic sedition. There is good evidence to suggest that radical Catholics had infiltrated and were overrepresented among the ranks of the junior officers. When they were informed that the king was under threat from the Huguenots and that they were to stand to the following day, many saw it as an opportunity not to be missed. The royalists hurriedly stitched white crosses to their hats or put on white armbands: anyone not wearing this insignia was a potential enemy.

Guise had no idea of the impending catastrophe as he mustered his troops at the Hôtel d'Aumale in the early hours of the 24th. As around sixty men, including his uncle Claude and the Duke of Angoulême, prepared to ride the short distance to the rue de Béthisy, he assured them that it was at 'the king's command'. In the duke's mind, he was dispensing justice. The assault began just before dawn. Anjou's guard withdrew and the admiral's bodyguard were easily overcome. Coligny ordered his household to escape across the roof. The first man to burst into the upstairs room was a German, Johann von Janowitz, called Besme, who was married to the Cardinal of Lorraine's bastard daughter: 'Oh Admiral, Admiral, You sleep too deeply... Are you not the Admiral?' Coligny replied: 'Yes, I am him. But you are too young a soldier to speak thus to an old captain. At least have respect for my age.' The last words he heard were: 'I am old enough to put you to rest.'[35] Coligny's body was then pushed out of the window and fell onto the courtyard below.

What happened next is a matter of some debate. There are claims that the corpse, in a feature common to contemporary sectarian and ethnic conflicts, was mutilated. Protestants claimed that Guise wiped blood from Coligny's face and then pushed it with his boot saying, 'Venomous beast no longer will you spit your venom.'[36] One story has it that Coligny's head was then severed and sent to the Queen Mother, who then had it embalmed for presentation to the Pope. All these stories wished to associate the Duke of Guise with the mob; to show that the vendetta and the Massacre were one and the same thing. But these actions are not consistent with the conventions of aristocratic revenge, nor with the duke's subsequent behaviour. One Protestant, Jean de Mergey, who witnessed the scene, does not make mention of mutilation and was certain that Guise did not get off his horse. It seems more likely, as Sassetti claims, that once he identified the corpse, he prevented his men from plunging their daggers into it, 'saying enough to the poor man'. The duke then left the scene and the corpse became a plaything to the mob, who cut off the hands, genitals and head, which was then sold for ten crowns to an Italian gentleman. The trunk was dragged around the streets for the next three days (as they had done to his effigy three years before). It was then displayed like that of a common criminal on the gibbet at Montfaucon, where the crowds flocked to see it. The vendetta was over; the Massacre was about to begin.

As dawn broke, residents in the neighbourhood, frightened by rumours of a Protestant rising, were stirred into action by the commotion in the rue de Béthisy. Alarm bells were sounded. Terror and confusion spread like a brushfire throughout the city. A similar episode had occurred in 1567 when the Huguenots had set light to windmills on the edge of Paris—even the Venetian ambassador had felt the need to buckle on his armour. As the duke and his men remounted and headed for their next mission across the river, he may have inadvertently set the touch paper to the powder keg, shouting words of encouragement to his men: 'Let us go on to the others, for the king commands it', which he repeated in a loud voice, 'the king commands it; it is his will; it is his express commandment.'[37] These words transformed a private feud into a public duty. It was precisely the order that many militiamen were waiting for. Instead of standing guard for the aristocrats, they turned imitator and formed their own death squads. With shouts of 'Kill, Kill', the time had come to clear God's city entirely of the Huguenot pestilence. The murder of the women and children is described in more detail than that of the men. Children are often described witnessing their parents' death. Thus the youngest daughter of Nicolas le Mercier was dipped 'stark naked in the blood of her massacred father and mother, with horrible threats that, if ever she became a Huguenot, the same would happen to her'.[38] Amid the orgy of killing and looting there was a cruel logic in operation. Among the first non-noble victims were the rich Protestant merchants who had been attacked and intimidated at the time of the Cross of Gastines affair. Hundreds more were rounded up and marched to the ancient Pont aux Meuniers to be executed. Not a conventional sixteenth-century bridge with housing on it, it was in fact a series of water mills; the farthest upstream of the three bridges that connected the Right Bank to the Ile de la Cité, it provided a modicum of seclusion for the killers and meant that the corpses were transported by the Seine out of the city as rapidly as possible and did not become snagged on mill wheels. 'It was necessary, they said, to send these fish to Rouen and other places inhabited by heretics.'[39] Sometimes the violence parodied royal justice, as in the case of Coligny's corpse, or mimicked the purificatory rites employed by the Catholic Church, such as the burning of a Protestant bookbinder. But elsewhere the motive was sheer vindictiveness. There were many tales of lawsuits and scores being settled at the point of sword or halberd. The wife of Philippe le Doux, who was about to give birth to her twenty-first child, was stabbed in the abdomen and her half-born babe left to die in the gutter. Her killer was a neighbour and militia sergeant, Pierre Coullon, a less successful professional rival of her husband. After killing husband and wife, he and his accomplices stole 4,000 crowns. This horror mingled with grisly carnivalesque games. Professor Ramus, the former friend of the Cardinal of Lorraine, was killed by the very students he taught; his corpse was flung out of an upper storey window on to the cobbles below, and then his entrails were spilled 'and dragged around the corpse whipped by some students, who were instructed by their masters'.[40]

At 3 pm the city aldermen arrived at the Louvre to tell the king that Paris was out of control. Charles ordered the violence to cease. But the genie had been let out of the bottle and the aldermen were unable to stop the violence. The official line was that the Crown was attempting to impose order and that the peace held. French embassies abroad were informed that the morning's events 'happened through a private quarrel long fostered between the two houses'.[41] This lie is further evidence pointing the finger at those who had a vested interest in portraying the Guise as scapegoats. The Massacre ruined their plans. Catherine and Anjou now argued that in order to restore the monarchy's reputation the king would have to declare that he ordered the admiral's death, and this is precisely what he did on the following day. There was a further reason for doing this beyond showing Europe that the king was still in control. To declare that the Massacre was the result of a private quarrel was to risk the continuation of the vendetta. Montmorency received news of Coligny's murder at Chantilly on the evening of 26 August. He remained 'undecided and cool as he could be'. If this was a private affair, he was bound by the laws of honour to march on the Hôtel de Guise. The king's volte-face was of the utmost strategic significance: Montmorency awaited news from Paris, 'hoping that the king would not admit to the murder of the deceased admiral, resolving in this case to pursue vengeance; but on news to the contrary, he resolved to submit himself to the will of the king'.[42] Even so, it was several days before order was fully restored. Charles IX seems to have had some form of nervous breakdown. The confusion in royal policy and the conflicting messages that emanated from Paris contributed to the spread of the killing to the provinces in the following weeks. Thousands more were killed, but the fate of Protestants in the regions varied from one town to the next, and depended much on how local officials interpreted the often opaque signals emanating from the capital.

* * * *

In murder investigations today, reconstructing the movements and behaviour of a suspect in the hours after a crime is imperative. We too can add to the psychological profile of our suspects and gain more of an insight into their motives. The scenes of carnage and slaughter did not elicit sympathy, sober reflection, or remorse from any of the chief suspects. Memoirs written later attempted to shift the blame. Charles could not resist riding out to Montfaucon to gawp at Coligny's corpse, 'a spectacle' which ambassador Walsingham thought revealed 'what good nature is in the King. It is much lamented to see his cruelty even by the Papists.'[43] The only culprit to express regret was the Duke of Guise. Walsingham, no friend, exonerated him: 'The duke of Guise is not so bloody, neither did he kill any man himself but saved divers. He spake openly that, for the admiral's death he was glad, for he knew him to be his enemy, but he thought for the rest that the King had put such to death as if it had pleased him might have done him very good service.' On leaving the rue de Béthisy, the duke crossed to the Left Bank, in order to carry out his second mission. But the Protestants here had been alerted, forcing Guise to conduct a furious and fruitless pursuit of the fugitives to Montfort l'Amaury, twenty-five miles away. He returned, exhausted, on the afternoon of the 25th. Guise had no wish to be cast as a scapegoat or to have the justice of his cause undermined by association with the rabble. In some respects this comes as no surprise. His mother's desire for Coligny's death was not at odds with her continuing sympathy for other Protestants. One target on day one was Coligny's chief counsellor, Arnaud de Cavaignes, who eluded his killers and made his way to Anne d'Este's residence, the Hôtel de Nemours, situated on the rue de Pavée on the Left Bank. Here he was hidden for two days until royal guards arrested him and he was led off to the Conciergerie, where he was tortured and, after confessing to treason, executed. Happier were those who, like Jacques de Crussol, made their way to the Hôtel de Guise. A girl was among the group which stayed there for a week until the atmosphere outside had calmed down. When her parents learned that the Guise planned to have her and her siblings re-baptized in the Catholic Church, they hastily reclaimed their young. News of this unlikely safe house circulated among those in hiding, since members of the ducal household, either because they feared for their Protestant kinsmen or because they were acting under the direct orders of the duke, were sent out amid the chaos and carnage to lend what assistance they could. Pierre de Foissy, whose father and brothers ranked among the duke's most trusted men, rescued Françoise de Languejoue. Jean de Mergey took refuge in Saint Thomas's church, from where he sent a note to the Baron of Cessac, the lieutenant of Guise's gendarmes, since 'he is my friend and would dare to do me a good turn'.[44] Cessac told him to sit tight. Another Guise man, a gruff Catholic ducal gendarme, Jean Pastoreau, Sieur de la Rochette, came to collect him. He was a good choice because, whereas Cessac was a southerner, Pastoreau was well known in the city and was 'a great enemy of those of the [Reformed] religion'. Pastoreau acted the part of a guard leading his prisoner and succeeded in getting Mergey across the Pont aux Meuniers and to safety. Compassion was not the prime motive for helping. Pierre de Foissy married the rich heiress he saved. Antoine Huyart from Troyes accepted an offer of help from a neighbour, another Guise household man, Charles des Boves. Boves welcomed him 'humanely enough', but it was soon clear from the soldiers that were sent to guard him that 'he would have to spit into the [money] pot, or otherwise it had been decided to finish him off like others of his ilk'.[45] Back in the Brie, too, men were taking advantage of the opportunities that the Massacre brought. Boves's brother, François, also a Guise servant, snatched Marie de Luzé, Dame de Lumigny, who had been hiding out dressed as a peasant, and took her off to Lorraine under the pretext of protecting her. She was only released and fled to Geneva after agreeing to sign over all her property.

Let us now contrast the actions of the duke and his men with the other main suspects. Many Catholics believed that the Massacre was a miracle. In the Saint-Innocents cemetery at midday on the 24th, a hawthorn bush—the traditional symbol of virgin purity—which had been shrivelled for months, suddenly burst into flower. Parisians flocked to see this sign of God's benediction, where women wailed and the sick were healed. The Saint Batholomew's Day Massacre was, for many Catholics, a mystical experience, a moment akin to resurrection, in which they came closer to God. At least this is how the Duke of Nevers described his feelings a few weeks later. For him the Massacre was an act which revealed the workings of divine will, to which men had no choice but to submit. His unshakeable belief in divine providence made him, the Counter-Reformation warrior, remarkably similar in outlook to his Calvinist enemies.[46] Unlike the unit that Guise had commanded which was only in the city briefly after the death of Coligny, the units commanded by Nevers and Anjou seemed to have played a major role in leading the popular violence. Despite the general disorder, Anjou's death squad was still carrying out killings in the city on the 25th.

The motive that Sassetti attributed to the main suspects after the Massacre was not faith but reason of state. What was the best way of stopping Coligny? How could the murder be done without ruining the Peace? Logically, the best solution for Catherine and her counsellors was to use the Guise and expect the backlash to fall on them. In allowing the private vendetta to run its course the monarchy would emerge as supreme arbiter. It was a classic example of divide and rule. If, on the other hand, Maurevert acted without orders from above, he did not do so alone; he had accomplices among the senior ranks of the Guise household. These men had a motive. Their own experience of the civil war in the Brie had sharpened their animosity to the admiral. They wished him dead as much as did the duke.

The history of the twentieth century has taught us that there are many levels of complicity in mass murder. We cannot completely absolve the aristocratic death squads from complicity in unleashing the popular religious violence. Some leaders, such as the dukes of Anjou and Nevers, had more blood on their hands than others. Both were extremely devout, representatives of the new militant Counter-Reformation piety. This was another reason why they despised the Duke of Guise. Like his father, Henri was rather more conventional: he showed little interest in matters of dogma. The duke was very careful to contrast the justice of his private quarrel with the actions of the Catholic mob. For him, this was not a crusade or a mystical experience; it was justice. He went out of his way to rescue defenceless Protestants. After all, his honour as a knight was at stake. The duke was not party to the initial deliberations to eliminate Coligny in the week after 9 August. His involvement in the massacre was based on opportunism, not religious fanaticism. Even his men seemed to have been more concerned with the material rewards that the violence brought, rather than bloody revenge.

Many Protestants accepted the duke's right to take revenge according to the laws of honour. They were also well aware of the steps he took to distance himself from the mob and his co-conspirators. He had no intention of being made a scapegoat. He was largely successful: it was the Crown which would be blamed and damaged by the events of August 1572. A plot which began as an attempt to ensure peace and stability ended up doing just the opposite. The Valois monarchy never again recovered its stature: Charles IX was revealed as a tyrant; Catherine de Medici and the Duke of Anjou as scheming hypocrites. The most widely read pamphlet about the Massacre, printed in Latin, Dutch, and German, as well as French, contrasts the regrets of the Duke of Guise to the bloody cunning of the royal family. It called for the overthrow of the Valois monarchy, who were mere descendants of the usurper Hugues Capet, and their replacement by the Guise. But the *Reveille Matin* was not a Catholic tract: it was Protestant—claiming to be published in Edinburgh it was dedicated to Elizabeth I. The Guise and the Protestants had both suffered at the hands of the monarchy: it was time to bury their differences in the common cause. If only, the author argued, the Guise would guarantee liberty of conscience, the Protestants would join them in overthrowing the Valois. This was fantasy in only one respect. In the years after the Saint Bartholomew's Day Massacre, the Duke of Guise would form a different alliance, which would overthrow one royal House and attempt to overthrow another.

FALSE KINGS AND TRUE CATHOLICS

The diarist Claude Haton observed the huge wedding party that crossed Champagne in September 1576. Like many Catholics, he was impressed, for though he considered most noblemen lazy and immoral, he was comforted that the Guise 'were not yet infected by heresy or false religion'.[1] They were celebrating not one but three weddings. The marriage of Charles de Mayenne had been celebrated at Meudon on 6 August and the family were on their way to celebrate a double wedding at Joinville: the 21-year-old Charles, Duke of Aumale, to his first cousin, Marie, daughter of the Marquis of Elbeuf—tall and pretty she would one day become the king's lover. The marriage of cousins was common, but first cousins less so, and the papal dispensation must have been expensive. The Duke of Guise also agreed to pay the dowry of 100,000 livres. Two days later, Aumale's sister, Diane, married François de Luxembourg, Duke of Piney, a neighbour whose credentials were that he was 'very rich, solvent and has a good house and furniture'.[2]

Many familiar faces had disappeared since the Massacre. Two years before, the Cardinal of Lorraine had died aged 49. His frail health had been unable to withstand the flamboyant devotions demanded by Henry III, who had recently succeeded his brother as king. On 8 December 1574, despite the advanced season, barefoot and carrying a black cross, the cardinal filed behind flagellants in white penitents' hoods. He caught a chill and died on 26 December. His body was laid to rest in Reims cathedral and his heart placed next to the tomb of his sister, the Queen of Scotland in the convent of Saint-Pierre de Reims. His death came just over a year after the death of the previous Duke of Aumale, who had been mown down by a cannon ball at the siege of La Rochelle. Only Cardinal Louis remained from the second generation, but though exceedingly rich he was no leader. The Spanish ambassador, Diego de Zuñiga, was more contemptuous: 'he had neither taste nor the intelligence for anything at all'.[3] And Zuñiga did not think much of the next generation either: 'the dukes of Guise and Mayenne and the [abbot] of Fécamp [soon to be cardinal] their brother, are not men of affairs'.

At the age of 25, court gossip had it that Henri de Guise would amount to little more than a gallant. It was an image sustained by his good looks. The Venetian ambassador described him as 'the same age as the king [in fact he was a year older], but taller and better built; his figure majestic, sharp-eyed with curly blond hair, a blond wispy beard...no one knows how to resist him in fencing'.[4] Of the two other Henrys who would decide the fate of France, he was more like Henri de Navarre than Henry III. Before Navarre's flight from the court and reconversion in 1576, the two men got on well; they hunted, diced, played tennis, and chased women together. To them religion was subordinate to politics: neither man was especially devout; there was something of the libertine about both. As soldiers, they believed that the existential and theological problems that pre-occupied Henry III were better left to the clergy. Guise was more refined than Navarre—even his enemies acknowledged his courtesy. He spoke Italian and German, which was essential, as his retinue was as cosmopolitan as his father's. He did not stand on ceremony with his social inferiors and his affability was buttressed by a sense of humour. When one of the Scots in his retinue began talking inappropriate and treasonous politics at a social event, demanding that the duke hurry and invade England, the ladies present, many of whom were Protestants, could only smile with polite embarrassment. The duke was able to rescue the situation: 'Ladies, he is talking Scotch; you do not understand it.'[5]

Henri's exaggerated sense of honour also added to his charisma. He took part in the new craze for duelling—a practice that should have been anathema to the truly pious, since it was banned by the Council of Trent. In December 1573 he fought with a mere esquire. One cannot imagine his father deigning to fight a social inferior. In other ways, too, Henri was beginning to emerge from his father's shadow. Henry III ascended the throne with a martial reputation, but Guise was the only royalist commander to distinguish himself in the disastrous offensive launched against the Protestants in 1575. At Dormans on the Marne, he showed immense bravery in checking an invasion of German mercenaries. As he pursued the fleeing enemy, a German pistolier, whom the duke had struck twice with his sword, replied with two pistol shots, grazing Guise's thigh and taking away part of his cheek and left ear. The wound was serious, but after six weeks of convalescence he was left with a scar to rival his father's and a nickname to match—*le Balafré* (scar-face). Unlike his grandfather after Pavia, the duke did not consider it important to undertake a pilgrimage of thanksgiving. Instead, his grandmother Antoinette had to send a servant to make the journey on foot to Saint-Nicolas du Port in Lorraine. The duke preferred to make political capital, much to the disapproval of the English ambassador in Paris, as he 'showed himself much in the place and around town to have the favour of the common people'.[6] Parisians clamoured for a popular hero and those sympathetic to him evoked the pain that tormented him and described the black velvet patch he wore, which rendered 'grace to the deformity'.[7]

That Henri was emerging as a man of substance and political skill is evident from the triple marriages which took place in 1576. With the passing of the older generation, which had been bound together by fraternal love and deference to the eldest, there was a danger that, as the new lineages established separate households, the ties that bind would weaken. Once again, the succession of the next generation was organized in such a way as to prevent squabbling and promote interdependence. The Duke of Guise's leadership was based on an agreement with his brothers and cousins, by which deference to strict principles of precedence was reciprocated with a fair distribution of estates, emoluments, and Church patronage. This began a year before the three marriages with a partition between the two elder Guise brothers. Charles was four years younger than his brother and a more straightforward character, a bluff soldier whom the English ambassador found 'not so full of treachery and dissimulation'. Like his brother, Charles showed little interest in the ascetic piety that was becoming fashionable at court. Unlike his brother he was a burly man, with hands 'like shoulders of mutton', the result of overindulgence that made him fat by the time he was 30. There was a dark side to him: in 1587 he stabbed to death a servant who displeased him. Charles received Mayenne, recently raised from a marquisate to a duchy, in the partition. Henri got the rest, but had to agree to pay all the family debts (which were considerable) and his mother's and grandmother's dowers. In addition, Charles inherited the governorship of Burgundy when his uncle Claude d'Aumale died—it had been in their continuous possession since 1543 and the Crown was in no position to refuse. Charles married a rich heiress, Henriette de Savoie.

Unusually, for a Guise it brought with it a significant inheritance in the south-west. Just as significant, the bride's father, Honorat de Savoie, promised to hand over the office of Admiral of France to his son-in-law when he died. The king was unable to prevent him doing so in 1578, thereby permitting the Guise to control three of the great offices of the crown: Admiral of France, Grand Master of the Household, which Guise had inherited from his father, and the Master of the Royal Hunt (*Grand Veneur*) which Claude, Duke of Aumale, passed to his eldest son, Charles. Their grip on high office was tightened in 1583 with the marriage of Charles d'Elbeuf to the daughter of the ageing Master of the King's Stables (*Grand Ecuyer*), who agreed to resign his post as part of the deal.

The cousins were brought up to behave like brothers, an arrangement sanctified by the marriage of Charles d'Aumale to Marie d'Elbeuf. Any reservations Charles had about marrying his first cousin were allayed by the substantial resources that the Church provided. His brother Claude (born in 1562) was first disqualified from the Aumale inheritance as a Knight of Malta and then compensated with a lucrative portfolio of monasteries by his uncles. Cardinals Charles and Louis had brought the second generation of the House to the pinnacle of its Church power and wealth; just as crucial was their ability to secure them for the next generation. Before his death, Cardinal Charles obtained Henry III's formal acceptance of his nephew, Louis II, the youngest of the three Guise brothers born in 1555, as his heir. Four years later, on Louis I's death, Louis II succeeded him as Cardinal of Guise.

Louis II's ability to pick up six benefices through his own youthful exertions between 1574 and 1588 suggests that he was a skilled ecclesiastical empire builder in the mould of his uncles. He was helped by the Pope's willingness to satisfy Guise ambition and Henry III's inability to curb them. The Counter-Reformation made greater demands of the clergy, and of bishops in particular. In this respect, Louis II was a throwback to an older era: his mistress, Aymerie de Lescherenne, gave him four bastard sons. The cardinal's education, at the hands of a conservative Benedictine scholar, was far removed from the humanist studies once championed by his uncle Charles. The English ambassador thought him 'as a Guise, not in show so cunning but given to vanities and disorders, but thought as crafty a head as [his brothers]'.[8] In other respects, however, he was a model Tridentine bishop. Canonical age requirements prohibited him from exercising the office of Archbishop of Reims until 1583. At the end of April that year he made his triumphal entry in Reims and sang his first Mass. He held a provincial synod in May that endorsed decrees of Trent. During the summer, his diocese became the epicentre of a vast number of penitential processions, in which pilgrims, dressed in white and singing hymns as they marched behind the Host, criss-crossed north-eastern France. Louis welcomed over 70,000 pilgrims into the city that summer. Thousands more made the journey to Notre Dame de Liesse, a pilgrimage of European significance, whose shrine to the Black Madonna was undergoing a revival thanks to the patronage of the Cardinal of Lorraine, who had bought the nearby château of Marchais and the land around Liesse in 1553. At the end of the century, Guise association with the shrine was confirmed by the gift of a magnificent black and white marble rood screen, on which was inscribed passages of scripture.

The 1583 processionals were a huge logistical operation and far from spontaneous. Many were led by their bishops and the cardinal, who led processions around the town, welcomed pilgrims at the cathedral with refreshments and small chapbooks of prayers that had been printed for the occasion. Louis was no innovator; he had been encouraged by the papal nuncio, Giovanni Battista Castelli, who arrived in France in 1581, to adopt the reform model introduced by Cardinal Borromeo in Milan. This was controversial to those who despised foreign, and especially Italian, innovations in devotion, but Louis was proud of his achievements and defended his reforming activities in a number of publications. The Marian Cult and the revival of shrines were particularly associated with the Jesuits: it is no coincidence that one hundred students from the English College in Reims took part in Louis's triumphal entry and that his summer's activities ended at the end of September with the mass-ordination of English missionary priests. Louis's campaign needs to be understood in a wider context: support for the English mission was the barometer of radical Catholic activism in France, while the revival of shrines and the cult of Mary were the chief symbols and agents of the Counter-Reformation throughout Europe.

The Jesuits exercised an influence over the third generation in another area too. Charles d'Aumale was among the first intake of 400 enrolled in the Jesuit University founded by Charles III, Duke of Lorraine and the Cardinal of Lorraine in 1572 at Pont-à-Mousson in Lorraine. The Duke of Lorraine was not himself a militant Counter-Reformation figure—the establishment of the university was an indication that he saw Catholic reconquest as a peaceful activity. He was on good terms with his Protestant neighbours, and tolerated Jews and those who kept their beliefs private, such as his chief minister, the Calvinist Count of Salm. The rigours of a Jesuit education turned out young men with a markedly different cast of mind. Charles d'Aumale, though not very able or intelligent, emerged from two years of study with a different world view from his cousins; he was more devout—he was the only member of the family to go on pilgrimage to Italy—and more uncompromising in his political and religious outlook. The Jesuits had taught him well. In contrast, his cousin turned brother-in-law, Charles, Marquis of Elbeuf, educated by the humanist Remy Belleau at Joinville, turned out to be the most libertine of the cousins: on friendly terms with several Protestants, he was not averse to employing heretics as servants. Friction must surely have existed between the cousins—Guise and Elbeuf did once come to blows at court—but was otherwise kept well hidden from public view. Continuity and harmony were assured by the severe presence of Antoinette de Bourbon, who continued to run family affairs from Joinville, where she was preoccupied by the upbringing of her great-grandchildren.

The festive mood that summer was threatened by the gathering financial storm. Guise had yet to liquidate the debts left to him by his father and uncle and this was aggravated by the agreements he made with his brothers and cousins. The amount of the indebtedness has been put at between 1 and 3 million livres, or between four and twelve times his annual income. The Venetian ambassador described his cousins as rich and the duke as a 'poor prince'. He was being sued by his treasurer, Pierre Hotman, and he owed his tailor 30,000 livres. There was absolutely no question of cutbacks: honour required that a prince lived and acted in accordance with his station: at ninety-eight people, his household was smaller than his father's and this was as far as he dared go without losing face. The parlous state of royal finances and his ambivalent relationship with Henry III ruled out help from that quarter. The 1575 campaign was financed out of his own pocket, borrowing 200,000 livres against the family silver. Antoinette, now well into her eighties, was left to sort the mess. In July 1577 she complained to her grandson that debt repayments were eating up so much of his income 'that not a sou of revenue was to be had'.[9] Her task was made worse by the death of Cardinal Louis I, whose affairs were found to be chaotic. The agent she dispatched to the abbey of Saint-Victor in Paris found 'everything in a bad state and was attempting to avoid complete ruin'.[10] In August 1578 the duke bowed humiliatingly to the inevitable and sold the county of Nanteuil to a courtier for 362,000 livres. But this did not clear all the debts, nor did it pay Aumale's dowry. In 1581 he sold the castle of Homburg and the fief of Saint-Avold in the Empire to the Duke of Lorraine for 288,000 livres, a huge return on an investment in properties that had been bought on the cheap from the Cardinal of Lorraine, during his tenure as Bishop of Metz. Though he was by no means solvent, the greatness of a prince was measured in the credit he was able to obtain. And there were plenty of rich Parisian merchants and bankers who continued to lend despite the risks. For some it was a long-term investment in the duke's political fortunes, for others akin to a religious duty. Money was also crucial to the duke's relationship with the Crown. He needed royal patronage to maintain himself; in order to do so he had to remain close to the king. The emergence of a radical Catholic opposition to royal policy provided both a challenge and an opportunity.

* * * *

At the accession of Henry III, Catholics had more hope for the future than at any time since the civil wars started. The mass conversions that had followed the Saint Bartholomew's Day Massacre seriously weakened Protestantism north of the Loire. As Duke of Anjou, the king had shown himself eager to spill blood in the quest for religious unity. The Guise shared these hopes. Excluded at the end of the previous reign, four of them were summoned by Henry to enter the new Privy Council. And then he joined their family. Unusually, it was not a political match. Quite simply he fell in love with their cousin, Louise, daughter of Nicolas de Lorraine-Vaudémont. They were married two days after he was crowned king by the Cardinal of Guise in February 1575. Such was the hope of the Catholics and the joy of the Guise that their dismay at the disastrous 1575 campaign and the Peace of Beaulieu which ended it in May 1576—the most generous to the Protestants so far—was all the greater. Henry III realized, like his mother before him, that the war was not only unwinnable, it was destroying monarchical authority: as provinces and their revenues fell under the control of aristocratic warlords, royal debts had risen to more than 100 million livres, ten times what it had been in 1559. In order to secure the peace, Henry also made a number of major political and financial concessions to them and their Catholic 'politique' allies. He agreed to call the Estates-General, pay off their mercenaries, reinstate them to the offices they had held before the Saint Bartholomew's Day Massacre, and in surety of his good intentions cede control of several strategic towns to them. The king's younger brother and heir, Alençon, who had allied himself with the heretics, was rewarded with the duchy of Anjou. To hard-line Catholics it was a humiliation. Opposition was immediate.

Opponents of the English Revolution had a horrible fascination for the Catholic League, viewing it as the most pernicious and significant development in modern history. To them it marked a revolutionary break with the past, ushering an era of religious fanatics who challenged the concept of divine-right monarchy. Sir William Dugdale considered that 'The Holy League in France, is so exact a Pattern of ours in England, as we have just reason enough to conceive, that the Contrivers of... [our] Rebellion, did borrow the Plott from theme. All the main parts, and many of the Material Circumstances, being the same in both: Only the scene is changed and the Actors divers.' The early Tories thought so too and, with reference to a flurry of books and plays on the subject compared their Whig opponents to the Duke of Guise. In one sense these reactionaries were right. The Catholic League was a radical break with the past because it went far beyond a call for the restoration of the Catholic Church. Drawing on the new science of history, its manifesto looked back with admiration to a mythic past, in which the first Frankish kings guaranteed the freedoms and liberties of the Three Estates. Its principles constituted a fundamental re-imagining of the state. The inviolability of royal Catholicity, not only ensured Henri de Navarre's exclusion, but it paved the way for a monarchy elected by the Estates-General, acting in the name of the people. The basis for this constitutional shift was the idea, first put forward by the Protestants, that sovereignty was shared. After the seventeenth century, the League was ignored by historians because it did not fit easily with the either liberal or Marxist notions of revolution. But since the 1979 Iranian Revolution we have become reacquainted with the revolutionary potential of theocratic and democratic ideas combined. We now know that the English Revolution was not the first Bourgeois Revolution, but a variant of religious revolution, whose European antecedents can be found in France in 1576 and in Germany during the Peasants War of 1525.

In another sense, however, English reactionaries got the Catholic League wrong. The Duke of Guise was not a precursor of Cromwell; the League was not initially a vehicle for princely ambition. Its origins were local and particular and the duke, though sympathetic, had to maintain a discreet distance. Opposition to the Peace of Beaulieu was strongest in Picardy and Normandy, provinces where Protestantism, decimated by the 1572 Massacres, was now being reintroduced by royal edict. In Normandy opposition centred on the reintroduction of Protestant worship to Rouen. Charles, Cardinal of Bourbon, archbishop of the city, took the lead. A man previously known as a courtier rather than a churchman, he now disowned his Protestant nephews, Navarre and Condé, and made one of his rare visits to his diocese. Reviving a dormant practice, he and his noble supporters invoked their rights to sit in the Parlement of Rouen, where they attempted unsuccessfully to stop the registration of the peace edict. On 23 July he confronted the Protestant congregation as they arrived for worship; they fled in terror.

The League's initial support came from the nobility. Men like François de Roncherolles, the Cardinal of Bourbon's chief adviser. Roncherolles would soon get himself into trouble with Henry III for publicly demanding that the non-Catholic princes of the blood be stripped by the Estates-General of their right to succeed. This would have had the effect of bringing the cardinal's Catholic nephew, the 10-year-old Count of Soissons, closer to the succession. Both men had a vested interest in the boy's career: the cardinal being his guardian; Roncherolles his governor.[11] The cardinal also saw himself as a potential candidate. Once before, in 1563, he had petitioned the Pope to dispense him from holy orders and now at the age of 53 the possibility was discussed again.

In Picardy the League took on a more dangerous form. Here resistance coalesced spontaneously around Henri, Prince of Condé's return as governor. The local gentry signed a manifesto at Péronne, a symbol of resistance to the peace since it had been assigned to Condé as surety, on 5 June. The signatories envisaged a network of secret associations, each with an elected head, pledged to defend both Catholicism and the 'rights and liberties' of Frenchmen, as had been enjoyed at the time of the first French king, Clovis. They sent agents to other towns in Picardy and made contact with fellow malcontents in Normandy. Henry III acted quickly and ordered the ringleaders to leave Péronne. He discovered that the Picards and Normans had joined together because 'neither wishes to have [Protestant] preachers, nor to observe the edict of pacification . . . there being little reverence for his majesty and hatred for the Queen Mother'.[12] In September he ordered the League to dissolve. But surveillance of a secret organization was otherwise difficult. Networks of kinship and sociability lent the conspirators cohesion and were hard to penetrate. There were regular secret meetings that coordinated the movement across Picardy and Upper Normandy. Letters were written in cipher, some of which fell into royal hands; but the League in turn intercepted royal correspondence. The League's organizational abilities were first put to the test in the electoral colleges that met to choose deputies to the Estates-General. This was the first time in French history that there was something approaching an electoral campaign. Traditionally, elections to the Estates were not contests; rather they were meetings which decided on a list of grievances and someone was delegated to carry them to the assembly. The League's mixture of bigotry and constitutionalist rhetoric injected an ideological element into the process. Henry III intervened in a number of cases to overturn the result and impose a royalist candidate. Things did not go all his way: the League managed to overturn the royalist candidate for the Second Estate of the Caux in Normandy on a technicality. The elections resulted in a League caucus being present at the opening of the Estates at Blois in December. Most of its noble leadership were present there, including François de Roncherolles, who was returned for the Second Estate of Gisors, and who now emerged as its chief negotiator with the king.

The king suspected the Guise were behind the agitation and he was right to be alarmed. The League of Péronne had been signed in the house of Jacques d'Applaincourt, an old family servant, who had to resign as the Cardinal of Lorraine's pantler in 1560 because of his conversion to Protestantism, before returning to the fold as ensign of the Duke of Aumale's gendarmes. His services would soon be further rewarded with his appointment as Governor of the duchy of Guise. This should not imply that the Guise were in day-to-day control of the organization. That would have been too dangerous. On 2 August the king made them swear an affidavit to uphold the peace, and they had no wish to break with him. Rather, it was hoped that the League would force a rethink in royal policy. While the duke dissimulated, his enemies tried to smoke him out. As the Estates-General opened he was accused of high treason. A memoir had apparently been discovered on an agent he had sent to Rome and published as *A Summary of the Guisian Ambassage to Rome*. Its contents and translation into English suggest it was the work of Protestants. It was a clever ruse and only at the end gives itself away as a piece of false propaganda, calling for the Pope to make Guise captain-general of the League, for the

Duke of Anjou to be arrested, and for the king and Queen Mother to be confined to monasteries. The Guise had never made a secret of their descent from Charlemagne. But the *Summary* stated that this claim would be the pretext for the overthrow of the Valois, whose ancestry could only be traced to the usurper of the Carolingians, Hugues Capet (*fl.* 940–96). Henry III was reassured and accepted the falsity of the *Summary*. But the first doubts about the duke's loyalty had been planted.

Having failed to stamp out the League, Henry adopted a ploy he would use again and again during his reign: unable to use force he would have to outsmart his opponents instead. On the eve of the Estates, Henry backtracked and announced that all his subjects should sign the League. In doing so, he significantly altered the original covenant, replacing subversive passages with new clauses that upheld the peace and Protestant worship and bolstered the royal authority. The League leadership responded by ignoring the alterations and continued to circulate the original text. However, they now faced a more stubborn opponent than the king. With some justification, taxpaying commoners viewed the king's co-option of the League as a cynical manoeuvre to squeeze more money out of them. The First and Second Estates were the most vociferous in favour of a renewal of war; but they would not have to pay for it. The revelations of the parlous state of royal finances made to them in January 1577 hardened the obduracy of the Third Estate to any more taxes. Even though they were sympathetic to the Catholic cause, most towns refused to sign the League outright, since 'it was a novelty, the like of which had never been used in France nor heard speak of'.[13] At Troyes, the presence of Guise in person could not induce any of the Three Estates to sign. A further embarrassment followed. The election of the duke's chief counsel, Pierre de Versoris, as spokesman for the Third Estate at the Estates-General was a major victory for the League. Unfortunately, Versoris, 'a famous and celebrated' Parisian lawyer, froze on the big occasion in front of the king and the assembly and gave a faltering performance. He, and by association his party, was made a laughing stock. The League's failure at Blois was orchestrated by another lawyer, Jean Bodin, an enlightened royalist, opposed to another calamitous civil war, who had just published, to widespread acclaim, the *Six Books of the Commonwealth*, where he argued that the king did not share power with the people. On the contrary, the sovereignty of the monarchy was absolute and undivided. For the king and the League the 1576 Estates were a failure, because they failed to vote fresh taxes. But they were significant in establishing some basic constitutional positions that would have immense implications for the future of the French monarchy, especially the incompatibility of representative government and religious tolerance. In the future, the choice would be between the League's vision of limited, constitutional monarchy, whose representative institutions would guarantee a theocratic state based on the principle of catholicity, or Bodin's vision of a monarchy, unfettered by custom and tradition, whose sovereignty was indivisible and thus strong enough to ensure peace and religious toleration.

As a result of Bodin's manoeuvres, the 1577 campaign began without the resources and was inevitably indecisive. It did, however, result in a peace that was more acceptable to the Catholics and was the basis for a significant reduction in intercommunal religious tensions in the years that followed. Article 56 of the pacification edict disbanded and outlawed all leagues and associations. The Catholic League was pushed underground and Henri de Guise continued to feign ignorance of its existence. Wherever it resurfaced, however, in Champagne in 1579, or Normandy and Picardy in 1580, it was led by the duke's lieutenants. It developed a clandestine regional command: the papal nuncio was sure that the Marquis of Elbeuf headed its organization in Normandy, Aumale in Picardy. In spite of this, the League was, as yet, little more than another faction of malcontent nobles, albeit possessed of a dangerous ideology. Henry III planned to make them an irrelevance: he was pressing ahead with an overhaul of government and administration; he remained on cordial terms with the Guise family; he was in the prime of his life and fully expected that the queen would soon produce an heir, quashing once and for all the prospect that Henri de Navarre, currently second in line to the throne, would succeed him as France's first Protestant king.

* * * *

The picture illustrated in Plate 24, completed from sketches taken at the marriage of the Queen's sister, Marguerite, to the Duke of Joyeuse, is one of the last depictions of Henri de Guise while he was alive. The six family members on the left are separated from the ball which whirls around them. They are, from the left, Mayenne, Henry III, Queen Louise, Catherine de Medici, Henri de Guise, and finally Cardinal Louis II, dressed not in his cardinal's robes but in fashionable clothes of a fetching pink topped off with a ruff. The picture crackles with tension. Guise, looking at the seated lady, gestures towards the dancers with his hat. Catherine appears to be doing the same, but on closer inspection we see that she is looking towards her son, her hand blocking the duke's advancement. The king, unusually for such a jolly occasion, rests a hand on his sword. Painted in 1582, the picture captures the moment when the strains in the relationship between the king and the duke could no longer be hidden. The reasons for the distance lay in the king's ambitious programme to transform his unruly subjects and reassert royal authority. His determination to alter the structure and personnel of his court accentuated the personality clash.

Henry III's divergence from the traditional model of French kingship made him a controversial figure in his own lifetime. He was an enigma to many of his subjects. Henry looked majestic: he was taller than average, comported himself with elegance and dignity; he was a good public speaker and, following the model set by Philip II, diligent and hard-working. He took the idea to heart that in order to reform the state Frenchmen would have to reform themselves. Who better to set an example than the king: for three years, beginning in January 1576, he instituted the practice of retiring after dinner to hear public lectures from the leading thinkers of the day on edifying subjects. But he did not always behave in the manner which was expected: he was notoriously free with his emotions in public and his sense of irony—he ennobled his court jester in 1584—was lost on many of his subjects. Without a child and dogged by ill-health his rule was precarious. He and the queen tried all sorts of quack fertility treatments. From the moment in March 1580 when Guise recommended a doctor from Dauphiné, the king would spend an increasing amount of time away from court taking thermal cures. The duke accompanied the king on the pilgrimages that he undertook to various shrines to assist the queen's conception. In 1582 Henry, already noted for his piety and convinced that divine wrath was the cause of his afflictions, underwent some form of spiritual conversion that manifested itself in abstinence. Regular dietary austerities had already become a significant part of his life and he now vowed to sleep with no other woman than the queen. On 11 August the king took leave of the court, leaving his mother in charge to go on a three month retreat. His immersion in the burgeoning penitential movement was crowned by the establishment of the new Confraternity of the Annunciation of Our Lady, which held its first procession at the feast of the Annunciation 1583. On Maundy Thursday, in pouring rain, the king, dressed in the grey serge cagoule of a simple brother, returned in procession from Notre Dame cathedral, imitating Christ's Passion with ritual flagellation. Many were shocked at the indignity of the spectacle; others, were more inclined to satirize what they saw as hypocrisy. The following ditty was one among dozens of lampoons:

> Having pillaged the kingdom France
> And all his people ripped off,
> Is it real penitence
> To cover yourself with a dripping sack cloth?[14]

The Cardinal of Guise, who carried the cross, and Mayenne, who was master of ceremonies, had more dignified roles. Their elder brother was not present: he mocked the king for 'living like a monk and not a king'. And there was something in this: the king spurned the traditional aristocratic pastimes, like hunting, tennis, and riding. As a consequence jousts and tourneys at his court were rare. The king was aware of Guise's scorn, turning it into a joke one day, as he leapt into his saddle, remarking afterwards to one of the duke's men nearby 'Does my cousin have monks like me in Champagne who mount their horses in one leap?'[15]

Henry was widely admired but he was not popular. Recent historians have found much to applaud too, but their judgement relies too much on the assessment of the educated elite. The people were less impressed. They blamed Henry for permitting heresy and thus bringing down on them God's wrath in the form of harvest failure and plague, which afflicted his reign and came on top of the economic dislocation caused by civil war. As early as 1578, Claude Haton overheard the townsfolk on Provins denouncing him as a tyrant and an atheist. And his reputation suffered further because one could not trust him; he said one thing and did another. He issued a grand edict in 1580 abolishing many recently created venal offices, which were hated as a form of stealth tax since the purchasers recouped their investments in gifts and bribes, only to invent all sorts of new ones to sell soon after. Even taverns were turned into venal offices, forcing their owners, who had to purchase them from the Crown, to pass the cost on to the poor customer! Haton thought Henry deceitful, about as trustworthy as a 'Turk' or a 'cunning whore'.[16] The perceived gap between the king's publicly declared virtue and privately practised vice was fertile ground for satire. Moralists railed against Henry's court as a den of immorality, profligacy, and corruption. They pointed the finger at the king's favourites, his *mignons*, or 'sweeties', a word with homosexual undertones. There was no truth in the rumours: but the king did little to stop tongues wagging; his ostentatious shows of affection towards them scandalized the public. The king's penchant for dancing, which he undoubtedly associated with dexterity and self-discipline, was a red rag to the priggish. The *mignons* were swaggering dandies, whose fashions marked them out from ordinary gentlemen and outraged the Parisian bourgeoisie, none more so than the misanthropic diarist Pierre de l'Estoile, who described:

> their hair like whores in a brothel, curled and recurled by artifice, sticking up under their bonnets, and their ruffs of their fine linen shirts stiffened and elongated so that their heads above them looked like the head of Saint John the Baptist on a platter. The rest of their clothes were the same; their pastimes were gaming, blaspheming, jumping about, dancing and vaulting, quarrelling and whoring, to follow the King around everywhere and do everything to please him.[17]

Anti-court feeling was strong among the middling sort and fuelled the righteous anger of the pious killjoys who made up the ranks of the Catholic League. Haton described how in 1581 the religious radicals in his parish refused to take part in public prayers for an heir, desiring Henry's 'death and the extermination of his entire lineage'. This was an extraordinary moment which shows that ordinary people, who surely had no acquaintance with the new Protestant literature justifying Tyrannicide, were imagining the king's death in the early 1580s.

* * * *

Far from being effeminate, the court dandies were violent and dangerous men. They were adepts of the new craze for duelling, where challenges were issued for the slightest offence. Duelling became dangerously entangled with faction politics. The *mignons* were intent on safeguarding the honour of the king and that meant cutting his rivals down to size; at first they provoked and fought against the king's brother, Anjou, but after he and his entourage quit court under the pressure in February 1578 they turned their attentions to the Guise. On 27 April at 5 am in the Paris horse market, the three *mignons* Caylus, Maugiron, and Livarot faced three Guisards, Entraguet, Ribérac and Schomberg. It was fierce combat: Maugiron and Schomberg were killed outright and Ribérac died the next day in the Hôtel de Guise where he had taken refuge; Livarot was severely wounded. The king was distraught at the death of his beloved companions: 'he kissed both of their dead bodies, had their locks cut off and took away and locked up their blond hair, took Caylus's earrings which he himself had given him'.[18] He wanted to punish the 'murderers', but the duke pledged to stand by his men. On the 10 May the whole Guise family and the Duke of Lorraine left court. The cause of the duel related to gossip about the Duchess of Guise, the object of the affections of another *mignon*, Saint-Mégrin, who knew that the best way to dishonour a man was to turn him into a cuckold. On 23 July at 11 pm he was attacked by a gang of masked assailants in the rue Saint-Honoré led, witnesses claimed, by the Duke of Mayenne. He was the victim of a savage assault; his corpse was mutilated by twenty blows.

The king's break, first with his brother and then with the Duke of Guise, had been sudden and violent. It was in order to revive a sense of obligation and brotherhood among his squabbling nobility that Henry III founded a new order of chivalry, the Order of the Holy Spirit, from which the Guise were excluded from the first promotion of new knights on 31 December 1578. But the king and the duke could ill afford to remain enemies for long. Henry III had no wish to add to the list of disgruntled princes, which included his brother and the King of Navarre. For his part, Guise needed royal favour to keep his creditors at bay. He had no wish to become yet another of the provincial warlords, who had benefited during the civil wars at the expense of royal power but, in the absence of favour, now eked out a precarious existence on plundered royal taxes and handouts from foreign princes. So the duke was happy, through the mediation of his mother, to return to court in March 1579; accompanied by 600 horse he would remain close to the king for the next three years. He entered the Order of the Holy Spirit in the second promotion of knights, re-entered the Privy Council and once more resumed the functions of the Grand Master of the King's Household.

The relationship between the duke and the king during the next three years was complex. Henry was far too clever to try to provoke or humiliate the Guise, but his desire to effect a fundamental transformation of the court and the kingdom would inevitably mean tackling vested interest groups. The king wanted to keep Guise at court so he could keep an eye on him, and to this end extended his generosity. Likewise, the traditional picture of Guise as a man driven by ambition, cynically manipulating the opposition to undermine the king does not hold. Only slowly, almost imperceptibly at first, would the duke find himself undermined and his pride damaged.

Henry III was fastidious and paid much attention to etiquette. He made significant changes to the structure of the court designed to break the Guise monopoly on high office. The Grand Master of the Household 'the first and cheifest office and dignitie', as the English-man Richard Cooke described it, had been in the hands of the Guise since 1559, and Cooke saw the duke perform the role:

> When the king maketh a great dynner with solempnitie & cere-monie, it is his charge to serve in person as stewarde and master of the house with awhite staffe in his hande, & must go before the meate which is served at the King's table ... [he] hath by virtue of his office the greatest allowance and the greatest table in the Court, that is for fowre & twentie persons, and to his table doe come ordinarily many younge noble men & others makinge profession of armes. And this table is allwaies covered whilest the King dynethe.[19]

A great privilege certainly. But Cooke was unaware that the control of the Grand Master over the court had been weakened in 1578 by the creation of a new official, the Grand Provost (*grand prévot de l'hôtel*), who was given responsibility for the policing of the court. It was entrusted to a *mignon*, François du Plessis, the father of Cardinal Richelieu. The same happened to the post of *Grand Ecuyer*. When this was in danger of falling into Guise hands, Henry diluted its authority over the royal stables by creating a new institution, the *Petite Ecurie*.

Purging the body politic of undue Guise influence was not just a question of bureaucratic organization; it was one of style. Those who did not share the king's intellectual pursuits felt left out; his disdain for traditional aristocratic pastimes hit the Guise particularly hard. Charles d'Aumale was Master of the King's Hunt, a post that, during the previous reign, had given his father control of 340 staff and a budget of 70,000 livres per annum, but Henry III rarely hunted and expenditure fell to 24,500 livres in 1584. Aumale was forced to sell land in order to make ends meet. Kings of France had traditionally lived their lives in public and been accessible to their subjects. Henry III followed the English model and took steps to restrict access thus 'avoiding the confusion that continually takes place in his chambers, where everyone without distinction wishes to enter without the ushers being able to stop them'. He and the Guise were seen together much on public occasions, but real business was increasingly con-ducted in private. In 1581, the king, against the advice of his mother, felt confident enough to establish a secret inner council. This was associated with the rise of two men from the pack of *mignons*, Jean-Louis de la Valette and Anne de Joyeuse, to positions of pre-eminence at court. They emerged as the principal ministers in the new cabinet. Henry set about turning these men, from the modest southern nobility, into great magnates, straining his relationship with the Guise to breaking point.

Guise had little to complain of publicly: he was regularly seen with the king; his pension and salaries were paid on time; he directly benefited from innovative and unpopular taxes. In the summer of 1581 he was awarded a gift of 200,000 livres, part of his cut from nine new fiscal edicts registered that summer, which enabled him to pay off many debts. But this was a sweetener to prepare him for his political exclusion. In September the viscounty of Joyeuse was raised to a duchy and negotiations opened with Mayenne to resign the office of Admiral of France. The king arranged Joyeuse's marriage to the queen's sister, Marguerite de Lorraine; and, once again, Guise could hardly complain, as Marguerite was his cousin. A deal was struck: Mayenne resigned the admiralty to Joyeuse for 360,000 livres, in return for which the marquisate of Elbeuf was created a duchy. Guise appeared for the marriage, where only the painting we have investigated records his displeasure at the extraordinary favour displayed to Joyeuse, who was given a gift of 1.2 million livres. The festivities, called 'Magnificences' lasted for two weeks, and stunned contemporaries with their sumptuousness. Even Pierre de l'Estoile, who was among the 50,000 spectators at one of the parades, was grudgingly impressed in his journal. And the king did not stop there. On New Year's Day 1582, Joyeuse and Epernon were appointed as alternating First Gentlemen of the Privy Chamber: henceforth no one could leave or enter the king's apartments without their consent. Resistance to the palace revolution coalesced around the figure of la Valette, who became Duke of Epernon in November 1581. His rise was even more remarkable than that of Joyeuse. During the 1580s he would accumulate something in the region of 3 million livres in salaries, pensions, and royal gifts, putting into perspective the crumbs with which Guise had to be content. While Joyeuse took care of the navy, Epernon was charged with reasserting royal control in the army; in July 1582 he became colonel-general of the infantry and was named commander of many important garrison towns, most notably Metz, from where he could keep an eye on the duchy of Lorraine.

With the country at peace and royal authority restored to a level it had not seen since the beginning of the civil wars, the king should have been delighted. But he was a troubled man; wracked by bouts of depression he went through a spiritual crisis. Partly this was due to his lack of an heir. Partly it was to do with the Guise. Everything seemed fine until Easter 1582. There was a frisson of excitement in January when the King took a fancy to the Duchess of Aumale. At Lent, the king was accompanied by Guise on a pilgrimage to Chartres to intercede for a child. The atrocious mud and rain forced the king and the other princes to turn back 'half-dead'. Only Guise, in a display as much of machismo as of piety, finished. For three years the king had humoured, managed, and skilfully out-manoeuvred the Duke of Guise, but now their relationship reached an impasse. Rumour had it that, in return for acquiescing to the promotion of his rivals, the duke was expecting to be made Constable of France, and he was now furious. As he wrote to his stepfather the Duke of Nemours: 'you cannot imagine the little pleasure that we have these days . . . you would not imagine how it irks me and if you were here you would find this company completely different from what it was formerly'.[20] At a family gathering in April at his mother's house in Paris, it was decided against following the court to Fontainebleau. Just before it departed a placard was pinned to Epernon's apartments in the Louvre:

> Braggard beware !
> For always taking more than your share.
> One morning you'll wake to bad luck,
> For that day we'll have you strung up.[21]

As his melancholy subsided the king made amends. In October he admitted that he 'lived too privately' and that he needed to make time for conversation. He ordered more feasting and dances.

These bread-and-circus entertainments masked the king's true feelings—he had finally been convinced that the Guise were planning to usurp the Navarre's legal right to the succession and seize the crown for themselves. The claims were not new; they were preposterous and easily exposed as fabrications. But during 1582 an obscure and little-read Latin genealogical compendium, the *Stemmatum Lotharingiae*, came to the king's attention. The claim that the Guise were directly descended from Charlemagne was uncontroversial; the legend had been put into print as early as 1510. In 1543 Edmond du Boullay had traced the dynasty back to Adam! The *Stemmatum* itself received the royal privilege. But here and there within its thousand pages its author, François de Rosières, Archdeacon of Toul, had inserted explosive allegations: he insinuated that Hugues Capet was a low-born usurper of the Carolingians, and that Provence and Anjou had been snatched from René II of Lorraine by extortion and false promises; he maintained that Elizabeth I was a bastard and that Philip II was the true heir to the kingdom of Navarre. Henry III was furious. On 23 December Rosierès was arrested in Toul and interrogated. Who had put him up to writing a book which 'condemns and dishonours Frenchmen'?[22] Rosières's reply that it was all his own work failed to appease the king and he was sent to the Bastille. On 26 April 1583 he appeared on his knees in front of the king, the council, the dukes of Guise and Mayenne, and begged pardon for having spread malicious lies detrimental to the kings of France and the House of Valois.

The enemies of the Guise capitalized on their misfortunes: wild accusations against the duke abounded—he was cleared of plotting to poison the king's brother. And yet there is good reason for thinking that the Guise were as shocked and disturbed by the *Stemmatum* as the king. For Rosières was not working for them, but for Charles III, Duke of Lorraine. He was the duke's genealogist and member of his Privy Council, and saved from execution at the duke's intercession. Charles III had two reasons for wanting the *Stemmatum* compiled. Partly, it was to refute a similar Protestant publication, which mocked the pretensions of the House of Lorraine to descend from Charlemagne, claiming instead that Hugues Capet, far from being the son of a butcher, was a true Carolingian and had saved France from German domination. The inference was clear: Henri de Navarre, the true heir, would save France, once again, from the 'Germans'. But the *Stemmatum* went far beyond a refutation. That it did so was because it reflected the vanity of Duke Charles III and the talk that circulated freely at his court. For Charles III was a man with great plans. He took to styling himself Count of Provence: the uncertainty into which the Dutch Revolt and the French Wars of Religion had plunged Europe provided opportunities for ambitious men like him. He dreamed of extending his duchy towards the Rhine. The same year that the *Stemmatum* was published, he plotted, with Calvinist support, to seize the Lutheran city of Strasbourg.

The controversy was a serious blow to Guise. Although the king no longer trusted him, he needed to keep him nearby. Nobody, least of all the astute English ambassador, Cobham, was fooled: 'The king dissembles exceedingly'. His flirtation with the Duchess of Aumale may also have been part of the ruse. The *mignons* took to poking fun at the cuckolded husband. Cobham described the tension between Guise and Epernon as a 'heartburning'. In May 1583 the feud turned violent: there was a punch-up between the two retinues and Guise issued a challenge. Later that year a squabble during a tennis match was even more dangerous: 'this will not be without blood, because the duke of Guise saith little, and then he commonly thinketh most'.[23]

* * * *

Life at court had steadily become unbearable. All the more so since, when the king married into the House of Lorraine in 1575, Guise prospects had seemed so good. Precedence was a precise indicator of power and the other princes, sensing the political wind, had won rulings that pushed the Guise further down the ceremonial pecking order. This was humiliating for a family that had once posed as the defender of the princes against parvenus. Even those Catholic princes to whom they were related—the Orléans-Longueville, the Nevers, the Montpensier—increasingly spurned them. One consequence of this was that the family turned in on itself more than ever before. Outside hostility and the intermarriage of first cousins strengthened the clan mentality. The rupture with the king in 1582 made solidarity imperative. The duke remained at court for one reason: he too was dissembling, humouring, and playing the king along. He was secretly plotting to win a kingdom. He was planning the invasion of England.

THE INVASION OF ENGLAND

We may hope that in time to come our England, which now through grievous torments lieth oppressed with the heavy burden of heresy, may, as it were, being called out of the ugly jaws of Satan and restored again to the bosom of the Catholic Church, make account of the receiving of their old and ancient religion at your hands.

William Gifford, considered the brightest prospect in the émigré community, had been teaching at Reims for less than a year when he wrote this eulogy to the Guise. The Giffords were an ancient and distinguished lineage with properties in Staffordshire and Gloucestershire, whose wider family circle contained many notable supporters of Mary Stuart, such as the Throckmortons. The Giffords encapsulated the dreams and dangers of exile. William's elder brother, George, 'the doublest knave that ever I knew', according to ambassador Stafford, was a soldier who harboured fantasies of assassinating Elizabeth I. Their cousin, Gilbert, was already a difficult and truculent 17-year-old when he left England and went into exile; he challenged a fellow student to a duel and stirred up division in the English College in Rome. On returning to France, he was a reformed character and joined the secret conspiracies of the Marian party. His fellow plotters were unaware that he was, in fact, a double agent, who was known to his controllers in London as Francis Hartley.

As for William, the Cardinal of Guise was impressed and granted him a pension. William's youthful optimism—he was no older than 25—captures the spirit of hope and expectancy that was surging through the ranks of English Catholic exiles at the beginning of 1583. Over a thousand exiles formed a militant and organized community centred on Reims, Paris, and Rouen. The move of the English College from Douai to Reims in 1578 had been a great success: by 1583 its size had quadrupled to over 200 students. The Cardinal of Guise facilitated the move and took a close interest in the institution, encouraging its mission, and ordaining many of the more than one hundred priests who made the return voyage across the Channel. It was a hazardous journey: seventeen priests had already been martyred since 1577. Those who returned to France were not disheartened however; they reported 'signs of revolt' everywhere, waves of conversions, and the readiness of people to rise up as soon as an army of liberation set foot on English soil. Once the exiles had looked to Spain as their saviour, now they saw the Duke of Guise as the man to lead them home. William proclaimed that 'the immortal fame of that noble family of Guise... should be blown and spread in the Christian world forever'.[1]

Elizabeth took the opposite view. She disapproved of Henry III's policy of keeping them at court; he 'should not favour her mortal enemy, to which she added some very foul words applied to Guise', which Mendoza, the Spanish ambassador in London, did not feel he could repeat to Philip II.[2] The Guise were up to something, and she knew more about it than Henry III or Philip II because with the influx of exiles had come double agents and spies. Mendoza complained to his master of how secretary Walsingham, an experienced observer of the Paris scene from his time there as ambassador, maintained 'such a multitude of spies in France'.[3] One of these was planted in the Guise household itself. His reports give us an unparalleled glimpse of the world of the Guise family: we can eavesdrop on the duke's jokes, participate in his *coucher*, the nightly ritual of his retiring to bed, or see the duke bite his lip in vexation as his invasion plans are postponed. This tale of spying and skulduggery has yet to be told in full partly because of the aversion of English historians for things continental; they refer to the invasion project as the 'Throckmorton Plot', as if Francis Throckmorton was something more than a parochial cog in a much bigger international mechanism.[4] In France, too, the English exiles evoke little interest, surprisingly so since the care of English refugees was an early opportunity for Paris radicals to demonstrate their solidarity with and commitment to the international Catholic cause. Exile propaganda was to be enormously important, not only in showing Frenchmen the terrifying fate that a Protestant succession would bring, but also in vilifying Henry III as the puppet of Elizabeth. What his ultra-Catholic critics wanted were less pilgrimages and processions and more action to help their British co-religionists.

* * * *

Guise interest in foreign affairs was stimulated by their deteriorating relationship with the king. In April 1578, in talks with the Spanish ambassador and letters to William Allen, the head of the English mission, the duke first spoke of his interest in the exile cause and of his concern for the plight of his cousins Mary Stuart and James VI. Guise found offers of Spanish assistance welcome as his reputation came under sustained attack from the *mignons*. Until then, the Spanish had been deterred by his inexperience and dilettante image. But the Duke of Anjou's flight from court in February and the danger that he would raise a French army to assist the Dutch rebels made it imperative that the Spanish find allies in France. Philip II was not fussy: he approached Henri de Navarre and paid pensions to Protestant noblemen. Guise was identified by the Spanish ambassador as an ideal ally, both because of the political pressure he was under and his enormous debts. The talks had no immediate political consequences but prepared the ground for future cooperation. Guise entered the world of international espionage with the Spanish code-name 'Hercules', which was later changed to 'Mucius'.

When he was finally forced to quit court in May the duke did not retire as usual to Joinville. Instead, he visited his wife's properties in Normandy. But this was no summer holiday. His first visit to the seaside was to pledge to build a new family residence at Eu: plans were quickly completed and the foundations laid. Eu was not just a pleasure palace; it was the beginning of the revival of interest in a British empire; this time backed by the Habsburgs rather than the Valois. Its proximity to Dieppe made Eu quickly and easily accessible to England. In the next few years he would spend more time in Normandy than in Champagne, improving Eu's anchorage so that it could receive vessels of up to 300 tons. One of the leading exiles, John Leslie, Bishop of Ross, who became suffragan and vicar-general of the diocese of Rouen in 1579, encouraged his interest. At the beginning of 1582 he invited Ross and a number of senior Jesuits to Eu, where he announced the donation of £100 towards the establishment of a new school for the sons of English Catholics. The duke had recently built there a new college for the French Jesuits and it remained almost empty. When Father Robert Persons, whose escapades in England the previous year captivated his French audience, begged it from Claude Mathieu, the Jesuit Provincial readily lent it to him. The small school, which never had more than thirty pupils, was the direct predecessor of the present Stonyhurst College.

The duke's conscience was untroubled by the English mission, which meant sending young and suggestible men into extreme danger. The Jesuits, in particular, adapted well to the cloak-and-dagger world of espionage, even though such activities were ostensibly forbidden by the Society. Guise chief agent, Hubert Samier, travelled disguised as a physician called la Rue, on his visits to Mary. Even on the continent he rarely wore his habit and travelled incognito, either as la Rue or Hieronymo Martelli. Guise was aware that he too was being watched and not just by the English. In 1579, Henry III appointed a new lieutenant in Champagne, Jean de Dinteville, with orders to keep an eye on the duke—it was another reason why he preferred to stay away from the province. Guise himself was compelled to adapt to the times: when he visited the Spanish ambassador he did so in disguise. He paid a bribe of 3,000 crowns to Stafford, the penurious English ambassador who replaced Cobham in the autumn of 1583, to look at diplomatic dispatches.

In January 1581 Guise was commissioned by Mary to form an association in her name. But it was Scottish domestic politics, as in 1560, that promised to transform Guise fortunes, this time for the better. The Earl of Morton's Protestant and Anglophile regime was shaken by the return of the Catholic, Esmé Stuart, Duke of Lennox. There were high expectations of James VI's return to the Catholic fold when Morton was hanged on 2 June and Lennox took control of power. Guise could barely contain his excitement. When he was not at court, he was in Normandy where he was a regular guest of the Bishop of Ross at the archiepiscopal palace of Gaillon, reputedly the most beautiful Renaissance palace in France. In December, an English spy followed him to a number of secret meetings with representatives of the Catholic League in Normandy; these included François de Roncherolles, who would soon be sent to Scotland as his plenipotentiary, the local vice-admiral, Jean de Moy, whose support in any overseas enterprise was crucial, and an old Guise acquaintance, Michel de Monchy, Archdeacon of Eu, who had taken responsibility for the care of the English exiles in Rouen. It was during this visit that the duke first encountered Persons, and another Jesuit, the Scotsman William Crichton. He entertained them at Eu, where he gave Crichton, who was about to depart to hold secret talks with the Earl of Lennox, final instructions. Persons had recently returned from England and told the duke about his narrow escape and the arrest of his fellow priest, Edmund Campion. Persons had since settled in Rouen, setting up a printing press and establishing himself as the chief propagandist for the English Catholic cause. Persons's report that the conversion of the entire British Isles depended on Scotland chimed with Guise's dynastic interests. Campion's martyrdom (1 December 1581) not only gave licence to propagandists like Persons to put Elizabeth on trial, but it played into the hands of Henry III's enemies and moved French hearts into active support for the exile cause. Until then, Henry and Guise had succeeded in disguising their mutual animosity. When the break finally came in the New Year, Guise would defy his king and plot Elizabeth's downfall.

* * * *

The key decisions took place in April and May 1582 as relations with Epernon came to a head and the court left for Fontainebleau without the Guise. On 14 May, in the house of the papal nuncio, Castelli, Crichton made a report of his visit and relayed Lennox's ambitious plans to restore Scotland to Catholicism with an invasion of 8,000 troops in September supported by a similar-sized local levy. This was preliminary to asserting the claims of James VI to the throne of England. Crichton read out a memoir, which denounced the machinations of the 'Puritan' faction under the earls of Leicester and Huntingdon to usurp the rightful Stuart succession. Beside the nuncio, sitting around the table were Guise; James Beaton, Archbishop of Glasgow, representing Mary; and Claude Matthieu, who, as well as Provincial, was also rector of the Professed Jesuits (the elite of the society distinguished by their personal oath of obedience to the Pope), whose house in the rue Saint-Antoine had, since its foundation in 1580, emerged as a leading centre of Catholic politics. After listening, Guise first made some modifications to the plan, before turning to the nuncio to ask him to inform the Pope that 'he would insist in going in person on this enterprise with all his friends and kinsmen, and that as things stood as they were he did not doubt that the enterprise was feasible'.[5] The meeting ended in agreement, but two weeks later the duke got cold feet. 'He had a great desire to take part in person', but was troubled that he would break the oath he had made to Henry III as a knight of the Order of the Holy Spirit not to employ himself in favour of a foreign prince. A meeting at Beaton's house was hastily arranged and, in typical Jesuit fashion, Matthieu was able to free the duke's troubled conscience. After all, his legitimacy would come from the Pope himself and, if necessary, an Italian commander would be placed nominally in charge, so as to avert domestic criticism. The next step was to raise the 400,000 crowns necessary, and the Spanish ambassador, Tassis, was duly contacted. Crichton was sent to Rome and Persons, disguised and under the pseudonym Richard Melino, was dispatched to Madrid to sell the enterprise. In July, Guise and Mayenne went to Normandy to begin preparations, discussing the logistics with their local contacts and procuring the necessary ships. Roncherolles was sent to Scotland in order to lay the groundwork for their arrival.

The enterprise suffered its first blow on 22 August with the seizure of James VI by Protestant lords in the Ruthven raid. Guise was not disheartened, as he still had great faith in Lennox. Worse news came from Rome, where the Pope was only prepared to offer 50,000 crowns, but especially from Madrid, where Philip II was distinctly cool. One of the most damaging accusations levelled at Guise was that he sold himself and later France to a foreign prince. This completely misunderstands the nature of sixteenth-century dynastic politics. The duke approached Philip as an equal and hoped that the Catholic cause would provide cover for Guise dynastic pretensions in the British Isles. But Philip had no intention of using Spanish money to install a Guise puppet regime in the British Isles. Above all, he wanted the Guise to remain in France for his nuisance value, distracting the attention of the English and French from the Netherlands, where the Duke of Anjou had arrived on 10 February with the blessing of Elizabeth and Henry III, who had been providing covert financial support for his brother for some time. Anjou, accompanied by an Anglo-French host, which included the Earl of Leicester, was sworn in as duke, count, or lord of the various Netherlands provinces. In September, Philip sent a meagre 10,000 crowns to Guise to support his espionage activities. What Philip wanted above all was a counterweight to the Anglophilia of the French court, and so he placed the duke on a pension of 40,000 crowns. Philip instructed Tassis to tell Guise his priority should be the threat posed by the possibility of a Protestant succession in France, and that the duke was assured of his protection should he require it. Being a foreign pensioner was not unusual in sixteenth-century Europe and it was difficult to refuse Spanish silver: even Stafford had his hands in the honey pot. What distinguished Guise's relationship with Philip was its scale. It was not yet a formal alliance, but the first steps had been made in a commitment that would inevitably grow as the Anglo-French entente strengthened. Meanwhile, at the beginning of the New Year, the arrival of Lennox in Paris, where he immediately fell ill, put invasion plans on hold.

Henry III too was receiving foreign assistance. There is a strong possibility that snippets of English intelligence were passed on to the

French. The enterprise was becoming compromised by leaks. In November 1582, Henry dismissed Claude Matthieu as the royal confessor for being 'too Spanish'. Guise's English agents were being followed: Walsingham learned in December of the arrival of one of the Throckmorton family in Paris, carrying letters from England. Who was the mole inside the Guise household? One suspect we can discount is Thomas Morgan, who had been in touch with Mary Stuart since his arrival in Paris in 1580, and who, from May 1581, was pensioned by her. As Beaton's cipher clerk, he had a position of considerable influence in the plot, administering all of Mary's secret correspondence. Trustworthy he may have been, but Morgan was also an ambitious chancer. He was heavily involved with Francis Throckmorton and it was probably through Morgan that Guise was put in contact with his fellow Welshmen, William Parry. Parry had been spying for the English since 1577, though the English ambassador at the time, Cobham, did not trust him. Having been received into the Roman Catholic Church in Paris in the summer of 1582, he became embroiled in exile politics and boasted to Lord Burghley of having 'shaken the foundacon of the English seminary in Rheyms and utterly overthrowen the credite of the English pensioners on Rome'.[6] It was through the offices of Morgan that he gained an interview with the Guise at the end of 1583, in which he made an extraordinary proposition. Parry offered to assassinate Elizabeth. Guise was not interested; he had heard it all before. In April he had been approached by George Gifford, a disgruntled gentleman pensioner of the queen, to kill her for 100,000 livres. He was initially enthusiastic and, encouraged by Robert Persons, promised to put up half the sum himself. Acquaviva, the General of the Jesuits in Rome, shocked that a member of the Society should countenance such a proposal, delivered a stiff rebuke to Persons. More directly, Guise's interest in assassination plots was tempered by the death of Lennox within a month of the offer, since it effectively ended hope of assistance from Scotland. He seems to have turned Parry's proposal down out of hand, and he was right to do so. Many of the exiles who thronged the Hôtel de Guise did not trust Parry, whose penury caused him to play the roles of both *agent provocateur* and traitor; it was as the latter that he would be executed in Westminster Palace Yard on 2 March 1585.

Guise was preoccupied by other affairs. His grandmother had finally died and in February 1583 he returned to Joinville for her funeral. The cash from her estate, estimated at 500,000 livres, was useful. This, added to his Spanish pension, made the duke solvent for the first time in his life and he was minded to put up with the indignities of court life. As the Spanish ambassador put it, 'the flood has nearly reached its full and threatens to burst the dam'.[7] The king was using the familiar *tu* with the hated Epernon. At the end of April he presented his favourite with a prayer book inscribed: 'I beg you, my friend remember me when you pray here, as he who loves no other in this mortal world as much as you.'[8] Guise announced that he intended to take his leave from the king 'to go to Eu to take the air of the sea', knowing that the king knew this to be no holiday.

His relationship with the king deteriorating once more, the duke plunged himself into plotting. Claude Matthieu became his confessor and took on the role of chief intermediary with the nuncio, in order, perhaps rather fancifully, not to arouse suspicion. In early June, the chief conspirators—Guise, Matthieu, Beaton, the nuncio, and Cardinal Allen—met in Paris to hear a report from François de Roncherolles, 'a very clever man, in whom Guise has entire confidence'. Roncherolles argued that there was no further prospect of invading Scotland and that a new strategy was required. Allen pressed for an invasion of England. Beaton objected, but was overruled. By the end of the month a new plan was drawn up and sent to the Spanish Ambassador. It called for a two-pronged attack on England. The main force would be international. Commanded by the brother of the Duke of Bavaria, it would consist of 12,000 men, equally of Spaniards, Germans, and Italians. This force, largely paid for by Spain, would sail from the Iberian peninsula and a port in Flanders and rendezvous at Dalton-in-Furness, using Lancashire as a base for a northern rising. Meanwhile, Guise would land a smaller army of his own men and English exiles in Sussex, where they could shelter in strongholds provided by the Percys and the Earl of Arundel and divert Elizabeth's attention while the northern uprising got under way. Tassis was cautious, telling Philip 'that it is always easier to spend other people's money'. So Guise sent Charles Paget, an Englishman in his household, to open a direct channel with Mendoza, Philip's more gung-ho ambassador in London. Paget visited Sussex under the codename 'Mope' and made contact with, among others, Henry Percy, Earl of Northumberland. Persons was sent to Rome.

Guise returned to Normandy to begin preparations. In July he stayed two weeks at Eu and was 'visited by sundry English gentlemen who are come over "pretending" to be papists'.[9] Why men who would take such a long journey were claiming to be Catholics we do not know. The spy reported by mid-August that fifteen ships were being readied at Honfleur, Le Havre, and Fécamp. Guise, accompanied by his brother, Mayenne, the Cardinal of Bourbon, and Thomas Morgan toured the province, and finally alighted at the residence of Vice-admiral Moy, upstream on the Seine from Rouen, 'where they stayed for five or six days holding council everyday'. Elizabeth complained in the strongest terms to Henry III. It was precisely this sort of activity that the king was trying to stop when he had made the Duke of Joyeuse admiral and Governor of Normandy earlier that year. Joyeuse energetically set about placing trusted men in command of the Channel ports. When news arrived from Le Havre of logistical problems, Guise had to suspend his preparations and withdraw the money he had advanced.

The major blow came not from Paris, but London, where Francis Throckmorton was arrested in November. The conspirators were not, however, deterred by the exposure of their plans and the expulsion of Mendoza. These setbacks were more than offset by the news smuggled from Scotland that James VI welcomed the plan, called for Guise assistance and would 'submit' to his cousin's counsel. The only problem to surmount was Philip's reticence—he refused to release more than 30,000 crowns. However, the arrival of Mendoza, who had sworn to be an 'instrument of vengeance' on Elizabeth, in Paris, gave Guise a more belligerent ally. Mendoza put his backing behind a smaller operation to rescue James VI. Guise declared that he would go himself, whether or not Philip came up with the 300,000 crowns that were necessary. There is no doubting his intent. During the winter of 1583 he issued 120 commissions and continued to hold secret meetings in Paris with Leslie, Beaton, Morgan, and the nuncio. In January 1584 the English spy reported that 'he never saw the duke of Guise more gallant or merry. And that talking with his mother, they fell in speech of Scotland . . . and that he hoped that there would be ere long, *beau jeu* in England.'[10] Discussions with the Pope about financing the operation were still going on in April when news of the Duke of Anjou's illness halted any plans to leave France.

* * * *

Guise persisted with his plans because they made sense in the domestic political scene. During the winter of 1583 Henry III made no secret of his preference for the Navarre succession. And in the spring, Elizabeth announced her decision to send the Order of the Garter, an honour reserved only for close friends and supporters of the English monarch, to Henry. In his role as chief patron of the exile cause, Guise mobilized his supporters in Paris against the Anglo-French entente, while a propaganda campaign advertised to the wider public the terror that was inevitable with a Protestant succession. For pious French Catholics there was a special fascination with England, which had produced the first martyrs of the Counter-Reformation Church. The diarist Guillaume Coton, librarian of the abbey of Saint-Victor, sought out the company of exiles to hear their tales of heroism, and assiduously recorded news of the mission and listed the names of English martyrs in his journal. Only later would reports of the missions from India, China, and Japan surpass the tales of English derring-do and adventure that filled the taverns and dining rooms of Paris in the 1580s.

The engraver, Richard Verstegan, who fled London to escape arrest in February 1582, quickly emerged as the most skilled broadcaster of the English Catholic struggle. As soon as he arrived in Paris he began work on a broadsheet with six woodcuts, depicting 'An Image of the Present State of the English Church' addressed to Catholics everywhere. The arrest, trial, torture, and dismemberment of the martyrs, most notably Edmund Campion, were depicted with gruesome precision. It was a companion piece to Persons's *An Epistle of the Persecution of Catholickes in Englande*, of which Guise commissioned a French translation. The text described the persecution, torture, and violent deaths perpetrated by Protestants. The following year Verstegan produced an engraving of Mary Stuart and by the end had completed an ambitious cycle of engravings the *Briefve Description des diverses cruautez que les Catholiques endurent en Angleterre pour la foi* (Plate 26). Its English story was made familiar to its French audience by the structure of the background buildings: the roofs, the shape of the windows, and the position of church spires were Parisian, suggesting that the action was taking place in Paris.[11] The Guise brothers took a close interest in his work. The following year they saw and approved of copies he had made of paintings in the English college of Rome portraying the sufferings of martyrs.

But Verstegan and his associates went too far. In November they posted a scurrilous image of Elizabeth in prominent places around the city, including the square in front of the Hôtel de Ville:

Last Monday a foul picture of the Queen was set up here, she being on horseback, her left hand holding the bridle, with her right hand pulling up her clothes; upon her head written *La reine d'Angleterre*; verses underneath signifying that if any Englishman passed that way, he could tell what and who the picture was. Under it was a picture of Monsieur [the Duke of Anjou] . . . on his fist a hawk, 'which continually baited and could never make her still'.

Parisians were being invited to laugh at the failed Anjou match. Stafford was not amused and in January Verstegan was imprisoned at his behest. His arrest became a cause célèbre among radical Catholics and he was eventually released at the intercession of the nuncio. In the duke's absence, the Hôtel de Guise was raided and a set of copper plates seized by the royal authorities.

The hôtel was the place where exile activity and domestic opposition came together and where future policy was coordinated. It was both a fortress and a palace. Separated from the rue de la Chaume by a wall and courtyard, it was three-stories high. From the ground floor one ascended by means of a monumental staircase to the first floor, from where one had access to the terrace and the steps that led down to the garden with its flowerbeds, fountains, orangerie, outbuildings, and stables. Banquets at the palace were famous social occasions at which court society mixed with well-to-do Parisians. Pierre de l'Estoile was scandalized by the wedding festivities that the duke put on for one of his servants, who came from a leading legal family, to the daughter of the city's former mayor. So rowdy did the revelry become that the more refined ladies among the wedding guests had to retire early. These social events now took on more overtly political overtones. In March 1584 the duke hosted a dinner for the most prominent exiles; it was chance for them to meet like-minded Parisians and discuss the international Catholic cause. These were public events, something not unlike a modern movie premiere, but in this case the crowd of onlookers were allowed inside 'like bats clinging to the rails to see the prince dine with the room still completely full of people'.[12]

At these social events the duke asked his guests to provide more than moral support. The English complained in June 1583 that he was daily 'practising' the city's aldermen and magistrates. With Philip II dragging his feet, Guise needed alternative sources of money and he invited a number of sympathetic bankers and financial experts to join his salon. One of these men, Etienne de Neuilly, President of the Paris Excise Court and city mayor between 1582 and 1584, joined the duke's council and emerged as a leader of the Paris's radical Catholics. Their friendship was abetted by the fact that they worshipped at the same church, Saint-Jean en Grève, just behind the Hôtel de Ville.

Perhaps Neuilly was among the mourners when the duke buried his 4-year-old daughter Marie there in 1582. When the duke was not in town the salon was run by his wife Catherine, whose abilities in business matters caused her to become known as 'the pretty advocate'. While he was away in Normandy, the duke wrote to his wife, reminding her to send his new friend a gift: 'send the rosaries to President Neuilly if my sister has not done so...and give him the best cheer that you possibly can, make a close friend of him for he is very important to me'.[13] In this manner, the dining club that the duke had started was maintained in his absence. Henri insisted that it was not just for men:

> I'm very pleased that you are striving as much as you can among everyone in order to win us friends. Give good cheer to one and all and ensure that the ladies of Paris come to eat and drink with you. But favour those who love us most over the rest, and make sure that everyone sees the difference.

The exiles clustered on the Left Bank, the obvious choice since many of them were students and priests. The cardinals of Guise and Bourbon had several palaces here. Dining rights in these establishments or the lease of rooms in one of many tenements that they owned in the vicinity were significant factors in creating a support network. Priests from all over the British Isles stayed in the dormitories of the abbey of Saint-Victor. It is no surprise that Giordano Bruno, who has been identified by John Bossy as Henry Fagot, Walsingham's spy in the French embassy in London, also passed through here.

Where the Guise led, their supporters followed. The exiles required accommodation, so Parisians welcomed them into their houses. The Left Bank was home to Paris's students, lawyers, and other legal officials. These educated bourgeois identified with the exiles' suffering, their support a badge indicating membership of the outlawed Catholic League. Many radicals in Paris, such as Pierre Acarie, a rich official in the Royal Chamber of Accounts (whose mystic wife, Barbe, was soon to be made famous for conversations with Christ) first got involved in oppositional politics by providing charity to English émigrés. The exiles themselves soon gained an institutional foothold in Left Bank life. They worshipped at Saint-Cosme et Damien church in the rue de la Harpe, and it was no surprise when the radical Scots preacher John Hamilton, became the parish priest in 1585. English and Scots students came to dominate the German Nation of the university, which was centred in Mignon College. The nobleman,

Charles Paget, cut a very different figure: he swaggered around the streets accompanied by a retinue of sixteen to twenty men and, sponsored by Pierre Acarie applied for letters of French naturalization. The community and many of its supporters gathered together once a year at Saint-Victor abbey on 29 December to celebrate the feast of the greatest English martyr of all, Thomas Becket.

Opposition to Henry III centred on three other Left Bank churches—Saint-Séverin, Saint-Benoît, and Saint-André des Arts. The curés here were sympathetic to or owed their careers to the Guise. From their pulpits they reinforced the message that it was a Catholic duty to give charity to and support the exiles. In these parishes lay radicals developed a strategy to control parochial office, infiltrating the city militia and dominating the election of churchwardens. Mary Stuart's council, which oversaw her legal and financial affairs in France, played a particularly important role in this process. The wealthy Nau clan, which dominated the council, lived near the Hôtel de Cluny and took responsibility for organization in the parish of Saint-Benoît. Henri de Guise knew Claude Nau, her secretary, as 'a man of worth and devoted servant of our family, among whom he had the honour of being raised'. More significant was her treasurer, Charles Hotman, an acquaintance of both Morgan and Paget, who in early 1585 was elected as the first leader of the Paris Sixteen, the name given to the Catholic League in Paris in honour of the city's sixteen neighbourhoods.

* * * *

Even before news that the Duke of Anjou had fallen seriously ill reached Paris at the end of March 1584, the strain between the king and Guise had become intolerable. As Stafford put it, 'he hateth extremely the dukes of Guise and Mayenne'. The succession was not simply a matter of religious principle: for both sides it was about the survival of their respective dynasties. Although Henry III was the last Valois, he saw Navarre as his rightful heir and had informed Navarre's envoy in a secret meeting in February 1584 that 'he loved him as a son'. In mid-April, as his brother's health deteriorated, he announced to his dinner guests, who included Mayenne: 'Today, I recognize the King of Navarre for my sole and unique heir.'[14] For the Guise, the stakes were equally high. Philip II reminded the duke 'of the treatment he may fear' if Navarre ever became king. And the ambassador of the Duke of Savoy spelled out such a future more clearly should Navarre be victorious: 'could [the Guise] have no other doubt than that their House would be ruined and, that as ancient enemies and Catholics, they would all be killed'.[15] In private the duke was candid about this. Several years previously he had admitted to Michel de Montaigne that the formation of an insurgent Catholic party was borne of necessity, for while Navarre lived 'neither he nor his House would ever be safe'. He personally favoured a religious compromise along Lutheran lines. Like Navarre, his posturing on matters religious was nothing more than a 'parade'.[16] On 10 June 1584 the Duke of Anjou died. The war of succession was about to begin. The 'parade' would lead to a thirteen-year war; the most destructive of the civil wars so far, it would claim the lives of two of the principal players and almost destroy France as a unitary state.

REVOLUTION

As they approached their destination, the exhausted riders, sporting the green livery of the Duke of Mayenne, could at last see the crenulated towers of the old château perched on top of a steep hill, which overlooked the town of Joinville and the new pleasure palace on the banks of the Marne. The stable lads and servants who rushed out to greet the duke as he entered the courtyard saw that he was in a foul mood; he had received some bad news, his plans had been thrown into confusion and he had made the two-day ride from Dijon for a show-down with his brother. Since the death of Antoinette de Bourbon, the family servants had not been used to such conferences and they busied with refreshments for the exhausted riders. But there was little time to waste on that 14 April 1585. The pressure was etched on the features of Henri de Guise too; at the age of 34 he was already prematurely grey.

The brothers followed by their counsellors entered the gallery of the old castle with its ornate columns, each decorated with a frieze and a cornice, and crossed the brightly coloured tile floor in order to take the stairs to the living quarters, which had been built by their grand-mother. They entered a room which jutted out from the main building, but had little time to admire the magnificent views it afforded towards the east of twelve summits, separated by streams, fields, woods, villages, and neighbouring castles; the conference, which would last a day and a night, had been called to resolve a crisis. The room in which it was set later became known as 'the cabinet of the League'.[1]

Mayenne was furious at his brother having 'too soon declared and taken up arms' against the king when he entered the town of Châlons with troops three weeks previously. The correspondence of the League leadership at this time has until now lain unknown and unread in the British Library. These letters, written in code, make clear that the brothers and their allies had initially planned to raise their standard on 18 April, a significant date for such a 'holy enterprise', as it was the day before Good Friday. They also make it clear that conspiracy was unfamiliar territory for some. Guise's cousin, the Duke of Mercoeur, was told to write in invisible ink on the back of the regular post, but he had to be reminded to make sure that his pen was clean of ink before he wrote![2] Mayenne charged his brother with a monumental blunder. In revealing themselves before they were ready, they would allow the king to represent them as the aggressors and buy off the town governors they themselves had been dealing with. He wanted to know why his brother had abandoned the plan to pressure the king into war against Protestants by working covertly, 'always to keep close without abandoning him...to maintain and conserve themselves in his good graces', while at the same time placing their partisans in positions of power. Instead, Guise and his troops had entered Châlons, where they had been confronted by the royalist lieutenant of Champagne, Joachim de Dinteville. Dinteville lost no time in dispatching a messenger to the king with the words: 'indubitably the die is cast and the Rubicon crossed'.

Guise explained to his brother that he had been forced by circumstance. In order to dispel claims of treason he had ordered his cousin, Elbeuf, to conduct the Cardinal of Bourbon to Péronne, birthplace of the Catholic League, to make a declaration. But the damage had already been done. A document purporting to be a speech that Guise had delivered to his troops outside Châlons was already being circulated. The contents were political dynamite. He, it was claimed, spoke of his ambition to cut the 'mocking *mignons*' down to size and referred brazenly to his claim on the throne, reminding his audience of Hugues Capet's usurpation of the Carolingian line and attacking those who denied his descent from Charlemagne from trying to 'stand in the way of the glory of our House'. The document was palpably false—Guise wished to be a kingmaker not a king—and had been put about by his Protestant enemies to blacken him in the eyes of moderate, law-abiding Catholics.[3] In contrast, the declaration made at Péronne was a model of constitutional legitimacy. No mention was made of the Guise. The Cardinal of Bourbon, as a prince of the blood, was indubitably leader of the association. The three obsessions of the Catholic League figured prominently: representative government, religious fundamentalism, and England. The adherents to the association called for renewal of contractual monarchy, one that was more receptive to the will of the people, who were, of course, overwhelmingly hostile to a

Protestant succession: 'The Estates-General, free and without management, should be held frequently and as the needs of the kingdom demand, with full liberty to make all complaints.' The cardinal declared himself not just against heretics, but against the enemy within: those Catholics who, in serving their own political interests, were subverting religion and the state. France, the cardinal exhorted his audience, must not be permitted to follow the example of England, which in League propaganda had become shorthand for tyranny.

Mayenne's frustration was understandable given that preparations had been under way for a year. Plans, which had initially involved a general muster of all League forces somewhere along the Loire Valley, now had to be hastily changed. Many of those they had been dealing with in secret now distanced themselves. They informed Mercoeur 'that our passage to join you in order to help and succour you is closed and the most important towns, where our coup would to be carried out, are lost'.[4] The brothers departed having agreed more limited objectives, but the conference pointed up their differences, which, as we shall discover, would be accentuated as the political crisis deepened.

* * * *

The war of succession was not just a civil war; it was a great European war. As soon as his brother was dead, the king sent the Duke of Epernon to Henri de Navarre to persuade him to convert, but Navarre had no intention of abandoning his power base. In Magdeburg on 15 December 1584 a Protestant alliance was signed by Navarre, Elizabeth I, an assortment of German princes, and Swiss Cantons to uphold the rightful succession. The king tried to keep the Guise in Paris, but after Anjou's funeral they made their excuses and left. In September the three brothers and Roncherolles, the Cardinal of Bourbon's chief advisor, held a conference at Nancy hosted by the Duke of Lorraine, where the decision was taken to revive the Catholic League. They reconvened at Joinville on 31 December with their cousins, Elbeuf and Aumale, and two representatives from Philip II, Tassis and Moreo, to sign a treaty that pledged to support the Cardinal of Bourbon as the heir to the throne. As the first Catholic prince of the blood, he provided a fig leaf of legitimacy. In fact, it was a radical step. The cardinal was 62 and, by claiming to alter the rules, the Catholic princes had struck a blow against the sacred and providential nature of the succession. For the first time it was possible to imagine the election of the monarch, candidates being endorsed by the Estates-General. Philip II agreed to fund the League army to the tune of 600,000 crowns a year payable in advance. However, because Philip was heavily committed in the Netherlands, the Duke of Lorraine agreed to advance two-thirds of the sum. For both men this was an opportunity not to be missed. They had both married French princesses, daughters of Henry II, and had children by them. Duke Charles was better placed: he had several sons by Claude de France, the eldest of whom, Henri, Marquis of Pont à Mousson, had been born in 1563, while Philip had only one daughter with Elizabeth de France, the Infanta Isabella born in 1566. At the time of the conference in Nancy, a medal was struck representing the marquis being crowned by Minerva and Mars with words *Crescenti Crescunt Coelestia Dona*, referring to the celestial gifts that the marquis was to come into. Of course, the Salic law excluded succession through the female line, but then the laws of succession had just been torn up.

The cousins embraced each other and left for their regions, where they were to raise money and recruit adherents: Guise remained in Champagne; Mayenne returned to his governorship of Burgundy; Elbeuf and Aumale were to organize the rebellion in Normandy and Picardy respectively. Their cousin, the Cardinal of Vaudémont, accompanied by the Jesuits, Matthieu and Samier, was sent to Rome to get the blessing of Gregory XIII. Paris was a special case. Guise initially saw his popularity in the city as an opportunity to raise funds. And so, at the end of 1584, he summoned his Left Bank friends to the palace of the Archbishop of Reims, his brother's Paris residence. The first Parisian branch of the Catholic League was made up of veterans of the English exile cause: Charles Hotman, Mary Stuart's treasurer; Boucher, curé of Saint-Benoît; Prévost, curé of Saint-Séverin, and Matthieu Launay, the translator of Robert Persons. They agreed to proceed by each recruiting two men among the legal and mercantile elite, who would in turn co-opt their friends. Like freemasonry, the Parisian League spread along networks of friends and colleagues: cells were rapidly established in all of the city's numerous civic and royal organs of government—Guise's friend President Neuilly took matters in hand among the excise men. The secret organization took the name of the Sixteen, in reference to the number of the city's districts. Its early members were overwhelmingly educated men of the middling sort—lawyers formed the backbone of the organization—precisely the sort of people who were able to contribute to League coffers. As the Sixteen spread, it required an organization. Its ruling council of ten, headed by Hotman, divided the city into five sectors: three on the Right Bank, one on the Ile de la Cité, and one on the Left Bank. Council meetings took place in Hotman's house in the rue Michel Lecomte, a stone's throw from the Hôtel de Guise, in the Sorbonne, or in the professed house of the Jesuits, behind Saint-Paul's in the Marais. Here Guise's letters were read out or verbal instructions given by Roncherolles, the duke's liaison in Paris. The Hôtel de Guise bustled with activity as the money and arms began to pile up. More beds had to be brought in to accommodate all the new people who came and went. The king had forbidden the sale of arms in the city, but the Sixteen's tentacles also reached into the organization of the city's provost and his archers. Nicolas Poulain, lieutenant of the provost, who joined the Sixteen on 2 January 1585, arranged for the transport of arms at night to the Hôtel de Guise. Delighted at the progress of the Sixteen, Guise ordered them to send emissaries to the provinces to establish cells in other towns. Hotman made the arrangements and earmarked 3,000 crowns for this purpose.

Henry III was aware of Guise plots, but not of their objectives. In the early months of 1585 he surrounded himself with a new guard, the *Quarante Cinq*, recruited from Epernon's homeland of Gascony, traditionally the birthplace of France's toughest soldiers. He tried to exploit differences between the brothers, tersely ordering Guise, who feigned ignorance, to stop his machinations, while being more emollient to Mayenne, writing to him of the 'singular love' that he had for him. And then the king had a stroke of luck. On 12 March a boat, loaded with 400 corselets and 1,200 arquebuses, was discovered on the Marne and brought back to Paris. An investigation was launched and orders for the arrest of Jean de la Rochette, an esquire of the Cardinal of Guise with close links to the Parisian legal world. Cardinal Vaudémont narrowly avoided being picked up as royalist units scoured the countryside looking for the suspect, who was finally arrested on 26 March. After his escape, Vaudémont wrote that 'never had a man had such good fortune', which was an understandable exaggeration since he had just returned from Rome with some news that would have stunned the whole of Europe and forced Henry III into a corner. According to Vaudémont, Gregory XIII had 'taken away all scruples that he could have had and gave full and plenary indulgence to all those who employed themselves in such a holy and good work'.[5]

Guise's decision to summon his forces to Châlons—which he had identified long before as his headquarters because of its excellent communications on the Marne—had been forced on him by la Rochette's arrest. It was a decision made easier by the Pope's blank cheque.

Over the next few weeks, Guise slowly extended his control over much of Champagne, though the capital, Troyes, remained in royalist hands. The League confined itself at first to plundering tax receipts and taking towns, which could be used to bargain with the king—the Governor of Verdun was bought for 10,000 crowns. A concentration of forces was attempted at Montargis, south of Paris. The Duke of Elbeuf left his base at Bayeux in mid-May and joined with the Count of Brissac at Angers, but in a skirmish outside Beaugency they were forced back by royalists under Joyeuse.

It had become apparent that the king did not possess the resources to defeat the League, and Guise had no wish to give battle and damage his image as the king's good servant. More seriously, the death of Gregory XIII and the election on 24 April of Sixtus V, a man known for his mistrust of Spain, removed papal approval for a *putsch*. Negotiations conducted under the auspices of Catherine de Medici had been under way for months before a peace was signed at Nemours on 7 July. At face value, the treaty was a royal capitulation. Henry rescinded the edicts in favour of Protestantism, promised to declare war on Navarre and accorded the Catholic princes towns for their security and bodyguards for their protection. During these years Henry's mood fluctuated between melancholic fatalism and a desire to retreat from the world: he spent several days a year between 1584 and 1586, living as a monk, wearing the coarse black habit of a Minim and meditating alone in his cell in the Franciscan Oratory. But it would be wrong to accept the general opinion that Henry did little to secure the succession for his preferred candidate. He had out-manoeuvred the League once before and thought he knew how to deal with the Guise: he would play for time, buy off their supporters, foster division between brothers and cousins, and wait for the League to blunder and crack.

This time, however, things were different. Since 1582, Henri de Guise had ceased to trust the king. He knew him as a hypocrite and what is more he had worked out his tactics. He was better informed than his adversary. He had a spy, le Bois, in the Duke of Epernon's household who slept in his master's chamber. Guise told Mercoeur, during the negotiations with the Queen Mother, that 'we are well advertised from all sides that their intention is to deceive us and we well believe it'.[6] Guise knew the rapprochement to be a fake, but he would make use of it to expand his power base and multiply the urban cells of the League. In private, he compared the king to Louis XI, the fifteenth-century king known as the universal spider for his treachery and double-dealing.[7] This reference is a clue that the duke was, like his mother, a student of history, and at the very least aware of the constitutional implications of contractual monarchy. In the resistance theories borrowed by the Catholic League from the Protestants, Louis XI was the archetypal tyrant, whose reign had witnessed the final overthrow of the sovereignty of the people, whose freedoms were enshrined in the ancient Frankish constitution.

* * * *

The first strains quickly began to appear as the campaign against the Protestants in the south got under way. Mayenne was given command of an army against Navarre, but it was poorly provided for and while he was occupied by fruitless sieges in the Dordogne, the king continued to conduct negotiations with the Protestants behind his back. Guise went to Paris to put pressure on the king. His entry on 15 February 1586 was carefully stage-managed. It took place almost a year to the day that the Earl of Derby and 200 English gentlemen had entered the city for the purpose of conferring the Order of the Garter on Henry III. Parisians had been excluded from these festivities for fear of violence. Public spectacles had been avoided and guards posted throughout the city, as even 'the best sort murmur not a little to finde this Kinge so disposed to entertayne Amity with Heretikes'. The Cardinal of Guise described the very different circumstances of their arrival on 'Saturday and very few or no courtiers rode in front of us, but a great host of the nobility that I guess there to have been five of six hundred... We did not see the king that day, and on our way to the Hôtel de Guise along the few streets one has to travel I have never seen such acclamation by the people, for all the houses and streets were crammed with men.'[8] The English ambassador reported, not without satisfaction, 'the strangest reception of the Duke of Guise that I ever saw... Not one gentleman went to meet him... He saw the King upon Sunday morning, who when he was coming in, spake all the worst he could of him... tarried not a quarter of an hour with him, but went his ways, and never saw him since but in the masque, where he never said a word to him... All [Guise's] people be marvellously out of countenance, and Madame de Montpensier [his sister], the virago of the League, crieth out extremely of this usage of him.'[9]

Despite this frosty start, Henry knew that, notwithstanding his popularity, the duke was short of funds and in a weak position. He thought he could charm him and use the war to his own advantage. He therefore agreed to step up the war effort, believing that a new round of taxes, especially the sale of more royal offices, would grind down the people and undermine support for the war. And he planned to channel the new funds to loyalist commanders and increase the defections from the League. Mayenne's struggling army would now have to compete with new forces sent into Auvergne under Joyeuse and Epernon in Provence. The rise of the latter was relentless. With his elevation to the governorship of Provence and command of the Mediterranean galley fleet, he was in command of what were considered the 'three keys' of the realm, the other being the fortresses of Boulogne and Metz.

Lucinge, the ambassador of the Duke of Savoy, who met and closely observed Guise during his stay, noted the disaffection of his Parisian supporters. Guise 'let himself be led by the nose . . . and enchanted by the practices of the king and his enemies . . . who played him along for weeks at a time with whoring and following all sorts of immoderate debauching'.[10] While this sort of behaviour may have scandalized the duke's pious constituency, such displays of virility played to a different gallery, pointing up the king's lack of manliness. The association of sexual and martial prowess was strong and it was an image that Henri de Navarre, too, cultivated with great success. Nevertheless, when Guise finally left Paris on 18 May his supporters were downcast. It seemed as though he had been outmanoeuvred once more. There was nothing he could do when Henry reopened negotiations with Navarre. He retuned to the eastern frontier. An invasion of German mercenaries paid for by English and Danish subsidies was expected at any moment and the duke was soon preoccupied besieging Jametz and Sedan, key fortresses on the Meuse, belonging to the Protestant Duke of Bouillon. His major concern was to keep his small army in the field in anticipation that the king would do a deal with the Protestants. He would not return to the city for another two years. As a result he would lose control of the Paris Sixteen.

During his absence the Sixteen became impatient. They did not wish to temporize with a king who did not keep his promises, and they wanted the *mignons* removed from power. They feared that a deal with Navarre and his English allies was about to be done and pamphlets, such as Louis Dorléans' *Advertissement des Catholiques Anglois* and the French translation of Robert Persons's scandal sheet, *Leicester's Commonwealth*, painted a hideous picture of life across the Channel under a heretical monarch. The opening sonnet of the *Advertissement* was so full of treason that l'Estoile considered it 'enough to send the author to the gallows'.[11] The authorities undertook rigorous investigations in order to suppress it. In Paris, resistance to censorship and new taxes, especially the sell-off of 139 grades of royal office to purchasers who bought the rights to sell them on for a profit or pass them to their heirs, was led by the lawyers and related professions. In the summer the city's solicitors went on strike. On 22 November the Sixteen had its first martyr when an attorney, François le Breton, was hanged for saying that the king 'was one of the greatest hypocrites that ever there was'. His critique went far beyond matters of faith: he accused the king of putting justice up for sale and taxing the poor to feed the rich. As the Sixteen developed a social and political pro- gramme, so its armed wing grew. It could count on 1,500 butchers, 600 horse-traders and 500 'bad boys' among the Seine's boatmen and river workers.

The plan to seize the king was however born of desperation. The arrest of one of its founding members, the notary Lamorlière, increased fears of a royal crackdown. How to do it? The leadership had no experience of organizing a coup, let alone street-fighting. The arrival of the Duke of Mayenne in January 1587 calmed their anx- ieties. Mayenne had returned from the south furious at his treatment by the king and determined to avenge his humiliation. His army, ill- supplied and underfunded, had been decimated. Desertions were made worse in a depopulated countryside denuded by famine and plague. Mayenne took up residence in the palace of the abbot of Saint-Denis among the Left Bank militants, and it was here that preparations for the coup were finalized. The plan was to overwhelm the strong points of the city, eliminate a number of royalists, and seize the king. In order to disrupt the movement of royalist reinforcements, a new weapon was to be deployed, one that would become synonym- ous with Paris's history of insurrection. For the first time, barri- cades—a word derived from the *barrique*, the barrels in which every household stored its comestibles—were to be built across the city's narrow streets, presaging the great events of 1648, 1794, 1848, 1871, and 1968. The day of the barricades was set for 15 March. The Duke of Guise, who was absent, was not informed.

Among the plotters there was however discontent. One of the founding members of the Sixteen, Nicolas Poulain, lieutenant of the city's provost, was aghast at what he considered to be social revolu- tion, 'using the lower orders to divest the king of his throne and put the House of Lorraine in his stead, having cut the throats of the rightful heirs'.[12] Thanks to Poulain's tip-off, the plot was foiled and several of the ringleaders arrested. The Sixteen were seriously compromised, and if the king had acted decisively he might have been able to break the movement altogether. That he did not do so may have been due to overconfidence. After all, his strategy of wearing the Guise down seemed to be working. And he now had a double agent providing excellent information about the divisions among his enemies. Mayenne denied any complicity and distanced himself from the coup. Poulain told the king that Guise was furious both with his brother and the Sixteen and that the latter, chastened by their failure, had begged the duke's pardon and sent him a gold chain worth 500 crowns. But the king was prevented from a full-scale repression in the city for another reason: news of the execution of Mary Stuart arrived in Paris on 1 March, providing the Paris League with a martyr of a different order.

* * * *

In the weeks following the news of Mary's execution hardly a parish church in the city was immune from the sound of Lenten preachers mourning the death of the dowager queen and screaming for revenge against those responsible for the cruelty. Even in a traditionally moderate parish like Saint-Eustache, the preacher, possibly Mary's former confessor, René Benoist, a man averse to extremism, was forced to leave his pulpit and abandon his sermon altogether, so great was the emotion that 'had won over the audience including himself'.[13] Interest in Mary's plight had always been strong among French readers and her death filled the bookshops with editions relating to her and more broadly to the persecution of Catholics in England. In 1587, Catholic polemic accounted for 60 per cent of all the editions printed in France. Of these 416 items no less than 91 or 22 per cent were related to events in the British Isles.[14] Rumour had it that the king had been complicit in Mary's execution, though no one dared to put such words into print until much later.

Guise was more sanguine. He did not travel to Paris for the memorial service, which took place in Notre-Dame on 13 March, nor join the clamour for revenge. He had momentarily turned his back on the city. Since the summer of 1586 he had been preoccupied with the international situation. His strategy was increasingly dictated by events out of his own control. He had become completely dependent on Philip II for funds and for political direction. Philip had no intention of elevating the Guise to a position of influence in England and during 1586 the Spanish had taken over control of attempts to save

Mary. It was they who had directed the last daring plot to overthrow Elizabeth which forced the queen to sign Mary's execution warrant. Philip was increasingly preoccupied by the Armada and subsidies to Guise were overlooked or not paid at all. During the winter of 1586 Guise insisted that Philip honour his obligations, but the duke was no longer a priority. 'Have patience', Philip told him, 'help will arrive. Don't shout in protest until you are sure you have been refused . . . the cause of religion is on the threshold of its greatest triumph, but requires time, and prudence.'[15] The duke had been reduced from the status of ally to that of client. In order to ensure the continued flow of subsidies, he agreed to provide the Armada with a deep-water port in France. But the spy Poulain got wind of the plot and on 17 March 1587 an attempt by the Duke of Aumale to seize Boulogne was foiled. Aumale went into open revolt. He blockaded the town and took control of three smaller towns in Picardy; it was the beginning of a campaign to bring this strategic province, which bordered the Spanish Netherlands and the Channel, completely under League control. Henry was furious at this flagrant challenge to his authority. He ordered Aumale to disband his troops and pleaded with Mayenne and Guise to reason with their cousin. On 10 April, at an assembly of notables in Paris, the king defended the Bourbon succession and attacked those who defied his authority. The failure to take Boulogne was to have serious consequence for the Armada; but the affair was equally serious for the relations between the king and the Guise. The manner of the fighting reveals a shift in the attitude of the League leadership to the use of force. Aumale had the royalist captain of Boulogne murdered and placed a price of 4,000 crowns on his successor. During May he conspired to seize Abbeville and Amiens. Henry responded by appointing the loyal Duke of Nevers as governor and assembling troops at Beauvais. France was on the threshold of its first full-scale Catholic civil war.

These manoeuvres did not induce Aumale to withdraw and Henry was unable to confront the League in the field for the simple reason that he was no longer secure in Paris. With their men-folk preoccupied elsewhere and the leadership of the Sixteen cowed by the failure of the March 15 coup, leadership of the League in Paris devolved upon a woman, the duke's 35-year-old sister, Catherine-Marie de Lorraine, dowager Duchess of Montpensier. Pierre de l'Estoile considered her to be 'queen of Paris'; to Brantôme she was 'a great lady of state'. A widow since 1582, her power in the city derived from the protection she provided for radical preachers. She had a violent dislike of the king and, in the wake of Mary Stuart's execution, encouraged priests to preach openly against him. From her palace in the rue de Tournon in the faubourg Saint-Germain she continued to sponsor the English exiles' cause. The king responded to protests by Stafford and in June several printers were arrested and books burned. Catherine kept up the pressure by arranging for an exhibition of pictures of six pictures from a book, the *Briefve Description*, which had been executed by the engraver Richard Verstegan (Plate 26). The exhibition began on the Feast of John the Baptist (24 June) in the cemetery of Saint-Séverin. It was a natural choice because the church was close to the English embassy on the Left Bank and the curé, Jean Prévost, a founding member of the Sixteen. Cemeteries in the sixteenth century were recreational and gathering places, natural arenas for games, promenading, and shopping. The engravings were enhanced for the exhibition by being enlarged and painted. Copies of the book were distributed to visitors. The event caused a sensation:

> I never saw a thing done with fury nor with that danger of great emotion as that hath brought; for I see not so few as five thousand people a day come to see it, and some English knave priests that be there, they point with a rod and show everything; affirm it to be true and aggravate it. Others aposted purposely for the matter, show then how likely Catholics are to grow to that point in France if they have a king a heretic, and that they are next door to it, which indeed is the chief intent that the thing set there to animate and mutiny the people.[16]

Henry's nickname for Catherine was the 'hunchback', and he ordered the dismantling of the exhibition at night 'for if the hunchback suspects anything she will prevent it, since she likes to cause me great fear'.[17] But the weakness of the king's position soon became apparent when he attempted to deal with her preacher friends. At the end of August a sermon was delivered in Saint-Germain l'Auxerrois church attacking the king in person and making the link between the lack of morality in France and high bread prices (the subject of recent riots) and venal office-holding. On 2 September, following rumours that the king intended to arrest a number of preachers, including Jean Prévost and Jean Boucher, the Sixteen gathered to protect the preachers. A riot ensued when the king's men entered the parish of Saint-Séverin. Henry's men were forced to withdraw and he to abandon any hope of arresting the preachers; they, emboldened by their defiance, refused to let up and there were incidences of them refusing communion to those they considered 'politiques'. On 16 December the Sorbonne issued a judgment stating that it was permissible to depose princes who did not act correctly. Henry saw the hand of Boucher, rector of the Sorbonne, behind this and at the end of the month he summoned him and the others for a personal audience, warning them that if they did not cease to attack him he would not hesitate to send them to the galleys. Then in the New Year he summoned the duchess and told her he was aware that 'she was making herself the Queen of Paris and of the monopolies, plots and seditions she was practising and how she was paying the wages of Boucher... and other priests and preachers to continue their seditious and bloody preaching'.[18] She was unrepentant and bragged that the League had advanced more by the words of her preachers than by the arms of her brothers. He ordered her to leave Paris. But he could not compel her to go. To arrest a woman and a princess would have antagonized the people. Just three days after her dressing down, Catherine was seen carrying a pair of scissors in her belt, supposedly in preparation for tonsuring the king before putting him in a convent. She joked that it would be his third crowning, a play on the king's device *Manet ultima coelo*. The third and last crown (after that of France and Poland, where Henry had briefly been elected king) is that of heaven.

Henry's inability to silence the duchess and her preachers was due to the utter collapse of royal power in France at the end of 1587. Unable to confront Guise openly and force him to surrender the towns he had seized in Picardy, the king had planned for the Protestants to do the work for him. In months of painstaking negotiations, using his mother as an intermediary and making substantial concessions, he tried to persuade Navarre to convert. With the invasion of France by the Protestant powers now imminent the king had no choice but to confront it. Consisting of 20,000 crack Swiss infantry, 10,000 German pistoliers and 3,800 French, it was an enormous force. Guise was persuaded to meet the king at Meaux on 4 July to discuss the defence of France. It was a tense affair. Epernon came out to greet Guise and the two embraced, but Epernon and the *Quarante Cinq* later accompanied the king to vespers with weapons concealed beneath their doublets. The trouble for Henry was that he had tried to dupe Guise once too often. All the ambassadors knew what he was up to. As Stafford put it, he 'was playing a mock holiday' with the duke, believing that he could outmanoeuvre him as he had done before. For three days the king and the duke worked on a strategy and, though Henry stubbornly refused to make the duke lieutenant-general of the royal armies, he made him a number of promises about men and materiel. Guise left Meaux expecting reinforcements and money. Within weeks he was complaining that not one of the promises made to him had been kept: only six of the thirty-two gendarmie companies he had been allocated had appeared. Henry never intended to keep them. Guise would have to fend for himself in the face of overwhelming numbers. In the meantime, the king would keep the main royal army fresh, ostensibly to prevent the union of Protestant forces, and send another army under Joyeuse to keep Navarre penned in the southwest. Success here would bring Navarre to his senses and silence the preachers in Paris who accused the king of pusillanimity.

With no help from the king, Guise had recourse to his friends and family. The charisma of the Guise name also attracted noblemen and volunteers from all over France and 120,000 crowns was raised by his friends in Paris. The duke also expressed his gratitude to Mendoza: 'I hold his Catholic Majesty as the common father of all Catholics and of me in particular.'[19] The core of the army, which assembled at Nancy in Lorraine, consisted of 6,000 pikemen, 3,000 arquebusiers, 1,000 light cavalry raised by the Duke of Lorraine, 2,000 gendarmes under Guise, and 3,000 horse sent from Flanders by the Duke of Parma. By mid-September he had assembled a formidable force of 22,000 men. His first inclination, once the Protestant army crossed into the duchy of Lorraine, was to give battle. But he was unable to force them to fight and once they had passed through his territory, the Duke of Lorraine had no intention of hazarding his own troops. When the Protestants crossed the frontier on 18 September and camped close to Joinville, in the region of the Cardinal of Guise's abbey of Saint-Urbain, Lorraine's forces remained in the Barrois and he refused to enter the kingdom of France. In the meantime, Henry III did his best to deprive Guise of reinforcements, summoning 'all his Catholic subjects' to his army headquarters at Gien on the Loire, where he now commanded a force larger than Guise's—some 20,000 men. Worse was to follow for Guise when the Protestant army was reinforced by 1,200 men under François de Coligny, son of the admiral.

A royal agent wrote with satisfaction of the duke's 'weakness', as he was unable to stop the Protestant advance. Guise wrote desperate letters, 'having been abandoned by all others', to Philip II, which were full of bitterness at the 'exquisite and convoluted devices' Henry III was using to undermine him. Even after he was joined by detachments sent by his relatives, Aumale, Elbeuf, and Mayenne, his army had shrunk by mid-October to 6,000 foot and 1,800 horse. Guise could do little more than shadow and harry the much larger force. Meanwhile the Protestant army moved closer to the king at Gien, passing through northern Burgundy, pillaging and ravaging the countryside en route. Henry III blocked the passage across the Loire, but he had no intention of going over to the offensive. Bad news from the south increased his timidity. On 20 October Joyeuse had offered battle to Navarre at Coutras. The two armies were evenly matched in numbers: Navarre had about 4,000 to 5,000 foot and 1,200 to 1,500 horse, Joyeuse had the same number of foot and slightly more horse (1,500 to 1,800). However, the Protestant army was a veteran force, which was compounded by Joyeuse's lack of experience. He made the fatal error of drawing his gendarmes in long line, *en haie*, in order that they could deploy their lances. The Protestant cavalry, armed with swords and pistols, were deployed in deep ranks, and to the sounds of their battle hymn, Psalm 118, 'This is the day which the lord hath made, we will rejoice and be glad in it', they smashed their way through, shattering the Catholics into fragments and rolling up the flanks. No quarter was given. It was a crushing victory: as many as 2,000 Catholics were killed, including hundreds of gentlemen loyal to the crown, and Joyeuse himself, whose death was a great personal loss to the king. Coutras was a significant battle. For the first time in the Wars of Religion the Protestants had won a victory in the field. For Henry III, who had invested so much in his devout image, the absence of divine approval was a serious reverse.

Fortunately for the king and for Guise, the main Protestant army could not decide on a strategy and there were divisions between the German mercenaries under the experienced Baron von Dohna and the French under the young Duke of Bouillon. With the season getting late and fatigued by their long marches, the Germans and Swiss now detached themselves from the rest of the army in order to replenish themselves on the rich farmland of the Beauce. This was the moment that Guise, who had been shadowing the Protestants since they had crossed the frontier, had been waiting for. Guise was lunching with his brother and cousins at Montargis on the 26 October when he heard that the Germans had arrived at Vimory, only one league distant. Despite Mayenne's caution, the army was ready to march within the hour. Guise was counting on surprise and the darkness of a moonless night. His attack was eventually repulsed, but he inflicted heavy casualties and, more significantly, seriously dented the enemy's morale. A month later Guise attacked them again, this time in broad daylight, at Auneau, between Chartres and Paris, destroying their baggage train, killing 2,000 and capturing 400 prisoners.

As Guise prepared to deliver the coup de grace, the king negotiated the withdrawal of the mercenaries. He gave them money and provided them with an escort for their protection. The duke was furious. He wrote to Mendoza on 16 December complaining 'of the strange favours and overt connivance that Epernon shows to the enemy…It is strange that the forces of Catholics should serve heretics as recompense for all the ills they have done to France.'[20] Henry's attempt to undermine the duke's victory was not lost on Parisians. Preachers attacked the king and proclaimed the duke as their saviour: 'without the prowess and constancy of the Duke of Guise the Ark would have fallen into the hands of the Philistines, and heresy would have triumphed over religion'.[21] Flushed with the success of their hero, the Sixteen sent a delegation to Guise's headquarters at Etampes, urging him to seize the king, but the campaign had not yet finished and the duke considered the moment unpropitious. Soon after the Sorbonne drew up its secret opinion that the government could be taken away from unsuitable kings, 'as could responsibility from a suspect guardian'.[22] The king hurried back to Paris. The silencing of the preachers was to be the first step in the reassertion of royal authority. Henry demanded the towns in Picardy be returned: 'I cannot endure my subjects seizing my towns, nor having intelligence with foreign princes.'[23] He sent agents to reason with the Guise, but he had an army at his disposal, and was prepared to use it.

* * * *

Guise was furious at his treatment and retired to Nancy at the end of January for a conference with his kinsmen which lasted until the middle of February. They resolved to force the king to adhere to the treaty he had made with the League, to force him to continue the war, and pay their troops. Above all, they demanded the dismissal of Epernon. Instead, Henry invested his favourite with the governorship of Normandy and the admiralty of France, which had been vacated by Joyeuse's death. It was an extraordinary and unparalleled concentration of power in the hands of one man and it caused Jean Boucher to pen one of the most scandalous pamphlets of the sixteenth century, the *Histoire tragique et memorable de Piers Gaverston*. Once again, the League made reference to English history to make its point, reminding readers that Gaveston, like Epernon, had risen from

Gascon obscurity to become the favourite of Edward II. Gaveston's terrible murder at the hands of the English aristocracy was warning to Epernon, who was also accused of homosexuality.

Both sides continued to negotiate, but trust had long since broken down. Guise had had enough of the king's artifices, which he compared to 'the temptations that the devil made to Our Lord on the mountain'.[24] Civil war loomed, as royalist troops moved into Picardy. At Nancy, Guise had formulated a plan for a series of coups d'état across the towns of northern France supported by armed insurgency. Plans were coordinated with Mendoza in Paris. The Armada was due to set sail in the spring and the duke was prepared to do the utmost to help Philip II take revenge on Elizabeth. A setback came when royalist reinforcements slipped into Boulogne, forcing Aumale to end his blockade. He turned his attentions to Abbeville, arriving there on 16 March, and stationed his troops in the suburbs in order to prevent a royalist garrison from entering. Henry ordered Aumale to leave the vicinity and reiterated that he must also surrender the other towns he was in control of or suffer the consequences. Guise's reason for refusing to do so reveals him to have been a student of Machiavelli:

> We must retain them and in this regard the most resolute will win. For if the towns perceive the least weakness their resolve will slacken and we shall lose all credit and authority. That which you hold from the king is only held through fear... for the majority of towns and provinces are looking at what we do in this affair, and what they fear most is that the king should go [to Picardy] in person... But if he does there lies our chance... I have troops ready... and before the king can reach Beauvais I will be at the Porte Saint-Antoine or the Porte Saint-Denis, and seeing Paris fall thus every town in France will do the same.[25]

At the end of March, Guise ordered the Sixteen to appoint the officers of a clandestine militia. A week before Easter (10 April) Poulain informed the king, who summoned prominent members of the Sixteen and threatened them with summary execution unless they ceased their machinations. The Sixteen, afraid for their lives, now urged the duke to come to Paris and told him that they would soon have to act 'whether the duke favours it or not, being extremely annoyed at his prevarication'. Guise continued to hope that Henry would be forced to leave the safety of Paris. Finally, on 15 April he sent instructions to the Sixteen to prepare an insurrection for the night of Quasimodo, Sunday 24 April. To this end he sent a number of veteran captains and promised to send more men to be housed in different parts of the city. In addition, he informed the Sixteen that he had secured the keys to the Porte Saint-Denis and that fifty horsemen would enter Paris, assassinate Epernon and seize the Louvre. The Sixteen were to erect their barricades and seize the strong points of the city. Poulain reported it to the king, who immediately took preventative measures, forbidding Guise to come to Paris and moving 4,000 Swiss troops closer to the city. In a frank letter to secretary of state, Villeroy, the king stated his readiness to use force against the insurgents:

> Only the sword brings peace! By baring our teeth we will make [Guise] ponder and search his conscience. You see this with men who rebel. Henceforth we must act the king, for too long we have been the valet. It is time that they were cut down to size in their turn ... speak to [the Guise] firmly with reason; for now that we have decided to act we can only finish it. And regarding their friends that they say they have warned, they are much more afraid than they acknowledge.

Through his informant Henry knew that the Sixteen were afraid. After hearing Poulain report in the Louvre on Tuesday 26 April, Epernon urged that Guise should be tried and executed. But Henry considered the measures he had taken were sufficient. After all, the new papal nuncio, Morosini, unlike his predecessors, was hostile to the League and assured him of papal support. Henry was sufficiently confident to leave the city that very day with his favourite. On the morning of 29 April they parted. Henry left for a week-long retreat of penance and contemplation in the Hieronymite monastery at Vincennes. News that the Duke of Elbeuf was in the vicinity of the Rouen with a small army and threatened to provoke an insurrection forced the king to dispatch Epernon with a portion of the royal army. Henry would soon rue their absence.

* * * *

While the king was at Vincennes, purging himself and drinking ass's milk, Guise, pressed by the Sixteen, made the momentous decision to come to Paris:

> The proximity of the king's forces makes our plan more difficult to execute—not that our Parisian friends do not still

have great courage. We still feel strong enough to achieve our objective but several of our friends have informed us that, because of the situation, it is necessary to declare openly against Epernon and to demand justice from the king. All those who willingly desist from these acts should be publicly named.

On his return to Paris, the king remained firm in his resolve to face down Guise, ordering units of horse to join the Swiss close to the city. He would view any attempt by the duke to come to Paris as a means 'to play out this tragedy' and he reiterated his prohibition on 5 May, making it clear that it would be considered an act of treason. On 8 May, Guise left Soissons at 9 pm with eight retainers and an emissary of the Sixteen and, after riding all night, entered Paris at midday the following day. Far from putting his personal device into action—*Ut Phoebus coelo, pax nubila terris discutit* (like Phoebus in the sky, peace disperses the clouds from the earth)—Guise's presence could only serve to darken the clouds of conspiracy that were swirling around Paris. He knew that his defiance of the king was risky, and might even cost him his life. That is why he did not go to the Louvre but instead to the palace of Catherine de Medici; he knew that she was jealous of Epernon's influence and guessed that she would shield him from the king's anger. As he crossed the city, he was quickly recognized and there were shouts of 'Long live Guise! Liberator of France, pillar of the Church, exterminator of heretics!' Flowers were thrown from widows. One lady shouted 'Good prince, now you are here, we are saved', and tried to kiss him. By the time he reached his destination in the rue Saint-Honoré the press was great as the crowd tried to reach out and touch his cloak.

Catherine took the duke in her carriage to the Louvre, where the king, forewarned, assembled his guards. Guise's murder was discussed, but the king may have been dissuaded by the fact that the duke had come to the city unaccompanied. There were the protestations of his beloved wife, the duke's cousin, to take into account. Once more he decided to play the duke along and embraced him when he was ushered into the Queen's chamber.[26] He accepted Guise's lie that he had been asked to come to Paris by Catherine and that, as a man of honour, he only wished to have satisfaction for the injuries done to him by Epernon. Henry replied that he loved Epernon and he wished the duke to do the same: 'He who loves the master should love his dog.' 'Provided that he does not bite', replied the duke, using humour to defuse the tension. Over the next two days Catherine did her best to reconcile the two men. They put on a good show. The king demanded a restitution of the Picard towns. Guise said this could only be done as part of a reformation of the kingdom and recommended the programme which his chief counsellor Pierre d'Epinac, Archbishop of Lyon and 'the *intellectus agens* of the League', had drawn up, beginning with the summoning of the Estates-General. The king agreed to look at it. At dinner on the evening of the 10th the duke performed his function as Grand Master of France. But neither man was a dupe. After dinner, the king held a meeting with a few close counsellors, at which his mother was not present. They discussed the possibility of summoning the Swiss and French regiments into Paris in order to frighten Guise and force him to leave the city. It was a high-risk strategy. The city had traditionally enjoyed the privilege of guarding itself. In the meantime, orders to search the city's taverns and arrest strangers were issued.

The royalists had to act because their position was deteriorating by the hour. Many of Guise's retainers had been in the city for weeks and more were arriving daily. When the duke arrived at the Louvre for dinner he was accompanied by forty horsemen. The outbuildings, garden, and courtyard of the Hôtel de Guise had been turned into an encampment and could barely contain the numbers. The Venetian ambassador noted the extraordinary number of soldiers arriving, and more were anticipated. A large contingent was lodged in and around the residence of the Duchess of Montpensier. The first skirmishes took place on Wednesday 11 May as the governor, François d'O, conducted sweeps in search of Guisard captains who had been distributed throughout the city. When the duke went to the Louvre to complain, the king could no longer dissimulate: 'as soon as he saw Monsieur de Guise arrive he turned to look away'.[27] Paris was on a state of high alert, and that evening the fateful decision to move troops into the city, in spite of its liberties, was taken. Despite periodic purges of the suspect officers, the royalists were unsure of the loyalty of the militia and so units were ordered into unfamiliar positions outside their neighbourhoods. Many captains refused. When Governor d'O did his rounds that night he found that many units had abandoned their posts. When he asked why he was told ominously that they had gone home to protect their families.

At 4 am a loyal alderman, Lugoly, opened Porte Saint-Honoré and in marched 4,000 Swiss and 2,000 French troops. They passed in silence to the cemetery of the Innocents, where they received their postings and, to the sound of fifes and drums, filed into the waking city. The plan seems to have been to bottle up the volatile Left Bank. Three ensigns of Swiss under Crillon crossed the Seine and occupied the market place on the Ile de la Cité. The two bridges that linked the island to the Left Bank were occupied by companies of French foot: one under de Gast crossed the Petit Pont and took up a position beneath the Petit Châtelet, a prison whose towers guarded the southern approach to the bridge; the other under Marivaux barred the Pont Saint-Michel. The rest remained on the Right Bank: six ensigns in the square in front of the Hôtel de Ville and a reserve at the cemetery of the Innocents.

It was an orderly takeover and the Parisian response was orderly too. From about 8 am people began to gather together and they began to build barricades. It was a defensive measure to protect their homes and property. In some parts of the Right Bank, such as the rue Saint-Honoré as far as the Innocents, there was little opposition and royalist control was quickly established. Resistance, as had been expected, was led by the University quarter and the Ile de la Cité. Royalist units which penetrated too far toward the university colleges on the Left Bank were forced back at the barricades though bloodshed was largely avoided and only one person was killed.

By 10 am a stalemate had developed as the sides confronted each other behind the makeshift barriers. The three militia colonels who had responsibility for the Left Bank and the Ile de la Cité were magistrates (two judges and a president of the Chamber of Accounts), and as such abhorred social unrest. They quickly took control of the situation and prevented violence. However, some of their junior officers were members of the Sixteen and several units unreliable. The loyalists knew that the best way to maintain order was to avoid bloodshed and they sent a delegation to the king, pleading with him to withdraw his troops. The rest of the morning was taken up with negotiations as each side sought to persuade the other to retire.

The duke was kept fully informed of these events. Three hours before the entry of the soldiers, he had been warned that the usual positions of the militia had been altered and that something was afoot. He arose early and went to hear seven o'clock Mass at the nearby Chapelle de Brac. Three hours later the purpose of the royal *putsch* was made clear: the king demanded that he leave Paris immediately. At the same time, the duke was being inundated with demands for assistance from across the city, and members of the Sixteen arrived at the Hôtel de Guise to offer their support. It was a momentous decision, but one that the duke took with remarkable coolness. Unlike the king, shut up in the Louvre, Guise came out of his palace to show himself to his supporters. At midday he was walking in the streets in the vicinity 'full of gaiety and confidence', chatting and mixing with soldiers and well-wishers. A plan of attack was quickly sketched out. He dispatched his captains into the city, most of them making for the hotspots on the Ile de la Cité and the Left Bank. The Count of Brissac was placed in overall command of the rebels there.

Brissac and his men passed the royalist guards on the bridges without difficulty. Why this should have been so is not difficult to ascertain. The position between the opposing forces had not changed since the morning. Negotiations were under way and there was, as yet, no reason for thinking that they would not succeed. Guise claimed to be acting as an honest broker between the two sides, and his lieutenants had no difficulty in persuading the royalists that their intentions were peaceable. As soon as he crossed to the Left Bank, however, Brissac's demeanour changed. He began to incite the crowds and called a meeting in the house of a wealthy supporter of the Sixteen, Mathurin Pigneron. Situated in the Place Maubert, it was just a short walk to the royalist position underneath the Petit Châtelet. The meeting, attended by a number of junior militia officers sympathetic to the Sixteen and former officers who had been purged for their role in previous acts of insurgency, began at around 1 pm. It was an educated group—many of those present were lawyers—with a shared history of dedication to radical Catholic politics. What they discussed we do not know. What we do know is that Brissac gave them a speech, and it must have been a rousing one. He pledged 'that willingly he would give his life for them and for liberty, and for the Holy Roman and Apostolic faith'. The word that stands out here is 'liberty'. The junior officers and legal officials who filed out of Pigneron's at around 3 pm on 12 May 1588 took a pledge to die fighting not just in defence of Catholicism, but to oppose a king, who had consistently trampled on their rights and liberties and whose absolutist principles had now been fully exposed by the use of force against his own subjects.

The effect these men had on returning to their units was electric. The magistrates and commanding officers on the Left Bank were brushed aside as the insurgents gathered their student and bourgeois supporters together and charged the advanced royalist pickets in the rue Saint-Jacques who quickly beat a retreat towards the Petit Pont. Brissac's mixed force of soldiers and bourgeois then assaulted the main position. Resistance quickly melted and he pushed on and seized the bridge and the Petit Châtelet. This defeat placed the royalists in the market place of the Ile de la Cité in peril, and they now found themselves under attack from the surrounding streets.

The victory galvanized the untrained bands of Parisians. An eye-witness in the rue de la Huchette, which ran parallel to the Seine, and was cut off by the royalist units on the bridges, recorded what happened next. The residents had dismantled their barricades and were in disarray, until two League soldiers emerged from the Angel tavern to rally them: 'Scoundrels! Where are you fleeing to? Abandoning your barricades so that in no time your daughters will be raped in their homes and you'll be slaughtered like pigs. Follow us! There are only half as many of them.' At the end of the street, another of Guise's lieutenants, François de Moy, began his attack on the Pont Saint-Michel. He too had animated the bourgeois with a rousing speech, 'having loudly ranted against the king and against those who surrounded him, whom he called scoundrels, he proclaimed the orders he had been given with the command of the duke to carry them out'. The assault seems to have been coordinated with Brissac, since bells were rung to announce the advance. The royalists were subjected to a fusillade of stones and shot from the surrounding houses. Brissac continued his advance and pushed the Swiss back through the Ile de la Cité to the Pont Notre-Dame. The royalists, demoralized and trapped in the narrow streets, were in disarray and in no position to counterattack. Even so, the failure was one of leadership: there was no coherent command and little coordination between the royalist units. In order to save his beleaguered troops the king pleaded with Guise to intercede and stop further bloodshed. It was the message that Guise had been waiting for. He could now live up to his device and disperse the clouds of dissension. Dressed in a white satin doublet, cap in hand and without arms, he left his palace in the Marais accompanied by only two pages, who preceded him on foot carrying his sword and buckler. At five o'clock he entered the heart of the city, pacifying his supporters and arranging the peaceful departure of the royalists. As he toured the streets he had some difficulty in controlling the passions around him. L'Estoile overheard one Left Bank radical, fresh from the fighting, say that it was time to 'go and barricade this bugger of a king in his Louvre'.[28] Others had taken to disparaging him as Brother Henry, or Sire Henry. Everywhere the duke went he was greeted with shouts of 'Long Live Guise!' 'My friends that's enough', he replied, 'Shout long live the King!' The duke's role as an honest broker suggested that a deal might be done. On the following day, the king, terrified and trapped inside the Louvre, was considering his options when a letter, intercepted by a royalist agent, was brought to him. It removed all hesitation. Guise was summoning reinforcements to Paris and bragging of how 'I defeated the Swiss, cut to pieces a part of the royal guard and keep the Louvre invested so closely that I will take good care of who is inside. This victory is so great that it will be remembered for ever.'[29] That evening Henry fled the city.

* * * *

The Sixteen took control of the city, occupying the Bastille, the château of Vincennes and the Arsenal. The royalist mayor and two Aldermen were thrown into prison. A few days after the barricades, Guise demonstrated his reform credentials, presiding over two popular assemblies that purged the city council and called for the abolition of municipal venal office and the free biennial election of all city officials. The principle that public office should be awarded on merit and not for cash was re-established. This was the first step in the restoration of representative institutions and civic authority throughout France, which envisaged an enhanced role for the Estates-General. Free and regular elections would transform it from a forum for the presentation of grievances into an assembly which would guarantee religious uniformity and scrutinize the royal council.

Guise's objectives, however, were different from his popular supporters. His intention had never been to overthrow the king of France, merely to obtain proper recognition of his worth and replace Epernon at the centre of power. Letting the genie of popular Catholic radicalism out of the bottle had proved remarkably easy; the test was whether Guise could control it for his own ends. All revolutions have their dark side, for the enemies of truth merit death, and it became quickly apparent that the Paris Sixteen were no exception. Years of anti-English propaganda boiled over into violence in the heady days after the fall of Paris. Mathurin Pigneron, whose reputation had been enhanced during the fighting, demanded that action be taken against the English ambassador. Located on the quai des Bernandins in the heart of Left Bank radicalism, the embassy was as potent a symbol of foreign intervention and heretical pollution as the US embassy in Teheran was in 1979. Guise placed a guard round the embassy and a diplomatic incident was avoided. But it was a powerful reminder of his tenuous hold on the people. Populist regimes must give their supporters what they want. No one had been executed for heresy since

1560. On Midsummer's Eve the new city authorities burned a huge effigy called 'heresy' in front of the Hôtel de Ville. Five days later the Parlement of Paris sentenced two daughters of a solicitor to be strangled and their corpses burned. One of them was burned alive 'by the fury of the mob, who cut the rope before she could be strangled and cast her into the fire'.[30] They had been in prison for eight months, during which time the authorities, including the king, had concentrated on persuading them to abjure. But the judges were now under intense scrutiny. Within days a number of bourgeois invaded the law courts and 'without respect for his quality' demanded that the First President of the Parlement execute another Huguenot who had been languishing in prison for a year.

Anyone with unorthodox views was now liable to arrest, or worse. In the days following the barricades, a teacher called Mercier was stopped in the street outside his house near Saint-André des Arts church by two radicals and, on suspicion of being a heretic, stabbed and his corpse thrown into the Seine—this, despite his doing his Easter devotions and receiving communion from the parish priest, a well-known supporter of the League. On 16 July l'Estoile watched an 'atheist' from Anjou burn. He mocked the mob for their credulity and not being able to tell the difference between Calvinists, Heretics, Politiques, and Navarristes. Witch-hunting was given a significant boost as the League took power. Parisian magistrates had traditionally been reticent and sceptical of popular beliefs about witchcraft. Louis Dorléans, the Sixteen's chief polemicist, who would soon become Attorney-General, now argued that 'in these times of misery, sorcery has crept into the realm and has become so common and widespread that something must be done about it'.[31] There were more arrests during the summer. In the spring of 1589 two Huguenot widows were burned alive by order of the Paris Parlement. No one at the time could have guessed that they would be the last two executions for heresy ordered by the greatest French appellate court.

COUNTER-REVOLUTION

Their first encounter after the revolution passed off as if nothing had happened. Guise, wearing a coat of mail under his clothes, accompanied by the Queen Mother, the Cardinal of Bourbon, the Archbishop of Lyon and 800 horse, arrived in Chartres on 1 August 1588 to make his submission. The town filled with people from the surrounding countryside who had come to applaud the duke for his role in saving them the previous year from 'robbing German heretics'. He was greeted with cheers and shouts of 'Long Live Guise!'[1] After the duke had gone down on one knee, the king helped him up and kissed him twice. Only at dinner that evening did the latent tension became palpable. The king asked, laughing, to whom they should drink:

> Guise: To whom you please, Sire, it is for your Majesty to propose.
>
> Henry: My cousin, let us drink to our good friends the Huguenots.
>
> Guise: Well said, Sire . . .
>
> Henry: [adding quickly] And to our good barricaders of Paris. Let's drink to them and not forget them!

The duke smiled through gritted teeth and retired angrily soon after. The papal nuncio, Morosini, who had been largely responsible for the reconciliation was undecided: 'I do not know if their hearts correspond to their embraces.' Guise, too, in a letter to Mendoza on 6 August did not know whether the king was displaying 'an extreme dissimulation' or 'a marvellous mutation of will, a new world as it were'; he would proceed with 'the circumspection required for his security, for the greater the king's caresses, the more he would have suspicion'.[2] But he dismissed warnings about his immediate safety for 'the sole and true danger he would run could only exist in the king's cabinet, where one is only admitted alone, and where the prince has every facility to have him attacked and killed by a dozen or twenty men posted for this purpose'. The duke was foretelling the manner of his own death.

* * * *

Guise's murder had been discussed before the barricades and it was discussed again in the months following, but the final decision was taken only a few days before the execution. All the indications are that it was planned in a hurry. Before the final act of the drama there were many scenes that suggested an entirely different outcome. Both men were fully committed to the reconciliation, but for very different reasons.

Guise should have been overjoyed by his success on 12 May. After all, he was the Tribune of the People, effectively the king of Paris. The seizure of royal revenues was the most satisfying aspect of the take-over. Bankers beat a path to his door to offer him credit, solving his financial problems at a stroke. Crucially for his sense of self-esteem he was no longer reliant on Philip II. But the duke was also embarrassed by his success. He was furious when he heard of the king's flight. He wanted to be the king's chief counsellor, not king of Paris. In the wake of the Day of the Barricades the duke presented himself as the natural mediator between king and people. His official pronouncements denied any foreknowledge of the barricades, noted the small size of his retinue, and reminded his audience that the only time he left his palace was to intervene to rescue the royal forces. One piece of propaganda stated that the only weapon to be found in the Hôtel de Guise was a rusty old pike belonging to his father! As a prince, the duke had no wish to be portrayed as a revolutionary. He put the events down to a 'miracle of God'.

The duke wanted to be close to the king for another reason: he was uncomfortable with his status as a client of Philip II. Guise was playing a double game. The Spanish wished above all for a complete rupture between Guise and Henry. As Mendoza wrote to Philip II, 'I am employing all means possible to prevent the reconciliation of Guise and the King... It is necessary to maintain the civil war in Picardy even if it is against Guise's interests.'[3] In a meeting with Mendoza at the end of July the duke reassured him, telling him that 'he regretted not have let the people off the leash during the tumult, in order to finish off what they had planned'. Despite Mendoza's insistence, he refused to march on the king at Chartres and satisfied himself with securing the approaches to Paris. With the imminent arrival of the Armada in the Channel Philip's overriding concern was a secure port. While Guise wished to work with Philip for the ruination of Elizabeth, his chief objective was to replace Epernon in the affections of the king. He acted in accordance with the interests of his own House and wished to avoid humiliation at the hands of any prince—Habsburg or Valois. He wanted to use his victory to wring concessions from the king, to get closer to him, not to widen the rupture. In March the king had already offered him 'great kindnesses and charges worthy of his dignity' if he ceased his intelligences with Spain and in Rome. With his position strengthened the duke was now prepared to do a deal.

This was not the advice of all members of his family. His sister Catherine, certainly, and possibly also his brother, Louis, counselled that he march on Chartres, seize the king and place him in a monastery. Signalling his intentions, Louis seized the city of Troyes. But Guise ignored them. On 15 July the king signed the Edict of Union, which confirmed the 1585 treaty with the League and renewed his commitment to the war on heresy. The League leaders were awarded more towns as surety and the king also agreed to adopt the decrees of the Council of Trent. Epernon was dismissed. Much to the irritation of Mendoza, the king declared that henceforth he wished 'to govern with his cousins of Guise'.[4] The duke was made lieutenant-general of the royal army. We know a great deal about the duke's state of mind as he made his way to Chartres for the formal reconciliation. The Archbishop of Lyon had emerged as the chief voice of moderation on the duke's council after the barricades and, in preparation for his return to court, composed a long memoir which outlined how his master should behave. It was from the archbishop that Guise learnt his Machiavelli. In order to maintain himself in power, the duke would need to control one of the great offices of state and win over suspicious royal courtiers. He would also have to work hard to obtain royal favour. The archbishop, who knew the king well, played on his psychology:

> The king's favour will be continued towards you and even grow day by day if you are able to maintain him between a state of love and fear, that is, if he always remains convinced as he is now that you have such power in his state that he has no power to rid himself of you and also that by your words and actions you let him know that you are far from wishing to abuse your power and that, on the contrary, you would employ it all in his service.[5]

Guise's principal objective on returning to court was the office of Constable of France: in abeyance since 1567, it was the highest office in the land and, unlike the title of lieutenant-general, was held for life and could not be revoked. News of the disaster that befell the Armada in early August 1588 confirmed the position of those on the duke's council who favoured cooling relations with the Habsburg and a return to court.

Henry III's intentions are much less easy to discern. There has been much speculation, though it seems most likely that it was a question of wait and see. The duke's behaviour at the Estates-General would be crucial. The decision to summon the assembly was forced upon Henry by the disastrous state of the finances—debts had risen from 101 million in 1576 to 133 million in 1588. Between a quarter and a third of all income was being spent on debt servicing and the Crown was finding it difficult to borrow. But there were political considerations too. The king had out-foxed the League once before, in 1576, by calling the Estates-General, and he now thought he could do so again. Summoning it would counter the propaganda which portrayed him a tyrant, the violator of privileges, and despoiler of the people. The Estates-General would be forced to provide the means to fight the war on heresy, or it would expose itself to attacks from precisely those radical Catholics who were its greatest champions. Now that he had his hands on the reins of power, Guise had less interest in pursuing the reforming agenda of the League. He advised against the calling of the Estates-General, which had been at the heart of League manifesto since 1585. He must have been aware that his position would be a difficult one: he would have to maintain his supporters while, if he wished to obtain the office he coveted, demonstrating at the same time that he was the king's good servant. Henry may have realized this too, and he ignored the advice of the newest member of the Privy Council.

As the election campaign got under way, Henry did something even more surprising. He dismissed every other member of the Council: Chancellor Cheverny; the superintendent of finances, Bellièvre; and the secretaries of state, Brulart, Villeroy, and Pinart were all relieved of their posts. They were replaced with new and relatively unknown men, who were characterized by their modest social status, but also by their probity—there was no question of them being bought by the Guise. It was the first time that such a wholesale change had been effected in the history of the monarchy. The failures of the past were blamed on the old ministers. As the Estates opened, Henry was announcing the beginning of a new era.

The Estates-General of 1588 was unlike any other before. It had more in common with the assembly of 1789 than the previous two assemblies of 1560 and 1576, which were still recognizably medieval representative institutions, summoned for the purpose of presenting grievances to the king, whose only obligation was to listen. The electoral campaign was a titanic struggle, the most divisive and intense ever fought. The king did his best to disrupt the League campaign and he intervened personally in a number of contests, in order to ensure his choice was returned. But the League was well organized and another novelty was the sight of the Guise, who left the court in order to help the campaign in the provinces. Though the king did better than expected among the clergy and the nobility, the results in the Third Estate were an overwhelming victory for the Catholic League. Many of the deputies from the Third Estate, who arrived at Blois for the opening session on 16 October, came not with the intention of presenting grievances in the traditional fashion but, inspired and justified by their intense Catholic faith, to establish a new constitutional arrangement between the king and his subjects. Reading the *cahiers* drawn up by the Parisian delegates, dominated by the Sixteen, one is struck by their extreme originality.[6] Using a religious language that was at times apocalyptic, their demands opened into a sustained critique of the current monarchical state. A thorough-going reformation of men and of the kingdom was essential if heresy was to be defeated and God's anger appeased. There were calls for placing the Estates-General on a regular constitutional footing. One provincial *cahier* suggested that it be summoned every six years. Others went further and called for a standing Council of State to 'advise' the king while the Estates were not sitting. Paris, as usual, went further, calling for it to be composed of twelve men—a number with biblical connotations—from each of the estates who would scrutinize the decisions of the royal council.

The inaugural session took place in the great hall of the château of Blois on 16 October. The king, with the two queens beside him on a dais and with Guise, who was dressed in white satin and a black velvet hat and holding the Grand Master's baton, at his feet, denounced past abuses and spoke of the financial needs that would have to be met if heresy were to be defeated. He was an accomplished public speaker and the speech was well received. It was also an opportunity to put pressure on the duke. After making explicit reference to 'some grandees of my kingdom [who] have made such leagues and associations', Henry promised to forget the past; but he reminded his audience 'that those of my subjects who do not leave them or get involved in them without my consent will be attainted and convicted of the crime of treason'.[7] At these words the duke was seen to go pale. Afterwards Guise was chided by his brother Louis for 'having only done things by half'. If they had followed his advice 'they would never have been in the difficulty they were now'.[8] Epinac said they should tell the king to remove the offending words from the published version. The king agreed to do so, but he had laid down the gauntlet.

The king could play the duke along, but he found his supporters much less easy to manipulate. The leaguer delegates demanded that the king swear to uphold the Edict of Union and declare that it was a fundamental law of the kingdom. The king agreed to do so, but inserted a qualifying phrase which referred to 'the authority, fidelity and obedience due to his majesty'. Once again, he was forced to back down. The offending words were replaced by 'only by the advice of the Estates does the king intend to make this law fundamental in his kingdom'. The consequences of this capitulation were potentially enormous. By depriving a heretic of the succession, another fundamental law, the Salic law, which assured the succession to the eldest male of the eldest line, was imperilled. The leaguers were jubilant; the royalists were dismayed. Everyone, however, understood the constitutional implications: the Estates were staking a claim to share sovereignty with the king. The debates on the issue were very different from those of previous Estates; the language and ideas that were expressed prefiguring those of 1789. The delegates argued that the law was above the king and that he could not modify it without consent.

What the new constitutional arrangement meant in practice soon became evident in the matter of taxation. One of the most significant features of the 1588 Estates was the manner in which the Third Estate, whose deliberations took place in the Hôtel de Ville of Blois, grew in confidence and, with the clergy and nobility quiescent, set the agenda. Leaguer activists ensured coordination and cooperation between the three chambers. Henry would have been prepared to put up with the humiliation over the issue of law-giving had the Estates performed the function it was called for and granted him money. But the taxpayers of the Third Estate were angry. Their moral outrage was stirred by a speech on 23 November from Lazare Coquelay, a Paris canon and member of the Sixteen, who came from the chamber of the clergy to encourage them 'to discharge the poor and seek out the real riches of the courtiers, financiers and other vermin, who must be squeezed like sponges'.[9] The deputies of the Third called for scrutiny of the royal accounts. The commission that was appointed for the task was openly hostile to the king; it included President Neuilly and la Chapelle-Marteau, a rich accountant who had succeeded to the leadership of the Sixteen on Hotman's death in 1587 and who had been elected Mayor of Paris in the wake of the barricades. Much to the king's annoyance they moved with the meticulous thoroughness of accountants. Perhaps not unsurprisingly they discovered that royal accounting procedures were chaotic. The workings of the sinews of power in sixteenth-century society depended on secrecy, nepotism, and baksheesh. But what made for an effective tool of royal power looked to the commissioners like simple incompetence and fraud. They came to the conclusion, with some justification, that the king already had the means at his disposal; he was just not making the proper use of it. Far from agreeing new taxes, the deputies demanded rebates and, in a move that anticipated the developments of the seventeenth century, the creation of an extraordinary chamber of justice to investigate and prosecute those who had enriched themselves at the expense of the state.

At the end of November Henry offered a compromise. He promised to reduce taxes, to create a chamber of justice (whose members would be chosen by the king), and to permit the provinces to oversee tax collection. These were significant concessions. But the king was exasperated further when the Third Estate dared to negotiate. Guise's claim to be arbiter between the king and his people was now put to the test. On the evening of the 28 November he dined with la Chapelle-Marteau, who had emerged as the leader of the opposition, and the heads of each provincial delegation. Guise pleaded with them to offer the king some relief. The debate was heated and the duke's arguments were 'vigorously' rebutted.[10] On the following day he warned the Third Estate that the 'rupture of the Estates was imminent . . . they should take care not to push things to the extremity for it would only be the cause of leaving the Edict of Union unexecuted'.[11] But the duke's prestige was insufficient to shake their resolve. The Third Estate, in particular, had long since ceased to trust Henry III. A master of manipulation, his reign was littered with broken promises. As Etienne Pasquier, an acute observer noted, the delegates no longer behaved like subjects; they were no longer content dealing with the king traditionally by means of 'supplication'; they now worked by 'resolution'. In order to avoid the failures of previous Estates, where the royal council had sifted through and cherry-picked grievances to suit its own agenda, the Third Estate, somewhat to the embarrassment of the clergy and the nobility, now demanded the right to publish their resolutions. It was tantamount to the power to make their own laws. Why not, they argued, in France? Other Christian peoples had long had this right:

> They said: was it not the Estates who gave kings their power and authority? Why is it necessary therefore for that which we debate and decide on to be scrutinized by the king's council? The English Parliament, the Estates of Sweden and Poland and all the Estates of neighbouring kingdoms, are assemblies whose kings are subject to observe that which they agree and decide on, without changing anything.[12]

The deputies threatened that if Henry did not reduce taxes they would walk out. He retorted on 3 December that 'the Queen of England, wicked though she is, was not maintained by this means' and that, though there was not a head-tax in England as there was in France, 'her subjects were more than willing to provide in case of necessity'.

* * * *

It was beginning to dawn on Henry III that he faced a full-scale constitutional revolution. He complained that the deputies' proposals would 'reduce him to the doge of Venice and make my state semi-democratic'.[13] Further humiliation came with the news that Charles-Emmanuel, Duke of Savoy, taking advantage of France's internal problems, had occupied the marquisate of Saluzzo, her last possession on the Italian side of the Alps. Henry blamed the Guise. Before the barricades they had had dealings with Charles-Emmanuel, who dreamed of acquisitions in Dauphiné and the Rhône valley should the kingdom of France, as many observers expected, begin to fracture into warring statelets.

Guise was acutely embarrassed by the situation in which he found himself. He was unable to deliver the compromise with the Estates he had promised: an impasse had been reached. The hours that Guise spent in consultation with his allies in the Third Estate now began to arouse suspicion. In the early days of December, the deputies were well aware of the stakes. Beauvais-Nangis, a noble deputy loyal to the king, warned Guise 'to consider how the king was being made jealous by the secret councils held every day in his chambers, where [the deputies] come to him to report on what had been resolved in the assembly of the Estates and where they decide all that should be proposed on the following day, and that it was sharing authority with the king'.[14]

In order to break the impasse and halt the march of constitutional change the king would have to move against the leaders of the Third Estate. But he could not do so without unleashing the opposition of the Guise, their clients and retinues. Guise was warned repeatedly that his life was in danger. The duke convened several council meetings to discuss the rumours. The duke, his brother Louis, the Archbishop of Lyon, three of Guise's captains, and five leaguer deputies, including President Neuilly and la Chapelle-Marteau, were present at one of these on 9 December. The majority urged him to leave Blois immediately for the safety of Orléans. But it was the Archbishop of Lyon who carried the day, since, as he put it, 'he who quits loses the game'.[15]

It was a serious mistake. The duke was losing his patience and the archbishop reassured him that his ultimate goal was within his grasp. Just a little more pressure on the king would deliver it. Guise himself was confident that a good Christian like Henry III would not contemplate murder. He had become overconfident. Within a fortnight relations between the king and the duke were stretched to breaking, as Guise pressed his advantage. He complained that the office of lieutenant-general was nothing more than 'parchment'. Henry III told him that 'he should content himself with the grade he had been given'.

The daily humiliation that the king had undergone during the Estates was taking its toll. Henry saw only one way of restoring his authority. His suspicion of the duke was confirmed on 17 December when, at a Guise family dinner, Cardinal Louis, always less discreet than his elder sibling, drank a toast to his brother as king, and their sister Catherine joked that she soon hoped to use her scissors (and tonsure Henry III). Guise's overconfidence had made him careless. An Italian actor, Venetianelli, who had been a dinner guest, reported these words to the king the following day. That evening Henry summoned a meeting of three of his most trusted captains, Marshal Aumont, the Marquis of Rambouillet, and Alphonse d'Ornano, and the decision to murder Guise was approved by three votes to one. On the evening of the 20th the plans were laid and the execution entrusted to the *Quarante Cinq*. Guise was always well accompanied, so it would be necessary to separate him from his men. The only place they were unable to follow him was when he was required to attend the Privy Council in the royal château. Counsellors were required to leave their retinues at the head of the grand staircase before entering the royal apartments in which the council chamber was situated.

The plot was not a secret for long. The duke received a steady stream of warnings to leave Blois immediately. On the evening of the 21 December the papal nuncio informed him his life was in danger. The following evening his mother told him that he would be killed in the king's chambers, and the following night between 10 and 11 pm it was the turn of the Duke of Elbeuf to beg him to leave. The duke was not about to abandon his plans on a rumour. Men of honour did not run at the first whiff of danger. Guise returned from the bedroom of his mistress, Madame de Sauves, at three in the morning to be handed five anonymous notes, all of which had the same message. 'He would not dare', Guise said to his surgeon, who was among those present at the duke's *coucher*. His aristocratic self-assurance and poise, once part of his charisma, had turned to arrogance. He dismissed his servants and went to bed.

The king was awakened at 4 am on 23 December. The duke had been asleep barely an hour. He dressed and went to inspect the *Quarante Cinq* who were divided into sections. He reminded them of Guise's insolence and ambition: 'I am reduced to such an extremity that this morning either he or I must die.'[16] Eight men, led by their captain, Loignac, were told to arm themselves with long daggers and take up a position in the royal bedchamber. After the 'Gascon devils', as the League called them, filed out the king, usually so calm and majestic, was wracked by doubt and reduced to pacing up and down, waiting for Guise's arrival in the council chamber to be announced.

Disturbed by the noise in the château, the duke's secretary, Péricard had awakened him at 4 am, but his master assured him that there was nothing out of the ordinary and insisted on going back to bed, not rising until comparatively late at 8 am, when he was roused by a message from the king. He dressed hurriedly in a grey satin doublet and, with no time for breakfast or his *lever*, rushed to the council meeting, stopping only for a brief prayer outside the oratory, which was locked. The December darkness and the noise of torrential rain hid the unaccustomed sights and sounds of units of soldiers scurrying around the castle. Had the duke been more alert and not still bleary from his nocturnal exertions he might have picked up the signals that not all was well as he hurried along the corridors. As he walked out on to the château's terrace, an Auvergnat gentleman told him about all the unusual activity and warned him to go no further. The duke thanked him: 'My good friend, it's a long time since I have been healed of this apprehension.' These prognostications were beginning to grate. When an old family retainer approached with the same news, he brushed him aside with the word, 'fool'.

At the top of the grand staircase he took leave of the two lackeys who had accompanied him. He seems to have had no idea what awaited him as the captain of the royal guard, Larchant, opened the door and he entered the council chamber. He had only minutes to live. Nonchalantly he warmed himself in front of the fire and ordered some breakfast. No Damascus raisins could be found for him, so he had to make do with Provençal prunes. If the duke had been the least suspicious or alert to the danger he would have noticed the pallor of Secretary of State Revol, who had been sent to summon him for a royal audience. The king had noticed, as he sent him on his way: 'Why you're so pale! You'll spoil everything! Rub your cheeks!'

Meanwhile the council meeting had got under way, discussing financial matters. The door connecting the council room to the royal chambers opened and Revol entered; unaccustomed as he was to such missions, he timidly told the duke that the king awaited him. Guise rose, picked up his gloves and hat, and, with his cape under his left arm, bid Adieu to his fellow counsellors with a courteous bow. He knocked on the door of the royal bedchamber, which connected the council to the king's cabinet, and entered. The door was firmly shut behind him. He greeted the squad of the *Quarante Cinq* posted there. They replied in the customary fashion and surrounded him as if to escort him to the king. He traversed the room and just before he put his hand to the door handle, he turned to face the guards who followed him. At that moment, fearing that the duke was about to defend himself, Montséry, seized his arm and plunged his dagger into the duke's breast with the words 'Traitor! You will die for it!' The Sieur d'Effranats launched himself at the duke's legs and clung on to stop him moving, while another member of the *Quarante Cinq*, Sainte-Malines, carried out the death blow close to the throat. For good measure, Loignac, the captain of the *Quarante-Cinq* thrust his sword into the duke's kidneys. Guise called for his friends, begged for mercy and, showing that he was a man of great physical strength, had the force, despite a final stab in the back from Sariac, to drag himself and his assailants from one side of the room to the other, where he fell dead at the foot of the king's bed. On the orders of the king, the corpse was taken by the grand provost, Richelieu, to a room on the first floor, where it was burned. The ashes were thrown into the Loire. Guise's father and cousin Mary were already martyrs and it was essential to prevent a tomb or relics around which the Catholic League could organize a cult.

Guise's death was not simply a political assassination; it announced a royal coup d'état. Unlike Louis XVI in 1789, Henry III was quick to see the dangers for his authority if the constitutional revolution was not opposed in its infancy by force. As he explained to his mother on the day, 'I wish to be king and not a prisoner and slave as I have been since the 13 May until now when I begin once more to be king and master.'[17] In the town of Blois, Richelieu and his archers burst into the assembly of the Estates, shouting 'No one move! Someone wanted to kill the king!' Eight members of the Third Estate were arrested, including the leaders of the Sixteen, Neuilly, la Chapelle-Marteau, and Louis Dorléans, and led through the rain to the château, where they were thrown into prison. Other units rounded up Guise's clients and other members of the clan, including the Duke of Nemours; the Duke of Elbeuf; Guise's son, the Prince of Joinville; several great ladies; and the ailing Cardinal of Bourbon, who was the League's preferred candidate for the throne.

That night Henry anguished about what to with Cardinal Louis and the Archbishop of Lyon. In deference to their high ecclesiastical status, his initial inclination was to spare both. In the end, remembering the threats made by the cardinal, he spared only the archbishop. Even the *Quarante-Cinq* bauked at this sacrilegious task. Henry had to cajole Michel de Gast, one of his most faithful gentlemen. The deed was done on the morning of the 24 December by six soldiers, who were paid 200 livres each. Louis's remains, too, were burned and his ashes scattered. The Guise brothers were dead. The Counter-Revolution had begun.

EPILOGUE

His dream of reclaiming the Anjou succession in ruins, Henri II, Duke of Guise, grandson of Henri I, turned away from the city of Naples on 7 April 1648 and rode north to safety. It was a desperate situation: he had only fifty men left; his esquire had abandoned him; his ensign had thrown away the ducal standard. He turned right off the Appian Way just before Capua and headed inland in order to cross the Volturno by ferry to Caiazzo. It was dangerous country. As he skirted to his left rose the wooded slopes of Mount Tifata, 620 metres high, and to his right the peak of San Leucio, whose castle dominated the region of Caserta with its magnificent views across the bay of Naples, loomed into view. As he made for the gap between the peaks, a squadron of Spanish cavalry, larger than his own, appeared from a wood with the intention of barring his route. The sounds of galloping horses from the rear announced the arrival of three more Spanish squadrons, cutting off his retreat.

There was no thought of surrender. The duke tossed off his cape and charged straight ahead, scattering the Spanish horse and, with his sword in his teeth and pistols in his hand, pushed passed thirty musketeers and made it to the other side of the ravine. After a couple of miles of hot pursuit, in which his lieutenant, the Baron de Mallet, was killed and the duke wounded in the shoulder, the troop halted and the remaining officers pleaded with the duke to change mounts and escape while he could. They were too few to hold the enemy for long and less than a mile from the ferry the duke's horse was hit and he tumbled to the ground. He looked for an officer to whom he could present his sword: two captains stepped forward, but they respectfully refused it, accepting as proof of his honourable surrender two ribbons which the duke took from his hat, one of buff, the colour of his lover,

Mademoiselle de Pons, the other green, the colour of the House of Anjou.

Henri II's dashing escapade reminds us that during the seventeenth century the Guise did not go into rapid decline; rather they continued to be a great princely House whose dynastic interests remained European in scope and whose opposition to the Habsburgs remained undimmed. Henri restored the honour and glory of the family, which had been eclipsed in recent years. His father, Charles, had been forced to leave France in 1631 and died in exile in 1640. Henri had initially been destined for the Guise ecclesiastical empire, which had been rebuilt after the Wars of Religion, under his uncle Cardinal Louis III, who became the fourth Guise Archbishop of Reims in 1605. Already Abbot of Saint-Urbain, Montier-en-Der, Corbie, Ourscamp, Saint-Denis, he added six others, including Cluny, Fécamp, and Mont Saint-Michel during the minority of Louis XIII.

Unfortunately, Louis III was wholly unsuited for a career in the Church. He was a rake and his appalling handling of the benefices strained relations with his more pious brother. Even as an archbishop, he did not bother with consecration. He devoted most of his time to an ex-mistress of Henry IV, and he seems to have contracted some form of marriage to her. She bore him five children. Louis's pre-Counter-Reformation attitudes caused a scandal and threatened the attempts by his brother to rebuild the family's fortunes and to erase the taint of rebellion associated with it.[1] His death in 1621 came as something of a relief. But the other branches of the family began to falter too: the Houses of Mayenne, Aumale, and Mercoeur were about to disappear for lack of male heirs. Charles's plans to pass the ecclesiastical empire, worth around 400,000 livres, to his second son, Henri, foundered in the 1630s partly because he was a bitter personal enemy of Cardinal Richelieu but perhaps more importantly because, although he had been Archbishop of Reims since the age of 15, Henri showed no interest in a religious vocation and was intent on emulating the dissolute ways of his uncle. When his elder brother died in 1639 he resigned his benefices and the century-old Guise ecclesiastical empire had come to an end.

Henri's desire to quit the Church was driven by his burning ambition to emulate his forebears. He revived the Guise-Coligny feud in 1643 when he fought and killed Maurice de Coligny, descendant of the admiral, in a duel. Next he revived the animosity with the Habsburgs. When Naples revolted against Spanish rule in 1647 he arrived with little money and few men, expecting that the cry of Anjou would still have meaning for Neapolitans a century after his great-grandfather had been forced out with a much larger army. Despite his ignominious failure and four years spent in Spanish captivity, he tried once again in 1654, this time backed by Cardinal Mazarin. The expedition was back in France within weeks. He spent the rest of his life at Louis XIV's court, where he was occupied by debts and love affairs until his death in 1664. The seventeenth-century Guise were not of the calibre of their sixteenth-century forebears. Henri was a reckless romantic, whose grand gestures and personal bravery were paid for by sacrificing his family's role in the Church, the bedrock of Guise fortunes. Behind the dashing façade, he was a libertine, utterly at odds with the soldierly demeanour of his grandfather and great-grandfather.

Though the Guise family survived and flourished after the Wars of Religion, the sense of clan feeling did not. Henri II's exaggerated sense of his own honour was no substitution for the lack of solidarity with his cousins. The absence of cohesion or of any attempt to build a network of obligation among brothers and cousins made the various branches of the House of Lorraine a much less significant political force as the seventeenth century progressed. The origins of this change can be traced back further, to the years following the murders of Blois when the family had the opportunity to replace the Valois as the next royal dynasty. Henry III's Counter-Revolution was an immense failure; rather than restoring royal authority it brought the monarchy crashing down. The reason for this was the genuinely popular outpouring of grief that greeted news of the assassinations. Emotions were whipped up further by preachers who turned the victims into Catholic martyrs and urged their congregations to resist the tyrant. 'The people', reported Pierre de l'Estoile, 'never left a sermon without having fire in their heads', and they turned their anger on the symbols of royal authority. On 29 December, St Thomas of Canterbury Day, the congregation of Saint-Gervais trampled the royal arms, which had adorned the door of the church, following a sermon by Dr Guincestre, one of the preachers maintained by the Duchess of Montpensier. The same preacher, during a sermon on 1 January, invited his congregation to take an oath that they would avenge the deaths of the brothers 'with the last taste of their blood'. The next day a group destroyed sepulchres and marble figures that the king had erected for his dead *mignons* close to the great altar of the church of Saint-Paul.

These emotions are also indicative of the success of the propaganda campaign of the Catholic League in the years preceding the murders at

Blois. News of the suffering of English Catholics had given St Thomas of Canterbury Day fresh significance for French Catholics. On the feast day, just six days after the murders, a Jesuit preacher in Rouen made the comparison between the murder of the Guise brothers and the murder of the Saint explicit. The impact that the sermon had on an emotionally charged audience was recounted by a refugee English nun:

> When he came unto the pulpytt, all eyeis and mowthes gapying upon hym, the good man was in such a passyion that he seemyd lyke to burst and could scars bring ouyt hys words for weepyng, the passion of that tyme had so altered his voice. Hys matter was of blessyd St. Thomas, declaring to the people the cause of hys martirdome in behalfe of Chrystes churche, and of the quarrel betwixt hym and the kyng, and how hys braynes were stroke out upon the pavement before ye alter. Thys thing was so apt for hys purpose that the people could by and by apply ytt that the preacher had no soner named the slaughter of theyr two princes but thatt all fell out into weepyng, and the preacher ther sobyng allowed could saye no more. Butt after a preatty space, striving with himself to speake, he clapyyng of hys hands cryed aloude, o pover eglese gallicane, and so came downe, the people all so movyd as we never have seene nor shall see ye lyke.[2]

In Paris, requiem Masses were hurriedly organized and churches decked out in mourning. On 8 January, the Duke of Aumale was present at the service in Saint-Jean-en-Grève, the family's Parisian place of worship, and a month later the same church, still covered in funeral hangings, hosted the baptism of Duke Henri's posthumously born son. The city aldermen and militia were prominent in the cortege which conducted the boy from the Hôtel de Guise to the church. The first alderman of the city, Nicolas Roland, held the baby at the font, symbolizing Parisian solidarity with the Guise. Rumour had it that the child had been born with the mark of divine grace. Across France in the early months of 1589 carefully managed funeral processions and ceremonies were staged in memory of the duke and the cardinal. These were highly unconventional in that ordinary people became participants, rather than simply spectators in the ritual. Thousands of small children played a prominent role. They walked two by two and proceeded from church to church. They carried candles, recited public prayers, and sang psalms and hymns. Despite the bitter cold, the majority of those who took part walked barefoot wearing only a shirt. Paris's dark, narrow, and icy streets were illuminated on many evenings by thousands of candles and filled with the sounds of prayer. At one such ceremony on 10 January, thousands of boys and girls wound their way up to the church and monastery of Sainte-Geneviève, at the entrance of which they 'threw ther candles to their feet and walked over them as a sign that this accursed tyrant [Henry III] had been excommunicated'. The presses rolled with pamphlets extolling the innocence of the murdered victims and vilifying the king. A new feature of this propaganda was the widespread use of simple pictures designed to shock; they consisted of gruesome pictures of the Guise brothers, their bodies riddled with injuries or the alleged mistreatment of their corpses by a gleeful Henry III.[3]

On 14 January 1589 a decree of the Sorbonne was registered in the Parlement deposing Henry III, and royal government was replaced by a Council composed of the Three Estates, as some deputies had envisaged at Blois. Mayenne was elected lieutenant-general and the Cardinal of Bourbon declared King Charles X. The murder of Henry III on 1 August 1589 by a Dominican monk was represented by the League as inspired by God; the murderer exulted as a new David killing the modern Goliath. Getting rid of Henry III failed to solve the essential contradiction of the League. Its democratic ideals were in conflict with the demands of wartime administration, which required not debate but bureaucratic management to feed insatiable Mars. The vacuum in resources was filled by Spanish silver. Increasingly Spanish troops were required to sustain the war effort. Despite his advantage on the battlefield, Henri de Navarre found himself unable to defeat the League militarily. Navarre's ultimate victory was far from inevitable. If the League had found a serious Catholic alternative, the likely scenario would have been the division of the kingdom, along similar lines to the Low Countries, into two mutually hostile states: a Catholic north, supported by Spain and organized, not unlike the Dutch Republic, according to the principles of representative government, and the Bourbon south, where the king's absolute authority guaranteed religious tolerance. The Cardinal of Bourbon died in captivity in 1590 but the wartime emergency ensured that it was only on 26 January 1593 that the Estates-General convened in the Louvre to elect a new monarch. The failure to find a consensus candidate was due to two factors: internal squabbling among the House of Lorraine and Spanish arrogance. Within the family, the Duke of Lorraine's son, Henri, and Charles, Duke of Guise, who had recently escaped captivity, both had their supporters. But Mayenne, now head of the family in France, had no wish to cede power to a younger man and after a six day family conference at Reims at the end of April no agreement was reached.

In order to claim his reward for propping up the League, Philip II now brought pressure to bear: on 16 May his ambassador officially solicited the Estates to elect the Infanta Isabella. Since the laws of succession had already been changed, the abolition of the Salic law, which her candidature would require, was relatively non-contentious. At this juncture, Philip, who had a tendency to overestimate his power, overplayed his hand. Spanish bribes circulated freely but their cajoling was another matter; it even upset Mayenne. Had the Spanish agreed to marry the Infanta to a French prince, most likely Charles de Guise, a deal could have been struck; but instead the Spanish ambassador insisted that she marry a Habsburg, Archduke Ernest, brother of the emperor, Rudolf II. The Estates refused under any circumstances to countenance the crown going to a foreign king. On 4 July the Spanish changed tack and agreed to the election of Guise and his marriage to the Infanta. The problem with the 22-year-old duke was that, although he had widespread support among the people of Paris, he was not taken seriously by his own relatives. Mayenne and the Duke of Lorraine were underwhelmed. Mayenne had tasted power and was not going to cede it to his young nephew without substantial guarantees. His demands were exorbitant and would have left him in effective control of the League kingdom, his nephew a mere puppet. Mayenne's only interest was to perpetuate his own authority and he fell out with the dukes of Aumale and Elbeuf too. The women, once a force for solidarity, now stirred the pot of discord: the dowager Duchess of Montpensier referred to her nephew sarcastically as 'the pretty king'; he reminded Mayenne's wife 'of a little boy who still needed a spanking', and even his mother seemed to prefer the children from her second marriage, especially the Duke of Nemours, who referred to Charles de Guise as a 'young fool who has his mother to help him get ahead'.[4] The clan mentality which had sustained and ruled the family since its foundation by the first duke, Claude, was at an end. As Henri de Navarre arrived at the royal abbey of Saint-Denis on the evening of 22 July with a huge retinue of nobles and counsellors, he was conscious of the divisions within the League. The date was carefully chosen, the drama masterfully orchestrated. After two days of instruction, on the seventh Sunday after Pentecost, a time in the liturgical calendar when 'there is signified and expressed this regenerated life, which is to be spent on the model of Christ's, and under the direction of his Spirit', Navarre abjured Protestantism. The

League, already undermined by war weariness and foreign domination, had lost its raison d'être. In the course of the next few years, all
the Guise clan, except the super-pious Duke of Aumale, who died in
Spanish exile, made their peace with Navarre, now King Henry IV.
Henry could afford to be generous to his former enemies, who were
crippled by enormous debts, but he was careful to deal with them
individually, thereby ensuring that the erosion of clan solidarity continued and was not revived by adherence to a single peace treaty.

* * * *

The death of the 4-year-old François-Joseph de Lorraine, the seventh
duke, from smallpox on 16 March 1675, ended the House of Guise in
the male line after a history of more than 160 years. The duchy and
peerage of Guise were extinguished and the inheritance divided.
History has not been kind to the Guise. Commentators have been
overwhelmingly hostile and there was plenty of ammunition at hand:
since the end of Francis I's reign there were anti-Guise printed polemics,
as well as songs and jokes, which reached a peak during the Catholic
League. Henri I de Guise, in particular, became synonymous with rebellion, ambition and Machiavellian scheming. It was in England that the
Black Legend was first popularized. Christopher Marlowe's *The Massacre at Paris, With the Death of the duke of Guise*, first performed in
1593 had good takings at its ten performances the following year. The
duke is 'a typical Machiavel, ambitious, ruthless, commonly dissimulat-
ing, yet possessed of courage and restless energy'.[5] The appetite for
contemporary French history had been whetted and did not wane in
the seventeenth century. John Webster's *Guise* and Henry Shirley's *The
Duke of Guise* are both sadly lost, but the English Civil War and
Revolution were, for many royalists in particular, a repetition of events
in France. After the Restoration there was a flurry of histories, plays, and
treatises about the French Wars of Religion that traced the roots of
seditious political association to the Catholic League, such as Thomas
Shipman's *Henry the Third of France, Stabb'd by a Fryer; with the Fall of
Guise: a Tragedy*, which was first performed in 1671–2. Most controversially, Dryden, in his *The Duke of Guise*, first conceived in 1661 but
only performed in 1682 as religious and political tensions mounted,
made the explicit link:

> Our Play's a Parallel: The Holy league
> Begot our Cov'nant: Guisards got the Whigg:

Whate'er our hot-brained Sheriffs did advance
Was, like our Fashions, first produc'd in France.

Polemical interest in the Wars of Religion was also undergoing a revival in France. Initially, under the Bourbons, histories contributed to the spirit of reconciliation, and had been balanced and judicious. But under Louis XIV criticism of the monarchy was tantamount to treason. A year after its publication in 1683, Dryden undertook a translation of the official version of the history of the Catholic League written by Louis de Maimbourg. For Dryden this was contemporary history: 'there is nothing but the Age that makes the difference, otherwise the Old man of an hundred and the Babe in Swadling-clouts, that is to say, 1584, and 1684, have but a century and a Sea betwixt then, to be the same'. What the early Tories found so satisfying in Maimbourg was the equation between Calvinism and radical Catholicism. The good guys were royalist Catholics. The Guise came out of Maimbourg badly, as abusers of religion, exhibiting 'Ambition under the masque of true zeal'. During the eighteenth century an image, which still persists, further distorted the Guise. They were now accused of selling out the 'nation', a term recently invented by patriots, for their own interests. In 1789 a catalogue of the crimes of the princes of Lorraine, who were deemed 'always to have been the enemies of the nation and the king's of France', appeared.[6] It traced the origins of France's misfortune on the eve of the revolution to Guise rule at the end of the 1550s! Sole responsibility for the civil wars of the sixteenth century was laid at their feet. Their story made great material for novelists (and later film-makers) and in the nineteenth century the Guise were romanticized. This was much better than their treatment for most of the twentieth century, as professional historians shunned the aristocracy as not worthy of study.

We can no longer ignore the Guise. While it is true that, unlike their contemporaries, the Valois, the Tudors, the Habsburgs, and the Bourbons, their legacy is often intangible and always ambiguous, they nevertheless left a significant mark on history. The Council of Trent, which defined Catholicism for 300 years, would not have succeeded without the Cardinal of Lorraine. Their outright hostility to Protestantism came later than commonly supposed, but they were a major factor in halting and turning back the Reformation tide in France. Consciously or unconsciously, they were convectors of a new form of politics that looked beyond the traditional elites to the people, in which the nature of the monarchical state was itself called into question. Dynastically, the Guise were among the sixteenth century's great losers: their dreams of empire proved elusive and they failed to grasp the crown of France when it was in their hands. And yet, the fact that, at one time or another, they opposed the greatest dynasties of the age and, at great personal sacrifice, emerged from the religious wars and dynastic convolutions of the sixteenth century intact, is evidence that henceforth the name of Guise deserves wider recognition.

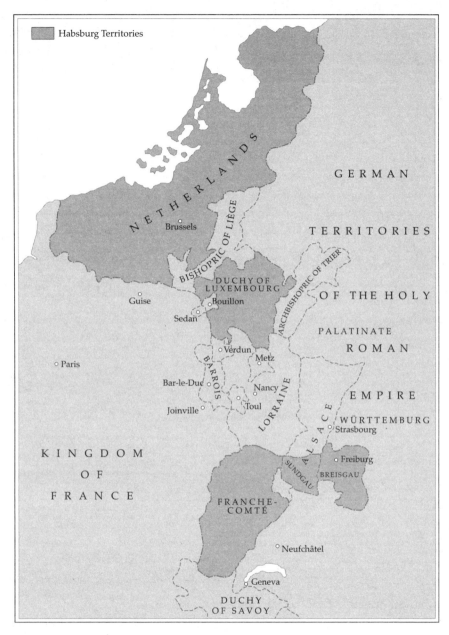

Map 1. The Franco-Imperial border

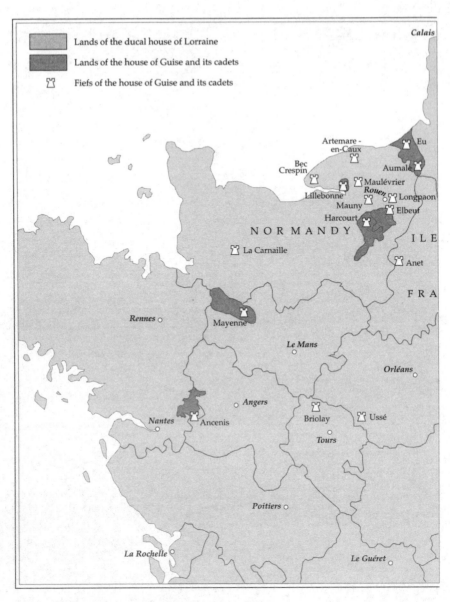

Map 2. Principal lands of the House of Guise

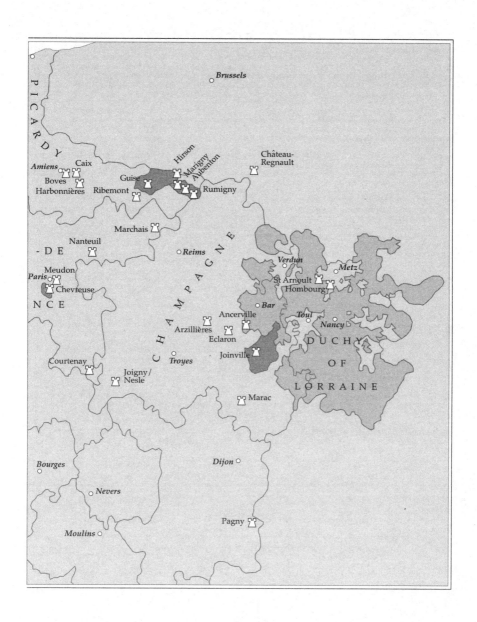

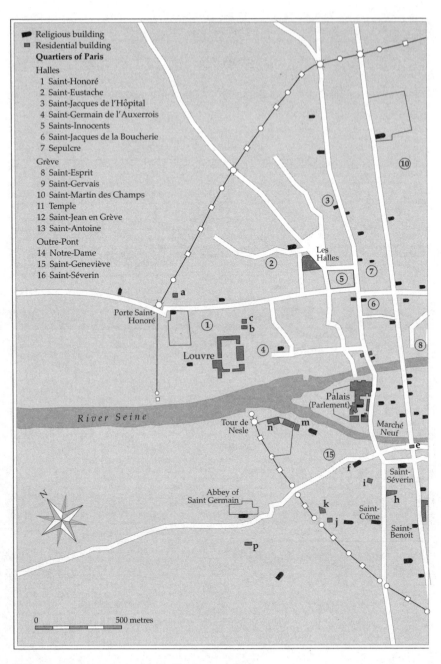

Religious building
Residential building
Quartiers of Paris

Halles
1 Saint-Honoré
2 Saint-Eustache
3 Saint-Jacques de l'Hôpital
4 Saint-Germain de l'Auxerrois
5 Saints-Innocents
6 Saint-Jacques de la Boucherie
7 Sepulcre

Grève
8 Saint-Esprit
9 Saint-Gervais
10 Saint-Martin des Champs
11 Temple
12 Saint-Jean en Grève
13 Saint-Antoine

Outre-Pont
14 Notre-Dame
15 Sainte-Geneviève
16 Saint-Séverin

Les Halles

Porte Saint-Honoré

Louvre

Palais
(Parlement)

River Seine

Tour de Nesle

Marché Neuf

Saint-Séverin

Abbey of Saint Germain

Saint-Côme

Saint-Benoît

0   500 metres

Map 3. Guise properties in Paris

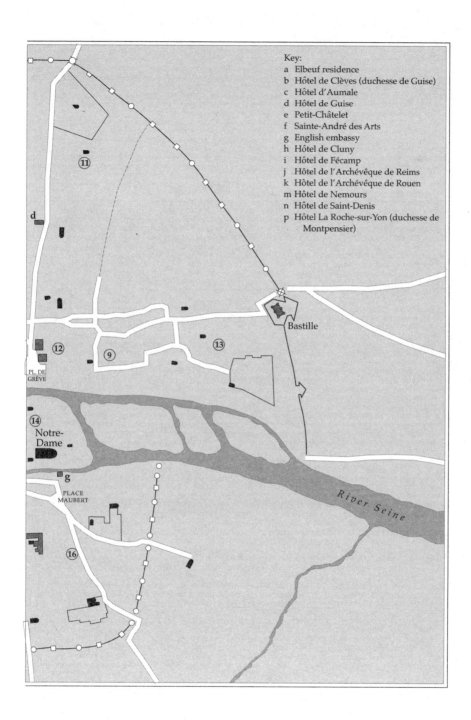

Key:
a Elbeuf residence
b Hôtel de Clèves (duchesse de Guise)
c Hôtel d'Aumale
d Hôtel de Guise
e Petit-Châtelet
f Sainte-André des Arts
g English embassy
h Hôtel de Cluny
i Hôtel de Fécamp
j Hôtel de l'Archévêque de Reims
k Hôtel de l'Archévêque de Rouen
m Hôtel de Nemours
n Hôtel de Saint-Denis
p Hôtel La Roche-sur-Yon (duchesse de
   Montpensier)

Bastille

PL. DE
GRÈVE

Notre-
Dame

PLACE
MAUBERT

River Seine

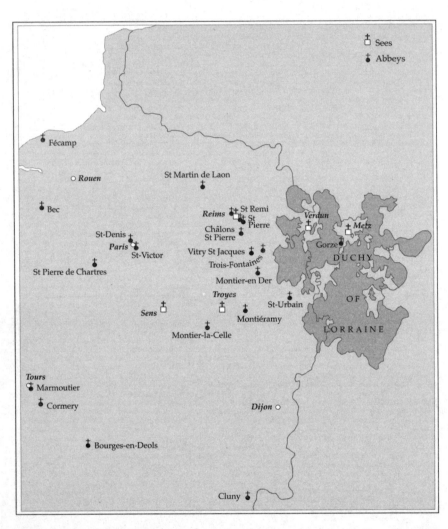

Map 4. The Guise ecclesiastical empire

GENEALOGICAL TABLES

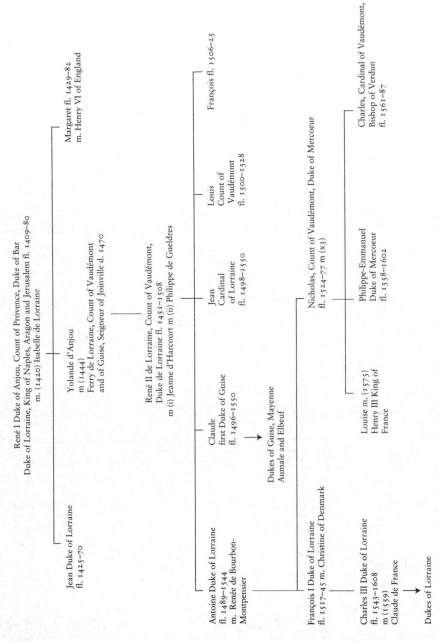

1. The House of Lorraine and the Angevin succession

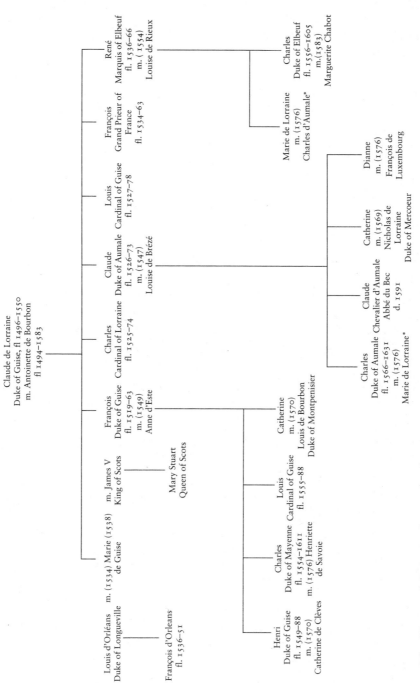

2. The House of Guise in the sixteenth century

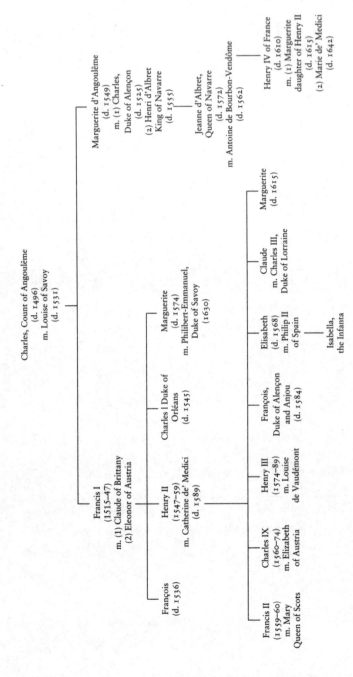

3. The later Valois

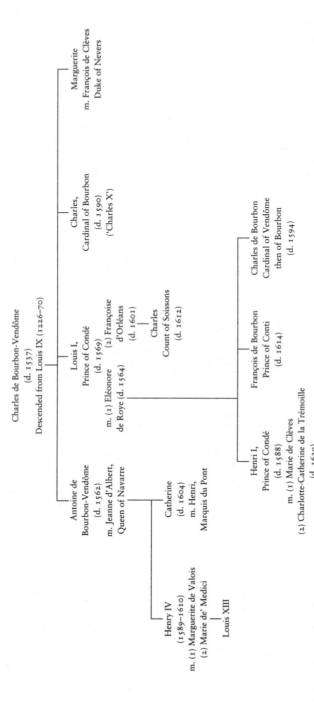

4. The House of Boubon-Vendôme

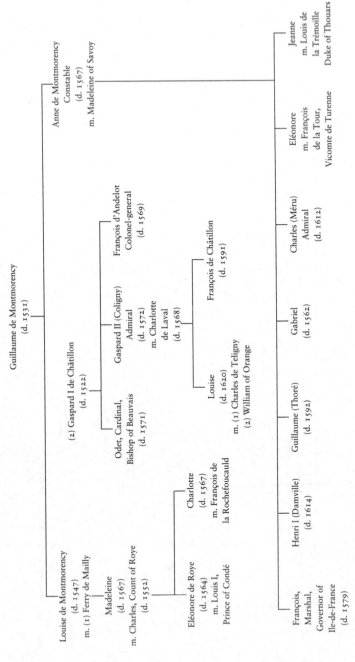

5. The House of Montmorency

FURTHER READING

Any serious investigation of the Guise family must begin with René de Bouillé du Chariol's monumental four volume *Histoire des ducs de Guise* (Paris, 1849–50), passages of which are translated and reproduced *in extenso* in Hugh Noel Williams's *The Brood of False Lorraine: The history of the Ducs de Guise, 1496–1588* (London, 1918). Henri Forneron, *Les ducs de Guise et leur époque*, 2 vols. (Plon, 1893) is more anecdotal and needs to be used with caution. The most recent work, Jean-Marie Constant's, *Les Guise* (Paris, 1985), concentrates largely on the period of the League and the figure of Duke Henri I.

Other male members of the family are surprisingly poorly served by biographers. The starting point for the Cardinal of Lorraine remains Outram Evenett, *The Cardinal of Lorraine and the Council of Trent* (Cambridge, 1930), but a projected follow-up volume was never completed. Duke François is the subject of Sylvia Castro Shannon, 'The political activity of François de Lorraine, duc de Guise (1559–1563): From military hero to Catholic leader', PhD thesis (University of Boston, 1988), which relies heavily on printed sources. The work of Eric Durot (see below) on François's career is only just beginning to appear in article form. In contrast, the Guise women are well served by biographies. Gabriel Pimodan, *La mère des Guises: Antoinette de Bourbon, 1494–1583* (Paris: Champion, 1925) contains numerous unpublished documents. Her eldest daughter, Marie, has been rehabilitated by Pamela Ritche in *Mary of Guise in Scotland, 1548–1560: A political career* (East Linton, 2002). Anne d'Este is also the subject of a recent German monograph: Christine Coester, *Schön wie Venus, mutig wie Mars: Anna d'Este von Guise und von Nemours, 1531–1607* (Munich, 2007). There are vast number of studies devoted to Mary Stuart. Antonia Fraser's, *Mary Queen of Scots* (London. 1969), is still valuable. John Guy, *My Heart Is My Own: The life of Mary Queen of Scots* (London, 2004), is the most recent biography.

The sinews of Guise power are the subject of Stuart Carroll, *Noble Power during the French Wars of Religion: The Guise affinity and the Catholic cause in Normandy* (Cambridge, 1998). On their ecclesiastical wealth and patronage, see Joseph Bergin, 'The decline and fall of the House of Guise as an ecclesiastical dynasty', *Historical Journal*, 25 (1982), 781–803 and 'The Guises and their benefices, 1588–1641', *English Historical Review*, 99 (1983), 34–58; Joanne Baker, 'Female monasticism and family strategy: The Guises and Saint Pierre de Reims', *The Sixteenth-Century Journal*, 28 (1997), 1091–108. Guise art patronage and their love of music is now well served by Yves Bellanger (ed.), *Le mécénat et l'influence des Guises* (Paris, 1997), which should be supplemented by Eric Durot, 'François de Lorraine (1520–1563): duc de Guise et nouveau Roi mage', *Histoire Economie Société*, 27 (2008), 3–16.

As for the key printed sources, the 'Mémoires-journaux de François de Lorraine duc d'Aumale et de Guise, 1547 à 1563', published in Michaud and Poujoulat, *Mémoires pour servir à l'histoire de France*, are misleading. They are not memoirs in the modern sense of the word, but rather a collection of documents, which include correspondence, related to the duke's public career. More intimate and anecodotal evidence is to be found in Pierre de Bourdeille, Sieur de Brantôme, *Oeuvres*, L. Lalanne (ed.), 11 vols. (Paris, 1864–82). Brantôme is notoriously unreliable, but he knew the Guise well and he had heard much of the gossip first hand. Some of the Guise's correspondence (which is particularly voluminous for the period before 1560) is available in print: M. Wood ed.), 'Foreign correspondence with Marie de Lorraine, Queen of Scotland, 1537–1548', *Scottish Historical Society*, 3rd series IV (Edinburgh, 1925); D. Cuisiat, *Lettres du Charles cardinal de Lorraine, 1525–1574* (Geneva, 1998); J de Croze, *Les Guises, les Valois et Philippe II*, 2 vols. (Paris, 1866), reproduces much correspondence of the Simancas archives in Madrid relating to Henri de Guise.

Diplomatic correspondence conveys a great deal of information about the Guise, but has to be used with care since it is often hostile. The major sources are *Calendar of State Papers, Foreign Series, of the Reign of Elizabeth I*, J. Stevenson et al. (eds.) (London, 1863–1950); M. N. Tommaseo, *Relations des ambassadeurs vénitiens sur les affaires de France au XVIe siècle*, 2 vols. (Paris, 1838); E. Alberi (ed.), *Relazioni degli ambasciatori veneti al Senato*, 3 vols. (Florence, 1839–1863); Archivo Documental Espanol, *Negociaciones con Francia (1559–1568)*, 11 vols. (Madrid, 1950–1960); the *Acta Nuntiaturae Gallicae*, a multi-volume work which publishes the correspondence of the papal nuncios in France.

The rise of the Guise under Henry II is covered in F. Baumgartner, *Henry II King of France, 1547–1559* (Durham NC and London, 1988); L. Romier, *Les origins politiques des guerres de religion*, 2 vols. (Paris, 1913–14); I. Cloulas, *Henri II* (Paris, 1985); D. Potter, 'The duc de Guise and the fall of Calais, 1557–8', *English Historical Review*, 98 (1983), 481–512.

The best short introduction to the French Wars of Religion is Mack Holt, *The French Wars of Religion*, 2nd edn (Cambridge, 2005). Eric Durot, 'Le crépuscule de l'*Auld* Alliance: la légitimé du pouvoir en question entre Ecosse, France et Angleterre (1558–1561)', *Histoire, Economie, Société*, 26 (2007), provides important detail on the French entanglement in Scotland. L. Romier, *La conjuration d'Amboise* (Paris, 1923) is still serviceable on the Calvinist threat to the regime of François II. Recent work is beginning to rediscover the radicalism of the Calvinist reformation: Philip Benedict, 'The dynamics of Calvinist militancy, 1555–63' in Benedict et al., *Reformation, Revolt and Civil War in France and the Netherlands* (Amsterdam, 1999); Mark Greengrass 'Regicide, martyrs and monarchical authority in France in the Wars of Religion' in Robert von Friedeburg,

Murder and Monarchy: Regicide in European history, 1300–1800 (Basingstoke: Palgrave, 2005).

On the Guise religious position in the early 1560s: Thierry Wanegffelen, *Ni Rome ni Genève: des fidèles entre deux chaires en France à XVIᵉ siècle* (Paris: Champion, 1997); Stuart Carroll, 'The compromise of Charles Cardinal of Lorraine: New evidence', *Journal of Ecclesiastical History*, 54 (2003), 469–83; Donald Nugent, *Ecumenism in the Age of the Reformation: The Colloquy of Poissy* (Harvard Mass., 1973); Alain Tallon, *La France et le concile de Trente* (Rome, 1997); Jean Harrie, 'The Guises, the body of Christ, and the body politic', *Sixteenth-Century Journal*, 37 (2006), 43–58.

For the background and context to Wassy: G. Baum and E. Caunitz (eds.), *Histoire ecclésiastique des églises reformées au royame de France*, 3 vols. (Nieuwkoop, 1974); C. Serfass, *Histoire de l'Église réformée de Wassy en Champagne depuis ses origines jusqu'à sa dispersion, 1561–1685* (Paris, 1928); Jules de la Brosse, *Histoire d'un capitaine Bourbonnais au XVIᵉ siecle: Jacques de la Brosse, 1485(?)–1562* (Paris, 1929).

The death of François, Duke of Guise, is covered by Nicola Sutherland, 'The assassination of François Duc de Guise, February 1563', *The Historical Journal*, 24 (1981), 279–95, and David El Kenz, 'La mort de François de Guise: entre l'art de mourir et l'art de subvertir' in *Société et idéologies des temps modernes. Hommage à Arlette Jouanna*, 2 vols. (Montpellier, 1996). The impact of the Guise–Montmorency feud on the civil wars is the subject of Stuart Carroll, *Blood and Violence in Early Modern France* (Oxford, 2006), Chapter 12, and 'Vengeance and conspiracy during the French Wars of Religion', in Julian Swann and Barry Coward (eds.), *Conspiracy and Conspiracy Theory from the Waldensians to the French Revolution* (Aldershot, 2004).

The most sensible guide to the Massacre of Saint Bartholemew is Arlette Jouanna, *La Saint-Barthélemy: les mystères d'un crime d'état* (Paris, 2007). Nicola Sutherland's *The Massacre of St. Bartholomew and the European Conflict, 1559–1572* (London, 1973) wears its confessional heart on its sleeve. Barbara Diefendorf, *Beneath the Cross: Catholics and Huguenots in sixteenth-century Paris* (Oxford, 1991) contains much of interest on popular violence. Denis Crouzet, *La nuit de la Saint-Barthélemy: un rêve perdu de la Renaissance* (Paris, 1994) is also valuable, especially on Maurevert and his circle.

Pierre Chevallier, *Henri III* (Paris, 1985) began the rehabilitation of the most complex and intriguing monarch ever to rule France. David Potter, 'Kingship in the Wars of Religion: The reputation of Henri III', *European History Quarterly*, 25 (1995), 485–528, surveys the literature up until the mid-1990s. Xavier Le Person, *Praticques et Praticqueurs: La vie politique à la fin du règne de Henri III (1574–1589)* (Geneva, 2002), continues the trend which sees Henri as a shrewd and manipulative politician.

On the invasion of England and the English Catholic exiles, see J. Kretzschmar, *Die invasionsprojekte der katholischen mächte gegen England zur zeit Elisabeths* (Leipzig, 1892); Leo Hicks (ed.), 'Letters and memorials of Robert Parsons SJ', *Catholic Record Society*, 39 (1942); John Bossy, 'Elizabethan Catholicism: The link with France', unpub PhD thesis (University of Cambridge, 1960); Catherine Gibbons, 'The experience of exile and English Catholics: Paris in the 1580s', unpub PhD thesis (University of York, 2006); Anne Dillon, *The Construction of Martyrdom in the English Catholic Community* (Aldershot, 2002); Alexander Wilkinson, *Mary Queen of Scots and French Public Opinion, 1542–1600* (Basingstoke, 2004).

Jean-Marie Constant's, *La Ligue* (1996), is a good synthesis on the rise and fall of the Catholic League. For a closer examination of the events of May 1588 in Paris: Stuart Carroll, 'The revolt of Paris, 1588: Aristocratic insurgency and the mobilization of popular support', *French Historical Studies*, 23 (2000), 302–37. De Lamar Jensen, *Diplomacy and Dogmatism: Bernardo de Mendoza and the Catholic League* (Cambridge Mass., Harvard University Press, 1964) has now been supplemented by Valentin Vázquez de Prada, *Felipe II y Francia (1559–1598): política, religión y razón de Estado* (Pamplona, 2004), which also falls into the trap of underestimating the level of 'operational overreach' in Spanish foreign policy and thereby of overestimating the control exercised by Spain over the Guise. The family's fortunes in the seventeenth century are sadly neglected—an imbalance in the historiography which will be rectified by the publication of Jonathan Spangler's *The Society of Princes: The Lorraine-Guise and the conservation of power and wealth in seventeenth-century France* (Aldershot, 2009).

NOTES

CHAPTER I

1. Pierre de Bourdeille, sieur de Brantôme, *Oeuvres*, L. Lalanne (ed.), 11 vols. (Paris, 1864–82), IV, 233.
2. M. N. Tommaseo (ed.), *Relations des ambassadeurs vénitiens sur les affaires de France au XVIe siècle* 2 vols. (Paris, 1838), I, 499.
3. Ibid.
4. G. Pimodan, *La mère des Guises: Antoinette de Bourbon, 1494–1583* (Paris: Champion, 1925).
5. R. Bouillé du Chariol, *Histoire des ducs de Guise*, 4 vols. (Paris: Duverger, 1849–50), I, 223.
6. Ibid., 224.
7. Ibid., 225.
8. *The New Catholic Encyclopedia*, G. Baum and E. Caunitz (eds.), *Histoire ecclésiastique des églises reformées au royame de France*, 3 vols. (Nieuwkoop: B. de Graaf, 1974), I, 806, C. Serfass, *Histoire de l'Église réformée de Wassy en Champagne depuis ses origines jusqu'à sa dispersion, 1561–1685* (Paris: Librairie Protestante, 1928), 17, 26.
9. Jacques-August de Thou, *Histoire universelle de 1543 jusqu'en 1607*, 16 vols. (London, 1734), III, 167.
10. P. Roberts, *A City in Conflict: Troyes during the Wars of Religion* (Manchester: Manchester University Press), 12.
11. Serfass, *Histoire de Wassy*, 17.
12. H. Dannreuther, 'Jean de Luxembourg (1537–1576) et la réforme dans le comté de Ligny-en-Barrois', *Bulletin de la Société de l'Histoire du Protestantisme Français*, XLIII (1894).
13. 'Mémoires-journaux de François de Lorraine duc d'Aumale et de Guise, 1547 à 1563', Michaud and Poujoulat (eds.), *Mémoires pour servir à l'histoire de France*, VI, 478.
14. Ibid.
15. Translations and music from the Genevan Psalter can be found at <http://genevanpsalter.redeemer.ca/> (accessed December 2006).
16. Nicolas Pithou, *Chronique de Troyes et de la Champagne (1524–1594)*, P.-E. Le Roy and I. Palasi (eds.), 2 vols. (Reims: Presses Universitaires de Reims, 1998–2000), I, 221.
17. Louis de Lorraine to Antoinette de Bourbon, Blois, 5 April 1551, cited in Pimodan, *La mère des Guises*, 338–9.
18. *Histoire ecclésiastique*, III, 252.
19. 'Mémoires-journaux de François de Lorraine duc d'Aumale et de Guise', 475.
20. De Thou, *Histoire Universelle*, III, 167.
21. A. Corbin, *Village bells: Sound and meaning in the nineteenth-century French countryside*, tr. Martin Thom (London: Papermac, 1998), 254.

22. 'Mémoires-journaux de François de Lorraine duc d'Aumale et de Guise', 484, 486.
23. Jules de la Brosse, *Histoire d'un capitaine Bourbonnais au XVIe siècle: Jacques de la Brosse, 1485(?)–1562* (Paris: Champion, 1929), 27.
24. 'Mémoires-journaux de François de Lorraine duc d'Aumale et de Guise', 481.
25. L-F. Lefèvre de Caumartin, *Recherche de la Noblesse de Champagne* (Paris, 1673), entry for the Marc family.
26. 'Mémoires-journaux de François de Lorraine duc d'Aumale et de Guise', 482.
27. I am persuaded by the arguments of Serfass, *Histoire*, 55–6.
28. Ibid., 207.
29. De Thou, *Histoire Universelle*, III, 167.
30. The figures range from 200 to 1,200.
31. 'Mémoires-journaux de François de Lorraine duc d'Aumale et de Guise', 482.
32. J. Stevenson et al. (eds.), *Calendar of State Papers, foreign series, of reign of Elizabeth I* (London: HMSO, 1863–1950), [hereafter CSPF], 1561–2.
33. Mémoires-journaux de François de Lorraine duc d'Aumale et de Guise', 474.
34. M. Greengrass, 'Hidden transcripts: Secret histories and personal testimonies of religious violence in the French Wars of Religion' in M. Levene and P. Roberts (eds.), *The Massacre in History* (New York and Oxford: Berghan, 1999).

CHAPTER 2

1. Why they preferred the more unusual feminine form is intriguing. Dumas employs the more conventional masculine, *Tous pour un, un pour tous*.
2. C. Michon, 'Les richesses de la faveur à la Renaissance: Jean de Lorraine (1498–1550) et François Ier', *Revue d'Histoire Moderne et Contemporaine* L (2003), 34–61.
3. Pimodan, *La mère des Guises*, 18.
4. Bouillé, I, 49.
5. R. Knecht, *Renaissance Warrior and Prince: The reign of François I* (Cambridge: Cambridge University Press, 1994), 70.
6. Ibid., 165.
7. Bouillé, I, 74.
8. Longueville (1510) was a *duché non-pairie*.
9. H. Forneron, *Les ducs de Guise et leur époque*, 2 vols. (Paris: Plon, 1893), I, 58, n. 3.
10. M. Wood (ed.), 'Foreign correspondence with Marie de Lorraine, Queen of Scotland, 1537–1548', *Scottish Historical Society*, 3rd series, IV (Edinburgh: Edinbrugh University Press, 1923), 11–12.
11. Forneron, *Les ducs de Guise*, I, 68.
12. Ibid., 71.
13. Bouille, *Histoire*, I, 117.
14. Ibid., I. 91, 144.
15. Ibid., I, 76.
16. Brantôme, *Oeuvres*, III, 232.
17. Pimodan, *La mère des* Guises, 51.
18. Ibid., 52.
19. D. Crouzet, 'Capital identitaire et engagement religieuse: aux origines de l'engagement militant de la maison de Guise ou le tournant des années 1524–5', in J. Fouilleron et al. (eds.), *Société et idéologies des temps modernes: hommage à Arlette Jouanna*, 2 vols. (Montpellier, 1996).

20. Brantôme, *Oeuvres*, IX, 481.
21. A. Collignon, 'Le mécénat du cardinal Jean de Lorraine (1498–1550)', *Annales de l'Est*, 23 (1910), 32.
22. Letter of Admiral Chabot quoted in Bouillé, I, 98.
23. J. Brooks 'Les Guises et l'air de cour: images musicales du prince guerrier' in Y. Bellanger (ed.), *Le mécénat et l'influence des Guises* (Paris: Champion, 1997).
24. F. Giacone, 'Les Guises et le psautier de David', in Bellanger (ed.), *Le mécénat*.
25. For this and following, A. Collignon, 'Le mécénat du cardinal Jean de Lorraine (1498–1550)', *Annales de l'Est*, 23 (1910), 23.
26. Ibid., 68.
27. Technically, Jean's nephew, Nicolas, was the bishop, but this was a fiction.
28. J. Cooper, 'Le rêve italien des premiers Guises' in Bellanger, *Le mécénat*, 121.
29. Bouillé, *Histoire*, I, 192.
30. Pimodan, *La mère des Guises*, 46.
31. Ibid., 30.
32. Bouillé, I, 125.
33. Ibid., I, 545.
34. R. Harding, *The Provincial Governors of Early Modern France* (Yale: Yale University Press, 1979), 27.
35. Pimodan, *La mère des Guises*, 33.
36. Ibid., 48.
37. Wood (ed.), 'Foreign Correspondence of Marie de Lorraine, 1537–1548', 33.
38. Pimodan, *La mère des Guises*, 105.
39. Wood, 'Foreign Correspondence of Marie de Lorraine, 1537–1548', 19.
40. J. Delaborde, 'Antoine de Croy, prince de Porcien', *Bulletin de la Société de l'Histoire du Protestantisme Français*, XVIII (1869), 2–26.
41. British Library, Additional MS 21361.
42. Pimodan, *La mère des Guises*, 125.
43. J-A. de Thou, *Histoire universelle de 1543 jusque'en 1607*, 16 vols. (London, 1734), I, 183.
44. Brantôme, *Oeuvres*, IV, 272.

CHAPTER 3

1. F. Baumgartmer, *Henry II King of France, 1547–1559* (Durham NC and London: Duke University Press, 1988), 25.
2. Ibid., 132.
3. Ibid., 30.
4. L. Romier, *Les origins politiques des guerres de religion*, 2 vols. (Perrin et Cie: Paris, 1913–14), I, 28.
5. P. Ritche, *Mary of Guise in Scotland, 1548–1560: A political career* (East Linton: Tuckwell, 2002), 67.
6. Ibid., 68.
7. I. Cloulas, *Henri II* (Paris: Fayard, 1985), 160.
8. D. Cuisiat (ed.), *Lettres du Charles cardinal de Lorraine, 1525–1574* (Droz: Geneva, 1998), 119.
9. M. Wood (ed.), 'Foreign correspondence with Marie de Lorraine, Queen of Scotland, 1548–1557', *Scottish Historical Society*, 3rd series, VII (Edinburgh: Edinbrugh University Press, 1925), 35.
10. British Library, Add MS 38031, fo. 181, copy.

11. N. Boucher, *La Conjonction des lettres et des armes des deux . . . princes lorrains* (Reims, 1579).
12. Brantôme, *Oeuvres*, IV 289.
13. Bouillé, *Histoire*, I, 276.
14. Brantôme, *Oeuvres*, IV 269.
15. Ibid., 188.
16. Wood (ed.), 'Foreign correspondence with Marie de Lorraine, 1548–1557', 19.
17. For this and following, C. Coester, *Schön wie Venus, mutig wie Mars: Anna d'Este von Guise und von Nemours (1531–1607)* (Munich: Oldenburg, 2007).
18. Cuisiat (ed.), *Lettres*, 173.
19. Romier, *Origines politiques*, I, 71–3.
20. Brantôme, *Oeuvres*, IV 276.
21. Bouillé, *Histoire*, I, 242.
22. Brantôme, *Oeuvres*, IV, 276.
23. Cuisiat (ed.), *Lettres*, 66 n. 235.
24. Ibid., 140, n. 3.
25. E. Alberi (ed.), *Relazioni degli ambasciatori veneti al Senato*, 3 vols. (Florence, 1839–1863), III, 440–1.
26. Cuisiat (ed.), *Lettres*, 168.
27. Wood (ed.), 'Foreign correspondence with Marie de Lorraine, 1548–1557', 237.
28. Ibid., 144.
29. Cuisiat, *Lettres*, 154.
30. Bouillé, II, 182.
31. Ibid I, 282.
32. Cloulas, *Henri II*, 308.
33. Baumgartner, *Henry II*, 147.
34. 'Mémoires-journaux de François de Lorraine duc d'Aumale et de Guise', 129.
35. Cuisiat (ed.), *Lettres*, 163.
36. Ibid., 507.
37. Baumgartner, *Henry II*, 165.
38. Cuisiat (ed.), *Lettres*, 184.
39. Baumgartner, *Henry II*, 173.
40. Ibid., 175.
41. Ibid., 176.
42. Cuisiat (ed.), *Lettres*, 270.
43. Romier, *Origines politiques*, II, 179.

CHAPTER 4

1. CSP, Venetian, 1556–7, 1341.
2. For this and following, D. Potter, 'The duc de Guise and the fall of Calais, 1557–8', *English Historical Review*, XCVIII (1983), 481–512.
3. Pimodan, *La mère des Guises*, 154.
4. A. de Ruble, *La première jeunesse de Marie Stuart* (Paris, 1891), 34.
5. John Guy, *My Heart Is My Own: The Life of Mary Queen of Scots* (London: Fourth Estate, 2004), 85–8.
6. Cuisiat (ed.), *Lettres*, 187.
7. J. Bergin, 'The decline and fall of the House of Guise as an ecclesiastical dynasty', *Historical Journal*, XXV (1982), 781–803.
8. Musée Condé Chantilly, A, liasse 7, Reglement d'habillement, 1 Jul 1576.

9. J. Bonnet, *Lettres de Jean Calvin*, 2 vols. (Paris, 1854), 186.
10. C. Haton, *Mémoires*, L. Bourquin (ed.), 4 vols. (Paris: Editions du comité des travaux historiques et scientifiques, 2001–7), I, 126.
11. Cuisiat (ed.), *Lettres*, 322–3.
12. Romier, *Origines politiques*, II, 265.
13. C. de L'Aubespine, 'Histoire particulière de la cour de Henri II', in Cimber and Danjou (eds.), *Archives curieuses de l'histoire de France*, 15 vols. (Paris, 1837), III, 287.
14. Baumgartner, *Henry II*, 220.
15. Romier, *Origines politiques*, II, 324.

CHAPTER 5

1. A. Desjardins (ed.), *Négociations diplomatiques de la France avec la Toscane*, 6 vols. (Paris, 1859–86), III, 404.
2. Cuisiat (ed.), *Lettres*, 353.
3. *Mémoires-journaux de François de Lorraine duc d'Aumale et de Guise*, 450.
4. Cuisiat (ed.), *Lettres*, 359.
5. Charles de Bourgeville, Sieur de Bras, *Les Recherches et Antiquitez de la Prince de Neustrie* (Caen, 1588), 166.
6. E. Durot, 'Le crépuscule de l'*Auld* Alliance: la légitimé du pouvoir en question entre Ecosse, France et Angleterre (1558–1561)', *Histoire, Economies, Société*, 26 (2007), 15.
7. Durot, 'Le crépuscule de l'*Auld* Alliance', 10.
8. Ibid., 23.
9. Forneron, *Les ducs de Guise*, I, 237.
10. Cuisiat (ed.), *Lettres*, 350.
11. For this and following: Mark Greengrass 'Regicide, martyrs and monarchical authority in France in the Wars of Religion' in R. von Friedeburg, *Murder and Monarchy: Regicide in European History, 1300–1800* (Basingstoke: Palgrave, 2005).
12. N. Roelker, *One King, One Faith: The Parlement of Paris and the religious reformations of the sixteenth century* (Berkeley: The University of California Press), 221.
13. Ibid., 229.
14. Cuisiat (ed.), *Lettres*, 370.
15. Forneron, *Les ducs de Guise*, I, 258.
16. *Histoire ecclésiastique*, I, 242.
17. Archivo Documental Espanol, *Negociaciones con Francia (1559–1568)*, 11 vols. (Madrid, 1950–1960), I, 106.
18. Roelker, *One King, One Faith*, 23.
19. Archivo Documental Espanol, *Negociaciones con Francia*, I, 150.
20. A. Jouanna, J. Boucher, D. Biloghi, and G. Le Thiec (eds.), *Histoire et dictionnaire des guerres de religion* (Paris: Laffont, 1998), 60.
21. H. Layard (ed.), 'Despatches of Michele Suriano and Marc Antonio Barbaro, Venetian ambassadors at the court of France, 1560–1563', *The Publication of the Huguenot Society*, 6 (1891), 17.
22. L. Romier, *La conjuration d'Amboise* (Paris: Perrin, 1923), 124.
23. Durot, 'Le crépuscule de l'*Auld* Alliance', 29.
24. Romier, *La conjuration d'Amboise*, 166.

25. S. Castro Shannon, 'The political activity of François de Lorraine, duc de Guise (1559–1563): From military hero to Catholic leader', unpublished PhD thesis (University of Boston, 1988), 175.
26. Jules de la Brosse, *Histoire d'un capitaine Bourbonnais au XVIᵉ siècle: Jacques de la Brosse, 1485(?)–1562* (Champion: Paris, 1929), 229.
27. Ibid., 180.
28. Durot, 'Le crépuscule de l'*Auld* Alliance', 35.
29. For this and following, S. Carroll, *Noble Power during the French Wars of Religion: The Guise affinity and the Catholic cause in Normandy* (Cambridge: Cambridge University Press, 1998), 96–101.
30. Ibid., 104.
31. 'Discours de Michel Soriano, Vénitien, touchant son ambassade de France' in M. Mennechet (ed.), *Histoire de l'Estat de France tant de la république que de la religion sous le règne de François II par Régnier, sieur de la Planche* (Paris, 1836), 391.
32. Ibid., 181.
33. *Negociaciones con Francia*, I, 228 ; Castro Shannon, 'The political activity of François de Lorraine', 197.
34. Tommaseo (ed.), *Relations des ambassadeurs vénitiens sur les affaires de France au XVIᵉ siècle*, 2 vols. (Paris, 1838), II, 153.
35. Cuisiat (ed.), *Lettres*, 420, 426, 431.
36. *Negociaciones con Francia*, I, 486.
37. A. Fraser, *Mary Queen of Scots* (London: Weidenfeld and Nicolson, 1969), 107.
38. Brantôme, IV, 228.
39. Layard (ed.), 'Despatches of Michele Suriano and Marc Antonio Barbaro', 8.

CHAPTER 6

1. CSPV, 1558–1580, 276.
2. M. Mennechet (ed.), *Histoire de l'Estat de France*, 208.
3. T. Wanegffelen, *Ni Rome ni Genève: des fidèles entre deux chaires en France an XVIᵉ siècle* (Paris: Champion, 1997), 157.
4. Cuisiat (ed.), *Lettres*, 48.
5. L. Taylor, *Soldiers of Christ: Preaching in late medieval and Reformation France* (Oxford: Oxford University Press), 223.
6. L. Taylor, 'The good shepherd: François Le Picart (1504–1556) and preaching reform from within', *Sixteenth Century Journal*, XXVIII (1997), 799.
7. See below p.210.
8. For this and following: D Crouzet, *La sagesse et le malheur: Michel de l'Hôpital, chancelier de France* (Paris: Champ Vallon, 1998).
9. Haton, *Mémoires*, I, 76–7.
10. Michel de Castelnau, *Mémoires*, Michaud and Poujoulat (eds.), IX, 431. He went on to become a celebrated Protestant captain and indefatigable foe of his former masters.
11. Cuisiat (ed.), *Lettres*, 377.
12. L. Romier, *Catholiques et Huguenots à la cour de Charles IX* (Paris: Perrin, 1924), 99.
13. R. Knecht, *Catherine de Medici* (London: Longman, 1998), 80.

14. G. Griffiths, *Representative Government in Western Europe in the Sixteenth-Century* (Oxford: Oxford University Press, 1968), 135.
15. Castro Shannon, 'Political Activity', 227.
16. CSPF, 1560–1, 61.
17. F. Giese, *Artus Desiré, Priest and Pamphleteer of the Sixteenth-Century* (Chapel Hill: University of North Carolina Press, 1973), 184.
18. A. de Ruble, *Antoine de Bourbon et Jeanne d'Albret*, 4 vols. (Paris, 1881–6), III, 86.
19. CSPF, 1560–1, 281.
20. A. Kluckhohn, *Briefe Friedrich des Frommen Kurfürsten von der Pfalz mit verwandten Schriftstücken*, 2 vols. (Braunschweig, 1868–72), I, 187.
21. S. Carroll, 'The Compromise of Charles Cardinal of Lorraine: New evidence, *Journal of Ecclesiastical History*, LIV (2003), 476.
22. Archivo Documental Espanol, *Negociaciones con Francia*, II, 295.
23. E. Pasquier, *Lettres Historiques pour les années 1556–1594*, D. Thickett (ed.), (Droz: Geneva, 1966), 65.
24. Ibid., 66.
25. D. Nugent, *Ecumenism in the Age of the Reformation: The Colloquy of Poissy* (Harvard Mass: Harvard University Press), 73.
26. Ibid., 85.
27. Ibid., 100.
28. Ibid., 152.
29. A. Tallon, *La France et le concile de Trente* (Ecole Française de Rome: Rome, 1997), 333.
30. CSPF, 1561–2, 487.
31. A. Muntz, 'Entrevue du duc Christophe de Wurtemberg avec les Guise à Saverne', *Bulletin de la Société de l'Histoire du Protestantisme Français*, IV (1856) 184–96.
32. Cuisiat (ed.), *Lettres*, 446.
33. Carroll, 'The Compromise'.
34. Tallon, *La France et la Concile de Trente*, 397ff.
35. Bouillé, *Histoire*, II, 327–9.
36. Cuisiat (ed.), *Lettres*, 508.
37. A. Tallon, 'Le cardinal de Lorraine au concile de Trente', in Bellanger (ed.), *Mécénat*, 341.

CHAPTER 7

1. A. Jouanna, J. Boucher, D. Biloghi, and G. Le Thiec (eds.), *Dictionnaire des guerres de religion*, 107.
2. Roelker, *One King*, 269.
3. B. Diefendorf, *Beneath the Cross: Catholics and Huguenots in sixteenth-century Paris* (Oxford: Oxford University Press, 1991), 63.
4. A. Jouanna, J. Boucher, D. Biloghi, and G. Le Thiec (eds.), *Dictionnaire des guerres de religion*, 117.
5. François II de Clèves had succeeded his dead father, François I, as duke earlier that year: both father and son shared similar religious beliefs.
6. A. Jouanna, J. Boucher, D. Biloghi, and G. Le Thiec (eds.), *Dictionnaire des guerres de religion*, 118.
7. Bouillé, II, 284.
8. Coester, *Schön wie Venus*, 174.

9. Brantôme, IX, 442.
10. BN MS Dupuy 324, fo. 113v.
11. Montaigne, *Essais*, 'De la Tristesse' (I: 2).
12. BN MS fr 17302 'Proposition par escrit presentee au conseil du roy Charles IX'.
13. Forneron, *Les ducs de Guise et leur époque*, II, 22.
14. Full citations for this section are to be found in Carroll, *Blood and Violence*, Ch.12.
15. Seong-Hak Kim, *Michel de L'Hôpital: The vision of a Reformist chancellor during the French Religious Wars* (Kirksville Mo: Truman State UP, 1997), 109.
16. Brantôme, IV, 277. Confirmed by Ambassador Chantonnay.
17. Kim, *Michel de L'Hôpital*, 144.
18. 'Lettres anecdotes écrites au cardinal Borromée par Prosper de Sainte-Croix', Cimber and Danjou (eds.), *Archives Curieuses*, VI, 145.
19. Boucher, *La Conjonction des lettres*, 64.
20. CSPF, 1564–5, 790.
21. Cuisiat (ed.),*Lettres*, 543.
22. Ibid., 555.
23. Ibid., 567.
24. Cuisiat (ed.), 573, 575.
25. Kim, *Michel de L'Hôpital*, 167.
26. CSPF [1568] 557.
27. Cuisiat (ed.), *Lettres*, 619.

INTERLUDE

1. Forneron, *Les ducs de Guise et leur époque*, II, 98.
2. M. Venard (ed.), *Les mémoires d'un curé de Paris (1557–1590) au temps des guerres de religion* (Geneva: Droz, 2004), 100.
3. Brantôme, V, 248.
4. Brantôme, III, 371.
5. Cuisiat (ed.), *Lettres*, 614.
6. Ibid., 611.
7. Brantôme, VII, 172.
8. For this and following: Cuisiat (ed.), *Lettres*, 614.
9. Bouillé, II, 464.
10. Ibid., 466.

CHAPTER 8

1. *The Massacre of St. Bartholomew and the European Conflict, 1559–1572* (London: Macmillan, 1973).
2. Cuisiat (ed.), *Lettres*, 643.
3. 'Relation des troubles excités par les calvinistes dans la ville de Rouen depuis l'an 1537 jusqu'en l'an 1582', *La revue de Rouen et de la Normande* (Rouen, 1837).
4. A. Boltanski, *Les ducs de Nevers et l'État royal: genèse d'un compromis (ca 1550–ca 1600)*. (Geneva: Droz, 2006), 381.
5. Bouillé, II, 481.
6. Jules Gassot, *Sommaire memorial (1555–1623)*, P. Champion (ed.) (Paris, 1934), 93–4.
7. Cuisiat (ed.), *Lettres*, 625.

8. Bouillé, II, 483.
9. Cuisiat (ed.), *Lettres*, 628.
10. Diefendorf, *Beneath the Cross, 1991)*, 156.
11. A Desjardins (ed.), *Négociations de la France avec la Toscane*, 6 vols. (Paris, 1859–96), III, 743.
12. Diefendorf, *Beneath the Cross*, 157.
13. Desjardins (ed.), *Négociations de la France avec la Toscane*, III, 784.
14. Cuisiat (ed.), *Lettres*, 632.
15. Ibid., 636.
16. A. Jouanna, *La Saint-Barthélemy: les mystères d'un crime d'état* (Paris: Gallimard, 2007), 86.
17. G. Parker, *The Dutch Revolt* (Penguin, 1985), 137–8.
18. E. de Noailles, *Henri de Valois et la Pologne en 1572*, 2 vols. (Paris, 1867) I, 8–9; 55–6.
19. Jouanna, *La Saint-Barthélemy*, 83.
20. Cuisiat (ed.), *Lettres*, 634.
21. *Mémoires et Correspondance de Duplessis-Mornay*, 12 vols. (Paris, 1824–5), II, 20–37.
22. BN MS Fr 3177, fo. 120–3. Thanks to David Potter for this reference.
23. Jouanna, *La Saint-Barthélemy*, 86.
24. D. Crouzet, *La nuit de la Saint-Barthélemy: un rêve perdu de la Renaissance* (Paris: Fayard, 1994).
25. BN MS Fr 8182, fo. 321.
26. AN Minutier Central étude VIII 388, fo. 445.
27. Etienne Pasquier quoted in N. M. Sutherland, *The Massacre of St Bartholomew and the European Conflict, 1559–1572* (MacMillan, 1973), 313.
28. J. Tedeschi, 'Tomasso Sassetti's account of the St. Bartholomew's Massacre' in A. Soman (ed.), *The Massacre of Saint Bartholomew: Reappraisals and documents* (The Hague: Kluwer Academic Publishers, 1975), 99–152.
29. Jouanna, *La Saint-Barthélemy*, 108.
30. AN Y 124, fo. 558, 14 Jun 1584.
31. Villemur is usually identified as canon Pierre de Piles, apparently the Duke of Guise's former preceptor. The notarial archives, however, refer to the Sieur de Villemur as François de Pilla or Piles. It seems likely that they are one and the same person. Villemur was a pensioner of the Cardinal of Lorraine in 1560 and charged with numerous diplomatic missions during this period. He is also confused with Jean de Piles, a secretary of the Cardinal of Lorraine.
32. And not his nephew and heir apparent, François de Villiers, master of the ducal household and the man who had let Maurevert into the house. BN Pièces Originales 595, nos. 15–19.
33. AN Minutier Central étude VIII 380, fo. 420.
34. La Boissière was married into the Raguier, the chief Protestant lineage in the Brie who were related to the Louviers. The civil war in the Brie was dominated by a feud between the Raguier and the Foissy, also servants of the Guise.
35. Crouzet, *La nuit de la Saint-Barthélemy*, 400.
36. Bouillé, II, 505.
37. Diefendorf, *Beneath the Cross*, 99.
38. R. Knecht, *The Rise and Fall of Renaissance France, 1483–1610* (Oxford: Blackwell, 2001), 363.
39. Crouzet, *La nuit de la Saint-Barthélemy*, 33.

40. Ibid., 43.
41. La Motte-Fénelon, *Correspondance diplomatique* (Paris, 1838, 1840), VII, 322–3.
42. Diefendorf, *Beneath the Cross*, 210.
43. SP70/125 no. 3112 sep 1572.
44. 'Mémoires de Jean de Mergey', Michaud and Poujoulat (eds.), IX, 577. Mergey's account is confused and I have altered his story slightly, especially since he mentions la Rochefoucauld, who had been lieutenant of the Duke of Lorraine in 1550s.
45. Nicolas Pithou, *Chronique de Troyes et de la Champagne (1525–1594)*, 2 vols. (Reims: Presses Universitaires de Reims, 2000), II, 692.
46. Sentiments shared by the Cardinal of Lorraine in Rome who was overjoyed at the news and thanked divine Providence.

CHAPTER 9

1. Haton, *Mémoires*, III, 340.
2. BN MS Fr 3338, fo. 38. Antoinette de Bourbon to Nemours, 22 November 1576.
3. Bouille, III, 4.
4. Tommaseo, *Relations*, II, 639.
5. CSPF, 1583–4, 57.
6. CSPF, 1575–7, 210.
7. C. Valois (ed.), *Histoire de la Ligue. Œuvre inédite d'un contemporain* (Paris, 1914), 77–8.
8. CSPF, 1583–4, 620.
9. Carroll, *Noble Power*, 172.
10. BL Add MS 30833, fo. 503, 26 September 1578, Poggio to the dowager duchess.
11. Inferred from the fact that Roncherolles was lieutenant of his gendarmerie company from 1579 to 1582.
12. Pierre Hurtubise (ed.), *Correspondance du nonce en France Antonio Maria Salviati (1572–1578)*, 2 vols. (Rome: Ecole Française de Rome, 1975), II, 506.
13. Haton, *Mémoires*, III, 394.
14. Pierre de l'Estoile, *Registre-Journal du règne de Henri III*, M. Lazard and G. Schrenck (eds.), 6 vols. (1992–), IV, 77.
15. P. Chevallier, *Henri III* (Paris: Fayard, 1985), 410.
16. For this and following Haton, *Mémoires*, IV, 112, 359, 445.
17. L'Estoile, *Registre-Journal*, II, 43.
18. Ibid., II, 189.
19. D. Potter and P. Roberts, 'An Englishman's view of the court of Henri III', *French History*, 2 (1988), 312–44.
20. Bouillé, III, 100–1.
21. CSPF, 1582, 3.
22. A. Cullière, *Les écrivains et le pouvoir en Lorraine au XVIe siècle* (Paris: Champion, 1999), 280.
23. CSPF, 1583–4, 217.

CHAPTER 10

1. CSPF, 1583–4, 288–9.
2. CSPS, 1580–6, 361.
3. Ibid., 471.

4. The exceptions are: J. Bossy, 'Elizabethan Catholicism: the link with France', unpublished PhD thesis (University of Cambridge, 1960); K. Gibbons, 'The experience of exile and English Catholics: Paris in the 1580s', unpublished PhD thesis (University of York, 2006).

5. J. Kretzschmar, *Die invasionsprojekte der katholischen mächte gegen England zur zeit Elisabeths* (Leipzing, 1892), 134.

6. Dictionary of National Biography.

7. CSPS, 1580–6, 485.

8. CSPF, 1583, 158.

9. CSPF, 1583–4, 36.

10. Ibid, 299.

11. A. Dillon, *The Construction of Martyrdom in the English Catholic Community* (Aldershot: Ashgate, 2002), 163.

12. X. Le Person *Praticques et Praticqueurs. La vie politique à la fin du règne de Henri III (1574–1589)* (Geneva: Droz, 1992), 67.

13. S. Carroll, 'The revolt of Paris, 1588: Aristocratic insurgency and the mobilization of popular support', *French Historical Studies*, XXIII (2000), 337.

14. Le Person, *Praticques et Praticqueur*, 53.

15. Boucher et al, *Dictionnaire des guerres de religion*, 311.

16. J.-A. de Thou, 'Mémoires', *Michaud and Poujoulat* (eds.), 1st ser., XI, 330–1.

CHAPTER 11

1. Inspired by the opening of Le Person's *Praticques et Praticqueurs,* my interpretation differs fundamentally.

2. British Library Add MS 21361, fo. 9. These letters are often misdated and clearly refer to the events of 1585.

3. Printed in Le Person, *Practiques et Praticqueurs*, 592. The survival of the manuscript in both the papers of the Chancellor of Navarre and Lord Burghley is instructive.

4. British Library Add MS 21361, fo. 9

5. Ibid., fo. 13.

6. Ibid., fo. 2.

7. Ibid., fo. 14.

8. BN MS Fr 5806, fo. 70, 18 Feb. 1586.

9. CSPF, 1586, 363.

10. René de Lucinge, *Lettres sur la cour d'Henri III en 1586* (Geneva: Droz, 1966), 203–4.

11. Quoted in A. Wilkinson, *Mary Queen of Scots and French Public Opinion, 1542–1600* (Houndmills: Palgrave, 2004), 113.

12. *Le Procèz-Verbal d'un nommé Nicolas Poulain*, in Cimber and Danjou (eds.), *Archives Curieuses*, XI, 301.

13. Quoted in Wilkinson, *Mary Queen of Scots and French Public Opinion*, 121.

14. Ibid., 111.

15. Quoted in De Lamar Jensen, *Diplomacy and Dogmatism: Bernardino de Mendoza and the French Catholic League* (Cambridge Mass.: Harvard University Press), 89.

16. CSPF, 1586–8, 315.

17. Quoted in Chevallier, *Henri III*, 390.

18. L'Estoile, *Registre-Journal*, VI, 13.

19. Quoted in Chevallier, *Henri III*, 600.

20. Ibid., 610.
21. L' Estoile, *Registre-Journal*, V, 328.
22. Ibid.
23. BN MS Nouvelles Acquisitions Françaises 2743 fo. 134–5, Henri to Pisani, 27 Jan. 1588.
24. Chevallier, *Henri III*, 624.
25. For this and following: Carroll, 'The revolt of Paris', where detailed references can be found.
26. There are several conflicting versions of this interview; I have discounted l'Estoile's account.
27. Chevallier, *Henri III*, 631.
28. Ibid., 635.
29. Ibid., 637.
30. L'Estoile, *Registre-Journal*, VI, 35.
31. Quoted in A. Soman, 'The Parlement of Paris and the great witch hunt (1565–1640)', *Sixteenth-Century Journal*, IX (1978), 30–44.

CHAPTER 12

1. Le Person, *Praticques et Practiquers*, 538.
2. Bouillé, III, 290.
3. Quoted in Constant, *Les Guise*, 191.
4. Ibid., 205.
5. J. Loutchitsky, *Documents inédits pour server à l'histore de la Réforme et de la Ligue* (Kiev, 1875), 225–7.
6. Constant, *Les Guise*, 166.
7. C.J. Mayer (ed.), *Des Etats Généraux et autres assemblées nationales*, 18 vols. (The Hague, 1789), XV, 350–1.
8. Chevallier, *Henri III*, 657.
9. Le Person, *Praticques et Practiquers*, 559.
10. Lalourcé and Duval (eds.), *Receuil des pièces originales et authentiques concernant la tenue des états-généraux*, 11 vols. (Paris, 1789), V, 125.
11. Constant, *Les Guise*, 223.
12. Ibid., 225.
13. Chevallier, *Henri III*, 661.
14. Constant, *Les Guise*, 226.
15. Ibid., 227.
16. Ibid., 10.
17. Chevallier, *Henri III*, 672.

EPILOGUE

1. J. Bergin, 'The Guises and their benefices, 1588–1641', *English Historical Review*, XCIX (1983), 34–58.
2. P. Benedict, *Rouen during the Wars of Religion* (Cambridge: Cambridge University Press, 1980), 178. See also A. Wilkinson, ' "Homicides Royaux": The assassination of the Duc and Cardinal de Guise and the radicalization of French public opinion', *French History*, XVIII (2004), 129–53.
3. Wilkinson, 'Homicides Royaux', 141.

4. Bouillé, IV, 201.
5. J. Briggs, 'Marlowe's Massacre at Paris: A reconsideration', *Review of English Studies*, XXXIV (1983), 257–78.
6. *Des Crimes commis par les Princes Lorrains depuis leur établissement en France, jusqu'aujourd'hui* (Lausanne, 1789).

PHOTOGRAPHIC ACKNOWLEDGEMENTS

Bibliothèque du Louvre, Paris/© Erich Lessing/akg-images: 12; © Hervé Champollion/akg-images: 25; Galleria Pallatina, Palazzo Pitti, Florence/© Rabatti-Domingie/akg-images: 3; Musée de Blois, Blois/© Erich Lessing/akg-images: 23; Musée Cantonal des Beaux-Arts, Lausanne/© akg-images: 22; Musée Condé, Chantilly/© Erich Lessing/akg-images: 19, 27; Musée du Louvre, Paris/© Erich Lessing/akg-images: 21, 24; Bibliothèque Nationale de France, Paris: 2, 6, 8, 11, 14, 16, 18, 26; Bodleian Library, University of Oxford: 1; British Library, London: 13; © Cameraphoto, Venice: 9; © The Frick Collection, New York: 17; Glasgow University Library, Special Collections Department: 10; © Musée National du Chateau de Pau: 4; © The National Trust for Scotland: 5; Chateau de Versailles et de Trianon/© Gerard Blot/RMN: 20; Musée du Louvre, Paris/© Gérard Blot/RMN: 15

INDEX

The letter n indicates an endnote.